D0712309

Siliceous Sedimentary Rock-Hosted Ores and Petroleum

EVOLUTION OF ORE FIELDS SERIES

Wilfred Walker, Series Editor

ORE FIELDS AND CONTINENTAL WEATHERING/
   Jean-Claude Samama
SILICEOUS SEDIMENTARY ROCK-HOSTED ORES
   AND PETROLEUM/*James R. Hein*
EVOLUTION OF CHROMIUM ORE FIELDS/*Clive W. Stowe*

Related Titles

GOLD: History and Genesis of Deposits/*Robert W. Boyle*
THE ENCYCLOPEDIA OF APPLIED GEOLOGY/
   Charles W. Finkl, Jnr.

Siliceous Sedimentary Rock-Hosted Ores and Petroleum

Edited by

JAMES R. HEIN

U.S. Geological Survey

A Hutchinson Ross Publication

 VAN NOSTRAND REINHOLD COMPANY
New York

Copyright © 1987 by **Van Nostrand Reinhold Company Inc.**
Library of Congress Catalog Card Number: 86–34029
ISBN 0–442–23250–0

All rights reserved. No part of this work covered by the copyright
hereon may be reproduced or used in any form or by any
means—graphic, electronic, or mechanical, including photocopy-
ing, recording, taping, or information storage and retrieval systems—without written permission of the publisher.

Printed in the United States of America

Van Nostrand Reinhold Company Inc.
115 Fifth Avenue
New York, New York 10003

Van Nostrand Reinhold Company Limited
Molly Millars Lane
Wokingham, Berkshire RG11 2PY, England

Van Nostrand Reinhold
480 La Trobe Street
Melbourne, Victoria 3000, Australia

Macmillian of Canada
Division of Canada Publishing Corporation
164 Commander Boulevard
Agincourt, Ontario MIS 3C7, Canada

16 15 14 13 12 11 10 9 8 7 6 5 4 3 2 1

Library of Congress Cataloging-in-Publication Data
Siliceous sedimentary rock-hosted ores and petroleum.
  (Evolution of ore field series)
  Includes bibliographies and index.
  1. Rocks, Siliceous. 2. Ore-deposits. 3. Petroleum—
Geology. I. Hein, J. R. (James R.) II. Series.
QE471.S556 1987   553′.1   86–34029
ISBN 0–442–23250–0

CONTENTS

PART III: BEDDED CHERT SEQUENCES

PREFACE

This book is a product of the efforts of the International Geological Correlations Project's (IGCP) research group 115, Siliceous Deposits of the Pacific Region. In 1981, IGCP 115 was extended for an additional 5 years as Project 187, Siliceous Deposits of the Pacific and Tethys Regions. Together, projects 115 and 187 will have been active for a total of 10 years at the time of their termination in September 1986. Project 187 involved 142 scientists from 33 countries. The IGCP program is sponsored by UNESCO and the International Union of Geological Sciences (IUGS).

This book can be considered as a companion volume to one edited by A. Iijima, J. R. Hein, and R. Siever (Elsevier, 1983), dealing with the geology, sedimentology, paleontology, and geochemistry of siliceous deposits. That volume, titled *Siliceous Deposits in the Pacific Region,* contains papers presented at the Second International Conference on Siliceous Deposits, which was held in Japan in 1981. That conference was the culminating event of IGCP 115 and the beginning of the expanded IGCP 187. The present volume is a direct outcome of the new phase, IGCP 187, that has placed emphasis on the ore and petroleum deposits associated with siliceous rocks. A discussion and integration of each chapter in this book is presented in Chapter 1, where each ore-deposit type is placed into a genetic model emphasizing coastal upwelling.

As international group leader of IGCP 187, I would like to thank all of our members for their consultations through the years, their contributions to some of the chapters in this book, and their reviews of other chapters presented here. I would also like to thank Lisa Morgenson, U.S. Geological Survey, for technical and editorial help. All the papers in this volume were critically read by at least two reviewers, as well as by me as volume editor.

International and interdisciplinary cooperation is valuable for the understanding of complex and widespread geologic phenomena. Because of the biological origin of many siliceous deposits, their geochemical transformation in the marine environment, and their occurrence in many formations around the world, it is essential that oceanographers, paleontologists, geochemists, and geologists work together to reach a holistic understanding about the origin and evolution of these deposits and their associated ore minerals and petroleum. Not only is integration of disciplines needed, but it behooves workers from all nations whose territories contain siliceous deposits to cooperate in comparative studies. In this spirit of cooperation, IGCP 187 has been a complete success.

JAMES R. HEIN

SERIES EDITOR'S FOREWORD

This series is concerned with both the evolution of individual ore fields and changes in ore field evolution in the 4 billion years of the Earth's history. As an explorationist, I have a need to identify those features of ore field development that control the position and nature of ore bodies. These features include the positioning of host lithologies; the boundaries of the ore field (which may or may not match those of the host lithology); and modification by plutonism, metamorphism, and deformation. Perhaps most intriguing is why some terrains bear ore while others, apparently identical, do not. This situation introduces consideration of metallogenic periods, metallogenic provinces, and the possibility of identifying new ore fields. An interest in developing understanding at the ore field scale is evident from the favorable reaction of experts to requests to write these volumes. We may expect, therefore, that first editions will set the course for further work and for second editions with new understandings.

The traditional Phanerozoic-Precambrian and Archean-Proterozoic classifications do not allow recognition of evolutionary patterns. Because they are so well known, it is almost mandatory that they be referred to, and we may expect to see more than one classification in these volumes. In a 1970 abstract of a 1971 paper, said to be the first on the dual topic of metallogeny and plate tectonics, I extended back to 3 billion years ago the Bilibin theme in which he related ore formation to Phanerozoic tectonic cycles. The current version (Walker, 1982) of my 1970 Table of Eras (Table 1) bears a strong resemblance to the legend of the Tectonic Map of the World (1972) (Table 2).

Table 1. Table of Eras

Era	Age in m.y. (approx.)
Alpine	200–present
Paleozoic	600–200
Katangan	900–600
Grenvillian	1600–900
Karelian	2200–1600
Superior	3000–2200
Swazian	3500–3000
Godthaabian	4000–3500
Enderbian	4400?–4000

Table 2. Legend of the Tectonic Map of the World (1972)

Areas of Continental Crust	Consolidated before
Mesozoic and Cenozoic	Present
Paleozoic	200–190 m.y.
Katangan-Baikalian-Cadomian	650–570 m.y.
Grenville-Dalslandian-Satpuran	1100–900 m.y.
Gothian-Elsonian	1500–1350 m.y.
Karelian-Hudsonian-Mayombian-Eburnian	2000–1700 m.y.
Kenoran-Belomorian-Rhodesian-Guiana	2600 m.y.
Transvaalian	3000 m.y.

Most workers today are comfortable with the concept of pre-, syn-, and post-tectonic stages of development in mobile belts. Many acknowledge it locally in their classifications, as Lucien Cahen has done in Africa and the Tectonic Map Committee in Australia. If Gastil is right, we can equate mobile belts worldwide, throughout the geological record. In contrast, the component tectonic stages are not necessarily equivalent worldwide, because local repetitions are common. As Cahen pointed out, a major problem is that existing classifications have breaks in the wrong places. Thus, repetitions of pre-tectonic volcanism and syn-tectonic granite emplacement in the Canadian Shield are called Archean, with the post-tectonic stage—the Huronian—being called Proterozoic. So, too, with Aphebian, Helikian, Hadrynian, and Precambrian W, X, Y, and Z: The pattern of mobile belt development and accepted classifications are out of phase.

The principal difference between the two tables is that the eras in Table 1 include post-tectonic stages whereas the heading "Consolidated before" in Table 2 implies that the eras in the legend of the Tectonic Map of the World terminate with cratonization, that is, the syn-tectonic stage. Nevertheless, each era represents a distinct period of mobile belt formation, as Gastil suggested. Since at least 4 billion years ago, the Earth appears to have evolved by a succession of eras of mobile belt formation. We should be able to recognize variations on this theme, both geologically and in the evolution of ore fields. This was the rationale that gave rise to this series of volumes.

The initial concept of the series was that each author would describe the evolution of ore fields of his or her specialty. For authors working on individual metals (such as chromite, nickel, uranium, and gold) or metal groups (such as platinum-palladium), this modus operandi is well suited. Some authors, however, made it evident in the titles and synopses of their proposals that they preferred to consider ore-forming environments, such as in porphyries, pegmatites and veins, skarns, evaporites, reefs and hot springs. The present volume is in the latter category.

James R. Hein, as editor and senior author of this volume, draws upon a different parameter, that of biologic evolution, and in so doing broadens our horizons. Further, in one volume, through the consideration of groups of plankton, Hein draws upon a phenomenon that controls the development of oil fields and ore fields of metallic and industrial minerals.

In his introductory note on temporal relations, Hein comments that in some Precambrian deposits: " . . . cherts may have been derived from a siliceous plankton of unknown affinity, and thus, the Precambrian may represent a third era of a dominant siliceous plankton group." I suggest that the 3 billion years of recorded pre-Paleozoic life may well have given rise to several bio-siliceous epochs. Siliceous deposits form the uppermost group in the Huronian of the northeast corner of Lake Huron. Mature sediments accompanied by products of glaciation are known in post-tectonic sequences, from the 3-b.y.-old Witwatersrand to the present. A concern with paleoclimates, particularly glaciation, is evident in several chapters in this volume. Banded iron formation, the theme of R. C. Morris in this volume, is the principal component of the oldest pre-tectonic rocks known (3.8 b.y.) at Isua, Greenland. It is economically important in the Swazian (3.4 b.y) near Havelock, South Africa, and in the 2.9-b.y.-old Keewatin volcanics of Ontario. The development of these siliceous deposits and some of those noted by Morris certainly follows an evolutionary pattern: Might parts be biologic?

In Chapter 2, Hein and J. T. Parrish compile all the occurrences of chert reported in the literature and display those data on paleogeographic maps for each period of the Phanerozoic. This chapter is an excellent source of raw data. The geologic periods, however, provide a rather arbitrary base: The Ordovician, for example, was established as the area of overlap between what Sedgwick called the Cambrian and what Murchison called Silurian. There must be some relationship of planktonic surges to other phenomena recorded in the geologic record, perhaps tectonic stages, perhaps an evolving system of plate tectonics during the 4 billion years of record, or perhaps to broader patterns of development in the solar system and galaxy.

I would encourage the authors to seek relationships. As each volume in the series adds new parameters, I trust that we will seek yet broader understandings of the evolution of ore fields. I certainly thank the authors and editor of this volume for the contribution.

WILFRED WALKER

References

Bilibin, Y. A., 1955 (translated by E. A. Alexandrov). *Metallogenic provinces and metallogenic epochs.* Queens College Press, Flushing, N.Y.

Cahen, L., 1970. Igneous activity and mineralization episodes in the evolution of the Kibaride and Katangide orogenic belts in Central Africa, in *African Magmatism and Tectonics*, T. N. Clifford and I. G. Gass, eds., Oliver and Boyd, Edinburgh.

Gastil, R. G., 1960. The distribution of mineral dates in time and space. *Am. Jour. Sci.* **258**(1):1–35.

Tectonic Map Committee, Geological Society of Australia, 1971. Tectonic map of Australia and New Guinea. Geological Society of Australia, 1:5,000,000.

Walker, W., 1971. Mantle cells and mineralization. Society of Mining Engineers, AIME, Preprint number 71-S-3 (and **Trans. 252:**314–327, 1972).

Walker, W., 1982. Evolving earth, Pacific opening, and related mineral belts. Society of Mining Engineers, AIME, Preprint number 82-319.

CONTRIBUTORS

Koichi Aoyagi
Japan Petroleum Exploration Co., Ltd., 3-5-5 Midorigaoka, Hamura-Machi
Nishitama-Gun, Tokyo, 190-11 Japan

John A. Barron
U.S. Geological Survey, 345 Middlefield Road, MS-915, Menlo Park,
California, 94025, U.S.A.

James R. Hein
U.S. Geological Survey, 345 Middlefield Road, MS-999, Menlo Park,
California, 94025, U.S.A.

Azuma Iijima
Geological Institute, University of Tokyo, 7-3-1 Hongo, Bunkyo-ku,
Tokyo, 113 Japan

Caroline M. Isaacs
U.S. Geological Survey, 345 Middlefield Road, MS-999, Menlo Park,
California, 94025, U.S.A.

Randolph A. Koski
U.S. Geological Survey, 345 Middlefield Road, MS-999, Menlo Park,
California, 94025, U.S.A.

Raul J. Madrid
U.S. Geological Survey, 345 Middlefield Road, MS-941, Menlo Park,
California, 94025, U.S.A.

Ryo Matsumoto
Geological Institute, University of Tokyo, 7-3-1 Hongo, Bunkyo-ku,
Tokyo, 113 Japan

Lisa A. Morgenson
U.S. Geological Survey, 345 Middlefield Road, MS-999, Menlo Park,
California, 94025, U.S.A.

Richard C. Morris
Division of Mineralogy, CSIRO, Wembley, Western Australia, 6014
Australia

Benita L. Murchey
U.S. Geological Survey, 345 Middlefield Road, MS-915, Menlo Park, California, 94025, U.S.A.

Judith T. Parrish
U.S. Geological Survey, Denver Federal Center, MS-940, P.O. Box 25046, Lakewood, Colorado, 80225, U.S.A.

Neil F. Petersen
Worldwide Geosciences, Inc. Houston, Texas, 77036, U.S.A.

Forrest G. Poole
U.S. Geological Survey, Denver Federal Center, MS-905, P.O. Box 25046, Lakewood, Colorado, 80225, U.S.A.

Richard P. Sheldon
Geologic Consultant, 3816 T. Street, N.W., Washington, D.C., 20007, U.S.A.

Rosemary E. Sliney
U.S. Geological Survey, 345 Middlefield Road, MS-999, Menlo Park, California, 94025, U.S.A.

Hsueh-Wen Yeh
Hawaii Institute of Geophysics, University of Hawaii, 2525 Correa Road, Honolulu, Hawaii, 96822, U.S.A.

SILICEOUS SEDIMENTARY ROCK-HOSTED ORES AND PETROLEUM

PART I

OVERVIEW

FINE-GRAINED SILICEOUS DEPOSITS: HOSTS FOR MULTIFARIOUS MINERAL DEPOSITS

James R. Hein

U.S. Geological Survey
Menlo Park, California

CONNECTION BETWEEN SILICEOUS DEPOSITS AND THE ASSOCIATED ORES

A wide variety of mineral deposits of potential economic value occur in association with fine-grained sedimentary siliceous deposits, including petroleum, iron, manganese, barite, phosphorite, uranium, and diatomite. The connection between these varied resources can be found in the characteristics of the depositional basin and the composition of the host siliceous deposit. Most siliceous rocks preserved in the geologic record were deposited in continental margin basins under zones of coastal upwelling (Jenkyns and Winterer, 1982; Hein and Karl, 1983; see also Chap. 2 in this book). Siliceous rocks that host ores and petroleum are characteristically an upwelling facies. Various amounts of siliceous plankton, terrestrial and marine organic matter, and detrital minerals were deposited together in basins beneath surface waters supporting high biological productivity.

Biogenic silica and organic matter are highly reactive phases and were integral participants in the creation of the accompanying ore and petroleum occurrences. Both reactive phases adsorb constituents from seawater and in the diagenetic environment adsorb elements from and release elements to the pore waters. During diagenesis, biogenic silica undergoes transformations to stabler silica phases, from opal-A (amorphous biogenic silica) to opal-A' (amorphous inorganic silica) to opal-CT (disordered cristobalite-tridymite) and finally to quartz (Hein et al., 1978). During very early diagenesis, organic matter is degraded by bacterial processes, which generate compounds such as carbon dioxide and methane used in the formation of secondary minerals. During later diagenesis and deeper burial, the organic matter can generate petroleum through thermocatalytic molecular cracking. During various stages in the evolution of the depositional basin, degradation of the organic matter provides barium for the formation of barite, phosphorus for the formation of phosphorite, carbon compounds for the generation of hydrocarbons, and a substrate for the adsorption of uranium. Biogenic silica provides the source of diatomite, an additional substrate for the adsorption of uranium, a source of fluids needed for the migration of hydrocarbons through hydrous silica dehydration reactions, and a reservoir in fractured chert and porcelanite for petroleum.

TEMPORAL RELATIONSHIPS

Petroleum, uranium, and diatomite are confined to Cenozoic and Latest Cretaceous siliceous deposits, and phosphorite is common in these Cenozoic rocks. Manganese and barite are dominant and phosphorite common in Mesozoic and Paleozoic bedded cherts; barite is more common, however, in Paleozoic siliceous sections. Iron ore is present in Paleozoic but dominant in Precambrian bedded chert sequences. The causes of these temporal variations can be related to the paleogeographic position of the depositional environment, the degree of diagenesis, the composition of the host sediment, rates of sedimentation, the evolution of siliceous and calcareous plankton, and unknown mechanisms. For example, diatomite is absent in older rocks because biogenic silica (opal-A from diatoms in these deposits) is metastable and easily transformed to opal-CT under shallow burial conditions at a continental margin. This mineralogic transformation destroys the properties of diatomite that make it commercially attractive—for example, its low density, high porosity, low thermal conductivity, light color, high specific area, high melting point, and strength and elasticity (Chap. 7). Likewise, uranium is lost during each of the diagenetic silica transformations and is found in only low concentrations in quartz chert, the dominant silica-phase lithology in pre-Cenozoic sections (Chap. 6).

The evolution of plankton has had a greater influence on the characteristics of siliceous deposits and associated ores than is commonly appreciated. For example, diatoms, the dominant siliceous plankton group during the Cenozoic, react differently during deposition and chemical change than radiolarians, which were the dominant plankton group during the Mesozoic and Paleozoic. Radiolarians, having more robust and less porous tests compared to diatom frustules, have a greater tendency to form mass flow deposits such as turbidites (Barrett, 1982); thus the mechanical and hydrodynamic characteristics differ for these two siliceous plankton groups, and as a result, so will the lithologic characteristics of the siliceous rocks they compose. In addition, diatoms possess a smaller size on the average and greater surface area than radiolarians; these characteristics may control the solution kinetics of silica-phase transformations during diagenesis (Williams et al., 1985).

During the so-called era of radiolarians, the Mesozoic and Paleozoic, siliceous plankton were probably deposited over a greater expanse of the seafloor and in more diverse depositional environments because of the lack of competition from calcareous plankton. This is in contrast to the era of diatoms, the Cenozoic, where calcareous plankton dominate in many marine depositional settings.

The silica composing Precambrian bedded cherts is thought to be of inorganic origin, unlike the biogenic silica in cherts of the Phanerozoic. In some Precambrian deposits an inorganic origin for silica is probably valid. In other deposits, however, the cherts may have been derived from a siliceous plankton of unknown affinity, and thus, the Precambrian may represent a third era of a dominant siliceous plankton group. Evidence for this suggestion is found in some Precambrian cherts that contain many structures reminiscent of radiolarians contained in Phanerozoic cherts (Imoto and Saito, 1973; LaBerge, 1973). Interpretation of the origin of the silica in these Precambrian deposits relates directly to the origin of the associated iron ores, also commonly thought to have been precipitated from seawater.

Commentary on Chapters

The eleven chapters in this book are organized into three groups: general overviews, Cenozoic siliceous deposits, and bedded chert sequences. As readers shall see from their review of these chapters, progress in the understanding of the genesis of the various ore deposits associated with siliceous rocks is at many different stages. Extensive literature exists concerning banded iron formations (BIF), phosphorite, and diatomite, whereas the publications on uranium in diatomite number only two; similarly, the barite-silica association has been little studied. A moderate number of papers have addressed the origin of chert-hosted manganese, most proposing a hydrothermal origin. Chapters 8 and 9 are the first to provide evidence for a bacterially mediated, diagenetic origin for these manganese deposits. Although a number of papers are available on petroleum associated with Tertiary siliceous rocks, a large part of the information obtained to date is proprietary company data.

The significance of the various ores and petroleum as resources is also variable. The iron ores form vast resources on all the continents, but the high-grade ores have been depleted in the United States, where now the less-enriched BIF are mined. Phosphorite associated with siliceous rocks is also extensive and provides significant percentages of this valuable commodity used by the agricultural community. Diatomite is mined extensively in the United States, the USSR, Denmark, France, Germany, and Italy and is used in many industrial applications. Likewise, extensive reserves of petroleum are associated with siliceous rocks, primarily in California, and have been recovered for many decades. The manganese deposits are commonly high to moderate grade and low-tonnage deposits and have been mined primarily during the world wars in the United States, Japan, Costa Rica, New Zealand, and elsewhere. Compared to fluvial sandstone-hosted and conglomerate-hosted uranium deposits, those derived from siliceous rocks are apparently minor, but they have been little sought after and larger deposits may be found.

The first three chapters, this one included, are general overviews. In Chapter 2, after a brief review of siliceous deposits, Hein and Parrish compile all the occurrences of chert reported in the literature and display those data on paleogeographic maps for each geologic period of the Phanerozoic. Each occurrence is also itemized and cross-referenced in Appendix 2-1. These plots demonstrate that biosiliceous epochs exist; the ones with the greatest production of siliceous debris occurred in the Late Jurassic, Late Cretaceous, Eocene, and Miocene. Bedded chert is least abundant in the Silurian and has low abundance in the Triassic and Permian. Chert occurrences are also not evenly distributed by latitude but rather concentrate between paleolatitudes of 0° and 30°. The locations of chert on paleogeographic reconstructions are usually in good agreement with predicted regions of paleo-upwelling. Chapter 2 represents a first attempt to provide a predictive upwelling model for the Phanerozoic and offers a tool for the exploration for upwelling facies including the associated mineral deposits. A more detailed and precise correspondence between chert occurrences and upwelling zones requires a better understanding of upwelling mechanisms in relation to various past continental configurations, knowledge of the paleogeographic setting of exotic terranes and amalgamated terranes such as Japan, and a better understanding of the history of global productivity and the response of siliceous plankton to the changes in seawater and to the evolution of various plankton groups.

In Chapter 3 Sheldon proposes a mechanism by which two different phosphorite families form during various stands of sea level and conditions of polar glaciation. Trade-wind-belt phosphorite formed during periods of polar glaciation at intermediate stands of first-order sea level variations and at low stands of second-order variations, whereas equatorial phosphorite formed during high stands of first-order sea level and low stands of second-order sea level, probably without significant polar glaciation. Trade-wind phosphorite of early Pliocene, Miocene, Oligocene, Jurassic, Permian, Early Carboniferous, and Late Ordovician ages is common, while equatorial phosphorite was deposited in Early Tertiary, Late Cretaceous, and possibly the Cambrian and Proterozoic. Sheldon further proposes that in some deposits the chert and phosphorite were deposited at alternating interglacial and glacial stages respectively. A direct link exists between glacial cover, sea level variations, and the intensity of oceanic circulation including upwelling. Chert commonly occurs stratigraphically above phosphorite and represents a deeper-water facies. The lithologic association of chert and phosphorite is characteristically an upwelling facies. Both the silica and phosphate were removed biologically from near-surface water and, on death of the organisms, were deposited on the seafloor as diatomaceous or radiolarian mudstone and phosphate-rich organic matter and fish debris. The typical diatomite, porcelanite, chert, and phosphorite beds seen in outcrop were formed through diagenesis. Phosphorite beds commonly formed earlier in the diagenetic history (shortly after burial) than chert and porcelanite beds (after hundreds of meters of burial). The precipitation of phosphate, and thus its separation from chert, is controlled by the pH, organic matter content, oxygen content, and perhaps bioturbation of the sediment in the depositional basin. Sheldon further points out that the easily recognizable associated chert may be a guide in the field during the exploration for some phosphate deposits. Individual deposits may contain hundreds of millions to billions of tons of phosphate rock important to the agricultural industries of the world.

Part II is divided into four chapters, two on petroleum, one on uranium, and one on diatomite. Organic matter, produced abundantly in zones of upwelling, is partly oxidized as it sinks through the water column. Organic matter is further oxidized at the seafloor and after burial, especially in areas of bioturbation of the sediment. This degradation of organic matter produces a low-oxygen zone in the water column that intersects the continental shelf and slope over an interval that varies between 75 m and 1,500 m water depth. Cenozoic diatomaceous sediment deposited beneath the oxygen-minimum zone is commonly laminated and rich in organic matter. In near-shore basins this marine organic matter may be augmented by various amounts of terrestrial organic matter. The marine organic matter in the diatomaceous deposits is the source of most of California's and Japan's petroleum resources.

Isaacs and Petersen, in Chapter 4, and Aoyagi and Iijima, in Chapter 5, show that the hydrocarbon source rocks are the Monterey Formation in California and the Onnagawa, Wakkanai, and age-equivalent formations in Japan. Isaacs and Petersen show that the decrease in the input of terrigenous debris relative to organic matter to the depositional basin produces the organic-rich siliceous deposits. They also show that Monterey Formation oil was generated under a temperature regime previously considered too low to produce abundant oil. One consequence of this early generation is the high sulfur content of the oil. The Monterey Formation and other siliceous deposits offer a unique set of characteristics that influences the generation and storage of oil. Examples include the following:

1. Overlying diatomites and diatomaceous shales act as thermal blankets on the sections.
2. The burial compaction of siliceous sections takes place in two discrete episodes rather than continuously as in carbonate or argillaceous sections. One manifestation of this situation is preservation of significant porosity to great depths of burial.
3. Extensive fracturing of brittle chert and secondary dolomite provides significant reservoir capacity.

The difficulties encountered in research and exploration for oil in siliceous deposits have also been unique. Examples include the following:

Uncharacteristic behavior of vitrinite alteration in the presence of abundant marine algal matter,

The disregard by most workers in considering precompaction stratigraphic thicknesses in their development of thermal models,

The difficulty of interpreting well logs because of the fine-scale lithologic variation in siliceous deposits.

Isaacs and Petersen further discuss these interesting (but often frustrating to the explorationist) characteristics of siliceous deposits.

Hein et al., in Chapter 6, show that organic matter not only is the essential ingredient for the petroleum resources but also acts as the substrate, along with biogenic silica, for the adsorption of uranium from seawater. Uranium is adsorbed more efficiently on terrestrial (humic) organic matter than on marine organic matter. During bacterial degradation of the organic matter and later diagenesis of biogenic silica, the adsorbed uranium is released and migrates to surrounding sandstone host rocks where, given the appropriate conditions, economic concentrations may develop. Siliceous deposits may be considered as a source rock of uranium deposits as they are for petroleum deposits. While uranium is enriched in all diatomites studied in the circum-Pacific, petroleum resources have not been identified in association with many of the Tertiary siliceous formations, such as the Pisco Formation of Peru.

In Chapter 7, Barron points out that diatomite has many unique qualities that make it useful for over three hundred industrial purposes. Its primary use as a filtering agent is possible because of the complex and small size of pores in the diatom frustule. The United States is the largest producer of diatomite, with most coming from California. Commercial-grade diatomite results from oceanic conditions that promote the vigorous production of diatoms; depositional conditions that exclude most terrigenous, volcanic, and calcareous biogenic debris; and a geologic history of little diagenesis or erosion. Phosphorus, nitrate, and silica are the primary nutrients required by diatoms and are supplied to the surface waters in areas of upwelling. Through the consumption of these nutrients and photosynthesis, the diatoms produce the opaline frustules and phosphorus-containing protoplasm that eventually go into the formation of some phosphorite, diatomite, petroleum, and uranium deposits.

Part III is divided into four chapters, two about manganese and one each on iron ore and barite. Chapter 8, by Matsumoto, and Chapter 9, by Hein et al. show that chert-hosted manganese deposits are of diagenetic origin. The manganese lenses formed at depth in the sediment column through bacterial processes rather than hydrothermally as proposed in the past. The Japan rhodochrosite deposit studied by Matsumoto was derived from the carbon dioxide produced during bacterial fermentation processes, which produced methane as well. The rhodochrosite from California formed from this same process in addition to oxidation of the methane produced by the fermentation and carbonate reduction. In both deposits, the manganese was derived from the hemipelagic shales and rhythmically interbedded siliceous turbidites (cherts) that host the manganese deposits. The depositional settings of these Mesozoic and Paleozoic siliceous deposits are the same as those for Tertiary siliceous deposits, but radiolarians rather than diatoms were the dominant type of plankton. It is not clear why manganese carbonate appears to be the predominant bacterially produced carbonate in Mesozoic and Paleozoic siliceous deposits, whereas dolomite is apparently predominant in Cenozoic siliceous deposits.

Even though the literature on BIF is extensive, much controversy exists about the origin of the various lithologies including chert, iron oxides, silicates, and carbonates. As discussed by Morris in Chapter 10, this controversy is partly the result of complexities brought on by textural and compositional changes due to metamorphism and supergene processes. More detailed studies of the chert and carbonate lithologies may bring about a better understanding of the origin and evolution of these large iron ore deposits. Morris details the sequence of events that lead to enrichment of the BIF, primarily through supergene processes. Goethite may replace chert, which in turn is replaced by hematite. A balance must be reached between the rate of silica solution and hydrous iron oxide precipitation. Migration and precipitation of iron at depth may be possible because of an electrochemical mechanism involving cathodic reactions at magnetite-groundwater interfaces that drives corrosion cells by drawing electrons from the anodic oxidation of ferrous iron at depth. Morris shows that although all the major BIF are Precambrian in age, as old as 3.6 b.y., the enrichment of these deposits did not begin until about 2 b.y. ago, with additional enrichments occurring in the Phanerozoic. These enriched BIF form vast iron reserves on all the continents and may constitute the largest and most concentrated accumulation of any single metal in the Earth's crust.

In Chapter 11, Murchey et al. briefly describe the association of bedded and nodular barite with bedded chert in mostly Paleozoic sequences of western North America. The barite-chert association was deposited in an upper to middle continental slope environment, paleogeographically between platform carbonates and deep-water chert-bearing sequences. These continental margin depositional environments were probably areas of intense coastal upwelling that provided the barium for barite, the silica for chert, the carbon for associated carbonaceous shales, and the phosphorus for associated phosphates.

REFERENCES

Barrett, T. J., 1982. Stratigraphy and sedimentology of Jurassic bedded chert overlying ophiolites in the North Apennines, Italy. *Sedimentology* **29**:353–373.

Hein, J. R., and S. M. Karl, 1983. Comparisons between open-ocean and continental margin chert sequences, in *Siliceous Deposits in the Pacific Region*, A. Iijima, J. R. Hein, and R. Siever, eds., Elsevier, Amsterdam, pp. 25–43.

Hein, J. R., D. W. Scholl, J. A. Barron, M. G. Jones, and J. Miller, 1978. Diagenesis of late Cenozoic diatomaceous deposits and formation of the bottom simulating reflector in the southern Bering Sea, *Sedimentology* **25**:155–181.

Imoto, N., and Y. Saito, 1973. Scanning electron microscopy of chert, *Natl. Sci. Museum Tokyo Bull.* **16**:397–402.

Jenkyns, H. C., and E. L. Winterer, 1982. Palaeoceanography of Mesozoic ribbon radiolarites, *Earth and Planetary Sci. Letters* **60**:351–375.

LaBerge, G. L., 1973. Possible biological origin of Precambrian iron-formations, *Econ. Geology* **68**:1098–1109.

Williams, L. A., G. A. Parks, and D. A. Crerar, 1985. Silica diagenesis, I. Solubility controls, *Jour. Sed. Petrology* **55**:301–311.

2

DISTRIBUTION OF SILICEOUS DEPOSITS IN SPACE AND TIME

James R. Hein

U.S. Geological Survey
Menlo Park, California

Judith Totman Parrish

U.S. Geological Survey
Denver, Colorado

ABSTRACT. The worldwide distribution of siliceous deposits for each geologic period back through the Cambrian is displayed on paleogeographic maps and listed in Appendix 2–1. We consider only on-land deposits of bedded chert and their prediagenetic equivalents, diatomaceous and radiolarian earths. The global production and preservation of siliceous deposits has been relatively high since the Jurassic peaking during the Cretaceous–Paleogene; especially important intervals include the Late Jurassic, Late Cretaceous, Eocene, and Miocene. Occurrences are low in Triassic and Permian sections, moderate in Carboniferous and Devonian rocks, and lowest in Silurian and Cambrian deposits. Chert is not evenly distributed by latitude but has a strong peak distribution between 0° and 30° paleolatitude. This latitudinal distribution varies somewhat with major changes in tectonic plate configurations. These patterns of chert occurrences can be related to areas of oceanic upwelling, under the influence of which abundant siliceous plankton are produced and preserved in rock-forming quantities. Equatorial-oceanic divergence and west-coast-type upwelling systems apparently account for the greater part of the biogenic-silica production preserved in the geologic record, although monsoonal upwelling is predicted to have been important during the time Pangea was in existence. The causes of the biosiliceous epochs involve a host of geologic, oceanographic, and tectonic conditions favorable to the production and preservation of biosiliceous debris and the isolation of the depositional basin from input of terrigenous material.

INTRODUCTION

The fundamental knowledge necessary for the exploration for ores and petroleum is of the host-rock lithologic associations and the distribution of that suite of host rocks in space and time. This introductory chapter briefly describes siliceous deposits and displays their distribution on paleogeographic maps for each geologic period back through the Cambrian. This compilation of bedded chert deposits encompasses all those deposits we could glean from the literature, from discussions with field geologists, and from personal experience. The last such compilation was completed by Grunau (1965) and was confined to radiolarites. More recent analyses of the global distribution of cherts (cf. Ramsay, 1973) relied heavily on Grunau's compilation for the distribution of cherts in orogenic belts. The literature on siliceous deposits has increased dramatically since the mid–1970s, partly in response to the development of a technique for the extraction of Radiolaria from cherts and their use in age dating (Pessagno and Newport, 1972).

DEFINITION OF
SILICEOUS DEPOSITS

Siliceous deposits as defined here are fine-grained, dominantly biogenic sediments and sedimentary rocks. They include diatom and radiolarian oozes, diatomaceous and radiolarian earths, porcelanite, and chert. As the names imply, these deposits are composed predominantly of diatoms or radiolarians but also lesser amounts of siliceous sponge spicules and silicoflagellates. Various amounts of detrital and authigenic minerals also occur in siliceous rocks.

ORIGIN OF SILICA

The biogenic origin of Phanerozoic cherts has been well established (cf. Ramsay, 1973; Hein et al., 1983). Volcanism, either from direct hydrothermal precipitation or from halmyrolysis of oceanic crust, and alteration of volcanic, pyroclastic, or volcaniclastic debris, all of which would add silica to the oceans and thus stimulate plankton productivity, are not required for the formation of siliceous deposits (cf. Garrison, 1974). Rather, siliceous organisms in the present oceans, and probably also in the past, are deposited in rock-forming quantities only in areas of upwelling in the oceans (excluding lacustrine deposits). The distribution of radiolarian-rich deposits on the pre-Jurassic ocean floor may have been widespread because of the lack of competition with the calcareous plankton that evolved during post-Triassic times; however, like today, radiolarian productivity would have been great enough to produce siliceous debris in rock-forming quantities undiluted by abundant terrigenous material only in areas of upwelling. In these areas of upwelling, phosphate and nitrate, not silica, are the limiting nutrients to plankton productivity. Siliceous plankton can efficiently extract silica from water at concentrations far less than those found in the oceans (Lewin, 1961). Thus, siliceous deposits should be an excellent indicator for zones of paleo-upwelling. Other rock types that also may denote zones of upwelling include phosphorite, glauconite, barite, and some black shales (Parrish, 1983; see Chap. 11).

DISTRIBUTION OF MODERN SILICEOUS DEPOSITS

Holocene siliceous ooze is distributed in three pan-oceanic belts and along the western margin of continents; these are all areas of upwelling in the oceans. The southern, circum-Antarctic, belt contains by far the greatest amount of deposited biogenic silica (Lisitzin, 1971). The equatorial belt extends from 20° north to 20° south latitude. Siliceous deposits occur in the high-latitude parts of this zone because, around the equator, deposition is above the calcite compensation depth (CCD) and biogenic calcite prevails in the sediment. The equatorial belt of siliceous ooze is well developed in the Pacific and Indian oceans but not in the Atlantic. The northern belt of diatom ooze spans the far north Pacific and adjacent seas. Finally, upwelling is vigorous along the west coasts of continents, most notably off Peru and southwest Africa where biogenic silica is common in shelf and slope deposits.

The more ancient the siliceous deposits are, the more difficult it becomes to fit them into the modern scheme of global silica distribution. The upwelling models and paleogeographic plots of Parrish (1982) and Parrish and Curtis (1982) and those used here, taken from the University of Chicago Paleogeographic Map Project (1984), are useful, therefore, in resolving the space-time distribution of chert and consequently the zones of paleo-upwelling.

DEPOSITIONAL MECHANISMS AND ENVIRONMENTS

Two long-standing problems concerning the origin of bedded cherts, also called ribbon cherts or ribbon radiolarites, are the origin of the rhythmic bedding and the environment of deposition. No modern analogues to bedded cherts exist. Bedded chert is certainly not analogous to deep-sea chert recovered by the deep-sea drilling project (Hein and Karl, 1983), but Mesozoic and Paleozoic bedded cherts are probably equivalents to Tertiary continental margin diatomaceous deposits; that is, bedded cherts formed in the same depositional, oceanographic, and tectonic settings where diatomaceous deposits formed during the Neogene (Ramsay, 1973; Jenkyns and Winterer, 1982; Hein and Karl, 1983). These environments include back-arc basins, such as the Bering, Philippine, and Japan seas; small ocean basins with transform-fault-dominated spreading centers (spreading basins rather than spreading ridges), such as the Gulf of California; and silled basins locally isolated from terrigenous material, such as the wrench basins of the California continental borderland.

The nature of the rhythmic bedding in the chert-shale sequences is more difficult to ascertain. The two prevailing ideas are that (1) the chert beds represent turbidites composed of siliceous microfossils, whereas the shale beds represent background pelagic or hemipelagic sedimentation (cf. Nisbet and Price, 1974; Hein and Karl, 1983), and (2) the chert beds represent climatically controlled episodes of high plankton productivity in surface waters, whereas the shale beds represent background pelagic or hemipelagic deposition (Jenkyns and Winterer, 1982). Most workers favor the former mechanism as an explanation for the production of ribbon cherts. Both depositional mechanisms have generated certain chert sequences, but at present it is not known which mechanism was most common.

Diagenesis

Clay-rich siliceous sediments are transformed to porcelanite and then to chert through diagenesis. These textural changes are commonly accompanied by the mineralogic changes opal-A (biogenic silica) to opal-CT (disordered cristobalite-tridymite) to quartz (Hein et al., 1978). Pure siliceous ooze transforms to opal-CT chert then to quartz chert. These transformations are controlled primarily by temperature, but time, pore water chemistry, and host lithology also play a part in the diagenesis (Kastner et al., 1977). When cherts in ophiolite sequences are incorporated into continental margins either by obduction or by the docking of exotic terranes, further reorganization or mobilization of silica occurs, and other modifications to the rocks may result from tectonism.

Distribution of Ancient Siliceous Sediments

Methods

We deal here only with on-land deposits of bedded chert (ribbon chert) and do not consider nodular chert or siliceous shale. Cenozoic diatomaceous and radiolarian earths are considered to be the prediagenetic equivalents of Mesozoic and Paleozoic bedded cherts and therefore have been included. We have not attempted to choose sequences included in this chapter based on any thickness criteria partly because, having specified bedded chert, data on thickness were not always available and partly because thickness is not likely to have a genetic significance, other than as a matter of degree, preservation, or length of time the depositional environment existed.

Data on cherts were compiled from the literature, from personal experience, and from discussions with colleagues. Principal literature sources were Bushinskii (1969) and Grunau (1965) and sources in Drewry et al. (1974) and Iijima et al. (1983). We were somewhat more conservative than Drewry et al.; for example, we did not include shales that contain some radiolarians. Cherts listed by Grunau (1965) are listed as radiolarian cherts in Appendix 2-1 only if Grunau specifically referred to them that way. Limitations of the data compiled for cherts include the quality and precision of the age dates, particularly the state of the development of radiolarian biostratigraphy of certain geologic periods, and the vastness and incompleteness of the literature. Also, some dates are based on fossils extracted from limestone blocks in mélanges rather than from radiolarians or conodonts extracted from chert and thus do not necessarily represent the time of chert deposition. This may be true for many of the southwest Pacific and southeast Asian sequences. In contrast, the United States and Japan sequences are based on fossils extracted directly from the cherts of interest. Further limitations involve the placement of microplates and exotic terranes on the paleogeographic reconstructions, especially with regard to the complexes of amalgamated terranes in western North America, Alaska, Japan, and China. Chert deposits reported from terranes in Japan by Iijima and Utada (1983) and in western North America by Murchey et al. (1983) posed special problems in that these authors usually did not identify formation names and their references to previous work in the various areas were inconsistent. Therefore, it is possible that some duplication of data exists. For example, Murchey et al. described Triassic cherts in their Kagvik–Brooks Range Terrane; these almost certainly include the cherts of the Otuk (formerly part of the Shublik) Formation of Mull et al. (1982), even though Murchey et al. did not refer to them by name. Cherts from terranes are listed by the terrane names and are followed, where known, by names of included formations.

Data are listed in Appendix 2-1 with references and reference numbers to the paleogeographic maps given as Figures 2-4 through 2-14. In general, each deposit has a separate listing, with one listing per deposit. However, those deposits that have particularly extensive ranges in time and space may have two or more listings. For example, the Durness Limestone of Scotland contains cherts of both Cambrian and Ordovician age and should be represented on both maps; therefore, it is listed twice. The Torlesse Terrane of New Zealand is found over a wide geographic range, on both North and South islands. For the purposes of paleogeographic analysis of chert distribution—for example, comparison with the upwelling predictions of Parrish (1982) and Parrish and Curtis (1982)—such a wide range should be noted. Therefore, cherts of the Torlesse Terrane have two listings for each age if they are distributed within the Torlesse Terrane on both islands. Each map symbol includes data from roughly 5° latitude and longitude, after the methods of Parrish.

Because siliceous sediments deposited in upwelling zones are more readily preserved in the deep ocean than are other upwelling indicators (i.e., phosphorite- and organic-rich rock), the maps of predicted upwelling (Parrish, 1982, and modifications in J. T. Parrish et al., 1986; Parrish and Curtis, 1982), which were constructed to indicate coastal upwelling zones, had to be used with some modification. Oceanic upwelling occurs under low-pressure zones and cells, particularly along the equator and at about 55° north and south (high-mid-latitude oceanic divergence; Parrish, 1982). To account for this oceanic upwelling, cherts that fall in (or near, to allow for obduction of oceanic sediments) these areas are considered to have been deposited in upwelling zones. In addition, to allow for changes in continental positions and shorelines, chert deposits that are within zones that would be influenced by short lateral extensions of the originally-predicted upwelling zones also are considered to have been deposited in upwelling zones.

Parrish et al. (1979; see illustrations in Parrish, 1982) defined three types of coastal upwelling: (1) meridional, such as the California upwelling zone, occurring along west-facing coasts at low mid-latitudes; (2) zonal, such as the upwelling off northern Venezuela, occurring along north- or south-facing coasts; and (3) monsoonal upwelling, such as the seasonal Somalian upwelling, which occurs along east-facing coasts. High biologic productivity associated with strong, steady currents such as the Gulf Stream, and therefore not strictly wind driven, constitute another type of east-coast upwelling that was not included in the original predictions and that also is not considered here since the prediction of ancient analogs of such currents is less certain. However, it is clear that this type of upwelling was important at some times in the past, as has been shown for the phosphate deposits of the southeastern United States (Riggs, 1984).

The continental reconstructions (see Figs. 2–4 through 2–14) are from the University of Chicago Paleogeographic Atlas Project (1984; Scotese, 1979; Scotese et al., 1979; Ziegler et al., 1983). Paleogeographic maps based on versions of these reconstructions have been used in several paleoclimatologic studies (e.g., Parrish et al., 1982; Doyle and Parrish, 1984; Raymond et al., 1985; Rowley et al., 1985). The latest reconstructions are used here, which are somewhat different from those used in the earlier paleoclimatologic studies.

Results

The global production and preservation of siliceous deposits has been relatively high since the Jurassic, peaking during the Cretaceous and Paleogene (Fig. 2–1). The occurrence of bedded cherts is low in Triassic and Permian sections, moderate in Carboniferous and Devonian rocks, and lowest in Sil-

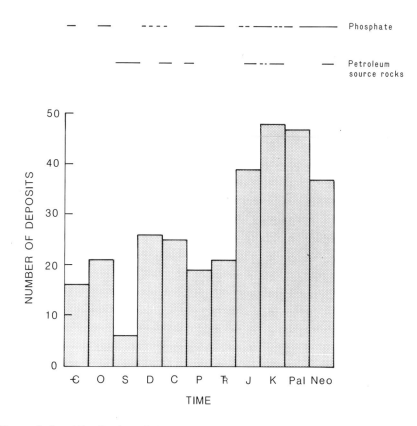

Figure 2–1. Distribution of chert through time (histrogram) compared with the distribution of petroleum source beds (Tissot, 1979) and phosphate (Cook and McElhinny, 1979), shown by horizontal lines. A space between lines indicates their absence, and short dashed lines indicates presence in minor amounts. Frequencies are derived from numbered entries in Appendix 2–1.

urian and Cambrian deposits. The Silurian is also poor in organic-rich rocks
and phosphorites. The occurrence of chert was moderate in the Ordovician.
A Jurassic–Cretaceous high is noted in Grunau's (1965) data. If only data
from the amalgamated exotic terranes in Alaska are considered (Murchey et
al., 1983), the occurrence of chert peaks in the Triassic and the Mississippian,
which may have some bearing on the history of the source of these exotic
terranes.

Chert is not evenly distributed by latitude but has a strong peak distribution
between 0° and 30° paleolatitude (Fig. 2-2). This latitudinal range includes
the equatorial-oceanic divergence and the west-coast upwelling zones, and the
data suggest that these settings account for the greater part of biogenic-silica
production, in contrast to the high-latitude oceanic divergences. However, this
trend is not even through time. The data in Figure 2-3 are broken down by
intervals that correspond to times of major global paleogeographic patterns—that is, before the assembly of Pangea, during Pangea's existence, and
after its breakup. It is notable that when Pangea was in existence, more chert
was deposited between 20° and 30° paleolatitude, whereas during the other
intervals, chert deposition declined poleward from the equator. This pattern
may be an indication of the intensity of the subtropical high-pressure cells in
eastern Panthalassa, suggested by J. M. Parrish et al. (1986) to be an effect
of the monsoonal circulation over Pangea—specifically, the contrast with sum-
mer temperatures in each hemisphere. Chert deposition also was more evenly
distributed by latitude when Pangea was extant (Fig. 2-3). The Pangean pattern may, however, be an artifact of the current positions of chert-bearing
allochthonous terranes.

More information is available for North America than for any other continent, so an examination of the history of chert deposition through time in
North America is particularly instructive and illustrative of some of the proc-

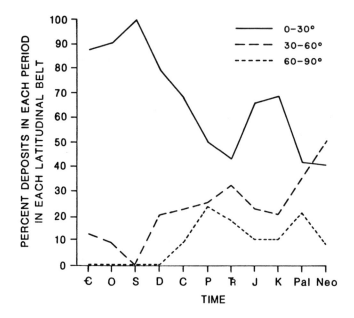

Figure 2-2. Distribution of chert by latitude.

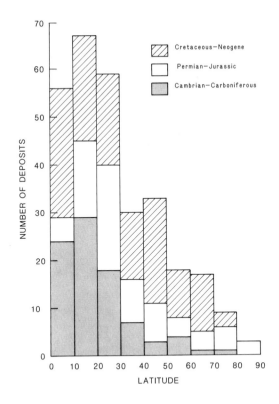

Figure 2–3.   Paleolatitudinal distribution of chert through time.

esses involved. North America has been influenced through its history by west-coast upwelling; equatorial upwelling on the western side; east-coast, probably Gulf Stream–type, upwelling; and high-latitude divergence (Parrish, 1982). In the Cambrian, North America straddled the equator and was rotated 90° clockwise relative to its present position (Fig. 2–4) (Scotese et al., 1979; J. T. Parrish et al., 1986). Through the early Paleozoic, North America rotated counterclockwise and gradually began drifting northward. As it did, it successively penetrated low- and then high-mid-latitude climatic zones. By the Ordovician, the rotation of the continent brought the northwestern corner into the subtropics, and a few chert deposits are known from that region (Fig. 2–5). With continued northward drift, chert deposits along the western side of North America, with the exception of a low in the Silurian (Fig. 2–6), became more numerous and widespread until the Triassic, when an apparent leveling off relative to the end of the Paleozoic occurred (Figs. 2–7 through 2–10). In the Jurassic, the number and geographic range of chert deposits again increased and maintained a high level through the Tertiary (Figs. 2–11 through 2–14). From this time on, however, the siliceous sediment probably was deposited in two separate systems, the meridional upwelling of low mid-latitudes and the oceanic divergence of the high mid-latitudes. A distinct gap exists between regions of chert deposition in the western United States and Alaska; chert deposits now found between these two regions may have been accreted to the continent after deposition on allochthonous terranes. Cherts that are likely to have been deposited in the equatorial-upwelling zones are present in North America in small numbers throughout the Paleozoic and Triassic, after

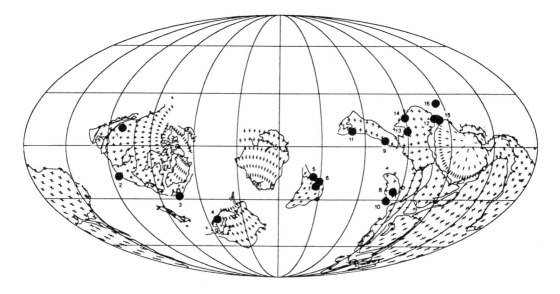

Figure 2–4. Cambrian paleogeography and chert distribution. Numbers correspond to entries in Appendix 2-1. Dots = age spanning entire period; the Late, Middle, or Early age designation for each point is listed in the appendix. The position of New Zealand is extrapolated. (Paleogeography from Scotese, 1979; Scotese et al., 1979; J. T. Parrish et al., 1986)

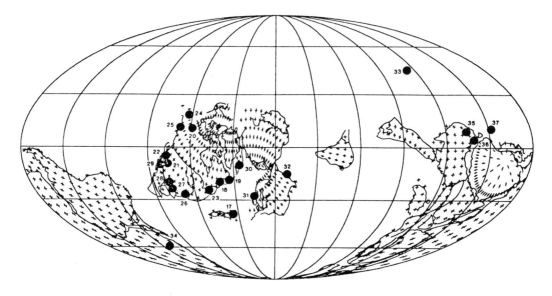

Figure 2–5. Ordovician paleogeography and chert distribution. Numbers and symbols are as explained in Figure 2-4. The position of New Zealand is extrapolated, and that of Malaysia is not known. (Paleogeography from Scotese, 1979; Scotese et al., 1979)

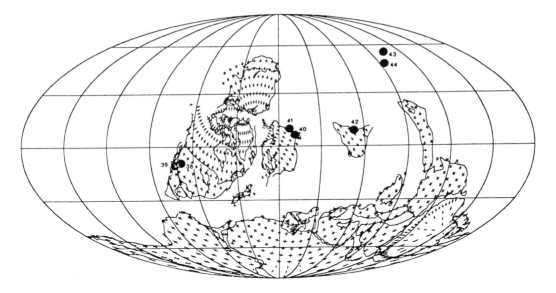

Figure 2-6. Silurian paleogeography and chert distribution. Numbers and symbols are as explained in Figure 2-4. The position of Malaysia and Thailand is not known. (Paleogeography from Scotese, 1979; Scotese et al., 1979)

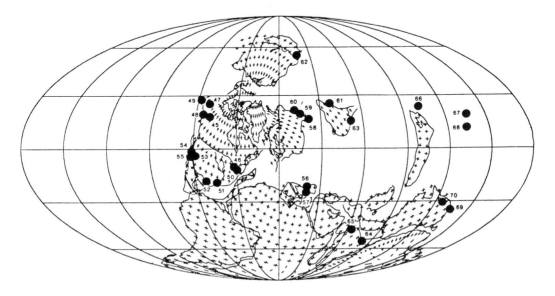

Figure 2-7. Devonian paleogeography and chert distribution. Numbers and symbols are as explained in Figure 2-4. The position of Japan is extrapolated, and that of Malaysia and Thailand is not known. (Paleogeography from Scotese, 1979; Scotese et al., 1979)

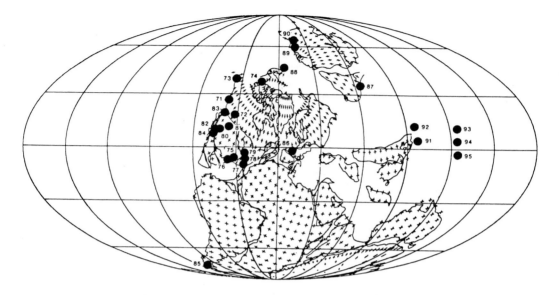

Figure 2–8. Carboniferous paleogeography and chert distribution. Numbers and symbols are as explained in Figure 2–4. The position of Japan is extrapolated, and the position of southeast Asia and Malaysia is not known. (Paleogeography from Scotese, 1979; Scotese et al., 1979)

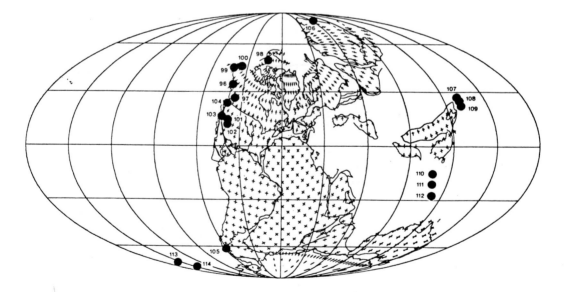

Figure 2–9. Permian paleogeography and chert distribution. Numbers and symbols are as explained in Figure 2–4. The position of Japan and New Zealand is extrapolated, and the position of Malaysia and Indonesia is not known. (Paleogeography from Scotese, 1979; Scotese et al., 1979)

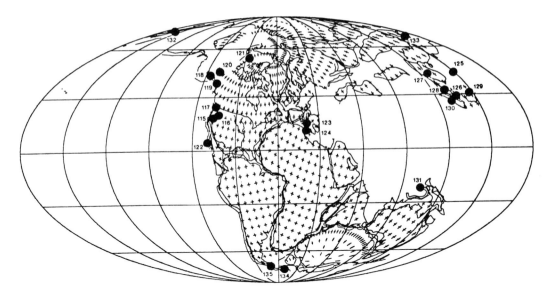

Figure 2-10. Triassic paleogeography and chert distribution. Numbers and symbols are as explained in Figure 2-4. The position of the Philippines is extrapolated. (Paleogeography from Scotese, 1979; Ziegler et al. 1983)

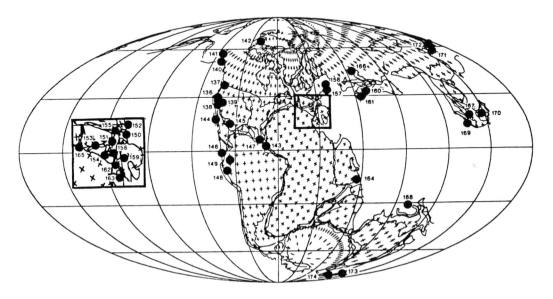

Figure 2-11. Jurassic paleogeography and chert distribution. Numbers and symbols are as explained in Figure 2-4. A detailed distribution of chert occurrences for the boxed area is inset on the left of the figure. The position of Sulawesi is extrapolated. (Paleogeography from Scotese, 1979; Ziegler et al, 1983)

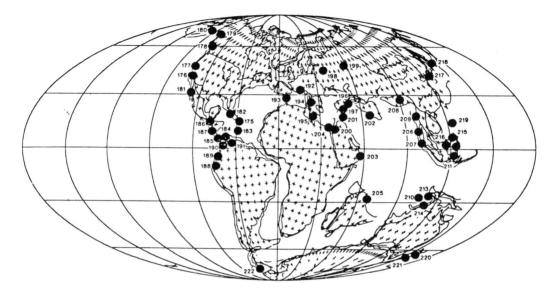

Figure 2-12. Cretaceous paleogeography and chert distribution. Numbers and symbols are as explained in Figure 2-4. The position of Sulawesi and the Philippines is extrapolated. (Paleogeography from Scotese, 1979; Ziegler et al., 1983)

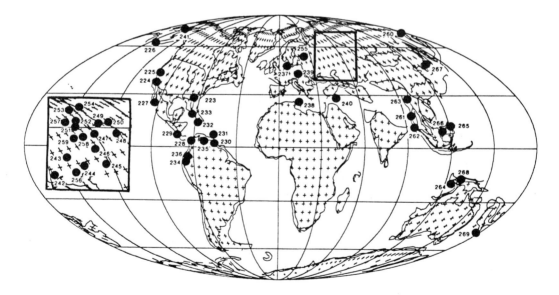

Figure 2-13. Paleogene paleogeography and chert distribution. Numbers are as explained in Figure 2-4. The Paleocene, Eocene, or Oligocene age designation for each point is listed in Appendix 2-1. A detailed distribution of chert occurrences for the boxed area is inset on the left of the figure. (Paleogeography from Scotese, 1979; Ziegler et al., 1983)

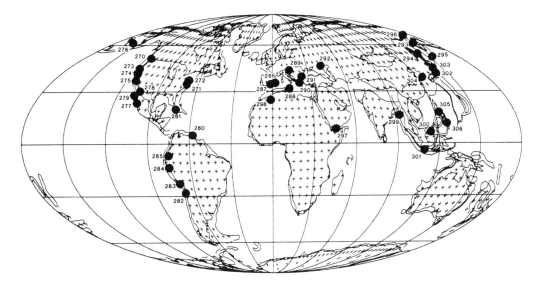

Figure 2-14.   Neogene paleogeography and chert distribution. Numbers are as explained in Figure 2-4. The Miocene or Pliocene age designation for each point is listed in Appendix 2-1. (Paleogeography from Scotese, 1979; Ziegler et al., 1983)

which time the continent drifted away from the equator. Equatorial cherts persisted, however, in northern South America, along with those associated with zonal upwelling (Parrish, 1982). Meridional upwelling is not much in evidence in western South America until the Neogene, even though the continent was in the proper latitudes from the Carboniferous onward; this lack of evidence may be because South America has been less intensively studied.

Monsoonal upwelling, though relatively unimportant in the Holocene is predicted to have been more important during the interval when Pangea was in existence—namely from the Permian to the Jurassic. Pangea is thought to have created intense monsoonal conditions in Tethys and eastern Pangea due to the seasonal contrast between the warm and cold halves of the continent, a contrast enhanced by the size of the exposed land areas (J. M. Parrish et al., 1986). However, chert deposition in Tethys was not extensive until the Jurassic (Fig. 2-11), even though monsoonal upwelling would be expected for the Permian and Triassic as well. By the Cretaceous, the monsoon had completely broken down because of the breakup of Pangea (Parrish and Doyle, 1984), and the continued chert deposition in the region is likely to have been beneath zonal coastal upwelling currents.

Judging by the distribution of chert, the paleo–Gulf Stream may have started as early as the Late Jurassic (see Fig. 2-11), about the time the monsoonal circulation in the Northern Hemisphere, which would have tended to disrupt normal oceanic-gyral circulation, is predicted to have disappeared. However, some of the cherts—for example, in Cuba—might be allochthonous terranes derived from the west (Pindell and Dewey, 1982), where they would have been deposited in the equatorial or meridional upwelling systems. Nevertheless, cherts on autochthonous terranes are common from the Cretaceous onward.

Cherts are exceptionally well studied in Japan (see Iijima et al., 1983). In the late Mesozoic and Tertiary, Japan's position would have been favorable for either Gulf Stream–type upwelling (the paleo–Kuroshio Current) or high-mid-latitude divergence if it was more or less in its current position relative to North China, or even somewhat farther south, as suggested by Jurassic floras (Kimura and Tsujii, 1984). For the earlier Phanerozoic, the depositional settings of Japanese cherts are difficult to interpret because the paleogeography of eastern Asia is so poorly known.

DISCUSSION

Data plotted on the paleogeographic reconstructions are usually in good agreement with predicted paleo-upwelling (Parrish, 1982; Parrish and Curtis, 1982). A quantitative evaluation cannot be made, however, until the circulation patterns are redone using the latest paleogeographic reconstructions. For the Phanerozoic as a whole, this correspondence appears especially good; the correspondence also holds for most of the individual geologic periods. Note that upwelling predictions were for specific geologic stages and corresponding paleogeographies, whereas the data used here are combined for each geologic period. Since siliceous plankton, the precursor of chert, are known to exist in rock-forming quantities only in zones of high-nutrient supply, the discrepancies between the observed distribution of chert and the areas of upwelling in the model can be explained as the result of several factors: (1) lack of knowledge of the original placement of exotic terranes that compose the margins of much of the circum-Pacific region, (2) errors in the upwelling model, (3) mechanisms other than upwelling that supply critical nutrients, and (4) inaccurate placement of continents.

Most previous discussions of the space-time distribution of siliceous deposits emphasize the remarkable Jurassic biosiliceous epoch (cf. Steinberg, 1981; Jenkyns and Winterer, 1982). In our global compilation and that of Grunau (1965), the Cretaceous is the height of the biosiliceous epoch. However, our compilation shows that the entire interval from the Jurassic to the present saw an abundant production of siliceous deposits. Especially important were the Late Jurassic, Late Cretaceous, Eocene, and Miocene. On a global scale, the Eocene and Miocene biosiliceous epochs rival any of those in the Mesozoic. It is interesting to note that the beginning of the great post-Triassic biosiliceous epoch coincided with the development of two widespread plankton groups, calcareous coccoliths and siliceous diatoms.

Perhaps the most mysterious element to the pattern of silica deposition through the Phanerozoic is the abundant siliceous deposits, mostly diatomite, deposited in the central USSR in the Paleogene. The position of these cherts in a central epicontinental setting is difficult to explain using known mechanisms of upwelling, including lacustrine turnover. Perhaps this basin received an unusual influx of nutrients from rivers, such as from eroding phosphate deposits.

Indeed, the uneven distribution of chert through time is only partly explained by paleogeographies favorable to upwelling. For example, the Silurian shows a marked low in chert; it is also extremely depauperate in phosphorite and organic-rich rock (Parrish et al., 1983; Fig. 2–1), suggesting some world-wide depletion of nutrients in the oceans at that time. Such fluctuations in nutrient levels have been discussed as being the cause of fluctuations in the abundance of phosphorite and organic-rich rock throughout the Phanerozoic (e.g., Arthur and Jenkyns, 1981; Arthur et al., 1984). However, chert, petroleum source rocks, and phosphate only roughly mirror each other in abundance through time (Fig. 2-1). All three tend to be high in post-Cretaceous time, but before then, they show quite different patterns. Therefore, either global productivity changes affect the three rock types independently or the mechanism of variations involves a complex interaction of variables.

The causes of these biosiliceous epochs involve a host of geologic, oceanographic, and tectonic conditions. The conditions most conducive for development of chert sequences include intense upwelling at continental margins in areas of basin development, specifically where new ocean basins are forming like the Gulf of California; in backarc basins; and in continental shelf and slope basins. The number of deposits preserved in the geologic record that formed in the open ocean is relatively small (Hein and Karl, 1983). The necessity of conditions of upwelling implies certain patterns of atmospheric and oceanic circulation (Parrish, 1982). A shallow CCD is important to eliminate biogenic carbonate from the depositional basin (Garrison, 1974), although the CCD commonly shoals near continents (Berger and Winterer, 1974) and diatoms can outproduce calcareous plankton under conditions of intense continental margin upwelling. The amount of detrital influx is equally important in that increases in terrigenous minerals to the continental margin basins dilute the siliceous debris. In turn, the detrital input is influenced by changes in sea level, climate, and tectonics (isolation of the basins).

APPLICATION TO RESOURCES

Chapter 1 contains a detailed discussion of the resources of siliceous deposits. The source rocks of many Cenozoic petroleum deposits are siliceous deposits—for example, the Miocene Monterey Formation of California. Most petroleum exploration has been in the Miocene siliceous sequences. The widespread occurrences of Eocene siliceous rocks may also provide good possibilities for petroleum exploration. The global distribution of all Cenozoic siliceous rocks offers a large variety of possible exploration targets.

Mesozoic and Paleozoic bedded chert is the host for high-grade, low-tonnage manganese deposits and for bedded barite (see Chaps. 9 and 11). Phosphorite is associated with siliceous rocks deposited throughout the Phanerozoic (see Chap. 3) and uranium in Tertiary diatomite (Chap. 1). Development of a predictive upwelling model for the Phanerozoic would provide an excellent tool for the exploration for upwelling facies and their associated resources: chert, phosphorite, black shale, glauconite, manganese, uranium, barite, petroleum, and iron.

ACKNOWLEDGMENTS

We thank the following people for providing information on chert localities: Lloyd Burckle and Connie Sancetta, Lamont-Doherty Geological Observatory, and John Barron, Benita L. Murchey, and David Jones, U.S. Geological Survey. Robert E. Garrison, University of California at Santa Cruz, and Benita L. Murchey provided helpful reviews.

Appendix 2–1. Compilation of Worldwide Chert Occurrences, Ages, Associated Lithologies, and References

Country	Locality[a]	Age[b]	Name[c]	Lithology	Reference
Cambrian					
1 United States	N NV	m, l	Indet.	Chert, limestone, shale	Roberts et al., 1958
2 United States	GA	e	Weisner, Shady Fms.	Chert, slate, dolomite, iron	O'Rourke, 1961
3 Great Britain	Scotland	l	Durness Limestone	Chert, limestone	Grunau, 1965
4 Norway	Dunderlandsdal	l	Indet.	Chert, schist, marble, hematite, magnetite	O'Rourke, 1961
5 USSR	SE Kazakhstan	e	Indet.	"Siliceous rock"	Vinogradov, 1968a
6 USSR	S Kazakhstan	e–m	Chulak-tau Suite	Chert, phosphate, dolomite	Kholodov and Khoryakin, 1961; Eganov, 1979; Bushinskii, 1969; Gimmel'farb and Tushina, 1966; Tushina, 1968; Meng, 1959; Kholodov, 1969; Smirnov, 1959
7 USSR	Alma-Ata	m–l	Narzykyl Suite	Chert, phosphate, shale, limestone, sandstone	Bushinskii, 1969
8 China	C Sichuan	e	Leipo Suite	Chert, shale, phosphate, marl	Bushinskii, 1969
9 China	E Tarim Basin	e	Indet.	Chert, limestone, phosphate	Bushinskii, 1969
10 China	Guizhou-Hunan boundary region	e	Indet.	Chert, shale	Bushinskii, 1969
11 China	Manchuria	e–m	Indet.	Chert, iron, schist, sandstone	O'Rourke, 1961
12 Australia	S N.S.W.	—	Wagonga Series	Chert, tuff, graywacke, schist	Grunau, 1965
13 Australia	Georgina Basin	m	Beetle Creek Fm.	Chert, carbonate, shale, phosphate	Fleming, 1974
14 Australia	NW Queensland	e–m	Camooweal Dolomite	Chert, limestone, siltstone, marl	Brown et al., 1968
15 Australia	Tasmania	m–l	Dundas Gp.	Chert, shale	Brown et al., 1968

#	Country	Location	Age	Formation	Lithology	Reference
16	New Zealand	N South Island	e–m	Balloon Fm.	Chert, sandstone, siltstone, siliceous limestone	Moore, 1983

Ordovician

#	Country	Location	Age	Formation	Lithology	Reference
17	Canada	E Newfoundland	e	Indet.	Chert, volcanics, shale, limestone	Strakhov, 1948
18	Canada	Gaspé Peninsula	e	Indet.	Chert, shale, conglomerate, limestone, sandstone	Poole et al., 1976
		New Brunswick	—	Austin Brook Iron	Chert, iron	Kimberley, 1978
		SE Quebec	—	Quebec Gp.	Chert, slate, iron	O'Rourke, 1961
19	Canada	NW Newfoundland	e	Snook's Arm, Lush Bight, Wild Bight Gps.	Chert, volcanics, sandstone, slate	Poole et al., 1976
20	Canada	W NW Territories	—	Road River Fm.	Chert, shale, siltstone, dolomite	Douglas et al., 1976
21	United States	N NV	e	Indet.	Chert, shale	Roberts et al., 1958; Ketner, 1969
			1	Vinini Fm., Roberts Mtn. terrane	Chert, shale, sandstone, limestone	Murchey et al., 1983
			1	Valmy Fm., Roberts Mtn. terrane	Chert, basalt, sandstone, graptolitic shale	Murchey et al., 1983
			—	Basco Fm.	Chert, shale, siltstone, limestone, sandstone	Ketner, 1969
			—	Jacks Peak Fm.	Chert, quartzite, shale, siltstone	Ketner, 1969
			—	Snow Canyon Fm.	Chert, quartzite, shale, greenstone, siltstone, sandstone, limestone	Ketner, 1969
			—	Clipper Canyon Gp.	Chert, shale, argillite	Ketner, 1969
22	United States	N CA, S OR	—	Chanchelulla Fm.	Chert, metaconglomerate, marble	Eardley, 1947

(continued)

Country	Locality[a]	Age[b]	Name[c]	Lithology	Reference
23 United States	NY	—	Indet.	Radiolarian chert, shale, sandstone, conglomerate	Grunau, 1965
24 United States	EC AK	l	Livengood Dome Chert	Chert, shale, siltstone, claystone, tuff, limestone	Chapman et al., 1980
25 United States	SE AK	e	Indet.	Chert, graywacke, volcanics	Eardley, 1947
26 United States	OK	—	Big Fork Chert	Chert, shale, carbonate, siltstone, coal	Goldstein and Hendricks, 1953
27 United States	SW TX	—	Fort Pena Fm., Maravillas Chert	Chert, conglomerate, limestone	Goldstein, 1959
28 United States	NM	—	Aleman Fm.	Chert, dolomite	Geeslin and Chaffetz, 1982
29 Mexico	Sonora	—	Indet.	Chert, barite, shale	Poole et al., 1983; B. Murchey, pers. comm.
30 Great Britain	N Scotland	e	Durness Limestone	Chert, limestone	Grunau, 1965
	S Scotland	e	Indet.	Radiolarian chert, volcanics, shale	Grunau, 1965
	Scotland	—	Indet.	"Greenalite"	James, 1966
	S Scotland	l	Indet.	Radiolarian chert, black shale, mudstone	Grunau, 1965
31 Norway	Trondheim	e	Indet.	Chert, volcanics	Grunau, 1965
32 USSR	Urals	l	Indet.	Radiolarian chert, shale	Grunau, 1965
33 Malaysia	NW peninsula	l	Indet.	Chert, limestone, siltstone, shale	Tan, 1983
34 Mauritania, Guinea, Liberia	Kayes District	—	Indet.	Chert, sandstone, schist, iron	O'Rourke, 1961
35 Australia	N.S.W.	l	Indet.	Radiolarian chert, shale	Grunau, 1965
		l	Girilambone, Tallebung Gps.	Chert, sandstone, shale	Brown et al., 1968

36 Australia	E Victoria	—	Mallacoota Beds	Chert, sandstone, siltstone, shale	Fenton et al., 1982
37 New Zealand	NW South Island	—	Anthill Black Shale	Chert, shale, sandstone	Moore, 1983
Silurian					
38 United States	NV	1	Roberts Mtn. terrane	Chert	Murchey et al., 1983
39 Mexico	Sonora	—	Indet.	Chert, barite, shale	Poole et al., 1983; B. Murchey, pers. comm.
40 USSR	S Urals	1	Indet.	"Siliceous rock"	Vinogradov, 1968a
41 USSR	Urals	—	Indet.	Radiolarian chert, shale	Grunau, 1965
42 USSR	Altai Sayan	1	Indet.	Chert, argillite	Grunau, 1965
43 Malaysia	NW peninsula	1	Indet.	Chert, limestone, siltstone, shale	Tan, 1983
44 Thailand	Peninsular	1	Indet.	Chert, shale, siltstone, sandstone, limestone	Tan, 1983
Devonian					
45 Canada	Yukon Territories	m	Prong's Creek Fm.	Chert, shale, limestone	Norris, 1967
46 Canada	SE Ontario	m	Grande Greve Fm.	Chert, limestone, siltstone, sandstone	Poole et al., 1976
47 United States	EC and C AK	e-m	Indet.	Chert, shale	Gryc et al., 1967
		e-m	McCann Hill Fm.	Chert, shale, limestone	Whalen and Carr, 1984
		1	Innoko terrane	Chert, sandstone, shale	Murchey et al., 1983
48 United States	SE AK	m	Indet.	Chert, limestone, slate, volcanics	Eardley, 1947
	AK panhandle	—	Hood Bay Fm.	Chert, argillite, limestone	Lathram et al., 1965
49 United States	SC AK	1	Chulitna terrane	Chert, ophiolite	Murchey et al., 1983
	Mystic terrane	1	Mystic terrane	Chert, carbonate	Murchey et al., 1983
50 United States	PA	e	Shriver Chert	Chert, claystone, sandstone	Waller, 1971
51 United States	OK	—	Arkansas Novaculite	Chert, shale, carbonate	Goldstein and Hendricks, 1953

(continued)

Appendix 2–1. (*continued*)

Country	Locality[a]	Age[b]	Name[c]	Lithology	Reference
52 United States	SW TX	l	Caballos Fm.	Chert, shale, sandstone, conglomerate, carbonate	Folk and McBride, 1976
53 United States	N NV	l	Havallah Seq.	Chert, greenstone, jasper	Silberling and Roberts, 1962; Snyder and Brueckner, 1983
		—	Indet.	Chert, limestone, shale	Roberts et al., 1958
		l	Schoonover Seq.	Chert, shale, sandstone, volcanics, conglomerate, dolomite	Grunau, 1965; Fagan, 1962; Miller et al., 1984
54 United States	CA	l	Sierra Buttes, Taylor, Elwell, and Peale Fms.	Chert, volcanics, shale, siltstone	D'Allura et al., 1977; Murchey et al., 1983
55 Mexico	Sonora	?e, l	Indet.	Chert, barite, shale	Poole et al., 1983; B. Murchey, pers. comm.
56 West Germany	C	—	Kieselschiefer	Chert, shale	Grunau, 1965
57 West Germany	SW	m–l	Konstanze/Lahn–Dill Iron Fm.	Chert, iron	Kimberley, 1978
58 USSR	S of Orsk	e	Indet.	"Siliceous rock"	Vinogradov, 1969
59 USSR	Yuzhnny Urals	m	Indet.	Chert, phosphate, shale, carbonate	Volkov, 1970
60 USSR	Urals	—	Indet.	Radiolarian chert, shale	Grunau, 1965
61 USSR	S Siberian Lowlands	m–l	Indet.	"Siliceous rock"	Vinogradov, 1969
62 USSR	Altai	e–m	Altai Iron Fm.	Chert, iron	Kimberley, 1978
63 China	Tien Shan	e	Indet.	Chert, carbonate	Breshnev et al., 1967
64 Nepal	Phulchoki District	—	Indet.	Chert, quartzite, siltstone, dolomite, iron	O'Rourke, 1961
65 Pakistan	Islamabad	l	Sirban Fm.	Chert, phosphate, carbonate, siltstone	Latif, 1972
66 Japan	Honshu	e	Indet.	Chert, volcanics, sandstone, conglomerate	Takai et al., 1963

(continued)

67 Malaysia	C peninsula	—	Karak Fm.	Chert, conglomerate, quartzite, sandstone	Tan, 1983
68 Thailand	NW	—	Bentong Fm.	Chert, shale, limestone, siltstone, quartzite	Haile et al., 1977
69 Australia	E N.S.W.-Queensland	e-m	Tamworth Series	Chert, limestone, volcanics	Brown et al., 1968
		l	Silverwood Series	Radiolarian chert, shale	Brown et al., 1968
70 Australia	Queensland	e-m	Etna Series	Chert, volcanics, shale, limestone	Brown et al., 1968
Carboniferous					
71 Canada, United States	W coast, SE AK	l	Wrangellia terrane	Chert, ophiolite, argillite, dolomite	Murchey et al., 1983; Eardley, 1947
72 Canada	Alberta	l	Kananaskis Fm.	Chert, siltstone, sandstone, dolomite	McGugan and Rapson, 1979
	S BC	e	Cache Creek terrane	Chert, limestone, volcanics, ophiolite, argillite	Murchey et al., 1983
73 United States	C AK	e	Broad Pass, Red Paint, Chulitna terrane	Chert, tuff, argillite, ophiolite	Murchey et al., 1983
		e-l	Mystic, Innoko terranes	Chert, ophiolite, limestone, shale, sandstone	Murchey et al., 1983
74 United States	NW AK	e	Angayucham terrane	Chert, basalt	Murchey et al., 1983
		e-l	Kagvik-Brooks Range terrane, incl. fms. below	Chert, argillite, shale, limestone	Murchey et al., 1983
		l	Siksikpuk Fm.	Chert, shale, siltstone	Siok, 1984
		l	Kuna Fm.	Chert, shale, limestone, dolomite, phosphate	Mull et al., 1982
75 United States	OK	—	Arkansas Novaculite	Chert, shale, limestone, dolomite	Goldstein and Hendricks, 1953

Appendix 2-1. (*continued*)

	Country	Locality[a]	Age[b]	Name[c]	Lithology	Reference
76	United States	TX	m	Marble Falls Fm.	Chert, sandstone, limestone	Namy, 1974
77	United States	AL, GA	—	Fort Payne Fm.	Chert, sandstone, limestone, dolomite	Chowns and Elkins, 1974
78	United States	KY, TN	—	Borden Fm., Fort Payne Fm.	Chert, sandstone, limestone, dolomite	Chowns and Elkins, 1974
79	United States	IN, IL	—	Borden Fm.	Chert, sandstone, limestone, dolomite	Chowns and Elkins, 1974
			—	Warsaw Fm.	Chert, sandstone, limestone, dolomite, anhydrite	Chowns and Elkins, 1974
80	United States	E NV	e-l	Golconda terrane incl. fms. below	Chert, basalt, limestone, sandstone, manganese ore	Murchey et al., 1983
			l	Schoonover Seq.	Chert, shale, sandstone, volcanics, conglomerate, dolomite	Grunau, 1965; Fagan, 1962; Miller et al., 1984
			e-l	Havallah Seq.	Chert	Silberling and Roberts, 1962; Snyder and Brueckner, 1983
81	United States	SW MT	l	Madison Gp.	Chert, limestone	Scholten, 1957
		ID	l	White Knobs Ls.	Chert, limestone, shale	Huh, 1967
82	United States	N CA	m	Sierra Buttes, Taylor, Elwell Fms.	Chert, volcanics	Murchey et al., 1983
83	United States	NW WA	e	San Juan terrane	Chert, ophiolite, mélange	Murchey et al., 1983
84	Mexico	Sonora	e-l	Indet.	Chert, barite, shale	Poole et al., 1983; B. Murchey, pers. comm.
85	Chile	S tip	l	Indet.	Chert, pillow lava	Dalziel, 1982
86	Great Britain	England	l	Namurian Fm.	Chert, shale, limestone	Oldershaw, 1968
		N Wales	e	Holy Well Shales	Chert, shale	Grunau, 1965
87	USSR	40.6°N, 75.7°E	e	Indet.	Chert	Vinogradov, 1969

	Location	Stage	Terrane/Formation	Lithology	Reference
88 USSR	62.5°N, 174.5°E	e	Indet.	Chert	Vinogradov, 1968a
89 USSR	70°N, 130°E	e	Indet.	Radiolarite, spiculite	Bulgakova, 1976
90 USSR	65°N, 135°E	e	Indet.	Radiolarite, spiculite	Bulgakova, 1976
91 Japan	SW Honshu, Kyushu, Shikoku	e–l	Chichibu terrane	Chert, sandstone, shale, limestone, basalt	Iijima and Utada, 1983; Takai et al., 1963
92 Japan	C Honshu	e–l	Chichibu terrane	Chert, sandstone, shale, limestone, basalt	Iijima and Utada, 1983
93 Laos, S. Viet Nam	C	e	Indet.	Chert, shale, quartzite, limestone	Tan, 1983
S. Viet Nam	S	e	Indet.	Chert, shale, siltstone	Tan, 1983
94 Malaysia	Malay Peninsula	e–l	Indet.	Chert, shale, limestone	Grunau, 1965
95 Malaysia	Sarawak	l	Indet.	Chert, limestone, shale	Tan, 1983

Permian

	Location	Stage	Terrane/Formation	Lithology	Reference
96 Canada, United States	W coast, SE AK	e–m	Wrangellia terrane	Chert, limestone, ophiolite, argillite	Murchey et al., 1983; Eardley, 1947
	AK panhandle	e	Cannery Fm. (Admiralty terrane)	Chert, argillite, graywacke, phyllite	Lathram et al., 1965
97 Canada	W BC	e–m	Cache Creek terrane	Chert, limestone, volcanics	Murchey et al., 1983
98 United States	NW AK	e	Kagvik–Brooks Range terrane (incl. Siksikpuk Fm.)	Chert, argillite, shale, limestone	Murchey et al., 1983
			Siksikpuk Fm.	Chert, shale, siltstone	Mull et al., 1982
99 United States	SE AK	—	Chulitna terrane	Chert, volcanics, conglomerate	Murchey et al., 1983
		e	Red Paint terrane	Chert, ophiolite	Murchey, et al., 1983
100 United States	NC AK	e	Innoko terrane	Chert, sandstone, shale	Murchey et al., 1983
101 United States	N NV	e	Beacon Flat Fm.	Chert, siltstone, limestone	Stewart et al., 1977; Fails, 1960
		e	Carlin Canyon Fm.	Chert, siltstone	Stewart et al., 1977; Fails, 1960

(continued)

Appendix 2-1. (*continued*)

Country	Locality[a]	Age[b]	Name[c]	Lithology	Reference
102 United States	E NV	e	Blue Mtns. terrane (prob. incl. Beacon Flat, Carlin Canyon Fms.)	Chert, tuff, ophiolite, mélange	Murchey et al., 1983
		e-m	Golconda terrane (incl. Havallah, Schoonover Seqs.)	Chert	Murchey et al., 1983
		e	Havallah Fms.	Chert, siltstone, sandstone, limestone	Stewart et al., 1977; Fails, 1960; Silberling and Roberts, 1962
		e	Schoonover Seq.	Chert, shale, sandstone, volcanics, conglomerate, dolomite	Miller et al., 1984
103 United States	N CA, S OR	e-m	Klamath Mtns. terrane	Chert, ophiolite	Murchey et al., 1983
104 United States	NW WA	e-m	San Juan terrane	Chert, ophiolite, mélange	Murchey et al., 1983
105 Chile	S tip	e	Indet.	Chert, pillow lava	Dalziel, 1982
106 USSR	60°N, 147°E	l	Indet.	Radiolarite, spiculite	Bulgakova, 1976
107 Japan	N Honshu, S Hokkaido	e-m	Sanbosan terrane, Kurosegawa-Ofunato belt	Chert, volcanics, limestone, shale	Iijima and Utada, 1983
108 Japan	C Honshu	e-m	Chichibu terrane	Chert, basalt, limestone, shale	Iijima and Utada, 1983
109 Japan	SW Honshu, Shikoku, Kyushu	e-m	Kurosegawa-Ofunato belt, Chichibu terrane	Chert, shale, basalt, limestone	Iijima and Utada, 1983
110 Indonesia	Bangka, Belitung Islands	l	Indet.	Chert, shale, sandstone, volcanics	Tan, 1983
111 Malaysia	Sarawak	e	Indet.	Chert, limestone, shale	Tan, 1983
112 Malaysia	NE peninsula	—	Indet.	Chert, shale	Tan, 1983

113 New Zealand	North Island	—	Waipapa terrane	Chert, argillite, volcanics	Moore, 1983
114 New Zealand	South Island	—	Torlesse terrane	Chert, sandstone, limestone, mélange	Moore, 1983
		—	Torlesse terrane	Chert, argillite, volcanics	Moore, 1983
		—	Caples terrane	Chert, volcanics, sandstone	Moore, 1983
Triassic					
115 United States	N CA	e-m	Pit Fm., Klamath Mtns. terrane	Chert, volcanics, shale, tuff	Murchey et al., 1983
116 United States	OR, ID	m-l	Blue Mtns. terrane	Chert, ophiolite, mélange	Murchey et al., 1983
117 United States	NW WA	m-l	San Juan terrane	Chert, ophiolite, mélange	Murchey et al., 1983
Canada	SW BC	m-l	Bridge River terrane	Chert, ophiolite, mélange	Murchey et al., 1983
		m-l	Cache Creek terrane	Chert, shale, ophiolite, limestone	Murchey et al., 1983
118 United States	S AK	?l	Uyak Fm.	Chert, basalt	Moore, 1969
119 United States, Canada	W coast, SE AK	e	Wrangellia terrane	Chert, limestone, shale, volcanics	Murchey et al., 1983
	AK panhandle	l	Hyd Fm. (Admiralty terrane)	Chert, limestone, slate	Lathram et al., 1965
120 United States	EC AK	l	Kamishak Chert, Innoko terrane	Chert, limestone, volcanics, shale, sandstone	Kelley, 1963; Murchey et al., 1983
	SC AK	l	McKinley terrane	Chert, basalt	Murchey et al., 1983
		l	Red Paint terrane	Chert, ophiolite	Murchey et al., 1983
	NC AK	l	Angayucham terrane	Chert, basalt	Murchey et al., 1983
121 United States	N AK	m	Otuk Fm.	Chert, shale, limestone	Mull et al., 1982
		—	Kagvik–Brooks Range terrane (prob. incl. Otuk Fm.)	Chert, limestone	Murchey et al., 1983

(continued)

Appendix 2-1. (*continued*)

Country	Locality[a]	Age[b]	Name[c]	Lithology	Reference
122 Mexico	Baja California	l	San Hipolito Fm.	Chert, volcanics, ophiolite, limestone	Pessagno et al., 1979
123 Yugoslavia	Dinarides	m–l	Indet.	Radiolarian chert, volcanics, shale, sandstone, limestone	Grunau, 1965
124 Greece	Othris	—	Neraida Chert	Chert, basalt, limestone	Price, 1977
125 Philippines	N Palawan	m	Indet.	Chert, limestone, sandstone, shale, tuff	Tan, 1983
126 Singapore		m–eJ	Indet.	Chert, mudstone, shale, sandstone, conglomerate	Tan, 1983
127 Thailand	N	—	Indet.	Chert, conglomerate, shale, sandstone, limestone	Tan, 1983
128 Malaysia	Malay Peninsula	—	Indet.	Chert, shale	Dietz and Holden, 1966
129 Malaysia	Sarawak, Sabah	l	Indet.	Chert, sandstone, shale, tuff, limestone	Tan, 1983
130 Indonesia	Sumatra	—	Indet.	Chert, marl, shale, limestone, sandstone	Tan, 1983
131 Indonesia	Ceram	—	Indet.	Radiolarian chert	Grunau, 1965
132 Japan	S Hokkaido, N Honshu	—	Sanbosan terrane (Konose Gp., Yoshio Fm.)	Radiolarian chert, shale, limestone, basalt	Ogawa et al., 1983; Iijima and Utada, 1983
133 Japan	SW Honshu, Kyushu, Shikoku	—	Nakaoi, Ishimi, Kamiyoshida, Yabuhara Fms.; Chichibu terrane; Kurosegawa-Ofunato belt	Chert, volcanics, basalt, argillite	Ogawa et al., 1983; Iijima and Utada, 1983; Igo and Koike, 1983
134 Antarctica	Peninsula	—	Trinity Peninsula Fm.	Chert, graywacke, shale, limestone, volcanics	Thomson, 1982

No.	Location	Region	Age	Unit	Lithology	Reference
135	S. Orkney Is.		l	Greywacke-Shale Fm.	Chert, graywacke, shale	Dalziel et al., 1981
Jurassic						
136	United States	N CA	e-m	Klamath Mtns. terrane	Chert, ophiolite, mélange	Irwin, 1972
137	United States, Canada	NW WA	—	San Juan terrane	Chert, ophiolite, mélange	Murchey et al., 1983
138	United States	SW BC	e	Bridge Creek terrane	Chert, ophiolite, mélange	Murchey et al., 1983
	United States	WC CA	—	Franciscan Complex	Radiolarite, shale, graywacke	Bailey et al., 1970
			—	Coast Range Ophiolite	Chert, basalt	Bailey et al., 1970
139	United States	E CA		Western Metamorphic belt	Chert, schist, greenstone, sandstone	Schweickert and Cowan, 1975
140	United States	SE AK	l	Chugach terrane	Chert, ophiolite, mélange	Murchey et al., 1983
141	United States	SC AK	e and l	West Fork terrane	Chert, tuff, shale, sandstone	Jones et al., 1980
			l	Chulitna terrane	Chert, shale, sandstone	Jones et al., 1980
			l	McKinley terrane	Chert, basalt	Murchey et al., 1983
142	United States	NW AK	e	Kagvik–Brooks Range terrane	Chert, limestone	Murchey et al., 1983
143	United States	Puerto Rico	l-eK	Bermeja Complex, Mariquita Chert	Chert, basalt, ultramafics	Mattson and Pessagno, 1979
144	Mexico	C Baja California	l	Indet.	Chert, graywacke, ophiolite, mélange	Cohen et al., 1963; Rangin, 1981
145	Mexico	Sierra Madre Oriental	l	La Caja Fm.	Chert, siltstone, limestone, phosphate	Rogers et al., 1956
146	Costa Rica		l-lk	Nicoya Complex Punta Conchal Fm.	Chert, shale, basalt, limestone	Hein et al., 1983; Gursky and Schmidt-Effing, 1983
147	Cuba		l-eK	Indet.	Chert, shale, limestone, manganese	Simons and Straczek, 1958

(continued)

Appendix 2–1. (*continued*)

Country	Locality[a]	Age[b]	Name[c]	Lithology	Reference
148 Peru	WC	e	Aramachay Fm.	Chert, limestone, phosphatic siltstone, shale	Loughman and Hallam, 1982
149 Ecuador	E	e	Santiago Fm.	Chert, shale, sandstone, limestone	Lewis et al., 1956
150 France	French Alps	l-ek	Gondran Series	Chert, marble, ophiolite	Grunau, 1965
151 France	Corsica	l-eK	Indet.	Radiolarian chert, limestone	Grunau, 1965
Italy	Elba Is.	l	Indet.	Radiolarian chert, limestone, ophiolite	Grunau, 1965
152 Switzerland, Austria, Germany	Alps	l	Indet.	Radiolarian chert, shale, limestone, sandstone, basalt	Grunau, 1965
153 Spain	S	l	Camarote Unit	Radiolarian chert	Grunau, 1965
154 Italy	Sicily	—	Indet.	Chert, limestone, shale	McBride and Folk, 1979
155 Italy	Romagna	—	Radiolarite, Jasper Fms.	Chert, shale, limestone	McBride and Folk, 1979
	Genoa area	l	Indet.	Chert, sandstone, volcanics	Jenkyns and Winterer, 1982
		l	Liguria Seq.	Chert, shale, limestone, volcanics	Folk and McBride, 1978
156 Italy	Calabria	l	Indet.	Chert, sandstone, volcanics	Jenkyns and Winterer, 1982
157 Hungary	C Trans-Danubian Mtns.	m-l	Indet.	Radiolarian chert, shale	Grunau, 1965
Romania	Carpathians	l	Indet.	Chert, shale	Jenkyns and Winterer, 1982
158 Poland	S	m-l	Pienny Klippen Belt	Radiolarian chert, limestone, shale	Grunau, 1965; Jenkyns and Winterer, 1982
159 Yugoslavia	Dinarides	l-eK	Indet.	Radiolarian chert, flysch, volcanics	Grunau, 1965
160 Turkey	SE	l	Radiolarite Series	Radiolarian chert,	Grunau, 1965; Tromp, 1947

Location	Region	Age	Terrane/Series	Lithology	Reference
				shale, limestone, volcanics	
161 Turkey	SW	l	Radiolarite Series	Radiolarian chert, shale, limestone, volcanics	Tromp, 1947
162 Greece	W	l	Indet.	Chert, shale, limestone	Jenkyns and Winterer, 1982
163 Greece	E	l	Indet.	Chert, shale, siltstone, limestone	Bernoulli and Jenkyns, 1974
164 Oman		l	Indet.	Radiolarian chert, tuff	Grunau, 1965
165 Morocco	N Rif	l	Indet.	Radiolarian chert	Grunau, 1965
166 USSR	W Ukraine	m	Indet.	"Siliceous rocks"	Vinogradov, 1968b
167 Singapore		mTr–e	Indet.	Chert, mudstone, shale, sandstone, conglomerate	Tan, 1983
168 Indonesia	Sulawesi	l	Indet.	Chert, mélange of sandstone, siltstone, shale, limestone, ultramafics	Tan, 1983
169 Indonesia	Sumatra	m–l	Indet.	Chert, shale, sandstone, limestone, volcanics	Tan, 1983
170 Malaysia, Indonesia	N Kalimantan, Sarawak	l	Indet.	Chert, mélange of sandstone, shale, limestone, basalt	Tan, 1983
171 Japan	C Honshu	l	Mazegawa Fm., Mino terrane	Chert, shale	Mizutani and Shabata, 1983
	Shikoku	l	Shimanto terrane	Chert, shale, sandstone, volcanics	Iijima and Utada, 1983
172 Japan	N Honshu, Hokkaido	e–m	Yoshio Fm., Sanbosan terrane	Chert, shale, siltstone, sandstone, volcanics	Iijima and Utada, 1983; Ogawa et al., 1983; Igo and Koike, 1983
	Hokkaido	l	Sorachi terrane	Radiolarite, shale, ultramafics	Iijima and Utada, 1983
173 New Zealand	North Island	—	Waipapa terrane	Chert, shale, limestone, dolomite	Moore, 1983
		—	Torlesse terrane	Chert, volcanics, sandstone	Moore, 1983

(continued)

Appendix 2-1. (*continued*)

	Country	Locality[a]	Age[b]	Name[c]	Lithology	Reference
174	New Zealand	South Island	—	Torlesse, Caples terranes	Chert, volcanics, sandstone	Moore, 1983
	Cretaceous					
175	United States	Puerto Rico	lJ–e	Bermeja Complex, Mariquita Chert	Chert, basalt, ultramafics	Mattson and Pessagno, 1979
176	United States	WC CA	—	Franciscan Complex	Radiolarite, shale, graywacke	Bailey et al., 1970
177	United States	C CA	l–Paleo-gene	Moreno Shale	Diatomite, shale, siltstone	Clark, 1978
178	United States	SE AK	l	Wrangellia terrane	Chert, limestone, shale, volcanics	Murchey et al., 1983
		SE AK	l	Schulze Fm.	Porcelanite	Jones and MacKevett, 1969
179	United States	SE AK	e	Chugach terrane	Chert, shale, sandstone, volcanics	Murchey et al., 1983
180	United States	SC AK	e	Chulitna terrane	Chert, sandstone, shale	Murchey et al., 1983
			e	McKinley terrane	Chert, basalt	Murchey et al., 1983
181	Mexico	C Baja California	e	Cedros Fm.	Chert, basalt, graywacke	Rangin, 1981
182	Cuba		lJ–e	Indet.	Chert, shale, limestone, manganese	Simons and Straczek, 1958
183	La Desiradé		e	Northeast Complex	Chert, basalt	Bouysse et al., 1983
184	Panama	E	l–ePal	Indet.	Chert, shale, igneous rocks	Bandy and Casey, 1973
185	Panama	SW	l	Ocu Fm.	Chert, shale	R. Miranda, pers. comm.
			l	Basic Igneous Complex	Chert, shale, basalt	R. Miranda, pers. comm.
186	Guatemala		e	Indet.	Radiolarian chert, ophiolite	Grunau, 1965
187	Costa Rica		lJ–l	Nicoya Complex, Punta Conchal Fm.	Chert, shale, basalt, limestone	Hein et al., 1983; Gursky and Schmidt-Effing, 1983

	Location	Age	Formation	Lithology	Reference
188 Ecuador	Nicoya and Osa Peninsulas	l–mEo	Sabana Grande Fm.	Chert, shale, limestone	Hein et al., 1983
	Guayaquil	l–ePal	Cayo Fm.	Chert, shale, limestone	J. Hein, unpubl. data
189 Colombia	SW coast	l	Basic Igneous Complex	Chert, shale, igneous rocks	Duque, 1972
190 Colombia	NW coast	l	Basic Igneous Complex	Chert, shale, igneous rocks	Duque, 1972
191 Venezuela	NC	l–ePal	Indet.	Chert, phosphatic limestone, siltstone, sandstone, conglomerate	Shagam, 1960
192 France	French Alps	lJ–e	Gondran Series	Chert, marble, ophiolite	Grunau, 1965
193 France	Corsica	lJ–e	Indet.	Radiolarian chert, limestone	Grunau, 1965
194 Yugoslavia	Dinarides	lJ–e	Indet.	Radiolarian chert, flysch, volcanics	Grunau, 1965
195 Greece	Achladi, E Evvoia	e	Diabase–Chert Fm.	Chert, siltstone, mudstone, graywacke	Baumgartner and Bernoulli, 1976
	Othris	e	Diabase–Chert Fm.	Radiolarite, shale, siltstone	Bernoulli and Jenkyns, 1974
196 Turkey	SE	l	Indet.	Radiolarian chert, shale, ophiolite	Grunau, 1965
197 Turkey	SW	e	Antalya Complex	Chert, basalt, siltstone, limestone	Robertson, 1981
198 USSR	SW of Moscow	e	Indet.	"Siliceous rocks"	Vinogradov, 1968b
199 USSR	Upper Tura River	l	Slavgorod Suite	Diatomite, shale	Glezer, 1966
200 Israel		l	Mishash Fm.	Chert, shale, limestone, chalk, phosphate	Bein and Amit, 1982; Kolodny et al., 1965
		l	Sayyarim Fm.	Chert, limestone, dolomite, shale, sandstone, phosphate	Steinetz, 1970
201 Cyprus		l	Indet.	Chert, shale	Jenkyns and Winterer, 1982
		l	Perapedhi Fm.	Chert, shale, volcanics	Robertson and Hudson, 1974

(continued)

Appendix 2-1. (*continued*)

Country	Locality[a]	Age[b]	Name[c]	Lithology	Reference
202 Iran	Beluchistan	l	Colored Mélange	Radiolarian chert, limestone	Grunau, 1965
		l	Pichakun Series	Chert, limestone, shale	Hallam, 1976
		l	Bachtegan Beds	Chert, basalt, limestone	Hallam, 1976
203 Oman		l	Hawasina Complex	Radiolarian chert, basalt, limestone	Grunau, 1965; Hallam, 1976
204 Egypt	NE	l	Indet.	Chert, shale, limestone	A. Sadek, pers. comm.
205 India	C Himalayas	—	Indet.	Radiolarian chert, shale	Grunau, 1965
206 India	Andaman Is.	l or Eo	Indet.	Radiolarian chert, limestone, serpentine	Grunau, 1965
207 India	Nicobar Is.	l or Eo	Indet.	Chert, limestone, serpentine	Grunau, 1965
208 China	Tibet	m	Indet.	Radiolarian chert	B. Murchey, pers. comm.
209 Burma	W	l or Eo	Negrai Series	Chert, ultramafics	Grunau, 1965
210 Indonesia	Sulawesi	—	Indet.	Chert, sandstone, siltstone, shale, limestone, ultramafics	Tan, 1983; Haile et al., 1979
211 Indonesia	S Kalimantan	—	Indet.	Chert, mélange	Tan, 1983
212 Indonesia	N Kalimantan	—	Indet.	Chert, mélange	Tan, 1983
213 Indonesia	Ceram	l-Eo	Cherty Limestone Fm.	Chert, limestone, marl, shale	Grunau, 1965
214 Indonesia	Timor	l	Sonnabait Series	Radiolarian Chert, limestone	Grunau, 1965
		e	Wai Bua Fm.	Chert, shale, marl, limestone	Audley-Charles, 1965
		—	Palelo Grp.	Radiolarite, volcanics, shale, limestone	Haile et al., 1979; Earle, 1983
215 Sabah		l or Eo	Danau Fm. of Brondijk, 1964	Radiolarian chert, ophiolite	Grunau, 1965

	Location	Age	Formation	Lithology	Reference
216 Malaysia	Sarawak	l or Eo	Danau Fm. of Brondijk, 1964	Radiolarian chert, ophiolite	Grunau, 1965
217 Japan	Shikoku, SW Honshu	—	Shimanto terrane	Chert, shale, siltstone, sandstone, basalt	Iijima and Utada, 1983; Sano, 1983; Nakazawa et al., 1983
218 Japan	Hokkaido	e	Sorachi terrane	Radiolarian chert, ultramafics, shale	Iijima and Utada, 1983
219 Philippines	Busuanga	—	Indet.	Chert, mélange of graywacke, shale, basalt	Tan, 1983
220 New Zealand	North Island	e	Tupou, Mohoiwi Fms.	Chert, basalt	Moore, 1983
221 New Zealand	South Island	e	Pahaoa Gp.	Chert, redbeds, shale	Moore, 1983
		—	Mead Hill Fm.	Chert, limestone, glauconite	Moore, 1983
222 Antarctica	Peninsula	e	Indet.	Chert	D. L. Jones, pers. comm.
Paleogene					
223 United States	SE coastal plain	Eo	Indet.	Diatomite, chert, shale	Wise et al., 1981
224 United States	S CA	Eo–Olig	Kreyenhagen Fm.	Diatomite, shale, siltstone	Clark, 1978
225 United States	C CA	lK–Paleogene	Moreno Shale	Diatomite, shale, siltstone	Clark, 1978
226 United States	Aleutian Is.	Eo	Andrew Lake Fm.	Chert, sandstone, shale	Hein and McLean, 1979
227 Mexico	S Baja California	lOlig	San Gregorio Limestone	Diatomite	H. McLean and J. Barron, pers. comm.
		mEo	Indet.	Diatomite	H. McLean and J. Barron, pers. comm.
228 Panama	E	l-ePal	Indet.	Chert, shale, igneous rocks	Bandy and Casey, 1973
229 Costa Rica	Nicoya Peninsula	lK–mEo	Sabana Grande Fm.	Chert, shale, limestone	Hein et al., 1983
230 Trinidad		Eo, Mio	Naparima Fm.	Diatomite	L. Burckle, pers. comm.

(continued)

Appendix 2-1. (*continued*)

Country	Locality[a]	Age[b]	Name[c]	Lithology	Reference
231 Barbados		Eo	Indet.	Radiolarian earths	Senn, 1940; R. Speed and D. Larue, pers. comm.
232 Jamaica		Eo	Indet.	Diatomite	L. Burckle, pers. comm.
233 Cuba		Eo	Indet.	Diatomite	L. Burckle, pers. comm.
234 Ecuador	Guayaquil	l-ePal	Cayo Fm.	Chert, shale, limestone	J. Hein, unpubl. data
235 Venezuela	NC	l-ePal	Indet.	Chert, phosphatic limestone, siltstone, sandstone, conglomerate	Shagam, 1960
236 Colombia	W	Pal	Indet.	Chert, graywacke, sandstone	Grunau, 1965
237 Denmark		Pal–Eo	Mohler Diatomite	Diatomite	Hansen, 1979
238 Italy	Sicily	Eo	Indet.	Radiolarite	Bernoulli and Jenkyns, 1974
239 Poland Czechoslovakia	W Carpathians	lEo–eOlig	Menelite	Chert, shale	Burchfield and Royden, 1982
240 Cyprus		Pal	Middle Lefkara Gp.	Chert, limestone, chalk	Robertson and Hudson, 1974
241 USSR	Anadyr region	lEo–Olig	Indet.	Diatomite	Koizumi, 1973
242 USSR	48°N, 36°E	Eo	Indet.	Chert, shale, sandstone, claystone	Vinogradov, 1967
243 USSR	52.5°N, 46°E	Pal	Indet.	Diatomite, siltstone, shale, sandstone	Vinogradov, 1967
244 USSR	50.5°N, 52.5°E	Pal	Indet.	Radiolarian chert, shale	Vinogradov, 1967
245 USSR	48.8°N, 64°E	Pal	Indet.	Chert, shale, sandstone	Vinogradov, 1967
246 USSR	53.5°N, 64.5°E	Eo	Indet.	Diatomite, shale, sandstone	Vinogradov, 1967
247 USSR	Kurgan, Koptelovo	Eo	Lyulimvor Suite	Diatomite, argillite	Glezer, 1966
	57°N, 70°E	e–mEo	Indet. (same as above?)	Chert, shale, sandstone	Vinogradov, 1967

248	USSR	54.5°N, 78.1°E	e-mEo	Indet.	Chert, shale, sandstone	Vinogradov, 1967
249	USSR	59.4°N, 74°E	e-mEo	Indet.	Chert, shale	Vinogradov, 1967
250	USSR	50°N, 81°E	Eo	Indet.	Diatomite, shale, sandstone	Vinogradov, 1967
251	USSR	Sosra River	lEo	Indet.	Diatomite, diatomaceous clay	Glezer, 1966; Vinogradov, 1967
252	USSR	lower Ob River	eEo	Indet.	Diatomite, argillite	Glezer, 1966; Vinogradov, 1967
253	USSR	Kazym	Eo	Indet.	Diatomite, argillite	Glezer, 1966; Vinogradov, 1967
254	USSR	65.8°N, 70°E	Eo	Indet.	Diatomite	Vinogradov, 1967
255	USSR	66°N, 80°E	Eo	Indet.	Diatomite, sandstone, shale	Vinogradov, 1967
256	USSR	Leningrad region	eOlig	Kharkou Suite	Diatomite, glauconite, sandstone, mudstone	Glezer, 1966
257	USSR	W North Caucasus	eOlig–eMio	Maikop Suite	Diatomite, shale	Glezer, 1966
258	USSR	Volgulka River	Eo	Indet.	Diatomite, argillite	Glezer, 1966
259	USSR	Sverdlovsk region	ePal	Marsyat Suite	Diatomite, argillite	Glezer, 1966
260	USSR	Malyi Atlym	eEo	Serov Suite	Diatomite, argillite	Glezer, 1966
261	USSR	Makhnevo village	ePal	Talitso Suite	Diatomite, glauconite, siltstone, sandstone, shale	Glezer, 1966
262	USSR	61°N, 169.6°E	Pal	Indet.	Chert, volcanics	Vinogradov, 1967
263	India	Andaman Is.	l or Eo	Indet.	Radiolarian chert, limestone, serpentine	Grunau, 1965
264	India	Nicobar Is.	l or Eo	Indet.	Chert, limestone, serpentine	Grunau, 1965
265	Burma	W	l or Eo	Negrai Series	Chert, ultramafics	Grunau, 1965
266	Indonesia	Ceram	l–eEo	Cherty Limestone Fm.	Chert, limestone, marl, shale	Grunau, 1965

(continued)

Appendix 2-1. (*continued*)

	Country	Locality[a]	Age[b]	Name[c]	Lithology	Reference
265	Sabah		l or Eo	Danau Fm. of Brondijk, 1964	Radiolarian chert, ophiolite	Grunau, 1965
266	Malaysia	Sarawak	l or Eo	Danau Fm. of Brondijk, 1964	Radiolarian chert, ophiolite	Grunau, 1965
267	Japan	C Honshu	lEo–eMio	Setogawa terrane	Radiolarian and diatomaceous chert, porcelanite, shale, volcanics	Iijima and Utada, 1983
268	New Guinea	N	Pal–Eo	Indet.	Radiolarian chert, limestone	Grunau, 1965
269	New Zealand	SE South Island	Eo	Oamara Diatomite	Diatomite, limestone, shale	Hornibrook, 1983

Neogene

	Country	Locality[a]	Age[b]	Name[c]	Lithology	Reference
270	Canada	Vancouver Is.	Mio	Indet.	Diatomite	Ingle, 1973
271	United States	VA, E coastal plain	Mio	Indet.	Diatomite	L. Burckle, pers. comm.
272	United States	DE, MD, VA	Mio	Calvert, Choptank Fms.	Diatomite	L. Burckle, pers. comm.
273	United States	NJ	Mio	Indet.	Diatomite	L. Burckle, pers. comm.
273	United States	S coastal OR	lMio	Empire Fm.	Diatomite	Orr, 1972
274	United States	C CA	Mio	Monterey Fm.	Diatomite, shale, siltstone, sandstone, limestone, tuff, dolomite, phosphate	Obradovich and Naeser, 1981; Bramlette, 1946
275	United States	S CA	Mio	Monterey Fm.	Diatomite, shale, siltstone, sandstone, limestone, tuff, dolomite	Bramlette, 1946; Obradovich and Naeser, 1981; Rowell, 1981
276	United States	Pribilof Islands	Plio	Indet.	Diatomite	Hanna, 1929
277	Mexico	S Baja California	lPlio Mio	Indet. Monterey Fm.	Diatomite Diatomite, shale, phosphate	J. Barron, pers. comm. IGCP 156 Field Trip Guide, 1981, unpublished

No.	Location	Age	Formation	Rock type	Reference
278 Mexico	San Felipe, Baja California	lMio, ePlio	San Felipe diatomite member, Llano el Moreno Fm.	Diatomite, ash	J. Hein, unpubl. data; Boehm, 1982
279 Mexico	Vizcaino Peninsula, Baja California	Mio	Indet.	Diatomite	Ingle, 1973
280 Trinidad		Eo, Mio	Naparima Fm.	Diatomite	L. Burckle, pers. comm.
281 Cuba		Mio	Indet.	Diatomite	L. Burckle, pers. comm.
282 Chile	Tiltil, Mejillones	Mio	Indet.	Diatomite	L. Burckle, pers. comm.
283 Peru	S coastal	lMio, ePlio	Pisco Fm.	Diatomite, ash	J. Hein and J. Barron, unpubl. data
284 Peru	N coastal	Mio	Zapallel Fm.	Diatomite, phosphate, ash	B. M. Arnoa, pers. comm.
285 Ecuador	C coastal	eMio	Villingota member, Tosagua Fm.	Diatomite, dolomite, ash	J. Hein and J. Barron, unpubl. data
286 Spain	Majorca	Mio	Tripoli equiv.	Diatomite	L. Burckle, pers. comm.
287 Spain	Andalusia	Mio, lPlio	Moron and Mors	Diatomite	J. E. Meulenkamp, pers. comm.
288 Italy	Sicily	eMio	Caltanisette Fm.	Diatomite	L. Burckle, pers. comm.
289 Hungary, Poland, Czechoslovakia	Vienna Basin, Moravia	Mio	Indet.	Diatomite	L. Burckle, pers. comm.
290 Greece	Aegean Sea Islands	Plio	Indet.	Diatomite	J. E. Meulenkamp, pers. comm.
291 Bulgaria	NE	Mio	Indet.	Diatomite	L. Burckle, pers. comm.
292 USSR	W North Caucausus	eOlig–eMio	Maikop Suite	Diatomite, shale	Glezer, 1966
293 USSR	Kamchatka Peninsula	lMio–Plio	Indet.	Diatomite	Koizumi, 1973
294 USSR	Sakhalin Is.	m, lMio	Indet.	Diatomite	Koizumi, 1973

(*continued*)

Appendix 2-1. (*continued*)

Country	Locality[a]	Age[b]	Name[c]	Lithology	Reference
295 USSR	S Kurile Is.	Mio–Plio	Indet.	Diatomite	Koizumi, 1973
296 USSR	64.7°N, 175°E	Mio	Indet.	Diatomite	Vinogradov, 1967
297 Yemen		?Mio	Indet.	Diatomite	L. Burckle, pers. comm.
298 Algeria		lMio	Beida Stage	Diatomite, marl, clay, shale, limestone, volcanics	Anderson, 1933
299 India	Andaman Is.	Mio	Indet.	Diatomite	Grunow, 1867
300 Malaysia	N Borneo	Mio	Indet.	Diatomite	Kirk, 1962
301 Indonesia	Java	Mio–Plio	Indet.	Diatomite	Reinhold, 1937
302 Japan	C Honshu	lEo–eMio	Setogawa terrane	Radiolarian and diatomaceous chert, porcelanite, shale, volcanics	Iijima and Utada, 1983
		Mio	Onnagawa, Funagawa Fms.	Diatomite, chert, shale, siltstone, sandstone, dolomite	Ingle, 1981; Iijima and Utada, 1983
303 Japan	Hokkaido	Mio	Masoporo Fm.	Chert, shale, sandstone, siltstone, conglomerate, volcanics	Mitsui and Taguchi, 1977; Iijima and Utada, 1983
304 Korea	Pohang area	e–mMio	Pohang Fm., Yeonill Gp.	Diatomite, dolomite, ash	J. Hein, unpubl. data; Garrison et al., 1979
	S peninsula	e–mMio	Indet.	Diatomite	J. Hein, unpubl. data
305 Philippines	S Luzon	Plio	Samalong Diatomite	Diatomite	Corby et al., 1951
306 Philippines	Mindanao	lMio	Indet.	Diatomite	Ranneft et al., 1960

Note: Although we tried to make this compilation comprehensive, other deposits undoubtedly exist. For example, Permian and Triassic cherts in Oman (Glennie et al., 1974) were brought to our attention subsequent to completion of our compilation and maps.

[a]E = east, W = west, N = north, S = south, C = central

[b]e = early; m = middle; l = late; Tr = Triassic; J = Jurassic; K = Cretaceous; Pal = Paleocene; Eo = Eocene; Olig = Oligocene; Mio = Miocene; Plio = Pliocene; — signifies that the deposit either represents the entire period or epoch or that a more resolved date was not given; - signifies "through"; and , signifies "and."

[c]Indet. means indeterminate and signifies that the name either was not given or the unit is unnamed.

References

Anderson, R. V. V., 1933. The diatomaceous and fish-bearing Beida stage of Algeria, *Jour. Geology* **41**:673–698.

Arthur, M. A., W. E. Dean, and D. A. V. Stow, 1984. Models for the deposition of Mesozoic-Cenozoic fine-grained organic-carbon-rich sediment in the deep sea, in *International Workshop on Deep-Sea Fine-Grained Sediments*, D. A. V. Stow and D. J. W. Piper, eds., Geological Society of London Special Publication, pp. 527–559.

Arthur, M. A., and H. C. Jenkyns, 1981. Phosphorites and paleoceanography, in *Chemical Cycles in the Ocean*, W. H. Berger, ed., Oceanologica Acta, pp. 83–96.

Audley-Charles, M. G., 1965. Some aspects of the chemistry of Cretaceous siliceous sedimentary rocks from East Timor, *Geochim. et Cosmochim. Acta* **29**:1175–1192.

Bailey, E. H., M. C. Blake, and D. L. Jones, 1970. *On-land Mesozoic Oceanic Crust in California Coast Ranges*, U.S. Geological Survey Professional Paper 700-C, pp. 70–81.

Bandy, O. L., and R. E. Casey, 1973. Reflectors, horizons, and paleobathymetric history, eastern Panama, *Geol. Soc. America Bull.* **83**:3081–3086.

Baumgartner, P. O., and D. Bernoulli, 1976. Stratigraphy and radiolarian fauna in a Late Jurassic–Early Cretaceous section near Achladi (Evvoia, eastern Greece), *Eclogae Geol. Helvetiae* **69**:601–626.

Bein, A., and O. Amit, 1982. Depositional environments of the Senonian chert, phosphorite, and oil shale sequence in Israel as deduced from their organic matter composition, *Sedimentology* **29**:81–90.

Berger, W. H., and E. L. Winterer, 1974. Plate stratigraphy and the fluctuating carbonate line, in *Pelagic Sediments: On Land and Under the Sea*, K. J. Hsu and H. C. Jenkyns, eds., International Association of Sedimentologists Special Paper 1, pp. 11–48.

Bernouilli, D., and H. C. Jenkyns, 1974. *Alpine, Mediterranean, and Central Atlantic Mesozoic Facies in Relation to the Early Evolution of the Tethys*, Society of Economic Paleontologists and Mineralogists Special Publication 19, pp. 129–160.

Boehm, M. C. F., 1982. Biostratigraphy, Lithostratigraphy, and Paleoenvironments of the Miocene-Pliocene San Felipe Marine Sequence, Baja California Norte, Mexico, Master's thesis, Stanford University, 826p.

Bouysse, P., R. Schmidt-Effing, and D. Westercamp, 1983. La Desiradé Island (Lesser Antilles) revisited: Lower Cretaceous radiolarian cherts and arguments against an ophiolite origin for the basal complex, *Geology* **11**:244–247.

Bramlette, M. N., 1946. *The Monterey Formation of California and the Origin of Its Siliceous Rocks*, U.S. Geological Survey Professional Paper 212, 57p.

Breshnev, V. D., V. B. Gorianov, R. V. Klishevitch, V. R. Martyshev, N. N. Nasybulin, and E. I. Zubstov, 1967. *International Symposium on the Devonian System*, D. H. Oswald, ed., Alberta Society of Petroleum Geologists, Alberta, Canada, pp. 433–450.

Brown, D. A., K. S. W. Campbell, and K. A. W. Crook, 1968. *The Geological Evolution of Australia and New Zealand*, Pergamon, Oxford, England, 409p.

Bulgakova, M. D., 1976. Siliceous complexes of the Verkhoyansk-Kolyma fold system and associated ores, *Akademia Nauk SSSR Doklady* **226**:180–182.

Burchfiel, B. C., and L. Royden, 1982. Carpathian Foreland fold and thrust belt and its relation to Pannonian and other basins, *Am. Assoc. Petroleum Geologists Bull.* **66**:1179–1195.

Bushinskii, G. I., 1969. *Old Phosphorites of Asia and Their Genesis*, Akadamia Nauk SSSR, Geologicheskogo Instituta, Israel Program for Scientific Translations, Jerusalem, 266p.

Chapman, R. M., F. R. Weber, M. Churkin, and C. Carter, 1980. *The Livengood*

Dome Chert, A New Ordovician Formation in Central Alaska, and Its Relevance to Displacement on the Tintinna Fault, U.S. Geological Survey Professional Paper 1126-F, 13p.

Chowns, T. M., and J. E. Elkins, 1974. The origin of quartz geodes and cauliflower cherts through the silicification of anhydrite nodules, *Jour. Sed. Petrology* **44**:885-903.

Clark, W. B., 1978. Diatomite industry in California, *California Geology*, **31**:3-9.

Cohen, L. H., K. C. Condie, L. J. Kuest, Jr., G. S. Mackenzie, F. H. Meister, P. Pushkar, and A. M. Stueber, 1963. Geology of the San Benito Islands, Baja California, Mexico, *Geol. Soc. America Bull.* **74**:1355-1370.

Cook, P. J., and M. W. McElhinny, 1979. A reevaluation of the spatial and temporal distribution of sedimentary phosphate deposits in the light of plate tectonics, *Econ. Geology* **74**:315-330.

Corby, G. W., et al., 1951. *Geology and Oil Possibilities of the Philippines*, Report of the Philippines Department of Agriculture and Natural Resources, Technical Bulletin 21, 363p.

D'Allura, J. A., E. M. Moores, and L. Robinson, 1977. Paleozoic rocks of the northern Sierra Nevada: Their structural and paleogeographic implications, in *Paleozoic Paleogeography of the Western United States*, J. H. Stewart, C. H. Stevens, and A. E. Fritsche, eds., Pacific Coast Paleogeography Symposium 1, Society of Economic Paleontologists and Mineralogists, pp. 395-408.

Dalziel, I. W. D., 1982. The early (pre-Middle Jurassic) history of the Scotia Arc region: A review and progress report, in *Antarctic Geoscience*, C. Craddock, ed., University of Wisconsin Press, Madison, pp. 111-126.

Dalziel, I. W. D., D. H. Elliot, D. L. Jones, J. W. Thomson, M. R. A. Thomson, N. A. Wells, and W. J. Zinsmeister, 1981. The geological significance of some Triassic microfossils from the South Orkney Islands, Scotia Ridge. *Geol. Mag.* **118**:15-25.

Dietz, R. S., and J. C. Holden, 1966. Deep-sea deposits in but not on the continents. *Am. Assoc. Petroleum Geologists Bull.* **50**:351-362.

Douglas, R. J. W., H. Gabrielse, J. O. Wheeler, D. F. Stott, and H. R. Belyea, 1976. Geology of western Canada, in *Geology and Economic Minerals of Canada*, R. J. W. Douglas, ed., Geological Survey of Canada Economic Geology Report No. 1, Part B, pp. 365-488.

Doyle, J. A., and J. T. Parrish, 1984. Jurassic-Early Cretaceous Plant Distributions and Paleoclimatic Models, *International Organization of Paleobotany Conference*, Edmonton, Alberta, Abstracts.

Drewry, G. E., A. T. S. Ramsay, and A. G. Smith, 1974. Climatically controlled sediments, the geomagnetic field, and trade wind belts in Phanerozoic time, *Jour. Geology* **82**:531-553.

Duque, C. H., 1972. Relaciones entre la bioestratigrafia y la cronoestratigrafia en el llamda geosynclinal del Bolivar, *Colombia Boletin Geologica* **19**:25-68.

Eardley, A. J., 1947. Paleozoic Cordilleran geosyncline and related orogeny, *Jour. Geology* **55**:309-342.

Earle, M., 1983. Continental margin origin for Cretaceous radiolarian cherts in western Timor, *Nature* **305**:129-130.

Eganov, E. A., 1979. The role of cyclic sedimentation in the formation of phosphorite deposits, in *Proterozoic-Cambrian Phosphorites: First International Field Workshop and Seminar*, P. J. Cook and J. H. Shergold, eds., International Geological Correlation Programme, Project 156 (UNESCO-IUGS), Canberra, Canberra Publishing and Printing Company, pp. 22-25.

Fagan, J. J., 1962. Carboniferous cherts, turbidites, and volcanic rocks in the northern Independence Range, Nevada, *Geol. Soc. America Bull.* **73**:595-611.

Fails, T. G., 1960. Permian stratigraphy at Carlin Canyon, Nevada, *Am. Assoc. Petroleum Geologists Bull.* **44**:1692-1703.

Fenton, M. W., J. B. Keene, and C. J. L. Wilson, 1982. The sedimentology and environment of deposition of the Mallacoota Beds, eastern Victoria, *Jour. Geol. Soc. Australia* **29**:107-114.

Fleming, P. J. G., 1974. *Origin of Some Cambrian Bedded Cherts and Other Aspects of Silicification in the Georgina Basin, Queensland*, Geological Survey of Queensland Publication 358, 9p.

Folk, R. L., and E. F. McBride, 1976. The Caballos Novaculite revisited, part I: origin of novaculite members, *Jour. Sed. Petrology* **46**:659-669.

Folk, R. L., and E. F. McBride, 1978. Radiolarites and their relation to subjacent "oceanic crust" in Liguria, Italy, *Jour. Sed. Petrology* **48**:1069-1102.

Garrison, R. E., 1974. Radiolarian cherts, pelagic limestones, and igneous rocks in eugeosynclinal assemblages, in *Pelagic Sediments: On Land and Under the Sea*, K. J. Hsu and H. C. Jenkyns, eds., International Association of Sedimentologists Special Paper 1, pp. 367-399.

Garrison, R. E., L. E. Mack, V. G. Lee, and H. Y. Chon, 1979. Petrology, sedimentology, and diagenesis of Miocene diatomaceous and opal-CT mudstones in the Pohang area, Korea, *Geol. Soc. Korea Jour.* **15**:229-247.

Geeslin, J. H., and H. S. Chaffetz, 1982. Ordovician Aleman ribbon cherts: An example of silicification prior to carbonate lithification, *Jour. Sed. Petrology* **52**:1283-1293.

Gimmel′farb, B. M., and A. M. Tushina, 1966. Principal phosphorite ore deposits of the Kara-Tau, *Lithology and Mineral Resources* **4**:88-102.

Glennie, K. W., M. G. A. Boeuf, M. W. H. Clarke, M. Moody-Stuart, W. F. H. Pilaar, and B. M. Reinhardt, 1974. *Geology of the Oman Mountains*, Verhandelingen van het Koninklijk Nederlandse Geologisch Mijnbouwkundig Genootschap, 423p.

Glezer, Z. I., 1966. Silicoflagellatophyceae, in *Cryptogamic Plants of the U.S.S.R.*, M. M. Gollerbakh, ed., Israel Program for Scientific Translations, Jerusalem, 1970; Izdatel′stvo Nauka 7, Moscow-Leningrad.

Goldstein, A., Jr., 1959. Cherts and novaculites of Ouachita facies, in *Silica and Sediments*, H. A. Ireland, ed., Society of Economic Paleontologists and Mineralogists Special Publication 7, pp. 135-149.

Goldstein, A., Jr., and T. A. Hendricks, 1953. Siliceous sediments of Ouachita facies in Oklahoma, *Geol. Soc. America Bull.* **64**:421-442.

Grunau, H. R., 1965. Radiolarian cherts and associated rocks in space and time, *Eclogae Geol. Helvetiae* **58**:157-208.

Grunow, A., 1867. *Reisses Seiher Majestat Frega Ha Novara um die Erde*, Bolansiche Theil, Bd. 1 edition, Algen, Vienna.

Gryc, G., J. T. Dutro, W. P. Brosgé, I. L. Tailleur, and M. Churkin, 1967. in *International Symposium on the Devonian System*, D. H. Oswald, ed., Alberta Society of Petroleum Geologists, Alberta, Canada, pp. 703-716.

Gursky, H.-J., and R. Schmidt-Effing, 1983. Sedimentology of radiolarites within the Nicoya ophiolite complex, Costa Rica, Central America, in *Siliceous Deposits in the Pacific Region*, A. Iijima, J. R. Hein, and R. Siever, eds., Elsevier, Amsterdam, pp. 127-142.

Haile, N. S., A. J. Barber, and D. J. Carter, 1979. Mesozoic cherts on crystalline schists in Sulawesi and Timor, *Geol. Soc. London Jour.* **136**:65-70.

Haile, N. S., P. D. Stauffer, D. Krishnan, T. P. Lim, and G. B. Ong, 1977. Paleozoic redbeds and radiolarian chert: Reinterpretation of their relationship in the Bentong and Raub areas, West Pahang, peninsular Malaysia, *Geol. Soc. Malaysia Bull.* **8**:45-60.

Hallam, A., 1976. Geology and plate tectonics interpretation of the sediments of the Mesozoic radiolarite-ophiolite complex in the Negriz region, southern Iran, *Geol. Soc. America Bull.* **87**:47-52.

Hanna, G. D., 1929. Fossil diatoms dredged from Bering Sea, *San Diego Soc. Nat. History Trans.* **5**:287-296.

Hansen, J. M., 1979. Age of the Mo-clay Formation, *Geol. Soc. Denmark Bull.* **27**:89–91.

Hein, J. R., and S. M. Karl, 1983. Comparisons between open-ocean and continental margin chert sequences, in *Siliceous Deposits in the Pacific Region*, A. Iijima, J. R. Hein, and R. Siever, eds., Elsevier, Amsterdam, pp. 25–43.

Hein, J. R., E. P. Kuijpers, P. Denyer, and R. E. Sliney, 1983. Petrology and chemistry of Cretaceous and Paleogene cherts from western Costa Rica, in *Siliceous Deposits in the Pacific Region*, A. Iijima, J. R. Hein, and R. Siever, eds., Elsevier, Amsterdam, pp. 143–174.

Hein, J. R., and H. C. McLean, 1979. *Paleogene sedimentary and volcanogenic rocks from Adak Island, central Aleutian Islands, Alaska*, U. S. Geological Survey Professional Paper 1126-E, 15p.

Hein, J. R., D. W. Scholl, J. A. Barron, M. G. Jones, and J. Miller, 1978. Diagenesis of late Cenozoic diatomaceous deposits and formation of the bottom-simulating reflector in the southern Bering Sea, *Sedimentology* **25**:155–181.

Hornibrook, N. deB., 1983. Upper Eocene, Oligocene and Lower Miocene biostratigraphy of North Otago and South Canterbury, *15th Pacific Science Congress and 3rd International Meeting on Pacific Neogene Stratigraphy*, Dunedin, New Zealand, 19p.

Huh, O. K., 1967. The Mississippian system across the Wasatch line, east-central Idaho and extreme southwestern Montana, in *18th Annual Field Conference Guidebook*, Montana Geological Society, pp. 31–62.

Igo, H., and T. Koike, 1983. Conodont biostratigraphy of cherts in the Japanese Islands, in *Siliceous Deposits in the Pacific Region*, A. Iijima, J. R. Hein, and R. Siever, eds., Elsevier, Amsterdam, pp. 65–78.

Iijima, A., J. R. Hein, and R. Siever, eds., 1983. *Siliceous Deposits in the Pacific Region*, Elsevier, Amsterdam, 472p.

Iijima, A., and M. Utada, 1983. Recent developments in sedimentology of siliceous deposits in Japan, in *Siliceous Deposits in the Pacific Region*, A. Iijima, J. R. Hein, and R. Siever, eds., Elsevier, Amsterdam, pp. 45–64.

Ingle, J. C., Jr., 1973. Summary comments on Neogene biostratigraphy, physical stratigraphy, and paleo-oceanography in the marginal northeastern Pacific Ocean, in *Initial Reports of the Deep Sea Drilling Project, Leg 18*, L. D. Kulm, R. von Huene, et al., U.S. Government Printing Office, Washington, D.C. pp. 949–960.

Ingle, J. C., 1981. Origin of Neogene diatomites around the north Pacific rim, in *The Monterey Formation and Related Siliceous Rocks of California*, R. E. Garrison and R. D. Douglas, eds., Pacific Section, Society of Economic Paleontologists and Mineralogists, pp. 159–179.

Irwin, W. P., 1972. *Terranes of the Western Paleozoic and Triassic Belt in the Southern Klamath Mountains, California*, U.S. Geological Survey Professional Paper 800-C, pp. C103–C111.

James, H. L., 1966. *Chemistry of the iron-rich sedimentary rocks*, U.S. Geological Survey Professional Paper 440-W, pp. 17–27.

Jenkyns, H. C., and E. L. Winterer, 1982. Palaeoceanography of Mesozoic ribbon radiolarites, *Earth and Planetary Sci. Letters* **60**:351–375.

Jones, D. L., and E. M. MacKevett, Jr., 1969. Summary of the Cretaceous stratigraphy in part of the McCarthy Quadrangle, Alaska, *U.S. Geol. Survey Bull.* **127 4K**:K1–K19.

Jones, D. L., N. J. Silberling, B. Csejtey, Jr., W. H. Nelson, and C. D. Blome, 1980. *Age and Structural Significance of Ophiolite and Adjoining Rocks in the Upper Chulitna District, South-Central Alaska*, U.S. Geological Survey Professional Paper 1121-A, 21p.

Kastner, M., J. B. Keene, and J. M. Gieskes, 1977. Diagenesis of siliceous oozes, I. Chemical controls on the rate of opal-A to opal-CT transformations—An experimental study, *Geochim. et Cosmochim. Acta* **41**:1041–1051.

Kelley, T. E., 1963. Geology and hydrocarbons in Cook Inlet Basin, Alaska, in *Backbone of the Americas*, O. E. Childs and W. B. Beebe, eds., American Association of Petroleum Geologists Memoir 2, pp. 278–296.

Ketner, K. B., 1969. *Ordovician Bedded Chert, Argillite, and Shale of the Cordilleran Eugeosyncline in Nevada and Idaho*, U.S. Geological Survey Professional Paper 650-B, pp. 23–34.

Kholodov, V. N., 1969. Secondary alterations of bedded phosphorites of Malyi Karatau in the hypergene zone, *Lithology and Mineral Resources* **1969**(3):276–288.

Kholodov, V. N., and A. S. Khoryakin, 1961. Origin of phosphatic conglomerate-breccia in Lesser Karatau, *Akad. Nauk SSSR Doklady* **135**:1140–1142.

Kimberley, M. M., 1978. Paleoenvironmental classification of iron formations, *Econ. Geology* **73**:215–229.

Kimura, T., and M. Tsujii, 1984. Late Jurassic (Oxfordian) flora of Northeast Japan, *International Organization of Paleobotany Conference*, Edmonton, Alberta, Abstracts.

Kirk, H. J. C., 1962. *Geology and Mineral Resources of Semfoma Peninsula, North Borneo*, British Borneo Geological Survey Memoir 14, 178p.

Koizumi, I., 1973. The Late Cenozoic diatoms of sites 183–193, Leg 9, Deep Sea Drilling Project, in *Initial Reports of the Deep Sea Drilling Project, Leg 9*, J. D. Hays, et al., U.S. Government Printing Office, Washington, D.C., pp. 805–838.

Kolodny, Y., Y. Nathan, and E. Sass, 1965. Porcellanite in the Mishash Formation, Negev, southern Israel, *Jour. Sed. Petrology* **35**:454–463.

Lathram, E. H., J. S. Pomeroy, H. C. Berg, and R. A. Loney, 1965. *Reconnaissance Geology of Admiralty Island, Alaska*, U.S. Geological Survey Bulletin 1181-R, pp. R1–R48.

Latif, M. A., 1972. An occurrence of Palaeozoic phosphate rock in Hazara district, West Pakistan, *Inst. Mining and Metallurgy Trans.* **81**:B50–B53.

Lewin, J. C., 1961. The dissolution of silica from diatom walls, *Geochim. et Cosmochim. Acta* **21**:182–198.

Lewis, G. E., H. J. Tschopp, and J. G. Marks, 1956. Ecuador, in *Handbook of South American Geology*, W. F. Jenks, ed., Geological Society of America Memoir 65, pp. 249–292.

Lisitzin, A. P., 1971. Distribution of siliceous microfossils in suspension and bottom sediments, in *Micropalaeontology of Oceans*, B.M. Funnell and W. R. Riedel, eds., Cambridge University Press, Cambridge, England, pp. 173–195.

Loughman, D. L., and A. Hallam, 1982. A facies analysis of the Purcara Group (Norian to Toarcian carbonates, organic-rich shale, and phosphate) of central and northern Peru, *Sed. Geology* **32**:161–194.

Mattson, P. H., and E. A. Pessagno, 1979. Jurassic and Early Cretaceous radiolarians in Puerto Rican ophiolite—Tectonic implications, *Geology* **7**:440–444.

McBride, E. F., and R. L. Folk, 1979. Features and origin of Italian Jurassic radiolarites deposited on continental crust, *Jour. Sed. Petrology* **49**:837–868.

McGugan, A., and J. E. Rapson, 1979. Pennsylvanian and Permian biostratigraphy, micropaleontology, petrography, and diagenesis, Kananaskis Valley, Alberta, *Bull. Canadian Petroleum Geology* **27**:405–417.

Meng, H. -H., 1959. The petrography of phosphorites of the Karatau Basin, *Akad. Nauk SSSR Doklady* **126**:524–526.

Miller, E. L., B. K. Holdsworth, W. B. Whiteford, and D. Rodgers, 1984. Stratigraphy and structure of the Schoonover sequence, northeastern Nevada: Implications for Paleozoic plate-margin tectonics, *Geol. Soc. America Bull.* **95**:1063–1076.

Mitsui, K., and K. Taguchi, 1977. Silica mineral diagenesis in Neogene Tertiary shales in the Tempoku district, Hokkaido, Japan, *Jour. Sed. Petrology* **47**:158–167.

Mizutani, S., and K. Shabata, 1983. Diagenesis of Jurassic siliceous shale in central Japan, in *Siliceous Deposits in the Pacific Region*, A. Iijima, J. R. Hein, and R. Siever, eds., Elsevier, Amsterdam, pp. 283–298.

Moore, G. W., 1969. *New Formations on Kodiak and Adjacent Islands*, U.S. Geological Survey Bulletin 1274-A, pp. A27–A35.

Moore, P. R., 1983. Chert-bearing formations of New Zealand, in *Siliceous Deposits in the Pacific Region*, A. Iijima, J. R. Hein, and R. Siever, eds., Elsevier, Amsterdam, pp. 93–108.

Mull, C. G., I. L. Tailleur, C. F. Mayfield, I. Ellersieck, and S. Curtis, 1982. New upper Paleozoic and lower Mesozoic stratigraphic units, central and western Brooks Range, Alaska, *Am. Assoc. Petroleum Geologists Bull.* **66**:348–362.

Murchey, B., D. L. Jones, and B. K. Holdsworth, 1983. Distribution, age, and depositional environments of radiolarian chert in western North America, in *Siliceous Deposits in the Pacific Region*, A. Iijima, J. R. Hein, and R. Siever, eds., Elsevier, Amsterdam, pp. 109–125.

Nakazawa, K., F. Kumon, K. Kimura, H. Matsuyama, and K. Nakajo, 1983. Environments of deposition of Cretaceous chert from the Shimanto Belt, Kii Peninsula, southwest Japan, in *Siliceous Deposits in the Pacific Region*, A. Iijima, J. R. Hein, and R. Siever, eds., Elsevier, Amsterdam, pp. 395–412.

Namy, J. N., 1974. Early diagenetic chert in the Marble Falls Group (Pennsylvanian) of central Texas, *Jour. Sed. Petrology* **44**:1262–1268.

Nisbet, E. G., and I. Price, 1974. Siliceous turbidites: Bedded cherts as redeposited ocean ridge-derived sediments, in *Pelagic Sediments: On Land and Under the Sea*, K. J. Hsu and H. C. Jenkyns, eds., International Association of Sedimentologists Special Paper 1, pp. 351–366.

Norris, A. W., 1967. Devonian of northern Yukon Territory and adjacent district of Mackenzie, in *International Symposium on the Devonian System*, D. H. Oswald, ed., Alberta Society of Petroleum Geologists, Alberta, Canada, pp. 753–780.

Obradovich, J. D., and C. W. Naeser, 1981. Geochronology bearing on the age of the Monterey Formation and siliceous rocks in Califiornia, in *The Monterey Formation and Related Siliceous Rocks of California*, R. E. Garrison and R. G. Douglas, eds., Pacific Section, Society of Economic Paleontologists and Mineralogists, pp. 87–95.

Ogawa, Y., K. Nakashima, and H. Sunouchi, 1983. Mesozoic accretion of siliceous deposits in southwest Japan, in *Siliceous Deposits in the Pacific Region*, A. Iijima, J. R. Hein, and R. Siever, eds., Elsevier, Amsterdam, pp. 413–425.

Oldershaw, A. E., 1968. Electron-microscopic examination of Namurian bedded cherts, North Wales (Great Britain), *Sedimentology* **10**:255–272.

O'Rourke, J. E., 1961. Paleozoic banded iron formations. *Econ. Geology* **56**:331–361.

Orr, W. N., 1972. Pacific Northwest siliceous phytoplankton, *Palaeogeography, Palaeoclimatology, Palaeoecology* **12**:95–114.

Paleogeographic Atlas Project, 1984. *Data and Software*, University of Chicago, Chicago, Illinois.

Parrish, J. M., J. T. Parrish, and A. M. Ziegler, 1986. Permian-Triassic paleogeography and paleoclimatology and implications for therapsid distributions, in *The Ecology and Biology of Mammal-like Reptiles*, N. Hotton, III, P. D. MacLean, J. J. Roth, and E. C. Roth, eds., Smithsonian Press, Washington, D. C., pp. 109–132.

Parrish, J. T., 1982. Upwelling and petroleum source beds, with reference to the Paleozoic, *Am. Assoc. Petroleum Geologists Bull.* **66**:750–774.

Parrish, J. T., 1983. Upwelling deposits: Nature of association of organic-rich rocks, chert, chalk, phosphorite, and glauconite (abstract), *Am. Assoc. Petroleum Geologists Bull.* **67**:529.

Parrish, J. T., and R. L. Curtis, 1982. Atmospheric circulation, upwelling, and organic-rich rocks in the Mesozoic and Cenozoic Eras, *Palaeogeography, Palaeoclimatology, Palaeoecology* **40**:31–66.

Parrish, J. T., and J. A. Doyle, 1984. Predicted evolution of global climate in Late Jurassic–Cretaceous time, *International Organization of Paleobotany Conference*, Edmonton, Alberta, Abstracts.

Parrish, J. T., K. S. Hansen, and A. M. Ziegler, 1979. Atmospheric circulation and upwelling in the Paleozoic, with reference to petroleum source beds (abstract), *Am. Assoc. Petroleum Geologists Bull.* **63**:507-508.

Parrish, J. T., A. M. Ziegler, and R. G. Humphreville, 1983. Upwelling in the Paleozoic Era, in *Coastal Upwelling: Its Sediment Record* Part B, J.Thiede and E. Suess, eds., Plenum Press, New York, pp. 553-578.

Parrish, J. T., A. M. Ziegler, and C. R. Scotese, 1982. Rainfall patterns and the distribution of coals and evaporites in the Mesozoic and Cenozoic, *Palaeogeography, Palaeoclimatology, Palaeoecology* **40**:67-101.

Parrish, J. T., A. M. Ziegler, C. R. Scotese, R. G. Humphreville, and J. L. Kirschvink, 1986. Early Cambrian palaeogeography, palaeoceanography, and phosphorites, in *Proterozoic and Cambrian Phosphorites*, J. H. Shergold and P. J. Cook, eds., Cambridge University Press, Cambridge, England, and International Geological Correlation Project 156, pp. 280-294.

Pessagno, E. A., W. Finch, and P. L. Abbott, 1979. Upper Triassic radiolaria from the San Hipólito Formation, Baja California, *Micropaleontology* **25**:160-197.

Pessagno, E. A., and R. L. Newport, 1972. A technique for extracting radiolaria from radiolarian cherts, *Micropaleontology* **18**:231-234.

Pindell, J., and J. F. Dewey, 1982. Permo-Triassic reconstruction of western Pangaea and the evolution of the Gulf of Mexico/Caribbean region, *Tectonics* **1**:179-211.

Poole, F. G., B. L. Murchey, and J. H. Stewart, 1983. Bedded barite deposits of middle and late Paleozoic age in central Sonora, Mexico, *Geol. Soc. America Abs. with Programs* **15**(5):299.

Poole, W. H., B. V. Sanford, H. Williams, and D. G. Kelley, 1976. Geology of southeastern Canada, in *Geology and Economic Minerals of Canada*, R. J. W. Douglas, ed., Geological Survey of Canada Economic Geology Report No. 1, Part A, pp. 227-304.

Price, I., 1977. Facies distinction and interpretation of primary cherts in a Mesozoic continental margin succession, Othris, Greece, *Sed. Geology* **18**:321-335.

Ramsay, A. T. S., 1973. A history of organic siliceous sediments in oceans, in *Organisms and Continents Through Time*, N. F. Hughes, ed., Special Papers in Palaeontology 12, The Palaeontological Association, London, pp. 199-234.

Rangin, C., 1981. Geochemistry of the Mesozoic bedded cherts of central Baja California (Vizcaino-Cedros-San Benito): Implications for paleogeographic reconstruction of an old oceanic basin, *Earth and Planetary Sci. Letters* **54**:313-322.

Ranneft, T. S. M., R. M. Hopkins, Jr., A. J. Froelich, and J. W. Gwinn, 1960. Reconnaissance geology and oil possibilities of Mindanao, *Am. Assoc. Petroleum Geologists Bull.* **44**:529-568.

Raymond, A., W. C. Parker, and J. T. Parrish, 1985. Phytogeography and paleoclimate of the Early Carboniferous, in *Geological Factors and Evolution of Plants*, B. R. Tiffney, ed., Yale University Press, New Haven, Conn., pp. 169-222.

Reinhold, T., 1937. Fossil diatoms of the Neogene of Java and their zonal distribution. Nederland en Kolonien Geology Mijnbouw, Genootschap, Verhandelingen, Geological Series, Deel 12, pp. 43-133.

Riggs, S. R., 1984. Paleoceanographic model of Neogene phosphorite deposition, U. S. Atlantic continental margin, *Science* **223**:123-131.

Roberts, R. J., P. E. Hotze, J. Gilluly, and H. G. Ferguson, 1958. Paleozoic rocks of central Nevada, *Am. Assoc. Petroleum Geologists Bull.* **42**:2813-2857.

Robertson, A. H. F., 1981. Metallogenesis on a Mesozoic passive continental margin, Antalya Complex, southwest Turkey, *Earth and Planetary Sci. Letters* **54**:323-345.

Robertson, A. H. F., and J. D. Hudson, 1974. Pelagic sediments in the Cretaceous and Tertiary history of the Troodos Massif, Cyprus, in *Pelagic Sediments: On Land and Under the Sea*, K. J. Hsu and H. C. Jenkyns, eds., International Association of Sedimentologists Special Publication 1, pp. 403-436.

Rogers, C. L., Z. DeCserna, E. Tavera, and S. Ulloa, 1956. *General Geology and*

Phosphate Deposits of Concepcion del Oro District, Zacatecas, Mexico, U.S. Geological Survey Bulletin 1037-A, 102p.

Rowell, H. C., 1981. Diatom biostratigraphy of the Monterey Formation, Palos Verdes Hills, California, in *The Monterey Formation and Related Siliceous Rocks of California*, R. E. Garrison and R. G. Douglas, eds., Pacific Section, Society of Economic Paleontologists and Mineralogists, pp. 55-70.

Rowley, D. B., A. Raymond, J. T. Parrish, A. L. Lottes, C. R. Scotese, and A. M. Ziegler, 1985. Carboniferous paleogeographic, phytogeographic, and paleoclimatic reconstructions, *Internat. Jour. Coal Geology* 5:7-42.

Sano, H., 1983. Bedded cherts associated with greenstones in the Sawadani and Shimantogawa Groups, southwest Japan, in *Siliceous Deposits in the Pacific Region*, A. Iijima, J. R. Hein, and R. Siever, eds., Elsevier, Amsterdam, pp. 427-440.

Scholten, R., 1957. Paleozoic evolution of the geosynclinal margin north of the Snake River Plain, Idaho-Montana, *Geol. Soc. America Bull.* 71:151-170.

Schweickert, R. A., and D. S. Cowan, 1975. Early Mesozoic tectonic evolution of the western Sierra Nevada, California, *Geol. Soc. America Bull.* 86:1329-1336.

Scotese, C. R., 1979. Phanerozoic continental drift base maps, in *Paleogeographic Reconstructions—State of the Art*, R. K. Bambach and C. R. Scotese, Geological Society of America Short Course, April 1979, Blacksburg, VA.

Scotese, C. R., R. K. Bambach, C. Barton, R. Van der Voo, and A. M. Ziegler, 1979. Paleozoic base maps, *Jour. Geology* 87:217-277.

Senn, A., 1940. Paleogene of Barbados and its bearing on history and structure of Antillean-Caribbean region, *Am. Assoc. Petroleum Geologists Bull.* 24:1548-1610.

Shagam, R., 1960. Geology of Central Aragua, Venezuela, *Geol. Soc. America Bull.* 71:249-302.

Silberling, N. J., and R. J. Roberts, 1962. *Pre-Tertiary Stratigraphy and Structure of Northwestern Nevada*, Geological Society of America Special Paper 72, 58p.

Simons, F. S., and J. A. Straczek, 1958. *Geology of the Manganese Deposits of Cuba*, U.S. Geological Survey Bulletin 1057, 289p.

Siok, J. P., 1984. A siliceous facies of the Siksikpuk Formation, north-central Brooks Range, Alaska, *Geol. Soc. America Abs. with Programs* 16(5):333.

Smirnov, A. I., 1959. New data of elemental constitution of the phosphorites in the Karatau Basin, *Akad. Nauk SSSR Doklady* 125:205-207.

Snyder, W. S., and H. K. Brueckner, 1983. Tectonic evolution of the Golconda Allochthon, Nevada: Problems and perspectives, in *Pre-Jurassic Rocks in Western North American Suspect Terranes*, C. H. Stevens, ed., Pacific Section, Society of Economic Paleontologists and Mineralogists, pp. 103-123.

Steinberg, M., 1981. Biosiliceous sedimentation, radiolarite periods and silica budget fluctuations, *Oceanologica Acta* SP:149-154.

Steinitz, G., 1970. Chert "dike" structures in Senonian chert beds, southern Negev, Israel, *Jour. Sed. Petrology* 40:1241-1254.

Stewart, J. H., J. R. MacMillan, K. M. Nichols, and C. H. Stevens, 1977. Deep-water upper Paleozoic rocks in north-central Nevada—A study of the type area of the Havallah Formation, in *Paleozoic Paleogeography of the Western United States*, J. H. Stewart, C. H. Stevens, and A. E. Fritsche, eds., Pacific Coast Paleogeography Symposium 1, Society of Economic Paleontologists and Mineralogists, pp. 337-347.

Strakhov, N. M., 1948. *Principles of Historical Geology, Parts I and II*, Israel Program for Scientific Translations, Jerusalem, 257p (I); 432p (II).

Takai, F., T. Matsumoto, and R. Turiyama, 1963. *Geology of Japan*, University of Califiornia Press, Berkeley, 279p.

Tan, D. N. K., 1983. Cherts of Southeast Asia, in *Siliceous Deposits in the Pacific Region*, A. Iijima, J. R. Hein, and R. Siever, eds., Elsevier, Amsterdam, pp. 79-91.

Thomson, M. R. A., 1982. Mesozoic paleogeography of West Antarctica, in *Antarctic*

Geoscience, C. Craddock, ed., University of Wisconsin Press, Madison, pp. 331–337.

Tissot, B., 1979. Effects on prolific petroleum source rocks and major coal deposits caused by sea-level changes, *Nature* 277:463–465.

Tromp, S. W., 1947. A tentative classification of the main structural units of the Anatolian Orogenic Belt, *Jour. Geology* 56:362–377.

Tushina, A. M., 1968. Lithofacies characteristics of the formation of the phosphorite stratum of Karatau, *Lithology and Mineral Resources* 4:456–465.

Vindogradov, A. P., ed., 1967. *Atlas of the Lithological-Paleogeographical Maps of the USSR. IV. Paleogene, Neogene, Pleistocene*, Ministry of Geology, Akademia Nauk, Moscow.

Vinogradov, A. P., ed., 1968a. *Atlas of the Lithological-Paleogeographical Maps of the USSR. I. Precambrian, Cambrian, Ordovician, Silurian*, Ministry of Geology, Akademia Nauk, Moscow.

Vinogradov, A. P., ed., 1968b. *Atlas of the Lithological-Paleogeographical Maps of the USSR. III. Triassic, Jurassic, Cretaceous*, Ministry of Geology, Akademia Nauk, Moscow.

Vinogradov, A. P., ed., 1969. *Atlas of the Lithological-Paleogeographical Maps of the USSR. II. Devonian, Carboniferous, Permian*, Ministry of Geology, Akademia Nauk, Moscow.

Volkov, B. N., 1970. Some aspects of phosphorite deposits, *Akad. Nauk SSSR Doklady* 192:63–65.

Waller, J. D., ed., 1971. *World Survey of Phosphate Deposits*, British Sulphur Corporation, London, 180p.

Whalen, P. A., and T. R. Carr, 1984. Devonian radiolaria and conodonts, McCann Hill Formation, east-central Alaska, *Geol. Soc. America Abs. with Programs* 16 (5):340.

Wise, S. W., M. P. Ausburn, D. A. Textoris, W. H. Wheeler, R. B. Daniels, and F. F. Gamble, 1981. Lithologic characteristics and diagenesis of some siliceous coastal plain rocks, *Scanning Electron Microscope* 1981/1.577–584.

Ziegler, A. M., C. R. Scotese, and S. F. Barrett, 1983. Mesozoic and Cenozoic paleogeographic maps, in *Tidal Friction and the Earth's Rotation, II*, P. Brosche and J. Sündermann, eds., Springer-Verlag, Berlin, pp. 240–252.

3

Association of Phosphatic and Siliceous Marine Sedimentary Deposits

Richard P. Sheldon

Geologic Consultant
Washington, D.C.

ABSTRACT. An empirical association exists between chert and major phosphorite deposits, although not all major phosphorites contain chert or vice versa. Chert and phosphorite deposits are not normally time-stratigraphic facies equivalents of each other but are deposited sequentially in shallow water cyclic sequences that usually show deepening of the basin upsection. The phosphorite is usually a shallower water deposit than the chert. The cyclic sequences show great lateral continuity along sedimentary facies strike.

The phosphorite-chert sequences were deposited on outer continental shelves and less commonly on inner continental shelves and in adjacent epicontinental seas. Phosphorite deposits on inner continental shelves and epicontinental seas have little or no associated chert. Phosphorites can be divided into at least two families. One family of phosphorites has the distribution pattern of the global Holocene phosphorites, occurring where the eastern-boundary current of the paleoceanic gyres crosses the paleo-trade-wind belt. This type of phosphorite was deposited in the early Pliocene, Miocene, Oligocene, Jurassic, Permian, Early Carboniferous, and Late Ordovician. A second family of phosphorites was distributed in a global belt near the equator, where it is found on paleocontinental shelves, epicontinental and intracratonic paleoseas, and seamounts. This type of phosphorite was deposited in Early Tertiary and Late Cretaceous time and possibly also in the Cambrian and Proterozoic time.

From a genetic consideration, phosphate and silica have similar exogenic geochemical cycles, including their predominant source from chemical weathering of rocks on the continents, storage in a deep-ocean geochemical sink, vertical circulation into the zone of photosynthesis, followed by biogenic sedimentation.

The cause of phosphogenic episodicity appears to be primarily variation in paleoclimates. The trade-wind-belt phosphorites, along with the trade-wind desert sand dunes, formed at times of polar glaciation at intermediate stands of the first-order sea level variations shown by Vail et al. (1977) and low stands of second-order sea level variations. The equatorial phosphorites were formed at high stands of the first-order sea level variations but low stands of second-order sea level and probably not at times of polar glaciation. The paleoclimate during times of equatorial phosphogenesis must have been different than that of trade-wind-belt phosphogenesis, but its nature is uncertain.

GENERAL RELATIONSHIP BETWEEN PHOSPHATIC AND SILICEOUS SEDIMENTS

Phosphorus and silica, along with organic carbon, are commonly associated in sedimentary rock sequences as organic-rich beds of phosphorite and chert or its equivalent in young rocks, porcelanite, or diatomite. This lithologic association is found in many places; however, not all phosphorites are associated with chert and not all cherts are associated with phosphorites.

The genetic reason for this limited lithologic association may result from similarities between the marine geochemical cycles of phosphate and silica. Both accumulate now, along with nitrate, in the oceanic geochemical sink below about 500–1,000 m of water depth. In areas of vertical circulation (upwelling), all three are supplied as nutrients to the photic zone, where they stimulate phytoplankton growth, which gives the potential for forming biogenic sediments.

It is beyond the scope of this chapter to deal with phosphorite genesis in detail, and this subject has been covered in some detail recently (Baturin, 1982; Cook and McElhinny, 1979; Bentor, 1980; Burnett, 1980; Slansky, 1980b; Kolodny, 1981; Sheldon, 1981). Both the empirical and genetic interrelations between phosphorite and chert, however, are examined in this chapter.

EMPIRICAL ASSOCIATION OF PHOSPHORITE AND CHERT

Both phosphatic and siliceous sediments occur in minor amounts in many different types of rocks in many areas. In general, there does not seem to be an association of the two in these minor occurrences. However, when major phosphorite deposits are considered, a distinct association appears (Table 3–1). Many of these phosphorite deposits are actively being mined and make up most of the world's phosphate rock production from marine sedimentary deposits. Most of the deposits of Table 3–1 are formed of phosphorite beds more than a meter thick and contain hundreds of millions to billions of tons of phosphate rock. In this sense they are major deposits.

A number of major phosphorite deposits exist that do not have a known association with siliceous sediments (Table 3–2). The economically most important of these is the Miocene deposit of Florida, which makes up the southern part of the southeastern U.S. phosphogenic province. The North Carolina deposit, which forms the northern part of the province, has a diatomite association in the deeper-water facies (S. R. Riggs, personal communication, 1984). It is possible that the Florida phosphorite also has a siliceous sediment association in its deeper-water facies that has not been identified. The stromatolitic phosphorite deposit of the Proterozoic Aravalli Group of western

Table 3–1. Major Marine Phosphorite Deposits Associated with Siliceous Sediment

Deposit	Locality	Reference
Lower Proterozoic		
Bijawar Gp.	Madhya Pradesh and Uttar Pradesh, India	Banerjee et al., 1982; Pant, in press; Sonakia and Kumar, 1982
Baraga Gp.	Michigan, United States	Cannon and Klasner, 1976
Upper Proterozoic and Cambrian		
Khubsugul Series	Khubsugul Basin, Mongolia	Ilyin and Ratnikova, 1981
Tamdy Gp.	Karatau Phosphorite Basin, Kazakhstan, USSR	Eganov et al., 1984
Yahucun Fm.	Yunnan Prov., China	Organizing Comm., IGCP, 1982; Liang and Chang, 1981
Kodjari Fm.	Northern Volta Basin, Upper Volta, Niger, and Benin	Trompette et al., 1980
Beetle Creek Fm.	Queensland, Australia	de Keyser and Cook, 1972
Tal Fm.	Uttar Pradesh, India	Pant, 1980; Azmi et al., 1981
Devonian–Lower Carboniferous		
Chattanooga Shale, Maury Shale, and Fort Payne Chert	Tennessee, United States	Smith and Whitlatch, 1940, pp. 301–354
Brazer Fm.	Utah, United States	Roberts, 1979, pp. 230–233; DeCelles and Gutschick, 1983; Sandberg, in press
Lisburne Group	Endicott Mtns. Alaska, United States	Armstrong and Mamet, 1978
Permian		
Phosphoria Fm.	Middle Rocky Mtns., United States	McKelvey et al., 1959
Triassic		
Shublik Fm.	North Slope, Alaska, United States	Detterman et al., 1975; Detterman, in press
Jurassic		
Aramchay Fm.	Central Andes, Peru	Szekely and Grose, 1972, pp. 407–428
La Caja Fm.	Zacatecas, Mexico	Rogers et al., 1956
Fernie Fm.	British Columbia, Canada	Christie, in press
Upper Cretaceous through Eocene		
Karabogaz Fm. and Mardin Fm.	Southeastern Turkey	Sheldon, 1964a

Table 3-1. (*continued*)

Deposit	Locality	Reference
Santonian to Eocene	Syria	Atfeh, 1966; Atfeh and Faradjev, 1963
Digma, Tayarat, Umm Er Radhuma, and Dammam Fm.	Iraq	Al-Bassam, 1976; Al-Bassam and Hagopian, 1983; Al-Bassam et al., 1983
Balqa Series	Jordan	Jallad et al., in press
Mishash Fm.	Israel	Wurzburger, 1968
Turayf Gp.	Saudi Arabia	Riddler et al., 1983; Meissner and Ankary, 1972; Berge and Jack, in press
Upper Cretaceous phosphatic series	Egypt	Omara, 1965; Faris and Hassan, 1959; Issawi, 1972; El-Tarabili and El-Sayed, 1969
Metlaoui Fm.	Tunisia	Fournie, 1980; Sassi, 1980
Djebel Onk deposit, Thanatian–Ypresian	Algeria	Oussedik et al., 1980
Maastrichtian–Lutetian phosphatic series	Morocco	Boujo, 1976
Bu Craa deposit, Maastrichtian, Paleocene	Western Sahara	Munoz Cabezon, in press
Eocene	Senegal	Monciardini, 1966
La Luna Fm.	Colombia and Venezuela	Cathcart and Zambrano, 1969; Rodriguez, 1984
Senonian phosphorites	Paris Basin, France	Jarvis, 1980
Ciply phosphatic chalk	Mons Basin, Belgium	Robaszynski, in press

Miocene (includes some Oligocene and Pliocene)

Deposit	Locality	Reference
Monterey Fm.	California, United States	Pisciotto and Garrison, 1981; Roberts, in press
Monterey Fm.	Baja California, Mexico	Ojeda Rivera, 1979, 1981
Sechura deposit	Sechura Desert, Peru	Cheney et al., 1979
Pungo River Fm.	North Carolina, United States	Riggs, 1984
Oligocene–Miocene	Cuba	Pokrishkin, 1967

Quaternary

Deposit	Locality	Reference
Continental shelf	Namibia	Bremner, 1983
Offshore	Global	Baturin, 1982

Table 3–2. Major Marine Phosphorite Deposits Not Associated with Siliceous Sediment

Deposit	Locality	Reference
Proterozoic		
Aravalli Gp.	Rajasthan and Madhya Pradesh, India	Banerjee et al., 1980; Choudhuri, in press
Ordovician		
Swan Peak Fm.	Idaho, United States	Mansfield, 1927
Kallavere Fm.	Estonia, USSR	Academy of Sciences of the Estonian SSR, 1984
Mesozoic		
Late Jurassic and Cretaceous	Moscow and Kirovsk regions, USSR	Soviet Union Delegation, 1968
Santonian (Cretaceous)	Aktubinsk region, USSR	Soviet Union Delegation, 1968
Gramame Fm. (Cretaceous)	Recife, Brazil	Cavalcanti de Albuquerque and Giannerini, in press
Tertiary		
Eocene	Togo–Benin	Slansky, 1962
Eocene	Mali	Karpoff and Visse, 1950
Kisil Kum deposit, Middle Eocene	Uzbekistan, USSR	Ilyin, in press
Capadave Fm., Middle to Late Miocene	Riecito deposit, Venezuela	Rodriguez, 1984
Miocene and Pliocene	Florida, United States	Riggs, 1984
Varswater Fm., Pliocene	Namibia	Hendey and Dingle, in press

India has no associated chert beds, although lateritic silcrete was formed during later times over the phosphorite and has been called chert.

STRATIGRAPHIC CHARACTERISTICS

McKelvey et al. (1953, p. 61) pointed out the close association between chert and phosphorite in the Phosphoria Formation of Permian age, which occurs in the Rocky Mountains of the western United States, and extended the association to other geosynclinal phosphorites, apparently for the first time. They stated:

The close association of chert and phosphorite in the (Phosphoria) formation and in other geosynclinal phosphorites was not reported by Kazakov but it deserves notice. Although both chert and carbonate-apatite occur together in some layers, the most important association is a geographic one—beds of chert and beds of phosphorite are more prominent near the margin of the geosynclinal belt. Their overlap but lack of precise coincidence indicates that their deposition is effected by similar but not precisely the same chemical conditions or that they are common products of other factors in the same environment.

A survey of the phosphorite and chert associations of the world (Table 3–1) confirms the McKelvey et al. (1953) hypothesis that geosynclinal phosphorites in general are associated with chert but lack precise coincidence. The first line of evidence for this is petrographic, and the second is stratigraphic.

Based on my observations, rocks made up of nearly equal mixtures of apatite and chalcedony or opal are rare, although phosphorite cemented by chalcedony is common. Rather, the association is characterized by interbedding of stratigraphic units of phosphorite with units of chert. These units do not show facies relationships—that is, time-rock lateral equivalence—as might be predicted from the lack of mixed rocks. Although an early interpretation of the U.S. Permian Phosphoria Formation (Sheldon, 1957, 1963) did hypothesize a facies relationship between phosphorite and chert, additional data and analysis give a model that better fits the data and indicates that chert and phosphorite were deposited respectively at alternating interglacial and glacial ages (Sheldon, 1984).

Sequences of phosphorite, chert, and associated rocks are commonly cyclically deposited. Cyclic sequences have been reported, for example, for Cambrian deposits of Australia and Asia (Eganov, 1979; Cook and Shergold, 1980), Permian deposits of the United States as noted previously, Upper Cretaceous through Eocene deposits of Africa and the Middle East (Salvan, 1985), and Upper Cretaceous deposits of Colombia (Maughan et al., 1979). The cyclic sequence is not the same in each of these phosphogenic provinces, but chert and phosphorite beds are commonly stratigraphically adjacent or nearly so. The stratigraphic sections commonly show a deepening upward sequence, with a lower unit of sandstone or shallow water carbonate rock, or a subaerial erosion surface. This lower unit is overlain by phosphorite, which in turn is overlain by a chert, carbonate rock, and/or black shale, marking the top of the cycle. Many of the phosphatic sequences contain organic-rich dolomite beds, commonly occurring with the organic-rich shale beds, but in Proterozoic–Cambrian rocks, the dolomite occurs with the phosphorites.

The individual beds of the cyclic sequences can be traced laterally for long distances along facies strike, but the sequence changes over short distances across facies strike. This change makes it possible to correlate cycles of sedimentation along facies strike for long distances, using only physical stratigraphic techniques. An outstanding example of lateral continuity of beds and cycles is the Phosphoria Formation in Idaho and adjacent states of the United States, which covers an area of over 350,000 km^2 (McKelvey et al., 1953). Within this area, thin individual beds can be traced for as much as 160 km along facies strike in western Wyoming (Sheldon, 1963, Plate 7). The individual beds and larger stratigraphic units of cyclic phosphatic sections tend to be laminated or layer cake units, particularly in the basinal parts of the area of deposition.

The differing distributions of chert and phosphorite beds, as discussed by McKelvey et al. (1953), show up on a broad paleogeographic view. Bentor (1979) pointed out that many ancient phosphorites were deposited in epicontinental seas adjacent to continental shelves (inner continental shelves adjacent to outer continental shelves). In North Africa and the Middle East, the epicontinental phosphatic sequences contain little, if any, chert, whereas the adjacent continental shelf deposits contain prominent chert. A strong chert-phosphorite association occurs in the deposits of Turkey, Syria, Israel, and Western Sahara, all of which were deposited on the outer continental shelf adjacent to the Tethys seaway. The phosphorites of Iraq, Jordan, and Saudi Arabia, which were deposited on the inner continental shelf, contain fewer chert beds, and the Egyptian deposits, which are farthest away from the Tethys seaway, contain the least amount of chert. The phosphorites of Morocco and Tunisia–Algeria were deposited in narrow inlets that opened northward into the Tethys seaway (Slansky, 1980a) and southward into a broad intracratonic sea in North Africa (Boujo, 1976, p. 129; Winnock, 1980), which at times was hypersaline, judging by the presence of evaporite deposits. The phosphate- and silica-rich water of the Tethys was drawn through the inlets, possibly by evaporation in the intracratonic sea, causing phosphorite and chert sedimentation. The heavy brines formed by evaporation presumably re-entered the Tethys seaway by other outlets, possibly the trough in northern Libya (Winnock, 1980). The phosphorite extends farther into the open epicontinental sea than the chert, which is concentrated at the mouth of the inlets near the Tethys Sea (Boujo, 1976, pp. 159–160). Comparable inner shelf phosphorites without a chert association exist in the Permian Phosphoria Formation in the United States, in the Late Cretaceous La Luna Formation in Venezuela and Colombia, and in the Miocene–Pliocene phosphorites of the southeastern United States. The earlier discussion of the empirical association of chert and phosphorite pointed out a number of phosphorite deposits with no chert association (Table 3–2). They all were inner shelf epicontinental sea or intracratonic sea deposits and, except for the Ordovician brachiopod phosphorites of the United States and the USSR, would fit into the general pattern of decreasing amounts of chert associated with phosphorites with increasing distance from the areas of upwelling on the continental shelf.

PALEOGEOGRAPHIC AND TEMPORAL DISTRIBUTION

Phosphatic and associated siliceous sedimentary rocks are distributed systematically both in their paleogeography and in geologic time (Cook and McElhinny, 1979; Sheldon, 1964b, 1980). Paleogeographically, they occur at the edges of major oceans, but they occur in two major paleogeographic families. Over geologic time, phosphorites were deposited episodically and alternate with periods of little or no phosphorite deposition.

PALEOGEOGRAPHY

In the geologic record, phosphatic and associated siliceous sediments were deposited at the structural hinge line between cratonic and geosynclinal areas, which is equivalent to the modern continental shelf-slope break but in some deposits is equivalent to the continental shelf-foreland basin break. They are normally further restricted to paleolatitudes lower than 40° north or south, with most lower than 30°. Within these distributional parameters, two major phosphorite families can be distinguished by their patterns of distribution.

The trade-wind-belt family occurs on the west side of continents (or the east sides of major oceans) in trade-wind-belt latitudes, which are typically lower than 30° latitude. This family includes the following deposits. On the western edge of the North American craton, phosphorite was deposited in Early Carboniferous, Permian, Jurassic, Oligocene–Miocene–Pliocene, and Quaternary times at paleolatitudes between 3° and 20° north. Similarly, Jurassic, Miocene, and Quaternary phosphorites were deposited on the western edge of the South American craton at paleolatitudes between 4° and 10° south (Sheldon, 1964b). On the western edge of the African craton, Miocene, Pliocene, and Quaternary phosphorite was deposited in the trade-wind belt at low paleolatitudes (Baturin, 1982; Summerhayes and McArthur, in press; Hendey and Dingle, in press). Figure 3–1 shows the global distribution of phosphorite of the Oligocene to Holocene phosphogenic episode.

The Oligocene–Miocene–Pliocene phosphorites of the United States–Cuba–Venezuela province occur on the western side of the Atlantic Ocean and do not fit the pattern of the trade-wind-belt family, which occurs on the eastern sides of the major oceans. As discussed later, both are related to surficial oceanic-gyral currents that are driven by the easterly trade winds and the westerly winds of higher latitudes. Thus, even though abnormal, the southeast United States–Caribbean Oligocene–Miocene–Pliocene province is a member of the trade-wind family.

The equatorial belt family of phosphorites was deposited in a global belt centered about the equator (Sheldon, 1980). The best example, and the only one for which the paleogeography can be deciphered with confidence, is the

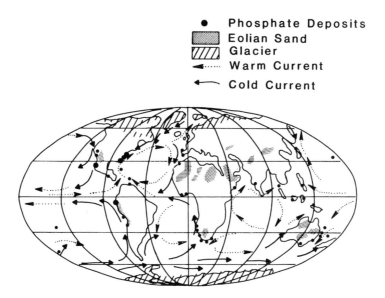

Figure 3–1.   Oligocene to Recent paleoceanography and distribution of deposits of glacial sediments, eolian sand, and marine phosphorite. (10 m.y.b.p. paleogeographic map from Ziegler, 1981; eolian sand distribution from McKee, 1980.)

Late Cretaceous–Early Tertiary phosphorites (Figs. 3–2 and 3–3). These include the Late Cretaceous and Early Tertiary phosphorites listed in Tables 3–1 and 3–2, which were deposited mainly on the continental shelves bordering the Tethys seaway. Additional members of this province include Late Cretaceous–Early Tertiary phosphatic sediment on seamounts (Baturin, 1982), which when restored to their original paleogeographic positions, lay close to the equator at the time of phosphate sedimentation (Sheldon, 1980).

Phosphorites deposited during the Proterozoic and Cambrian phosphogenic episodes were possibly members of the equatorial family, but the inherent errors of paleogeographic and paleoceanographic reconstructions are too large to be certain on these grounds alone. However, other characteristics suggest that they belong to the equatorial belt family. First, the Proterozoic and Cambrian continents were arrayed at low latitudes, and their continental shelves were the sites of phosphorite sedimentation on all sides, not preferentially on west sides. Second, the phosphorites were deposited at a high stand of the first-order sea level variations (Vail et al., 1977), which as discussed later, is also characteristic of the Late Cretaceous–Early Tertiary equatorial belt family.

The lithologic and stratigraphic characteristics of the two phosphorite families are essentially the same, including the chert-phosphorite relationship, although the distributions of the two families are different. For example, the trade-wind-belt region of the west coasts of continents was not the site of significant phosphate sedimentation during the Late Cretaceous and Early Tertiary phosphogenic episode that deposited phosphorite in the equatorial belt. Likewise, the Tethyan seaway continental shelves were not the sites of phosphorite sedimentation during the Late Jurassic trade-wind phosphogenic episode, even though the Tethys seaway was open at that time. However, the distributions of the two families do overlap at some paleogeographic locations. For example, shelf and slope drilling west of Morocco showed Eocene

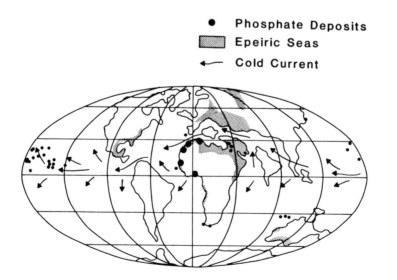

Figure 3–2. Early Tertiary paleoceanography and distribution of phosphorite. (40 m.y.b.p. paleogeographic base from Ziegler, 1981; distribution of seamount phosphorite from Baturin, 1982.)

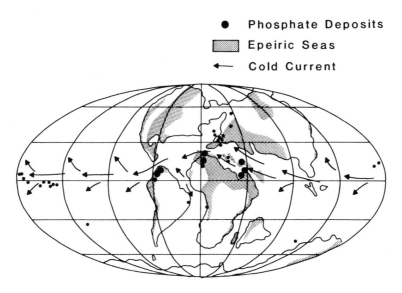

● Phosphate Deposits

▓ Epeiric Seas

← Cold Current

Figure 3–3. Late Cretaceous paleoceanography and distribution of phosphorites. (80 m.y.b.p. paleogeographic base from Ziegler, 1981; distribution of seamount phosphorite from Baturin, 1982.)

and Cretaceous phosphorites of the equatorial belt family overlain by Miocene phosphorite of the trade-wind-belt family (Summerhayes and McArthur, in press). In Venezuela, Miocene phosphorite of the Riecito deposit of the trade-wind-belt family occurs 250 km northeast of Upper Cretaceous La Luna phosphorites of the equatorial belt family (Rodriguez, 1984).

PHOSPHOGENIC EPISODES

Major phosphate sedimentation did not occur randomly throughout geologic history but during certain phosphogenic episodes, a concept first introduced by Gimmel'farb (1958). Strakov (1960), Bushinskii (1969), Cook and Mc-Elhinny (1979), and Sheldon (1980) added data and discussed the concept. Phosphogenic episodes occurred during the Early Proterozoic, Late Proterozoic to Cambrian (and perhaps into the Earliest Ordovician), Late Ordovician, Early Carboniferous, Permian, Late and Early Jurassic, Late Cretaceous to Early Tertiary, and Oligocene to Holocene (with major phosphogenesis in the middle Miocene). These episodes include the great majority of marine phosphorites, particularly the large deposits. Minor deposits of other ages do occur, however. For example, minor deposits of Devonian age are found in many parts of the world although the phosphorite of the Devonian-Carboniferous Chattanooga Shale is listed in Table 3–1. The Shublik Formation phosphorite of Alaska is also listed in Table 3–1, but no other Triassic phosphorite has been reported. The Baja California, Mexico, phosphorite has been widely regarded as Miocene, but paleontologic and radiometric studies date it as one of the few Oligocene deposits (Hausback, 1984). A Cuban phosphorite is dated as Oligocene–Miocene (Pokrishkin, 1967). The uppermost phosphorite of the North Carolina district, economically insignificant, is dated as Pliocene (Riggs, 1984). The Varswater phosphorite of Namibia is also Pliocene (Hendey and Dingle, in press). Thus, the temporal distribution of phosphorite is not simple, and it is best at this stage of knowledge to regard the record of phosphorite sedimentation as one of major episodes interspersed with periods of minor, isolated, or nonphosphorite deposition.

GENETIC CONSIDERATIONS

The marine geochemical cycle of phosphate and silica that leads to the deposition of phosphorite and chert consists of five basic processes: (1) delivery of phosphate and silica to the ocean, (2) storage of dissolved phosphate and silica in the deeper waters of the ocean, (3) circulation of deep water to shallow levels, (4) concentration of phosphate and silica in organic remains on the sea bottom, and (5) reprecipitation of phosphorite and silica. The supply of phosphate and silica to the ocean is predominantly from subaerial chemical weathering of rocks and transport to the ocean by rivers and in minor amounts by volcanic activity (Baturin, 1982; Froelich et al., 1982; Wollast and MacKenzie, 1983).

The phosphate is used by phytoplankton and zooplankton at the ocean surface, and on dying, the plankton sink. It is mainly through settling of fecal pellets (Porter and Robbins, 1981) and through oxidation of the protoplasm that the plankton transfer their contained phosphate to deeper levels of the ocean. In a similar way, silica, which comprises the frustules and tests of plankton, is also transferred intact to deeper levels, primarily by diatom-filled fecal pellets, and released back to the seawater by dissolution. These processes lead to a buildup of phosphate in the deep ocean below 500–1,000 m, to about 70 μg of phosphorus per liter and silica to 3,000–5,000 μg silicon per liter, whereas at the surface their concentrations approach zero, except at high latitudes in the winter months.

The dissolved phosphate and silica would remain trapped in the deeper-water masses of the ocean, due to the density stratification of the ocean, unless brought back to the surface by vertical circulation. Vigorous vertical circulation occurs in several ways in the ocean and mostly affects water only in the upper several hundred meters (Parrish, 1982). The zonal wind system of the Earth sets up major oceanic-gyral currents in each hemisphere in each ocean. Where the eastern boundary currents of these gyres cross through the trade-wind belt off the west coasts of continents, the combination of the Coriolis force and the equatorward-blowing surface winds causes the surface waters to move offshore, and they are replaced by upwelling of deeper nutrient-rich water. Where the shallow currents are impeded by bathymetric highs, the phenomenon of dynamic or obstruction upwelling occurs, also bringing nutrient-rich deeper water to the surface. Obstruction upwelling occurs where the Gulf Stream, which is the western boundary current of the north Atlantic gyre, flows along the southeastern U.S. continental shelf (Riggs, 1984). Minor equatorial upwelling occurs associated with the equatorial currents. Phosphate sedimentation is associated with these low-latitude vertical circulation systems. Phosphorite and diatomite are deposited beneath the eastern boundary current trade-wind upwelling zone and also in the southeastern U.S. offshore associated with the Gulf Stream (Riggs, 1984). Phosphate rock, derived from bird guano formed on raised limestone islands in the dry climatic zone, is the direct result of high biological productivity associated with the equatorial upwelling near the equator. Other types of upwelling occur in the ocean but are not generally connected with significant phosphatic sedimentation, although at places they are connected with significant phosphatic sedimentation. These include high-latitude divergent upwelling caused by the sinking of cold saline polar water and coastal upwelling caused by monsoonal offshore winds.

Where the surface waters are fertilized by the nutrient-rich upwelling waters, blooms of phytoplankton support prolific populations of zooplankton. The fecal pellet rain of organic matter (Porter and Robbins, 1981) from this zone of high productivity on shallow sea bottoms results in the concentration of phosphate and silica in the bottom sediment because the settling organic matter does not have time to be microbially degraded completely, and the siliceous frustules and tests do not dissolve completely.

Sediment offshore of Peru and Chile was deposited beneath the upwelled waters of the Humboldt current and is a major site of phosphorite sedimentation today. Quaternary carbonate fluorapatite pellets are precipitated in the upper 20–30 cm of the sediment column (Froelich, 1983; Froelich et al., 1983; Burnett and Kim, 1983). The precipitation is driven by an enormous downward flux of phosphate into the sediment. The phosphate ion is released below the sediment-water interface most probably by organic matter decay beneath a filamentous bacterial mat. Flourine concentration is the limiting factor in the apatite precipitation. The depth within the sediment of the precipitation reaction is limited by the rate at which flouride, aided by bioturbation, can diffuse into the sediment column from the overlying seawater.

Separation of Phosphate and Silica during Sedimentation

Silica and phosphate must be separated during sedimentation to give relatively pure siliceous and phosphatic sediments. Before diatoms evolved, the process seems straightforward. For example, in the Permian Phosphoria Formation, the chert is made up primarily of siliceous sponge spicules, so that the immediate source of half to two-thirds of the silica in the chert was siliceous sponge spicules (Cressman and Swanson, 1964). The matrix silica was probably originally incorporated in the sediment in the form of siliceous skeletal remains, which may have been microscleres and small megascleres of sponges, now conspicuously absent in the chert, or the relatively delicate siliceous remains of planktonic organisms such as silicoflagellates and Radiolaria, both known to be more susceptible to dissolution than sponge spicules (Hein et al., 1978). The chert and phosphorite of the Phosphoria Formation were deposited sequentially under different climatic conditions (Sheldon, 1984). During glacial stages, sea level was low, trade winds and upwelling were intense, and phosphorite was deposited. During interglacial stages, sea level was high, winds and upwelling were moderate, and chert was deposited. At both times, organic-rich shale was deposited in the deeper basinal areas, but the shales were richer in organic matter during the glacial periods. It seems logical that when upwelling was intense, planktonic productivity was prolific, producing bottom sediment rich enough in organic matter to allow for the deposition of phosphorite, but the low oxygen content of the bottom water was incompatible to benthic fauna. When upwelling was moderate, planktonic productivity was insufficient to produce bottom sediments rich enough in organic matter to allow the formation of phosphorite, and an increased oxygen content of the water allowed a prolific sponge benthic fauna.

The chert of the Lower Carboniferous Brazer Formation of Utah is made up primarily of radiolarians with minor sponge spicules (C. A. Sandberg, personal communication, 1984). However, most Paleozoic and Proterozoic cherts associated with phosphorites have been so altered during diagenesis that original textures have been destroyed, and the origin of the chert is problematic, although most appear to have a biogenic origin.

After diatoms evolved in the Early Cretaceous or possibly the Late Jurassic (Tappan, 1980), the process of separation of silica from phosphate is more uncertain. It may have been caused by a difference between dinoflagellate and diatom ecology. Eocene phosphorites of the Gafsa Basin in Tunisia, the Albian and Senonian phosphorites of the Paris Basin, and the Cretaceous of Egypt contain abundant dinoflagellates (Fauconnier and Slansky, 1980), which are nonsiliceous but contained originally 0.7–3% phosphate, similar to the diatoms. The phosphorite of the Gafsa Basin is not correlated with the opaline beds, which were derived presumably from the siliceous matter of diatoms. Slansky (1982) postulated that the phosphorite was formed from dinoflagellates, whereas the chert was formed from diatoms.

Baturin (1982) and Burnett (1977) emphasized the role of diatoms in supplying phosphorus to the seafloor to form Neogene to Holocene phosphorites. The association of diatomite and phosphorite is clear. For example, diatomite is interbedded with phosphorite in the Miocene Sechura deposit of Peru (Cheney et al., 1979), and thick sequences of organic-rich diatomite in the Miocene Monterey Formation of California contain thin beds of phosphorite (Pisciotto and Garrison, 1981). Baturin hypothesized that reworking of the sediment in which apatite pellets had formed during earlier diagenesis concentrated the apatite pellets to form phosphorite and washed away the diatom remains; however, stratigraphic and sedimentologic relationships of most ancient phosphorites and associated sediments do not support this hypothesis as the general case. For example, many phosphorites are widespread, tabular beds that show little thickness variation and are not commonly current bedded.

A separation of phosphate and silica from diatomite during diagenesis should be considered. If phosphorite originated from bacterial breakdown of diatom protoplasm, the silica of the diatoms would have been released and migrated out of the sediment back into the water column or perhaps would have cemented earlier-formed phosphorite. Conversely, diatomite probably originally contained up to 3% phosphate, so that the phosphorus would have been released by bacterial breakdown of the organic matter and migrated out of the sediment. It seems possible that pH variations could have controlled which process prevailed. Perhaps at high pH, silica migrated out of the sediment and phosphorite was formed, and at low pH, phosphate migrated out of the sediment and the silica of the diatoms remained. D. Z. Piper (personal communication, 1985) postulated that calcium carbonate in the sediment would buffer the diagenetic environment and raise the pH, allowing the formation of apatite. Without the calcium carbonate, phosphorus would not form apatite and would be fluxed back into the water column. The occurrence of calcareous phosphate rock in the Monterey Formation (Pisciotto and Garrison, 1981) as well as many other phosphorites gives some evidence for this process. However, many post-Triassic phosphorites are not calcareous—for example, the Miocene Sechura phosphorite.

The accumulation of phosphorite may not be dependent on the presence of calcium carbonate but may have formed directly by the bacterial decay of organic matter. Humic acid is present in phosphorites of the Paleocene–Lower Eocene sequence of the Gafsa Basin of Tunisia, indicating that the evolution of the organic matter stopped at the humic acid stage, even though it continued beyond this point to the kerogen stage in the nonphosphatic rocks (Belayouni and Trichet, 1981; Slansky, 1982). Laboratory experiments of apatite precipitation in sterile seawater show, moreover, that humic acid plays a direct role in the formation of apatite, without any bacterial contribution. In the evolution of organic matter from protoplasm to fulvic acid to humic acid and then to kerogen (Nissenbaum, 1974), phosphorus is released during the fulvic acid to humic acid transition. Humic substances predominate in the phosphorite and chert of the Mishash Formation of Israel, but kerogen predominates in the overlying oil shale of the Ghareb Formation. The humic acids of the phosphorite are more oxidized than they are in the chert, which may be attributed to more intensive microbial alteration (Bein and Amit, 1982). Nitrogen-reducing bacterial activity produces NH_4 and other nitrogenous bases, which possibly could raise the pH values within the range of apatite formation (Garrison et al., 1979).

The control on whether a diatomaceous sediment evolves during diagenesis into phosphorite or diatomite may depend on whether or not the sediment was deposited within or outside the oxygen-minimum layer in the ocean. On the continental margin off Peru and Chile, phosphorite is forming in the sediments near the upper and lower boundaries of the oxygen-minimum zone (Burnett et al., 1980). In contrast, diatomite of the Monterey Formation probably formed within the oxygen-minimum zone (Govean and Garrison, 1981). The process of precipitation of apatite and separation of silica and phosphorus in diatom-rich sediment clearly needs additional research to be understood.

PHOSPHOGENIC EPISODES

The cause of the episodicity of phospho-siliceous sedimentation is not clear. It appears to be caused by a number of factors including paleoceanographic conditions, paleogeographic position, relative sea level, paleocurrents, and paleoclimate (Sheldon, 1980). The underlying cause of much of this episodicity would appear to be plate tectonic processes that reconfigure oceans and continents and change ocean basin geometry and land/sea surface area ratios. Arthur and Jenkyns (1981) advanced the hypothesis that phosphogenic episodes are due to elevated sea level and warm climate, and they correlated phosphorite sedimentation with transgressions. They further stated that the warm climate may cause increased flux of phosphorus to the ocean during time of increased chemical weathering on land and development of widespread oxygen-depleted waters because rates of oceanic circulation and oxygen solubility were reduced. Consistent with the hypothesis of increased nutrient supply to the oceans at, or just before, major Cenozoic phosphogenic episodes is the coeval development of widespread biogenic silica deposits. A problem with the Arthur–Jenkyns hypothesis is that only the equatorial phosphorite family is associated with high stands of the first-order sea level variations (Vail et al., 1977), shown in Figure 3–4, but may be associated with low to intermediate stands of second-order sea level variations. The trade-wind phosphorites are associated with low to intermediate stands of first-order sea level variations and low stands of second-order sea level variations. A relatively good correlation between trade-wind phosphorite, polar glacial deposits, low stands of second-order sea level variations, and trade-wind desert dune sand deposits (Fig. 3–4) indicates that polar-glacial paleoclimate was probably the driving force of oceanic vertical circulation and phosphate sedimentation. A discussion of the cause of the deposition of equatorial phosphorites is beyond the scope of this chapter, but it seems clear that polar glaciation was not the cause because of the correlation of equatorial phosphorite with warm polar regions and the insignificance or absence of coeval trade-wind desert dune sands. However, high-elevation lower-latitude glaciation cannot be ruled out. A significantly different paleoclimate existed during deposition of equatorial phosphorites than that of trade-wind phosphorites. The locus of upwelling ocean currents was different as indicated by the different distributional patterns of the two families of phosphorites.

Some phosphorites fall into neither the trade-wind or equatorial phosphorite families nor one of the major phosphogenic episodes. The Triassic Shublik

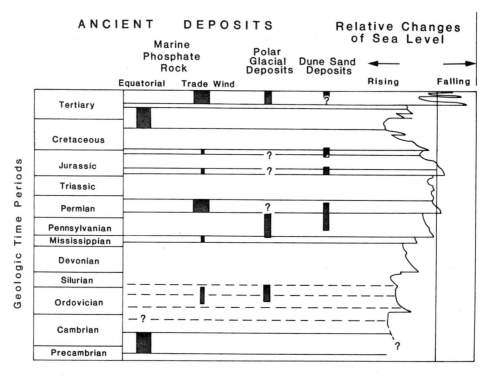

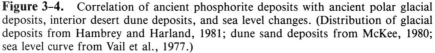

Figure 3–4. Correlation of ancient phosphorite deposits with ancient polar glacial deposits, interior desert dune deposits, and sea level changes. (Distribution of glacial deposits from Hambrey and Harland, 1981; dune sand deposits from McKee, 1980; sea level curve from Vail et al., 1977.)

Formation of Alaska contains a phosphorite–chert–black shale sequence (Detterman, in press; Detterman et al., 1975) that was perhaps deposited at high latitudes (Sheldon, 1964*b*). However, original paleolatitudes of the individual accretionary blocks of northern Alaska are not satisfactorily established (D. L. Jones, personal communication, 1985). The Shublik phosphorite was deposited at a time of low stand of first-order sea level variation and at normal stands of second-order sea level variation and also was deposited at a time when no phosphorite episode was occurring at lower latitudes. Much the same can be said for the Early Carboniferous Lisburne Group phosphorite, also of Alaska (Armstrong and Mamet, 1978), which was deposited significantly later (Chesterian) than the Lower Carboniferous phosphorites of Utah and Tennessee (Osagian–Meramecian) (Table 3–1). Thus, the Shublik and Lisburne phosphorites do not seem to be a part of either a phosphogenic episode or a phosphorite paleogeographic family based on low-latitude phosphorites. Despite their anomalous location and age, they show a strong chert association.

Conclusion

Chert, phosphorite, and organic-rich shale are genetically associated because of the similarities of the geochemical cycles of phosphorus and silica. The genetic link is through upwelling ocean currents that bring both silica and phosphate into the photic zone where they serve as nutrients to phytoplankton.

This association is very useful in exploration for phosphorite. Chert is an easily recognized hard rock that is resistant to weathering and commonly crops out in most climate zones. Phosphorite, in contrast, is a nondescript rock that is easily confused with other rocks such as limestone, dolomite, and even chert. It is soft, easily weathered and eroded, and usually covered in stratigraphic sections. For these reasons chert is normally reported in measured stratigraphic sections and serves as a useful guide rock to phosphorite, which is normally covered. This association has been used in aiding successful exploration for phosphorite in Turkey, Saudi Arabia, India, and Australia and promises to be useful in exploration elsewhere. The association has exploration limitations, however, in that epicontinental phosphorite has a weak to no chert association. Also, much chert exists that is not associated with phosphorite. In the first case, phosphorite would be missed, and in the second case, the exploration would be futile. Other exploration tools for phosphorite are available that help in overcoming the limitations of the phosphorite-chert association.

Acknowledgments

It is a privilege to acknowledge the input of Vincent E. McKelvey to this chapter, not only for constructively reviewing the manuscript but also for his original contributions to the phosphorite and chert problem. His early insights at a time when relevant data were scarce have been proved thirty years later and with much additional data to be correct. Critical reviews by David Piper, Eleanora Robbins, and Z. Samuel Altschuler were very helpful and are gratefully acknowledged.

REFERENCES

Academy of Sciences of the Estonian SSR, 1984. *Guidebook to the Geology and Mineral Deposits of Lower Palaeozoic of the Eastern Baltic Area*, International Geological Congress, Moscow.

Al-Bassam, K. S., 1976. The mineralogy, geochemistry and genesis of the Akashat phosphorite deposit, western Iraq, *Jour. Geol. Soc. Iraq* 9:1–33.

Al-Bassam, K. S., A. A. Al-Dahan, and A. K. Jamil, 1983. Campanian-Maastrichtian phosphorites of Iraq, *Mineralium Deposita* 18:215–233.

Al-Bassam, K. S., and D. Hagopian, 1983. Lower Eocene phosphorites of the western desert, Iraq, *Sed. Geology* 33:295–316.

Armstrong, A. K., and B. L. Mamet, 1978. Microfacies of the Carboniferous Lisburne Group, Endicott Mountains, Arctic Alaska, in *Western and Arctic Canadian Biostratigraphy*, C. R. Stelck and B. D. E. Chatterton, eds., Geological Association of Canada Special Paper 18, pp. 352–354.

Arthur, M. A., and H. D. Jenkyns, 1981. Phosphorites and paleoceanography, *Oceanologica Acta*, Proceedings 26th International Geological Congress, Geology of Oceans Symposium, No. S.P., pp. 83–96.

Atfeh, S. A., 1966. Phosphatic deposits in Syria and Safaga District, Egypt—Discussion, *Econ. Geology* 61:1142–1161.

Atfeh, S. A., and V. A. Faradjev, 1963. Position stratigraphique des phosphates en Syrie. *Soc. Géol. France Bull.* 5:1076–1084.

Azmi, R. J., M. N. Joshi, and K. P. Juyal, 1981. Discovery of the Cambro-Ordovician conodonts from the Mussoorie Tal phosphorite: Its significance in correlation of the Lesser Himalaya, *Contemp. Geoscientific Res. Himalaya* 1:245–250.

Banerjee, D. M., P. C. Basu, and N. Srivastava, 1980. Petrology, mineralogy, geochemistry, and origin of the Precambrian Aravallian phosphorite deposits of Udaipur and Jhabua, India, *Econ. Geology* 75:1181–1199.

Banerjee, D. M., M. W. Y. Khan, N. Srivastava, and G. C. Saigal, 1982. Precambrian phosphorites in the Bijawar rocks of Hirapur-Bassai areas, Sagar District, Madhya Pradesh, India, *Mineralium Deposita* 17:349–362.

Baturin, G. N., 1982. *Phosphorites on the Sea Floor*, Elsevier, Amsterdam, pp. 185–218.

Bein, A., and O. Amit, 1982. Depositional environments of the Senonian chert, phosphorite and oil shale sequence in Israel as deduced from their organic matter composition, *Sedimentology* 29:81–90.

Belayouni, H., and J. Trichet, 1981. Preliminary data on the origin and diagenesis of the organic matter in the phosphate basin of Gafsa (Tunisia), in *Advances in Organic Geochemistry*, John Wiley & Sons, New York, pp. 328–335.

Bentor, Y. K., 1979. Modern phosphorites—Not a sure guide for the interpretation of ancient deposits, in *Marine Phosphatic Sediments Workshop Report*, W. C. Burnett and R. P. Sheldon, eds., East-West Center, Honolulu, Hawaii, 29p.

Bentor, Y. K., 1980. Phosphorites—The unsolved problems, in *Marine Phosphorites—Geochemistry, Occurrence, Genesis*, Y. K. Bentor, ed., Society of Economic Paleontologists and Mineralogists Special Publication 29, pp. 3–18.

Berge, J. W., and J. Jack, in press. The phosphorites of West Thanayat, Saudi Arabia, in *World Phosphate Resources*, A. Notholt, R. P. Sheldon, and D. F. Davidson, eds., Cambridge University Press, Cambridge, England.

Boujo, A., 1976. *Contribution a l'étude géologique du gisement de phosphate crétacé-éocène des Ganntour (Maroc Occidental)*, Université Louis Pasteur de Strasbourg, Institute de Géologie Memoire 43, 227p.

Bremner, J. M., 1983. Biogenic sediments on the South West African (Namibian) continental margin, in *Coastal Upwelling: Its Sediment Record. Part B*, J. Thiede and E. Suess, eds., Plenum Press, New York, pp. 73–104.

Burnett, W. C., 1977. Geochemistry and origin of phosphorite deposits from off Peru and Chile, *Geol. Soc. America Bull.* **88**:813-823.

Burnett, W. C., 1980. Oceanic phosphate deposits, in *Fertilizer Mineral Potential in Asia and the Pacific*, R. P. Sheldon and W. C. Burnett, eds., East-West Center, Honolulu, Hawaii, pp. 119-144.

Burnett, W. C., and K. H. Kim, 1983. Growth history of a Quaternary phosphatic crust, abstract, *Sixth International Field Workshop and Seminar on Phosphorites*, International Geological Correlations Programme, Project 156, Morocco-Senegal.

Burnett, W. C., H. H. Veeh, and A. Soutar, 1980. U-series, oceanographic and sedimentary evidence in support of Recent formation of phosphate nodules off Peru, in *Marine Phosphorites—Geochemistry, Occurrence, Genesis*, Y. K. Bentor, ed., Society of Economic Paleontologists and Mineralogists Special Publication 29, pp. 61-72.

Bushinskii, G. E., 1969. *Old Phosphorites of Asia and their Genesis*, Israel Program for Scientific Translations, 266p. Originally published in Russian, 1966.

Cannon, W. F., and J. S. Klasner, 1976. *Phosphorite and Other Apatite-Bearing Sedimentary Rocks in the Precambrian of Northern Michigan*, U.S. Geological Survey Circular 746, 6p.

Cathcart, J. B., and O. F. Zambrano, 1969. *Phosphate Rock in Colombia—A Preliminary Report*, U.S. Geological Survey Bulletin 1272A, pp. A1-A77.

Cavalcanti de Albuquerque, G. de A. Sa., and J. F. Giannerini, in press. Paulista phosphate deposit in Pernambuco State, Brazil, in *World Phosphate Resources*, A. Notholt, R. P. Sheldon, and D. F. Davidson, eds., Cambridge University Press, Cambridge, England.

Cheney, T. M., G. H. McClellan, and E. S. Montgomery, 1979. Sechura phosphate deposits, their stratigraphy, origin and composition, *Econ. Geology* **74**:232-259.

Choudhuri, R., in press. Proterozoic phosphorites around Udaipur, Rajasthan, India, in *World Phosphate Resources*, A. Notholt, R. P. Sheldon, and D. F. Davidson, eds., Cambridge University Press, Cambridge, England.

Christie, R. L., in press. Jurassic phosphorite of the Fernie synclinorium, southeastern British Columbia, in *World Phosphate Resources*, A. Notholt, R. P. Sheldon, and D. F. Davidson, eds., Cambridge University Press, Cambridge, England.

Cook, P. J., and M. W. McElhinny, 1979. A re-evaluation of the spatial and temporal distribution of phosphorites in the light of plate tectonics, *Econ. Geology* **74**:315-330.

Cook, P. J., and J. H. Shergold, 1980. Proterozoic and Cambrian phosphorites of Asia and Australia—A progress report, in *Fertilizer Mineral Potential in Asia and the Pacific*, A. Notholt, R. P. Sheldon, and D. F. Davidson, eds., East-West Center, Honolulu, Hawaii, pp. 207-223.

Cressman, E. R., and R. W. Swanson, 1964. *Stratigraphy and Petrology of the Permian Rocks of Southwestern Montana*, U.S. Geological Survey Professional Paper 313-C, pp. 275-569.

DeCelles, P. G., and R. C. Gutschick, 1983. Mississippian wood-grained chert and its significance in the western interior United States, *Jour. Sed. Petrology* **53**:1175-1191.

de Keyser, F., and P. J. Cook, 1972. *Geology of the Middle Cambrian Phosphorites and Associated Sediments of Northwestern Queensland*, Bureau of Mineral Resources Bulletin 138, 77p.

Detterman, R. L., in press. Triassic phosphate deposits, northeastern Alaska, in *World Phosphate Resources*, A. Notholt, R. P. Sheldon, and D. F. Davidson, eds., Cambridge University Press, Cambridge, England.

Detterman, R. L., H. N. Reiser, W. P. Brosge, and J. T. Dutro, Jr., 1975. *Post-Carboniferous Stratigraphy, Northeastern Alaska*, U.S. Geological Survey Professional Paper 886, pp. 14-16.

Eganov, E. A., 1979. The role of cyclic sedimentation in the formation of phosphorite deposits, in *Proterozoic-Cambrian Phosphorites*, P. J. Cook and J. H. Shergold, eds., Canberra, Canberra Publishing and Printing Co., pp. 22-25.

Eganov, E. A., G. H. Ergaliev, A. V. Ilyin, and A. A. Krasnov, 1984. *Guidebook, Karatau Phosphorite Basin*, Field Workshop and Seminar of the International Geological Correlations Programme, Project 156, August 1984, Kazaksthan, USSR, 69p.

El-Tarabili and El-Sayed, 1969. Paleography, paleoecology and genesis of the phosphatic sediments in the Quseit-Safaga area, United Arab Republic, *Econ. Geology* **64:**172-182.

Faris, M. I., and M. Y. Hassan, 1959. Report on the stratigraphy and fauna of the Upper Cretaceous-Paleocene rocks of Um el Heutat, Safaga area, *Ain. Shams. Sci. Bull., Cairo* **4:**191-207.

Fauconnier, D., and M. Slansky, 1980. Relations entre le developpement des dinoflagelles et la sedimentation phosphatée du bassin de Gafsa (Tunisie), in *Géologie comparée des gisements de phosphates et de petrôle,* Bureau de Recherches Géologiques et Minières Document 24, pp. 184-204.

Fournie, D., 1980. Phosphates et pétrole en Tunisie, in *Géologie comparée des gisements de phosphate et de pétrole*, Bureau de Recherches et Minieres Document 24, pp. 157-166.

Froelich, P. N., Jr., 1983. Modern precipitation of carbonate fluorapatite in the upper 20 cm of Peru shelf muds: Pore water geochemistry, abstract, *Sixth International Field Workshop and Seminar on Phosphorites*, International Geological Correlations Programme, Project 156, Morocco-Senegal.

Froelich, P. N., M. L. Bender, and N. A. Luedtke, 1982. The marine phosphorus cycle, *Am. Jour. Sci.* **282:**474-511.

Froelich, P. N., K. H. Kim, R. Jahnke, W. C. Burnett, A. Soutar, and M. Deakin, 1983. Pore water fluoride in Peru continental margin sediments: Uptake from sea water, *Geochim. et Cosmochim. Acta* **47:**1605-1612.

Garrison, R. E., R. G. Stanley, L. J. Horan, 1979. Middle Miocene sedimentation on the southwestern edge of the Lockwood High, Monterey County, California, in *Tertiary and Quaternary Geology of the Salinas Valley and Santa Lucia Range, Monterey County, California*, S. A. Graham, ed., Pacific Section, Society of Economic Paleontologists and Mineralogists Field Guide 4, pp. 51-65.

Gimmel'farb, B. M., 1958. Regularity of the tectonic distribution of phosphorite deposits in the USSR. Zakonomern. Razmescheniya Pelezn. Iskop. **1:**487-516.

Govean, R. M., and R. E. Garrison, 1981. Significance of laminated and massive diatomites in the upper part of the Monterey Formation, California, in *The Monterey Formation and Related Siliceous Rocks of California*, R. E. Garrison and R. Douglas, eds., Pacific Section, Society of Economic Paleontologists and Mineralogists Special Publication, Los Angeles, pp. 181-198.

Hambrey, M. J., and W. B. Harland, 1981. *Earth's Pre-Pleistocene Glacial Record*, Cambridge University Press, Cambridge, England, 1004p.

Hausback, B. P., 1984. Cenozoic volcanic and tectonic evolution of Baja California, Ph.D. dissertation, University of California, Berkeley.

Hein, J. R., D. W. Scholl, J. A. Barron, M. G. Jones, and J. Miller, 1978. Diagenesis of late Cenozoic diatomaceous deposits and formation of the bottom simulating reflector in the southern Bering Sea, *Sedimentology* **25:**155-181.

Hendey, Q. B., and R. V. Dingle, in press. Onshore sedimentary phosphate deposits in southwestern Africa, in *World Phosphate Resources*, A. Notholt, R. P. Sheldon, and D. F. Davidson, eds., Cambridge University Press, Cambridge, England.

Ilyin, A. V., in press. The Kisil Kum phosphorite deposits, Soviet Middle Asia, in *World Phosphate Resources*, A. Notholt, R. P. Sheldon, and D. F. Davidson, eds., Cambridge University Press, Cambridge, England.

Ilyin, A. V., and G. I. Ratnikova, 1981. Primary, bedded, structureless phosphorite of the Khubsugul Basin, Mongolia, *Jour. Sed. Petrology* **51:**1215-1222.

Issawi, B., 1972. Review of Upper Cretaceous-Lower Tertiary stratigraphy in central and southern Egypt, *Am. Assoc. Petroleum Geologists Bull.* **568**:1448-1463.

Jallad, I., E. Murry, and R. Sadaqah, in press. Upper Cretaceous Jordan phosphate, in *World Phosphate Resources*, A. Notholt, R. P. Sheldon, and D. F. Davidson, eds., Cambridge University Press, Cambridge, England.

Jarvis, I., 1980. *The initiation of phosphatic chalk sedimentation—The Senonian (Cretaceous) of the Anglo-Paris Basin*, Society of Economic Paleontologists and Mineralogists Special Publication 29, pp. 167-192.

Karpoff, R., and L. Visse, 1950. Les phosphates du Sahara soudanais, *Soc. Géol. France Bull.* **20**:125-131.

Kolodny, Y., 1981. Phosphorites, in *The Sea*, vol. 7, C. Emiliani, ed., John Wiley & Sons, New York, pp. 981-1023.

Liang, T. Y., and A. C. Chang, 1981. *On the characteristic and genesis of Late Pre-Cambrian phosphorites associated with Gondwana*, Geological Institute for Mining and Chemical Industrial Minerals, Zhuo Xian, Hepeh Province, China, 68p. Published for the 4th International Workshop, International Geological Correlations Program, Project 156, India, November 1981.

Mansfield, G. R., 1927. *Geography, Geology, and Mineral Resources of Part of Southeastern Idaho*, U.S. Geological Survey Professional Paper 152, 453p.

Maughan, E. K., O. F. Zambrano, G. P. Mojica, M. J. Abozaglo, P. F. Pachon, and R. R. Duran, 1979. *Paleontologic and Stratigraphic Relations of Phosphate Beds in Upper Cretaceous Rocks of the Cordillera Oriental, Columbia*, U.S. Geological Survey Internal Report, 97p.

McKee, E. D., 1980. *A Study of Global Sand Seas*, U.S. Geolgical Survey Professional Paper 1052, 290p.

McKelvey, V. E., R. W. Swanson, and R. P. Sheldon, 1953. The Permian phosphorite deposits of western United States, International Geological Congress, 19th Algiers, 1952, Comptes rendus, sec. 11:45-64.

McKelvey, V. E., J. S. Williams, R. P. Sheldon, E. R. Cressman, T. M. Cheney, and R. W. Swanson, 1959. *The Phosphoria, Park City and Shedhorn Formations in the Western Phosphate Field*, U.S. Geological Survey Professional Paper 313A, 47p.

Meissner, C. R., Jr., and A. Ankary, 1972. *Phosphorite Deposits in the Sirhan-Turayf Basin, Kingdom of Saudi Arabia*, Directorate General of Mineral Resources, Mineral Resources Report of Investigations 2, 27p.

Monciardini, C., 1966. *La Sédimentation éocène au Sénégal*, Bureau de Recherches Géologiques et Minières Memoire 43, 65p.

Munoz Cabezon, C., in press. Bu-Craa phosphate deposit, Western Sahara, in *World Phosphate Resources*, A. Notholt, R. P. Sheldon, and D. F. Davidson, eds., Cambridge University Press, Cambridge, England.

Nissenbaum, A., 1974. The organic geochemistry of marine and terrestrial humic substances: Implication of carbon and hydrogen isotope studies, in *Advances in Organic Geochemistry*, B. Tissot and F. Beinner, eds., Paris, pp. 39-52.

Ojeda Rivera, J., 1979. Resumen de datos estratigraficos y estructurales de la Formacion Monterrey que aflora en el area de San Hilario, Baja California Sur, *Consejo de Recursos Minerales, Revista Geomimet* **100**.

Ojeda Rivera, J., 1981. General geology and phosphate deposits of southern Baja California, Mexico, Notes prepared for the Baja California phosphate field trip, International Geological Correlations Programme, Project 156, La Paz, Baja California.

Omara, S., 1965. Phosphatic deposits in Syria and Safaga District, Egypt, *Econ. Geology* **60**:214-227.

Organizing Committee, International Geological Correlations Programme, Project 156, 1982. *Guidebook to Field Excursions*, Fifth International Field Workshop and Seminar on Phosphorite, Kunming, China, 50p.

Oussedik, M., N. Ousmer, and M. Belkhedim, 1980. Les minéralisations phosphatées éocènes en Algerie, et le gisement de phosphate du Djebel Onk, in *Géologie Comparée des gisements de phosphates et de pétrole*, Bureau de Recherches Géologiques et Minieres Documents 24, pp. 141–156.

Pant, A., 1980. Resource status of rock phosphate deposits in India and areas of future potential, in *Fertilizer Mineral Potential in Asia and the Pacific*, R. P. Sheldon and W. C. Burnett, eds., East-West Center, Honolulu, Hawaii, pp. 331–358.

Pant, A., in press. Phosphorite in the Bijawar Group of rocks of Hirapur and Lalitpur Basins of central India, in *World Phosphate Resources*, A. Notholt, R. P. Sheldon, and D. F. Davidson, eds., Cambridge University Press, Cambridge, England.

Parrish, J. T., 1982. Upwelling and petroleum source beds, with reference to Paleozoic, *Am. Assoc. Petroleum Geologists Bull.* **66**:750–774.

Pisciotto, K. A., and R. E. Garrison, 1981. Lithofacies and depositional environments of the Monterey Formation, California, in *The Monterey Formation and Related Siliceous Rocks of California*, R. E. Garrison, and R. G. Douglas, eds., Pacific Section, Society of Economic Paleontologists and Mineralogists Special Publication, pp. 97–122.

Pokrishkin, V., 1967. Areas de prospeccion y estudio de fosforitas en la Republica de Cuba, Ministerio de Industrias de la Republica de Cuba, *Technologica* **5**:3–16.

Porter, K. G., and E. Robbins, 1981. Zooplankton fecal pellets link fossil fuel and phosphate deposits, *Science* **212**:931–933.

Riddler, G. P., H. Khallaf, and A. Farasani, 1983. Exploration for phosphate in the Sirhan-Turayf region, northwest Saudi Arabia, Deputy Ministry for Mineral Resources paper presented at Rabat Morocco, International Geological Correlations Programme, Project 156, Oct. 23, 1983.

Riggs, S. R., 1984. Paleoceanographic model of Neogene phosphorite deposition, U.S. continental margin, *Science* **223**:123–131.

Robaszynski, R., in press. The phosphatic chalk of the Mons Basin (Belgium), in *World Phosphate Resources*, A. Notholt, R. P. Sheldon, and D. F. Davidson, eds., Cambridge University Press, Cambridge, England.

Roberts, A. E., 1979. Northern Rocky Mountains and adjacent Plains region, in *Paleotectonic Investigations of the Mississippian System in the United States*, L. C. Craig and C. W. Connor, coordinators, U.S. Geological Survey Professional Paper 1010, part I, chapter N. pp. 221–248.

Roberts, A. E., in press. Geology and resources of Miocene Coast Ranges and Cenozoic OCS phosphate deposits of California, U.S.A. in *World Phosphate Resources*, A. Notholt, R. P. Sheldon, and D. F. Davidson, eds., Cambridge University Press, Cambridge, England.

Rodriguez, S. E., 1984. Phosphate districts in Venezuela, Paper presented at workshop on phosphate potential of the Caribbean Basin and Central America, East Carolina University, Grenville, North Carolina, July 9–13, 1984.

Rogers, C. L., Z. De Cserna, E. Tavera, and S. Ulloa, 1956. General geology and phosphate deposits of Concepcion del Oro District, Zacatecas, Mexico, *U.S. Geol. Survey Bull.* **1037-A**, 102p.

Salvan, H. M., 1985. Particularités de répartition stratigraphique des dépôts phosphatés de la Mésogée et de la bordure atlantique du continent africain. Nouvelles possibilités d'interprétation, in *Phosphorites*, L. Lucas and L. Prevot, eds., *Sciences Géologiques*, Universite Louis Pasteur de Strasbourg, Mem. 77, pp. 93–98.

Sandberg, C. A., in press. Deep-water phosphorite in Lower Carboniferous Desert starved basin, Utah, U.S.A., in *World Phosphate Resources*, A. Notholt, R. P. Sheldon, and D. F. Davidson, eds., Cambridge University Press, Cambridge, England.

Sassi, S., 1980. Contexte paléogéographique des dépôts phosphatés de l'Eocène de Tunisie, in *Géologie comparée des gisements de phosphates et de pétrole,* Bureau de Recherches Geologiques et Miniere Document 24, pp. 167–184.

Sheldon, R. P., 1957. Physical stratigraphy of the Phosphoria formation in northwestern Wyoming, *U.S. Geol. Survey Bull.* **1042-E**:105–185.

Sheldon, R. P., 1963. *Physical Stratigraphy and Mineral Resources of Permian Rocks in Western Wyoming*, U.S. Geological Survey Professional Paper 313-B, pp. 49–273.

Sheldon, R. P., 1964a. Exploration for phosphorite in Turkey—A case history, *Econ. Geology* **59**:1159–1175.

Sheldon, R. P., 1964b. *Paleolatitudinal and Paleogeographic Distribution of Phosphorites*, U.S. Geological Survey Professional Paper 501-C, pp. C106–C113.

Sheldon, R. P., 1980. *Episodicity of Phosphate Deposition and Deep Ocean Circulation—A Hypothesis*, Society of Economic Paleontologists and Mineralogists Special Publication 29, pp. 239–248.

Sheldon, R. P., 1981. Ancient marine phosphorites, *Ann. Rev. Earth and Planetary Sci.* **9**:251–284.

Sheldon, R. P., 1984. *Polar Glacial Control of Sedimentation of Permian Phosphorites of the Rocky Mountains, USA*, Proceedings 27th International Geological Congress, Moscow, pp. 223–243.

Slanksy, M., 1962. *Contribution a l'étude géologique du bassin sedimentaire cotier du Dahomey et du Togo*, Bureau de Recherches et Miniere Memoire 11.

Slansky, M., 1980a. Ancient upwelling models, in *Fertilizer Mineral Potential in Asia and the Pacific,* R. P. Sheldon and W. C. Burnett, eds., East-West Center Honolulu, Hawaii, pp. 145–158.

Slansky, M., 1980b. *Géologie des phosphates sédimentaires*, Bureau de Recherche Geologique et Minieres Memoire 114, 92p.

Slansky, M., 1982. Importance du role des organismes et de la matiere organique dans la sédimentation phosphatée, in *Memoires géologiques de l'université de Dijon*, pp. 215–224.

Smith, R. W., and G. I. Whitlatch, 1940. *The Phosphate Resources of Tennessee*, Tennessee Department of Conservation, Division of Geology Bulletin 48, pp. 301–354.

Sonakia, A., and B. Kumar, 1982. *An Interim Report on Assessment of Phoshorite Occurrences in Bijawar Group, District Sagar and Chhatarpur (M.P.)*, Geological Survey of India, Internal Report.

Soviet Union Delegation, 1968. Geological characteristics of commercial deposits of main kinds of mineral raw materials for fertilizer in the USSR, *Proceedings of the Seminar on Sources of Mineral Raw Materials for the Fertilizer Industry in Asia and the Far East*, United Nations Mineral Resources Development Series 32, pp. 100–109.

Strakov, N. M., 1960. *Fundamentals of the Theory of Lithogenesis*, Akad. Nauk SSR Inst. Geol. 1, Moscow, Geological Institute, 212p.

Summerhayes, C. P., and J. M. McArthur, in press. Moroccan offshore phosphorite deposits, in *World Phosphate Resources*, A. Notholt, R. P. Sheldon, and D. F. Davidson, eds., Cambridge University Press, Cambridge, England.

Szekely, T. S., and L. T. Grose, 1972. Stratigraphy of the carbonate, black shale, and phosphate of the Pucara Group (Upper Triassic-Lower Jurassic), Central Andes, Peru, *Geol. Soc. America Bull.* **83**:407–428.

Tappan, H., 1980. *The Paleobiology of Plant Protists*, W. H. Freeman, San Francisco, 637p.

Trompette, R., P. Affaton, F. Joulia, and J. Marchand, 1980. Stratigraphic and structural controls of Late Precambrian phosphate deposits of the northern Volta Basin in Upper Volta, Niger and Benin, West Africa, *Econ. Geology* **75**:62–70.

Vail, P. R., R. M. Mitchum, Jr., and S. Thompson, III, 1977. Global cycles of relative change of sea level, in *Seismic Stratigraphy—Applications to Hydrocarbon Exploration*, C. E. Payton, ed., American Association of Petroleum Geologists Memoir 26, pp. 83–89.

Winnock, E., 1980. Les depôts de l'Eocène intérieur au North de l'Afrique: Aperçu paléogéographique de l'ensemble, in *Géologie comparée des gisements de phosphates et de pétrole*, Bureau de Recherche Geologiques et Minieres Document 24, pp. 210–244.

Wollast, R., and R. G. MacKenzie, 1983. The global cycle of silica, in *Silicon Geochemistry and Biogeochemistry*, S. R. Aston, ed., Academic Press, New York, pp. 39-76.

Wurzburger, U. S., 1968. A survey of phosphate deposits in Israel, in *Proceedings of the Seminar on Sources of Mineral Raw Materials for the Fertilizer Industry in Asia and the Far East*, United Nations Mineral Resources Development Series 32, pp. 152-164.

Ziegler, A. M., 1981. *Paleogeographic Atlas Project,* Department of Geology, University of Chicago, Progress Report.

PART II

CENOZOIC SILICEOUS DEPOSITS

4

Petroleum in the Miocene Monterey Formation, California

Caroline M. Isaacs

U.S. Geological Survey
Menlo Park, California

Neil F. Petersen

Worldwide Geosciences, Inc.
Houston, Texas

ABSTRACT. The Miocene Monterey Formation of California (United States), a bio-genous deposit derived mainly from diatom debris, is important both as a petroleum source and petroleum reservoir. The formation is a principal petroleum source in California coastal basins, which are among the most prolific oil provinces in the United States. Oil generated from the Monterey tends to be sulfur rich and heavy ($<20°$ API), and chemical characteristics resemble immature source extracts more closely than they do normal oil. Thermal maturity indicators in Monterey kerogens appear to behave anomalously, and several lines of evidence indicate that the oil is generated at lower than expected levels of organic metamorphism.

As a reservoir, the Monterey is important due to both conventional production from permeable sandstones and fracture production from fine-grained rocks with low matrix permeability. Fractured reservoirs are difficult to identify, and conventional well-log analysis has not proven to be very useful in exploring for and evaluating these reservoirs.

Introduction

The Miocene Monterey Formation of California is unusual in that it is both a major petroleum source and an important petroleum reservoir. A distinctive unit of thin-bedded marine rocks derived mainly from diatom debris, the Monterey is widely regarded as the principal petroleum source rock in California (Taylor, 1976), an area in which 20 billion barrels of oil were produced from the earliest oil production in the 1860s through 1983 (California Division of Oil and Gas, 1984). Long a significant petroleum reservoir in onshore California, the formation has become a major target of offshore exploration. Since 1969, an estimated 2 billion barrels of recoverable oil have been discovered in the offshore (Fig. 4–1), mainly in fractured Monterey reservoirs (*Oil & Gas Journal,* 1981, 1984; Wilson and Williams, 1981; Williams, 1985*b*).

Similar Miocene and early Pliocene deposits derived from diatom debris are widely present in the circum-Pacific region, including Peru, Japan, the Bering Sea, the Soviet Far East, the Sea of Japan, the Philippines, and North Borneo (MacDonald, 1956; Garrison, 1975; Ingle, 1981). Despite their broad distribution, however, these deposits produce almost no oil outside California. The one exception is Akita (northeastern Honshu Island), Japan, where cumulative production of crude oil through 1979 was less than 50 million barrels, with reservoirs composed principally of tuff, tuffaceous sandstone, and volcanic rocks (Aoyagi and Iijima, 1983; see Chap. 5 of this book). Major fractured reservoirs are either absent or undiscovered in Japan.

On the one hand, geologically reasonable differences in depositional or diagenetic histories may explain the paucity of discovered oil in most Miocene diatomaceous deposits of the Pacific. On the other hand, the history of exploration and discovery in the Monterey Formation shows that fractured siliceous reservoirs may not be readily discovered by conventional exploration approaches. For example, despite long recognition of the Monterey Formation as a major oil source and fracture production in the onshore Santa Maria

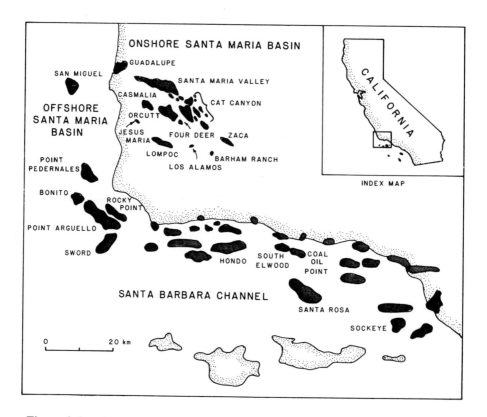

Figure 4-1. Oil and gas fields in the Santa Maria and Santa Barbara–Ventura areas, California, and adjacent offshore areas, showing fields (labeled) with significant production from Monterey fractured reservoirs. The Point Arguello field and adjacent offshore fields are included in the offshore Santa Maria basin. (Adapted from California Division of Oil and Gas, 1974; Williams, 1985a)

Basin dating back to 1902, Monterey fractured reservoirs did not become exploration targets in other areas until the 1970s. Earlier, oil shows in fine-grained Monterey strata were generally ignored, and strata were frequently drilled and even cased without production tests. In 1969, however, major oil reserves were inadvertently discovered in Monterey fractured zones in the South Elwood and Hondo offshore fields. As a result, fractured siliceous reservoirs became a target of widespread exploration in California, with the subsequent discovery of numerous other fields including the giant Point Arguello field (Fig. 4-1).

The long neglect of Monterey fractured reservoirs as an exploration target can be attributed mainly to their anomalous production characteristics. Conventional indicators of petroleum production potential are commonly useless in fractured reservoirs (Drummond, 1964), and the Monterey Formation has the additional complexity of unusual lithotypes that have atypical well-log responses. Another factor that discouraged exploration in the Monterey was conventional interpretation of organic matter maturity, which indicated that Monterey source rocks were too immature to have generated oil, even in places where major discoveries were subsequently made.

Exploration and production problems in these rocks may therefore serve as valuable examples in other parts of the world where siliceous rocks are present. This chapter summarizes geologic and petroleum-related research on the Monterey Formation, emphasizing characteristics that have discouraged or delayed petroleum production. Topics include geology, deposition and character of organic matter, organic matter maturity indicators, petroleum generation, fracture production, and well-log analysis.

LITERATURE OVERVIEW

The Monterey Formation has been the object of considerable geologic research in California. Bramlette's (1946) major study is still a classic on the Monterey, and research for many years after its publication focused mainly on local stratigraphy. More recent research began with Murata and co-workers' studies on dolomite and silica diagenesis (Murata et al., 1969, 1972, 1977; Murata and Nakata, 1974; Murata and Larson, 1975). Since 1980, extensive stratigraphic and topical work on the Monterey has been published, including volumes on general geologic research (Garrison and Douglas, 1981), oil-related research (Isaacs and Garrison, 1983), and dolomite (Garrison et al., 1984). Research focused on many areas, including the onshore Santa Maria Basin (Pisciotto, 1981), Santa Barbara–Ventura Basin (Isaacs, 1982, 1985; Keller, 1984), Cuyama Basin (Lagoe, 1984, 1985), San Joaquin Basin (Williams and Graham, 1982; Graham and Williams, 1985), Huasna–Pismo Basin (Surdam, 1984), and Salinas Basin (Mertz, 1984a, b). For the offshore Santa Maria Basin, an important source of data is the Point Conception deep stratigraphic test well (OCS-Cal 78-164 No. 1), informally known as the Point Conception COST well (Claypool et al., 1979; McCulloh, 1979). Additional topical research has been published on source rock characteristics (Orr, 1983, 1984a, b; Williams and Reimers, 1983; Williams, 1984), oil characteristics and generation (Milner et al., 1977; Curiale et al., 1985; Petersen and Hickey, 1986), thermal models (Heasler and Surdam, 1985), silica geothermometry (Keller and Isaacs, 1985), borehole gravity (Beyer, 1986), and dolomite formation

(Compton and Siever, 1986). Extensive research has also been conducted in the petroleum industry but is largely unpublished.

Geology

Occurrence

The term *Monterey* is generally applied to Miocene strata in California that are unusually siliceous (Bramlette, 1946). Monterey strata are widespread in coastal California, presently extending 1,200 km north to south and originally deposited in most of the Neogene marine basins in California (Fig. 4–2). The formation is typically about 300–500 m thick, though it is locally thinner and in some areas—such as the San Joaquin Basin—thicker. Strata were deposited in the late early Miocene and throughout the middle Miocene, but upper Miocene (11–5.5 Ma) deposits are areally most extensive and are of principal economic importance.

Best known as a varved organic-rich diatomaceous deposit, the Monterey is actually lithologically complex and regionally variable. Rock types include diatomite, diatomaceous shale and mudstone, chert, porcelanite, siliceous mudstone and shale, chalk, marl, phosphatic shale, dolostone, limestone, shale, and sandstone. Variations in composition among fine-grained Monterey rocks are particularly marked in the Santa Barbara and Santa Maria areas (Isaacs, 1984b, 1987). Here, individual beds represent widely varying admixtures of three main original components: (1) biogenous silica (principally diatom frustules), (2) biogenous calcite (principally coccoliths and some foraminifera), and (3) fine terrigenous detritus (principally illite-smectite mixed-layer clay minerals, feldspar, and quartz). In some rocks, organic matter is a major primary constituent, representing as much as 34% of the rock by weight. Nodular apatite is a major early (near-surface) diagenetic constituent (up to 25%), mainly in middle Miocene strata.

Deposition

The Monterey is thought to have been deposited on the slopes or bottoms of basins similar to those in the present southern California borderland or the Gulf of California (Blake, 1981; Pisciotto and Garrison, 1981). Although predominantly fine grained (silt or mud size), Monterey strata locally include interbedded coarse and fine terrigenous clastic sedimentary rocks deposited by turbidity flows (e.g., Lagoe, 1985). All the depositional basins were part of an active continental margin, but the paleogeography varied; settings included an interior marine basin with multiple sources of clastic debris (e.g., San Joaquin Basin; see Graham and Williams, 1985), comparatively near-shore basins (e.g., the Cuyama Basin; see Lagoe, 1984, 1985), as well as comparatively offshore basins (e.g., the western part of the Santa Barbara–Ventura Basin; see Isaacs, 1984b). Inferred depths range from outer neritic (50–150 m) to lower bathyal (>2,000 m) (Ingle, 1980).

Two conditions are thought to be required to form a diatom-rich deposit: (1) high diatom productivity and (2) low dilution, especially by terrigenous

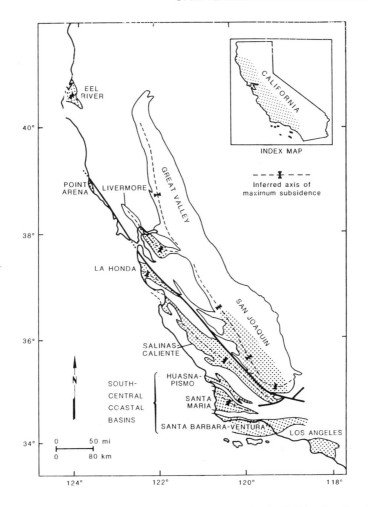

Figure 4-2. Present location of Neogene marine basins in California, showing the approximate distribution of the Monterey Formation (dot pattern). (After Blake et al., 1978.) The map is not representative of Miocene locations, which may have been affected by block rotations, formation of pull-apart basins, as much as 300 km of lateral fault movement, and other tectonic events (Blake et al., 1978; Howell et al., 1980; Heasler and Surdam, 1985). The Salinas Basin is the northwest portion and the Cuyama, or Caliente, Basin is the southeast portion of the Salinas–Caliente Basin as shown; the Santa Barbara Basin is the western portion and the Ventura Basin is the eastern portion of the Santa Barbara–Ventura Basin. Dots in the Eel River Basin indicate Monterey equivalent rocks.

influx (Ingle, 1980). The silica abundance in the Monterey Formation was for many years attributed to volcanic eruptions (Taliaferro, 1933). This theory of marine diatomaceous deposits, proposed long before oceanographic and marine-geologic investigations clarified the controls on diatom productivity, was disproven by Calvert's (1966) milestone study of the present-day Gulf of California. Production of diatoms is now known to result from upwelling of water from 300 m to 500 m below the surface, where nitrate and phosphate, nutrients critical for plankton growth, are abundant (see also Chap. 7).

Although diatom productivity is required to produce a diatom-rich deposit, recent work shows that silica accumulation rates were not necessarily unusually high during Monterey deposition. In the Santa Barbara Basin (Isaacs, 1985), for example, silica accumulated during most of the Miocene at moderate rates ($0.5–3.5$ mg/cm^2/yr) comparable to present-day rates ($1–3$ mg/cm^2/yr) in productive oceanic areas such as the Bering Sea rather than at the high rates characteristic of major present-day silica sinks such as the Gulf of California ($8–174$ mg/cm^2/yr; mean, 50 mg/cm^2/yr) and the Sea of Okhotsk (Calvert, 1966; Lisitzin, 1972). In fact, clay-rich latest Miocene and Pliocene strata overlying the Monterey Formation actually reflect much faster silica accumulation ($15–20$ mg/cm^2/yr) than do Monterey strata (Isaacs, 1985).

The critical change that resulted in the biogenous deposits of the Monterey was a restriction of terrigenous debris. In the Santa Barbara coastal area, terrigenous influx was markedly restricted at the base of the Monterey, with an elevenfold decrease (from 11 mg/cm^2/yr to 1 mg/cm^2/yr) in rates of accumulation of fine terrigenous debris during the early Miocene, a period when rates of silica accumulation were about constant (Fig. 4-3). Resulting terrigenous accumulation rates during the deposition of the Monterey in that area were much lower than present-day rates in the southern California continental borderland ($5–50$ mg/cm^2/yr). In Miocene strata of California, low terrigenous dilution was apparently caused by a combination of tectonic basin formation and marine transgression during a period thought to represent globally rising sea level (Vail and Hardenbol, 1979; but see Pitman, 1978). Basin formation apparently resulted from major plate tectonic readjustments in the Oligocene (Atwater, 1970; Blake et al., 1978; Howell et al., 1980) and thus may have had a Pacific-wide influence (Ingle, 1980).

INORGANIC DIAGENESIS

Diagenesis is a major influence on the reservoir characteristics of the Monterey Formation. Of particular importance is the geochemical instability of biogenous silica, a hydrated form of amorphous silica known as opal-A, which is synthesized by diatoms at temperatures where quartz is the stable silica phase. The opal-A that escaped dissolution in the water column and on the seafloor and that was buried sufficiently in the sediment column transformed to a metastable form of silica composed of interlayered α-cristobalite and α-tridymite and known as opal-CT (Jones and Segnit, 1971, 1972, 1975). With sufficiently greater burial, opal-CT in turn transformed to quartz. This mineralogic sequence has been widely observed in the Monterey Formation (Murata and Larson, 1975; Pisciotto, 1981; Isaacs, 1982) and in other diatomaceous sequences (Hein et al., 1978; Mitsui and Taguchi, 1977; Iijima and Tada, 1981) and has also been produced experimentally (Mizutani, 1970, 1977; Ernst and Calvert, 1969, Stein and Kirkpatrick, 1976; Kastner et al., 1977).

Because silica phase transformations markedly enhance the brittleness and fracturability of diatomaceous strata, they are extremely important to fractured reservoir characteristics. Silica phases typically transformed in diatomaceous sequences by rapid nearly in situ solution–precipitation (Hein et al., 1978; Isaacs, 1982). When opal-CT formed, the original shape and structure of the diatom frustules were completely destroyed, resulting in hard, brittle rock without recognizable diatom remains. In the Bering Sea, this transformation is marked by a prominent acoustic reflector (a bottom-simulating re-

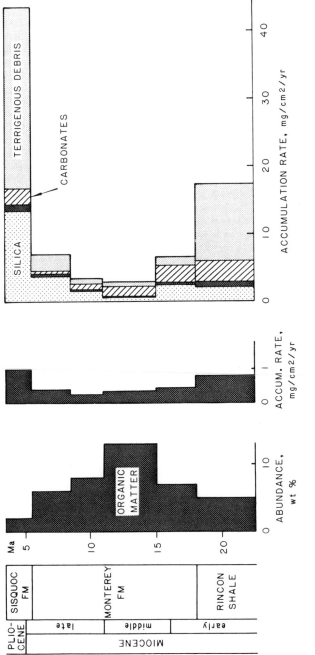

Figure 4-3. Comparison of mean abundance of organic matter (left) with long-term accumulation rates of organic matter (center) and of major sedimentary components (right), Santa Barbara coastal area. (From Isaacs, 1987)

flector, BSR) that in many places crosses lithostratigraphic boundaries (Hein et al., 1978; Hammond and Gaither, 1983; Cooper et al., 1987). As in the Bering Sea, silica phase transformations in the Monterey are accompanied by abrupt changes in physical properties and abrupt step reductions in porosity caused by compaction (Fig. 4-4; Murata and Larson, 1975; Isaacs, 1981). The transformation of opal-A to opal-CT usually occurs at about 45–50°C and from opal-CT to quartz at about 75–85°C (Murata et al., 1977; Pisciotto, 1981; Isaacs et al., 1983; Keller and Isaacs, 1985). In addition, sediment composition, principally clay mineral abundance, directly or indirectly influences the kinetics of silica phase transformations in the Monterey Formation (Isaacs, 1982).

In some areas, carbonate diagenesis also influences the physical properties of the Monterey. Where low-magnesium coccolith calcite is abundant (as in the Santa Maria and Santa Barbara areas), little carbonate cementation occurred during near-surface diagenesis, and the bulk of the calcite-rich rocks persists as moderately cohesive chalks or marls (Isaacs, 1984a). However,

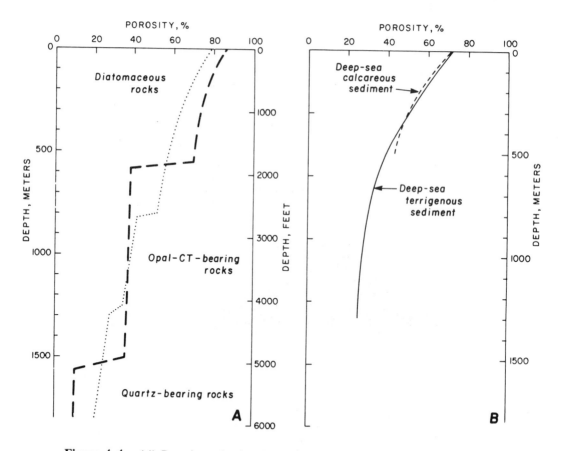

Figure 4-4. (A) Porosity reduction for highly diatomaceous rocks (dashed line), showing two abrupt step reductions corresponding to the two silica phase transformations. The dotted line shows the pattern for sparsely siliceous calcareous rocks of the Monterey Formation. Depths are illustrative only. (After Hamilton, 1976; Isaacs, 1981) (B) Porosity reduction in terrigenous and calcareous deep-sea sediments. (After Hamilton, 1976)

highly cemented beds of diagenetic calcite or dolomite formed widely (Bramlette, 1946; Murata et al., 1969, 1972) and have been the focus of considerable recent research (e.g., Pisciotto, 1978; Garrison et al., 1984; Compton and Siever, 1986). In places, dolostones are complexly brecciated and may be important reservoirs (Redwine, 1981; Roehl, 1981). Disseminated dolomite also formed locally; in regions where calcite is abundant, dolomite abundance locally averages as much as 34% in sequences 100 m or more thick (Isaacs, 1984a), over five times more than in analogous present-day settings (Baker and Burns, 1985). The formation of this dolomite, which is mainly in rocks other than dolostones, usually increases brittleness and fracturing in the Monterey and thus may also enhance reservoir potential.

DEPOSITION AND MATURATION OF ORGANIC MATTER

Monterey organic matter is commonly thought to be derived from marine algal debris deposited in anoxic bottom waters during periods of high plankton productivity. Geochemical characteristics for the most part confirm the marine origin and reducing environment, but the geologic distribution and abundance of organic matter suggest that controlling depositional factors were complex. Both the geology and geochemistry are discussed in the following sections.

GEOLOGIC CHARACTERISTICS

The Monterey Formation and related units are commonly rich in organic matter. Values of organic carbon average between 2% and 4% (range, 0.4% to 10.2%) in the San Joaquin Basin (Kruge, 1983; McGuire et al., 1983; Graham and Williams, 1985), between 2% and 3% (range, 1% to 5.4%) in the Pismo syncline (Surdam and Stanley, 1981), between 0.2% and 5% (range, 0.1% to 7.1%) in the western Salinas Basin (Mertz, 1984b), and about 3% in the Los Angeles Basin (Philippi, 1965). In Monterey deposits of the Santa Barbara–Ventura coastal area and the onshore Santa Maria Basin, organic carbon is especially abundant (Fig. 4–5), averaging more than 5%, with a maximum of as much as 23% (34% organic matter) in some beds (Taylor, 1976; Keller, 1984; Isaacs, 1987). Inasmuch as 0.5–1% organic carbon is recognized as the threshold for a good petroleum source rock, these values show that the Monterey is an excellent petroleum source.

High abundance is commonly equated with rapid deposition, but the abundant organic matter in the Monterey does not necessarily reflect unusually rapid accumulation of organic matter. In the Santa Barbara–Ventura Basin, for example, average rates of Monterey organic matter accumulation were in the range of 0.2 mg/cm^2/yr to 0.5 mg/cm^2/yr (Isaacs, 1987), less than values in underlying and overlying clay-rich strata (0.8–>1 mg/cm^2/yr) or in Holocene analogs (see Pao, 1977; Malouta et al., 1981; LeClaire and Kelts, 1982);

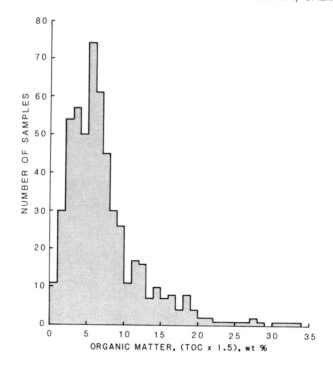

Figure 4–5.   Histogram of the abundance of organic matter (1.5 × organic carbon) in the Santa Maria and Santa Barbara–Ventura basins. (From Isaacs, 1987)

the Monterey's highly abundant organic matter in this area reflects slow, not fast, accumulation of organic matter. What concentrated the organic matter was low dilution, resulting from unusually low rates of total sediment accumulation (see Fig. 4–3). Inverse relationships between organic matter abundance and total sediment accumulation rates have also been noted in other organic-rich units (Gautier and Pratt, 1986; see also Doyle and Garrels, 1985).

Postdepositional and early diagenetic conditions are widely recognized as important influences on the preservation and distribution of organic matter. Low-oxygen bottom water, evidenced by well-preserved lamination that indicates the absence of burrowing organisms, is usually credited with the preservation of abundant organic matter in the Monterey (Demaison and Moore, 1980; Ingle, 1980; Summerhayes, 1981). However, layering and burrowing characteristics show that bottom water oxygen levels varied among Monterey deposits and through time in single sequences (Govean and Garrison, 1981; Pisciotto and Garrison, 1981). Locally, some strata have varvelike lamination (indicating anaerobic conditions), but persistent widespread anoxia seems unlikely inasmuch as such strata are rarely more than 1 m thick and represent a small percentage of beds (Isaacs, 1987). In any case, comparison of organic matter abundances with layering has produced mixed results. Monterey strata in the Salinas Basin show the expected relationship, with best laminated strata containing more abundant organic matter (average 4.6%) that is hydrogen-rich, and massive or bioturbated strata containing much sparser organic matter (average 0.2%) that is hydrogen-poor (Mertz, 1984b). In the Santa Barbara Basin, in contrast, varvelike strata commonly contain much sparser organic matter (average 2.3%) than interbedded massive strata (average 4.3%) (Isaacs,

1987). In Quaternary strata deposited in analogous depositional environments in the Gulf of California, by contrast, interbedded varved and massive strata have equally abundant organic matter (LeClaire and Kelts, 1982). Such differences suggest that depositional controls on organic matter distribution may vary significantly from basin to basin.

An intriguing aspect of Monterey organic matter is its bed-to-bed variability (see Fig. 4–5). The distribution of organic matter abundances is puzzling from the consensus viewpoint that Monterey organic matter is debris from highly productive surface waters deposited in anoxic bottom waters. For example, in the Miocene Santa Barbara–Ventura Basin, organic matter abundances are typically highest in slowly deposited chalks and marls with sparse ($<10\%$) biogenic silica, reflecting periods of moderate to low rather than high surface productivity. Moreover, the abundance of organic matter in this area is closely associated with clay and calcareous debris and is inversely related to silica abundance (Fig. 4–6). Even more remarkable is the fact that silica-rich strata with varvelike lamination (reflecting highest plankton productivity and lowest bottom water oxygen) commonly have the least abundant organic matter in this area (Isaacs, 1987). Although this relationship is not true of all Monterey deposits (see previous discussion), the Monterey in the south-central coastal basins is an especially significant source of oil and includes most discovered fractured reservoirs, so its organic matter variations deserve special attention.

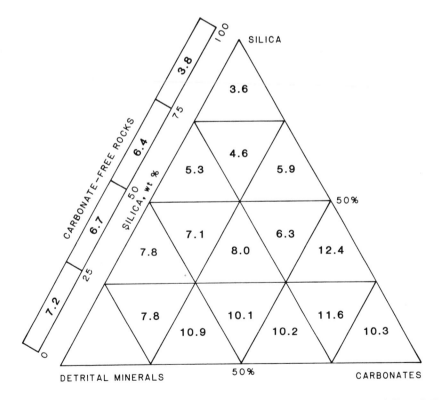

Figure 4-6. Average organic matter abundance [total organic carbon (TOC) × 1.5] of beds with various sedimentary compositions in the Monterey Formation of the Santa Barbara coastal area. Excludes rocks in which dolomite is the predominant carbonate mineral. (From Isaacs, 1987)

These variations may be particularly important to understanding oil generation because sulfur isotopes indicate that limited facies of the Monterey sequence sourced most oil in this area (Orr, 1984b, in press).

ORGANIC MATTER TYPE AND GEOCHEMICAL CHARACTERISTICS

Based on visual kerogen analysis, organic matter in the Monterey is mainly amorphous material interpreted as algal debris (e.g., Graham and Williams, 1985). For example, in Monterey outcrop samples from the Santa Barbara coastal area, the organic matter is 80–100% amorphous-algal (Petersen and Hickey, unpublished data). However, Monterey strata in some areas contain significant amounts of other organic materials. In the onshore Santa Maria Basin, for example, twenty-nine Monterey kerogens average 65% amorphous (algal), 20% herbaceous (pollen, spores, etc.), 10% humic (woody material or vitrinite), and 5% inertinite (coaly) particles (Isaacs and Magoon, 1984). Herbaceous, humic, and inertinite particles, which comprise an average 35% of these kerogens, are regarded to be of terrestrial origin (Staplin, 1969; Hunt, 1979). Although dominantly amorphous (marine), kerogens in the central San Joaquin Basin also have sparse to moderately abundant terrestrial organic matter (Graham and Williams, 1985).

As classed by elemental composition (Tissot and Welte, 1978), Monterey kerogen is typically type II, with minor contributions of type III in the near-shore San Joaquin Basin (Surdam and Stanley, 1981; Isaacs et al., 1983; Kruge, 1983). Type II kerogen is regarded variously as marine debris deposited in a reducing environment (Tissot and Welte, 1978), mixed marine and terrigenous debris (Milner, 1982), and marine and/or terrestrial debris (Hunt, 1979).

In terms of hydrocarbon source indicators, the relative abundance of C_{27}, C_{28}, and C_{29} steranes ($5\alpha,14\alpha,17\alpha20R$) has been proposed as an indicator of marine versus terrestrial organic matter contributions (Huang and Meinschein, 1976, 1979). A dominance of the C_{27} sterane in both Monterey oils and source rocks suggests a dominance of marine organic matter with little terrigenous input (King and Claypool, 1983; Curiale et al., 1985). Carbon-isotopic values for the saturated and aromatic hydrocarbon fractions in Monterey oils (Magoon and Isaacs, 1983; Sofer, 1984; Curiale et al., 1985) also indicate that the organic matter that sourced the oil was mainly marine according to the criterion of Sofer (1984). The compound oleanane, a land plant derivative, may be present in Monterey samples from the Point Conception COST well (offshore Santa Maria Basin), suggesting a contribution of land plant organic matter to the organic matter (Curiale et al., 1985; see also King and Claypool, 1983). $17\alpha(H),18\alpha(H),21\beta(H)$-28,30-bisnorhopane, a pentacyclic triterpane biological marker compound, is unusually abundant in some Monterey oils and source rocks (Seifert et al., 1978; Katz and Elrod, 1983; Curiale et al., 1985). Although its specific origin is unknown, this compound may be derived from sulfur-oxidizing bacterial mats, suggesting a bacterial contribution to the organic matter (Katz and Elrod, 1983; Williams, 1984).

In terms of environment indicators, the low pristane/phytane ratios (<1) of many of the oils and source rock extracts from the Monterey are considered indicative of a highly reducing depositional environment (Powell and Mc-Kirdy, 1973; Welte and Waples, 1973; Connan, 1981). Most oils from the Santa Maria Basin have pristane/phytane ratios less than 1 (Milner et al., 1977; Magoon and Isaacs, 1983; Petersen and Hickey, 1984, 1987; Curiale et al., 1985). Most analyzed Los Angeles Basin oils, in contrast, have pristane/phytane ratios between 1 and 2, indicating a more oxic depositional environment (Petersen and Hickey, 1984, 1987).

ORGANIC MATTER MATURITY INDICATORS

A number of indicators are widely used to evaluate the level of diagenetic maturity in organic matter. Partly because of compositional characteristics and partly because much Monterey oil is probably generated at levels of organic metamorphism normally considered as immature (see "Monterey Oil"), these indicators appear to be misleading or difficult to interpret in the Monterey Formation. Published data on the indicators are briefly summarized in the following sections.

VITRINITE REFLECTANCE

Vitrinite reflectance (R_O) is probably the most widely used parameter for judging kerogen maturity. Values of 0.6–1.3% are generally accepted as representing the main oil-generating window (Hunt, 1979; Waples, 1981).

Interpretation of vitrinite reflectance data in the Monterey Formation has proven to be controversial. Anomalously low vitrinite reflectance values associated with oil-generating Monterey strata were first reported in the Point Conception COST well near the giant Point Arguello field (McCulloh, 1979). A study of the Monterey-equivalent Modelo Formation in the northwestern Los Angeles Basin showed that these source rocks for reservoired oil have R_O values of only 0.13–0.41%, and the study suggested that reflectance values may be suppressed in hydrogen-rich organic matter (Walker et al., 1983). Further study of the Point Conception COST well, where oil appears to be generating at anomalously low R_O values of 0.3–0.4% (Fig. 4–7), concluded that vitrinite reflectance in the Monterey accurately reflects low thermal exposure because oil is generated after comparatively short time-temperature histories (Petersen and Hickey, 1984, 1987).

In addition to lower than expected values in oil-generating strata, another problem with using vitrinite reflectance in the Monterey Formation is that vitrinite is sparse and virtually absent in some areas (e.g., Kruge, 1984). Moreover, because of the common presence of reworked material, interpretation requires considerable care and expertise.

THERMAL ALTERATION INDEX

Another parameter widely used as a maturity indicator is the Thermal Alteration Index (TAI), a measurement of kerogen on a color scale defined by

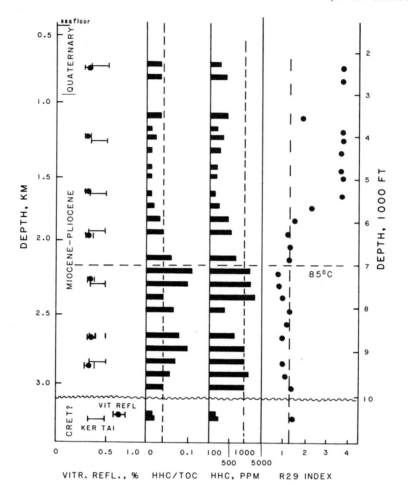

Figure 4–7. Depth profile of the Point Conception COST well (OCS–Cal 78–164 No. 1) near the Point Arguello field (for location, see Fig. 4–1). Shown are chemical maturity parameters, including the ratio of extractable heavy hydrocarbons to total organic carbon (HHC/TOC), the concentration of extractable heavy hydrocarbons (HHC), and the R29 index (Philippi, 1965) of the normal paraffins. Also shown are two organic metamorphism indicators, vitrinite reflectance (R_o) and kerogen slide TAI (Thermal Alteration Index) values. Maturity parameters exceed thresholds normally considered indicative of commercial oil generation at about 85°C. (Adapted from Petersen and Hickey, 1984, 1987)

Staplin (1969). Values are usually expressed on an integer scale from 1 to 5, with intermediate values expressed by + or − (e.g., 2−) and mixtures expressed as combinations (e.g., 1+/2−); however, some workers use an interpolated decimal scale. Because calibration varies somewhat from laboratory to laboratory, not all TAI values are exactly comparable (Waples, 1981). For the main oil-generating window, Tissot and Welte (1978) show values between 2−/2 and 3−/3; Waples (1981) cites values between 2.65 and 3.2; and Bayliss and Magoon (in press) cite values for type III kerogen between 2.2 and 2.9.

Only a few measurements of TAI in the Monterey have been published, with mixed results. Among twenty-nine Monterey kerogens buried at various depths in the onshore Santa Maria Basin (Isaacs and Magoon, 1984), TAI shows a consistent increase with depth, with values in deepest strata (thought to be well within the oil-generating zone) averaging 2.3 (on the same scale used by Bayliss and Magoon, in press). In cuttings from the Point Conception COST well (offshore Santa Maria Basin), however, TAI values show little discernible change through 2.5 km of Miocene-Pliocene strata (see Fig. 4-7), averaging $1+/2-$ even in strata 45°C hotter (and 900 m deeper) than the top of the apparent oil-generating zone (Petersen and Hickey, 1984, 1987).

Hydrogen/Carbon Ratio

Another parameter used to evaluate kerogen maturity is the atomic hydrogen/carbon (H/C) ratio. For type II kerogen, this ratio decreases from values of 2 or more to values in the range 1.25 to 0.7 within the main oil-generating zone (Tissot and Welte, 1978, p. 455).

In Monterey kerogens of the Santa Maria Basin, H/C correlates poorly with depth or maximum temperature, and values at greatest depth (in strata thought to be well within the oil-generating zone) average 1.2 (Isaacs and Magoon, 1984). In Miocene-Pliocene strata in the Point Conception COST well, between 700 m and 2,400 m subseafloor depth (about 40-120°C; McCulloh and Beyer, 1979), values of H/C do not vary significantly and are all within the range 1.23 to 1.36 (Claypool et al., 1979). Because values do not change across the boundary at 2,200 m well depth (1,750 m subseafloor depth) where other indicators (see Fig. 4-7) suggest that oil is being generated (McCulloh, 1979; Petersen and Hickey, 1984, 1987), H/C ratios do not appear to be particularly useful as maturity indicators in the Monterey.

Rock-Eval Pyrolysis

This widely used technique simulates oil generation, yielding values interpreted as bitumen already generated (S_1), future bitumen generative capacity (S_2), and temperature of maximum bitumen yield (T_{max}) (Espitalie et al., 1977). Both T_{max} and S_1/S_1+S_2 (the transformation ratio) are used as maturity indicators, with the main oil-generating zone represented by values of 430-460°C for T_{max} and 0.1-0.4 for S_1/S_1+S_2.

In the Monterey Formation, results of rock-eval pyrolysis appear to be problematic. The major difficulty is that the Monterey generates abundant nonhydrocarbons and high-molecular-weight hydrocarbons that are measured in the S_2 peak and thus incorrectly included in the future generating potential of the source rock (Orr, 1983). As a result, rock-eval parameters (including T_{max}) are thought to be unreliable as maturity indicators in the Monterey Formation (Kablanow and Surdam, 1983; Kruge, 1983). To obtain reliable data, extraction prior to rock-eval pyrolysis may be required (Orr, 1983), a process that makes the technique much more time consuming.

Thermal Models

A widely used parameter for estimating source rock maturity is the time-temperature index (TTI), derived from Lopatin-type geologic models of temperature through time (Waples, 1980, 1981). TTI values of 15–160 encompass the main oil-generating zone, with values of 75 representing peak oil generation.

Whether Monterey source rocks reached accepted values of time-temperature exposure prior to generation is controversial. Petersen and Hickey (1984, 1987) conclude that TTI can be as low as 1 for commercially generative source rocks. Other studies suggest values just below or within the conventional oil window (King and Claypool, 1983; Walker et al., 1983; Heasler and Surdam, 1985).

Some of the uncertainty results from thermal models, which are problematic in the Monterey for several important geologic reasons. One is the marked variability of present-day geothermal gradients in coastal and offshore California. Gradients based on equilibrium temperature measurements range from 24°C/km in the Ventura Basin to as high as 67°C/km in the Santa Maria Basin and vary significantly (by 25°C/km) over comparatively short (<20 km) distances (French, 1940; Bostick et al., 1978; Keller, 1984). This variability makes accurate present-day thermal modeling extremely difficult. Another major problem with thermal models is uncertainty over past geothermal gradients. The California coastal area is an active continental margin, Neogene structural histories are complex and controversial, and onshore basins have been uplifted—all factors making uniform thermal regimes throughout the Neogene unlikely. Significant underestimation of past geothermal gradients has been postulated for the Pismo–Huasna area, based on a model for thermal subsidence resulting from lithospheric cooling (Heasler and Surdam, 1983, 1985). Another major problem with thermal models of the Monterey is that diatomaceous rocks undergo uncommonly large changes during the process of burial and diagenesis, a ninefold compaction and a doubling in thermal conductivity from surface sediment to quartz rock (Murata et al., 1977; Isaacs, 1981, 1984b). Inasmuch as conventional thermal models are usually based on present thickness and gradients, they fail to account for these unusual physical properties of diatomaceous sediments, underestimating past temperatures by as much as a factor of two (Isaacs, 1984b; Heasler and Surdam, 1985).

MONTEREY OIL

The Monterey Formation and its equivalents are considered to be the source for much of the oil from the prolific oil provinces of the California coastal basins (e.g., Taylor, 1976). In most of these provinces, older source rocks are also present. In the Ventura Basin, for example, some Miocene oils may have been sourced by Eocene or older strata, and potential source rocks other than the Monterey are also present in the San Joaquin Basin and much of the Los Angeles Basin. Because of this ambiguity, oils from the onshore and offshore Santa Maria Basin are of special interest inasmuch as the Monterey Formation is the only significant source rock in this area.

Monterey oils have been studied extensively in the petroleum industry, but most data are proprietary. The following discussion is summarized from Petersen and Hickey (1984, 1987). Published data on specific oils can be found mainly in Milner et al. (1977), Magoon and Isaacs (1983), and Curiale et al. (1985).

General Characteristics

A significant percentage of production in California coastal basins is heavy oil (<20° API gravity). Through 1973, production from the Santa Maria Basin (entirely Monterey sourced) was over 90% heavy oil; from the Los Angeles Basin, 25% heavy oil; and from the Ventura Basin, 8% heavy oil (Fig. 4–8; Petersen and Hickey, 1984, 1987). More recent Monterey discoveries in the offshore Santa Barbara–Ventura Basin and the offshore Santa Maria Basin, although containing economically significant amounts of oil in the range 30° to 34° API, are also mainly heavy oil (Crain et al., 1985; Williams, 1985a).

In gross composition, Monterey oils differ remarkably from the worldwide average of six hundred oils reported by Tissot and Welte (1978) (Fig. 4–9). The major class of compounds in Monterey oils is in fact nonhydrocarbons, organic compounds containing oxygen, nitrogen, or sulfur atoms (NSO compounds, including asphaltenes and resins). Sulfur concentrations as high as 9 weight-percent have been measured.

Evidence of Early Generation

Oil that is heavy, sulfur rich, and asphaltic may result from biodegradation, the microbial alteration of crude oil. In many places, however, oils with these characteristics are recognized as representing immature oils or early expulsion products (Powell and Snowdon, 1983, and references therein).

For Monterey oils, increasing evidence suggests that their low gravity and unusual compositions are due to early generation. Milner et al. (1977) were among the first to suggest that Monterey oils are immature, and one of their key lines of evidence was a predominance of normal paraffins (n-alkanes) with even numbers of carbon atoms. Source rocks that have reached the normal oil-generating zone have a smooth distribution of normal paraffins, with virtually no odd or even predominance. By contrast, source rocks that have not reached the conventional maturity levels have either an odd or even predom-

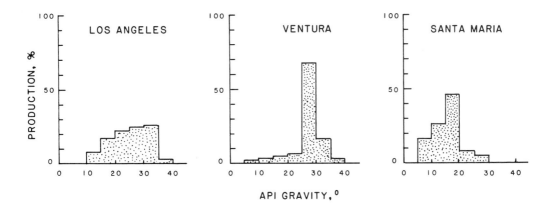

Figure 4–8. API gravity distribution of oil produced in California through 1973. (From Petersen and Hickey, 1984, 1987; distribution based on field summaries in California Division of Oil and Gas, 1974)

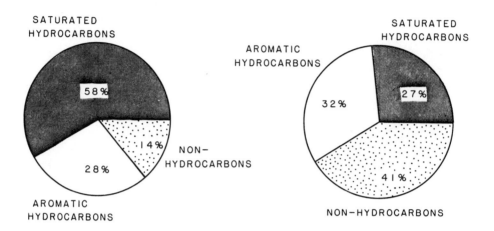

Figure 4-9. Gross composition of worldwide average oil compared with gross composition of Monterey oils from the California coastal basins. (Worldwide oil figures from Tissot and Welte, 1978; Monterey oil figures from Petersen and Hickey, 1984, 1987)

inance in the normal paraffin distribution (Bray and Evans, 1961; Philippi, 1965; Tissot and Welte, 1978). Because this characteristic is not induced as the result of biodegradation, it is an excellent indicator of immaturity.

Monterey oil samples from the Santa Maria Basin show a strong even predominance, indicating immaturity. Moreover, the intensity of the even predominance decreases with increasing API gravity (Fig. 4-10). This relationship suggests that the relative maturity level reached at the time the oil was generated exerts a strong control on the overall compositional quality of the oil; the lower the level of organic metamorphism at the time of generation, the lower the gravity.

A variety of other characteristics have now been proposed by a number of authors as being indicative of early oil generation (e.g., Ho et al., 1974; Van Dorsselaer et al., 1977; Ensminger et al., 1977; Seifert and Moldowan, 1978; Baker et al., 1984; Palacas et al., 1985). Monterey oils display nearly all these characteristics (Table 4-1).

Evidence of early generation also derives from the source rocks per se. Although vitrinite reflectance levels of 0.6-0.7% are widely accepted as the start of the oil generative window (e.g., Dow, 1977; Hunt, 1979; Waples, 1981), source extracts reach chemical characteristics similar to Monterey oils at vitrinite reflectance levels as low as 0.3-0.4% (Petersen and Hickey, 1983, 1987). At the same time, several oil generation indicators reach levels above the threshold normally considered indicative of commercial oil generation, including the concentration of extractable bitumen, the concentration of hydrocarbons, and the ratios of extractable bitumen and hydrocarbons to total organic carbon (see Fig. 4-7).

Early generation of petroleum from Monterey kerogens may be due to a low-activation kerogen, which would be more temperature dependent rather than time-temperature dependent (Petersen and Hickey, 1983). Because of the

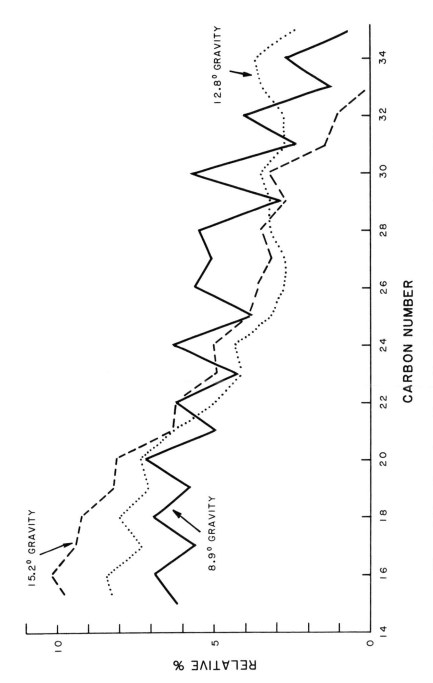

Figure 4–10. Normal paraffin profiles of three oils from Santa Maria Valley field. Note the decrease in even predominance with increasing API gravity. (From Petersen and Hickey, 1984, 1987)

Table 4–1. Characteristics of Early Oil Compared with Characteristics of Monterey Oil

Characteristic	Early Oil	Monterey Oil
API gravity	Heavy ($<20°$)	Heavy
Sulfur content	High	High
Gas/Oil ratio	Low	Low
Nonhydrocarbon compounds (as % of C_{15+} fraction)	High (>20)	High (av. 41)
Heavy fraction of oil (C_{15+} as % of oil)	High (>60–70)	High
Relative concentration of isoprenoids (IP_{19}/NC_{17} and IP_{20}/NC_{18})	High (>1)	High
Relative amount of polycyclic biomarkers	High	High
Odd or even normal alkane predominance	Prominent to moderate	Prominent to moderate
Biomarker maturity ratios		
Pentacyclic terpanes		
T_m/T_s	>0.9	1.4–4
C_{31}, C_{32}, C_{33} 22S/22R	<1.3	1.0–1.6
Steranes		
20S/20R	<1	0.2–1
Naphtheno-sulfur compounds		
Benzothiophene/Dibenzothiophene	>1	1.3+
Naphthene ring distribution	3–5 rings dominate	4 rings dominate
Porphyrins		
DPEP-type/Etio-type	>1	>1

Source: Adapted from Petersen and Hickey (1984, 1987).

relative ease of breaking carbon-sulfur bonds, the critical factor causing early generation may be the presence of high concentrations of sulfur in the kerogen (Orr, 1984*b*, in press).

Early generation of Monterey oils accounts for many of their unique chemical characteristics that cannot be attributed to biodegradation (see Table 4–1; Petersen and Hickey, 1984, 1987). Some Monterey oils are biodegraded (e.g., Milner et al., 1977; Curiale et al., 1985), but this postaccumulation process is not the principal cause of low API gravities or high sulfur contents. The level of organic metamorphism or maximum temperature reached by the source rock is probably the major control on oil quality. Other parameters affecting oil quality include whether or not the oil was actually expelled from a source bed into an adjacent reservoir bed or was produced as the result of a fracture network from a bed that is both source and reservoir. Expulsion from source to reservoir bed would result in an improvement in oil quality due to fractionation during the primary migration phase. Whether the rock is clay rich or clay poor could also be a contributing factor to oil quality. Clay-rich matrices tend to complex some of the heavy nonhydrocarbon compounds. The resulting migratable or producible oil is consequently lighter and contains a lower percentage of nonhydrocarbon compounds.

PETROLEUM RESERVOIRS

In terms of prospecting for oil reserves in siliceous rocks, the difficulties of identifying fractured reservoirs cannot be overemphasized. As an illustration, the 1980 discovery well for the giant Point Arguello offshore field (see Fig. 4–1) had only minor oil shows and a "not particularly exciting" mud log (Crain et al., 1985). According to the operating company, the well was tested mainly because of "past experience" (Crain et al., 1985). Apparently discouraging prospects are typical of fractured reservoirs.

RESERVOIR CHARACTERISTICS

Petroleum reservoirs in the Monterey are of two general types: (1) conventional reservoirs in sandstone interbedded with fine-grained rocks and (2) reservoirs in fine-grained strata. Sandstone reservoirs within fine-grained sequences, the ideal arrangement of permeable rock adjacent to oil-generating strata, are common in the San Joaquin, Los Angeles, and Salinas–Caliente basins but occur only locally in the Santa Maria and the Santa Barbara–Ventura basins.

Reservoirs composed of fine-grained Monterey strata are the principal target of current offshore exploration (Crain et al., 1985; Williams, 1985*b*). Most petroleum production from fine-grained rocks in the Monterey is from fractured reservoirs in diagenetically mature sequences—where silica is either opal-CT or quartz. Highly porous diatomaceous rocks also have high oil saturations locally in the Santa Maria and San Joaquin basins; because the rocks have low matrix permeabilities and are not usually sufficiently brittle to fracture, these oil accumulations can be produced by conventional methods only locally, but they can be easily strip-mined (Farley and Wilson, 1983; Mulhern et al., 1983).

Worldwide, fractured reservoirs typically have rather low bulk fracture porosity values, usually less than 3% and in some cases as low as 0.3% (Drummond, 1964). Because average matrix porosity in Monterey reservoirs is typically in the 10–35% range (Isaacs, 1981, 1984b; Isaacs et al., 1983), fracture porosity in most cases provides a relatively insignificant addition to total pore volume. Fractures are critical, however, in connecting isolated pore space (Stearns and Friedman, 1972), and fracture permeabilities can be extremely high. In the Santa Maria Valley field, where initial production rates early in the field's development were commonly 2,500 barrels/day and as high as 10,000 barrels/day, average permeabilities are estimated at 10–15 darcys, with a maximum of 35 darcys (Regan and Hughes, 1949). Productivities of thousands of barrels per day suggest feeder fractures 0.5–6 mm wide, and productivities of hundreds of barrels per day may correspond to feeder fractures only hundredths of a millimeter wide (Regan and Hughes, 1949). In the Point Arguello field (see Fig. 4-1) under current development, productivities average 6,000 barrels/day in rocks with matrix porosity values of 13.5%, fracture porosity values of 1.5%, negligible matrix permeability values (<0.1 md), and average in situ permeability estimated to exceed 750 md (Crain et al., 1984, 1985).

Identification of the principal reservoir rock type(s) in the fine-grained reservoirs of the Santa Maria and Santa Barbara areas has been difficult. Outcrop study of fractures shows that fracture intensity is commonly higher in quartz-bearing rocks than in opal-CT-bearing rocks and is closely related to rock type, with fracture intensity decreasing in the following sequence: (1) chert, clay-poor vitreous siliceous rock; (2) porcelanite, clay-bearing matte siliceous rock; (3) dolostone; and (4) marl (Belfield et al., 1983a, b). Regan and Hughes (1949) concluded that fractured zones have the following economic rank in the Santa Maria Basin: (1) chert zones; (2) calcareous shale zones; and of minor importance, (3) platy siliceous and porcelaneous shale zones. Several more recent studies suggested that dolostone is an important reservoir rock in the Santa Maria Basin (Redwine, 1981; Roehl, 1981), and a reservoir model for the South Elwood offshore field also includes both vertical and bedding-parallel breccia zones as important reservoir types (Belfield et al., 1983a, b). However, most workers (e.g., Crain et al., 1985) consider vitreous quartz chert to be the most important fractured reservoir rock type in the offshore.

All rock types in a fractured reservoir are probably important to production characteristics. According to Drummond (1964), reservoirs with both fracture and matrix porosity commonly have complex production characteristics, because matrix porosity that is ineffective in transmitting oil in initial production stages may contribute to oil transmission in later production stages.

WELL-LOG ANALYSIS

Petroleum exploration and production in the Monterey Formation have been significantly hampered by problematic well-log responses related to three general characteristics of the Monterey: (1) atypical rock types with distinctive physical properties, (2) thin beds of widely varying composition, and (3) production from fractures. Problems with well-log interpretation are common in fractured reservoirs. Because horizons producing petroleum from fractures differ in character from horizons producing due to high matrix permeability, conventional indications of petroleum production potential (such as high porosity) are nearly useless in fractured reservoirs; Drummond (1964) recommends mud loss and drill stem tests as the best general indications of petroleum-producing horizons in fractured reservoirs but states that neither of these tests is infallible.

One of the few available summaries of well-log responses in the Monterey Formation (Cannon, 1981) summarizes several years of study of the Monterey Formation in the mid-1970s by researchers at Schlumberger. This research concluded that rock types could not be identified from well-log responses and that all conventional indicators of potential petroleum-producing horizons fail for some reason in the Monterey Formation (Cannon, 1981).

Some of the interpretive problems are illustrated by a typical log for the Monterey in the offshore Hondo field (Fig. 4–11). The spontaneous potential (SP) curve shows lower values in the Monterey than in underlying and overlying formations, a response that is normally interpreted to indicate permeable beds, but SP in the Monterey does not actually distinguish permeable from nonpermeable beds (Cannon, 1981). The resistivity curve shows higher values in the Monterey than in underlying and overlying formations, a response suggesting high hydrocarbon saturation. However, resistivities measured in the Monterey are as much affected by porosity as oil saturation, and values in good producing horizons in the Monterey vary widely (from 3 ohm-m to 1,000 ohm-m) (Cannon, 1981).

Other problems with conventional well-log analysis in the Monterey include the following: (1) because of thin beds of rapidly varying lithology, most well-log data represent an interval-average encompassing a variety of rock types; (2) gamma ray log responses, usually interpreted in terms of clay mineral abundance, apparently reflect uranium in apatite; (3) responses from density logs are not easily interpreted in terms of porosity because of highly varying values of grain density (2.1–2.8 g/cm^3); and (4) porosity values derived from porosity logs do not reflect effective porosity, and in any case, high porosity does not indicate petroleum-producing horizons.

Because of the importance of effectively using log analysis in identifying petroleum-producing horizons in the Monterey, research in this area is currently active. One method that has reportedly had some success is the identification of zones having high values of movable hydrocarbons (determined by using two resistivity tools having different depths of investigation) and divergent values of apparent matrix density derived by conventional interpretation of sonic logs and of neutron logs (Cannon, 1981). Also recently tested in the San Joaquin Basin is a facies log based on comparison of conventional logs (Mulhern et al., 1985). Further refinements of log detection of fractured zones and petroleum-producing zones can be expected in the near future.

Summary

The Miocene Monterey Formation of California is a distinctive unit of organic-rich biogenous marine rocks derived largely from diatomaceous debris.

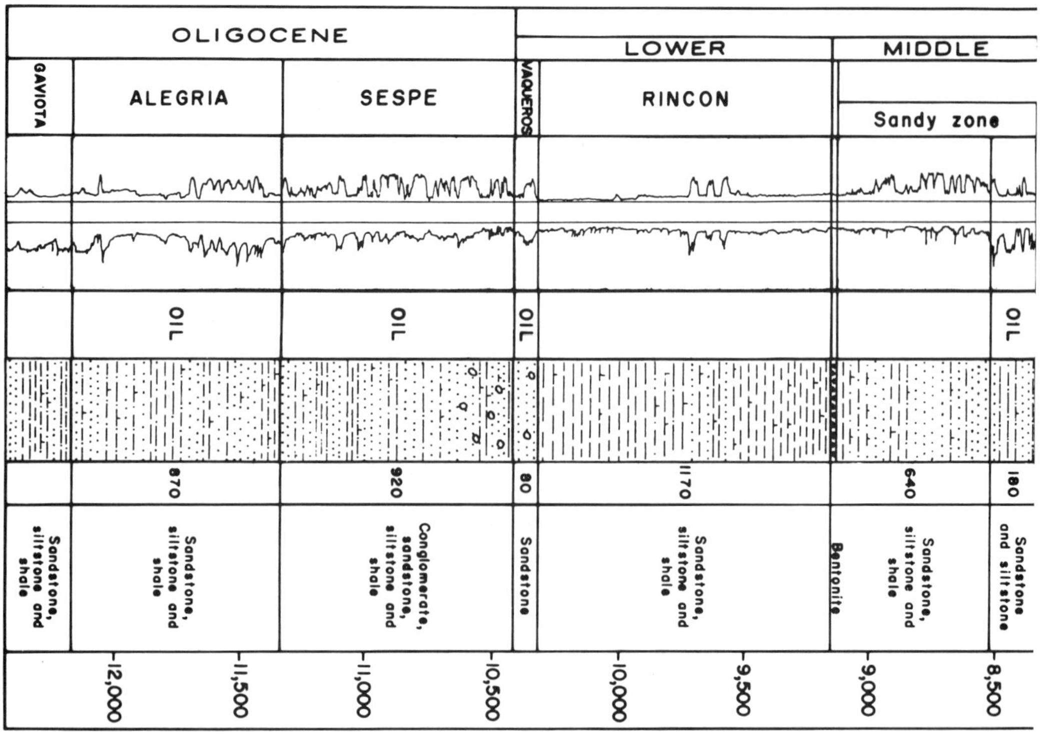

	OLIGOCENE			LOWER	MIDDLE
GAVIOTA	ALEGRIA	SESPE	VAQUEROS	RINCON	Sandy zone

OIL — OIL — OIL — OIL

870 — 920 — 80 — 1170 — 640 — 180

Sandstone, siltstone and shale — Sandstone, siltstone and shale — Conglomerate, sandstone, siltstone and shale — Sandstone — Sandstone, siltstone and shale — Bentonite — Sandstone, siltstone and shale — Sandstone and siltstone

12,000 — 11,500 — 11,000 — 10,500 — 10,000 — 9,500 — 9,000 — 8,500

Figure 4–11. Typical log of the Monterey Formation from the Hondo Field (for location, see Fig. 4–1) showing curves of spontaneous potential (left) and resistivity (right). (From U.S. Geological Survey, 1974)

The formation is unusual in that it is a major petroleum source rock as well as an important petroleum reservoir.

Monterey organic matter is abundant, with total organic carbon averaging 2–5% and ranging in individual beds as high as 23%. Its abundance is commonly regarded as a reflection of high plankton productivity, rapid deposition, and preservation in anoxic bottom waters, but patterns of distribution are complex and may vary from basin to basin. For example, in some basins Monterey organic matter is most abundant in silica-poor rocks, reflecting periods of moderate productivity, unusually slow sedimentation, and slightly oxygenated bottom water. Monterey kerogen is commonly amorphous (interpreted as marine), although distinct terrestrial particles may locally represent a third or more of the total, and is usually classified by elemental composition as type II. Characteristics of the hydrocarbons suggest that they are mainly derived from marine debris deposited in a reducing environment with a possible bacterial contribution.

Monterey oils tend to be heavy ($<20°$ API gravity) and contain more non-hydrocarbons (asphaltenes and resins) than hydrocarbons. Increasing evidence suggests that the gravity and composition of Monterey oils is due to early generation rather than biodegradation. Because of both early generation and unusual compositional characteristics, conventional maturity indicators such as vitrinite reflectance, thermal alteration indexes, hydrogen/carbon ratios,

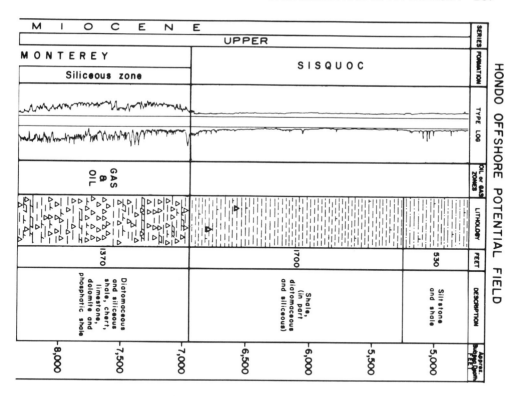

rock-eval pyrolysis, and thermal models are misleading or difficult to use in evaluating the maturity of Monterey source rocks.

The lithotypes of the Monterey Formation result in many unconventional characteristics that affect petroleum exploration and production. In contrast to most reservoirs, Monterey strata are extremely fine-grained. Excellence as a petroleum reservoir comes from comparatively high matrix porosity (10–30%) combined with fracturing. Matrix permeabilities are extremely low (<0.1 md), but effective permeabilities resulting from fracturing are commonly much higher (as much as 1–35 darcys). Other notable characteristics of the Monterey that affect petroleum exploration and production include prominent seismic reflections from diagenetic boundaries caused by silica-phase transformations, which in places cut obliquely across stratal boundaries, and anomalous well-log responses, which result in the failure of all normal log indicators to define potential petroleum-producing horizons.

ACKNOWLEDGMENTS

We thank Kenneth J. Bird, Margaret A. Keller, Thane H. McCulloh, and Wilson L. Orr for many valuable discussions. James R. Hein and Leslie B. Magoon made helpful critical reviews of a preliminary manuscript. Brigitta V. Fulop, Lee Bailey, and Phyllis A. Swenson drafted the figures.

References

Aoyagi, K., and A. Iijima, 1983. Reservoir characteristics and petroleum migration in the Miocene Onnagawa Formation of Akita, Japan, in *Petroleum Generation and Occurrence in the Miocene Monterey Formation, California,* C. M. Isaacs and R. E. Garrison, eds., Pacific Section, Society of Economic Paleontologists and Mineralogists Publication 33, pp. 75–84.

Atwater, T., 1970. Implications of plate tectonics for the Cenozoic tectonic evolution of North America, *Geol. Soc. America Bull.* **81:**3513–3535.

Baker, E. W., J. W. Louda, and W. L. Orr, 1984. *Porphyrins in Monterey Crudes,* Division of Geochemistry Abstracts, American Chemical Society, 187th National Meeting.

Baker, P. A., and S. J. Burns, 1985. Occurrence and formation of dolomite in organic-rich continental margin sediments, *Am. Assoc. Petroleum Geologists Bull.* **69:**1917–1930.

Bayliss, G. S., and L. B. Magoon, in press. Organic facies and thermal maturity in the National Petroleum Reserve in Alaska—Intercalibration of visual kerogen assessment, vitrinite reflectance, and C_1-to-C_4 hydrocarbons, in *Geology of the National Petroleum Reserve in Alaska,* G. Gryc, ed., U.S. Geological Survey Professional Paper 1399, 34p.

Belfield, W. C., J. Helwig, P. R. La Pointe, and W. K. Dahleen, 1983a. Monterey fractured reservoir, Santa Barbara Channel, California, *Am. Assoc. Petroleum Geologists Bull.* **67:**421–422.

Belfield, W. C., J. Helwig, P. R. La Pointe, and W. K. Dahleen, 1983b. South Ellwood oil field, Santa Barbara Channel, California, a Monterey Formation fractured reservoir, in *Petroleum Generation and Occurrence in the Miocene Monterey Formation, California,* C. M. Isaacs and R. E. Garrison, eds., Pacific Section, Society of Economic Paleontologists and Mineralogists Publication 33, pp. 213–221.

Beyer, L. A., 1987. Porosity of the oil-bearing formations in selected oil fields of the Santa Maria and San Joaquin basins, California, in *Exploration for Heavy Crude Oil and Bitumen,* R. F. Meyer, ed., American Association of Petroleum Geologists, Studies in Geology 23 (in press), Tulsa, Okla.

Blake, G. H., 1981. Biostratigraphic relationship of Neogene benthic foraminifera from the southern California outer continental borderland to the Monterey Formation, in *The Monterey Formation and Related Siliceous Rocks of California,* R. E. Garrison and R. G. Douglas, eds., Pacific Section, Society of Economic Paleontologists and Mineralogists Publication 15, pp. 1–13.

Blake, M. C., Jr., R. H. Campbell, T. W. Dibblee, Jr., D. G. Howell, T. H. Nilsen, W. R. Normark, J. G. Vedder, and E. A. Silver, 1978. Neogene basin formation in relation to plate-tectonic evolution of San Andreas fault system, California, *Am. Assoc. Petroleum Geologists Bull.* **62:**344–372.

Bostick, N. H., S. M. Cashman, T. H. McCulloh, and C. T. Waddell, 1978. Gradients of vitrinite reflectance and present temperature in the Los Angeles and Ventura basins, California, in *Symposium in Geochemistry: Low Temperature Metamorphism of Kerogen and Clay Minerals,* D. F. Oltz, ed., Pacific Section, Society of Economic Paleontologists and Mineralogists Publication 3, pp. 65–96.

Bramlette, M. N., 1946. *The Monterey Formation of California and the Origin of Its Siliceous Rocks,* U.S. Geological Survey Professional Paper 212, 57p.

Bray, E. E., and E. D. Evans, 1961. Distribution of *n*-paraffins as a clue to recognition of source beds, *Geochim. et Cosmochim. Acta* **22:**2–15.

California Division of Oil and Gas, 1974. *California Oil and Gas Fields, South, Central Coastal, and Offshore California,* California Division of Oil and Gas Report No. TR12, vol. 2.

California Division of Oil and Gas, 1984. *69th Annual Report of the State Oil and Gas Supervisor,* California Division of Oil and Gas Publication No. PR06, 147p.

Calvert, S. E., 1966. Accumulation of diatomaceous silica in the sediments of the Gulf of California, *Geol. Soc. America Bull.* **77**:569–596.

Cannon, D. E., 1981. Log evaluation of a fractured reservoir Monterey Shale, in *The Monterey Formation and Related Siliceous Rocks of California,* R. E. Garrison and R. G. Douglas, eds., Pacific Section, Society of Economic Paleontologists and Mineralogists Publication 15, pp. 249–255.

Claypool, G. E., J. P. Baysinger, C. M. Lubeck, and A. H. Love, 1979. Organic geochemistry, in *Geologic Studies of the Point Conception Deep Stratigraphic Test Well OCS-Cal 78-164 No. 1 Outer Continental Shelf Southern California, United States,* H. E. Cook, ed., U.S. Geological Survey Open-File Report 79-1218, pp. 109–124.

Compton, J. S., and R. Siever, 1986. Diffusion and mass balance of Mg during early dolomite formation, Monterey Formation, *Geochim. et Cosmochim. Acta* **50**:125–135.

Connan, J., 1981. Biological markers in crude oils, in *Petroleum Geology in China,* J. F. Mason, ed., PennWell Books, Tulsa, Okla., pp. 48–70.

Cooper, A. K., D. W. Scholl, and M. S. Marlow, 1987. Structural framework, sedimentary sequences, and hydrocarbon potential of the Aleutian and Bowers Basin, Bering Sea, in *Geology and Resource Potential of the Continental Margin of Western North American and Adjacent Ocean Basins—Beaufort Sea to Baja California,* D. W. Scholl, A. Grantz, and J. G., Vedder, eds., American Association of Petroleum Geologists Memoir (in press).

Crain, W. E., W. E. Mero, and D. Patterson, 1985. Geology of the Point Arguello discovery, *Am. Assoc. Petroleum Geologists Bull.* **69**:537–545.

Crain, W. E., W. E. Mero, and C. Wilkenson, 1984. Geology of Point Arguello discovery, *Am. Assoc. Petroleum Geologists Bull.* **68**:467.

Curiale, J. A., D. Cameron, and D. V. Davis, 1985. Biological marker distribution and significance in oils and rocks of the Monterey Formation, California, *Geochim. et Cosmochim. Acta* **49**:271–288.

Demaison, G. J., and G. T. Moore, 1980. Anoxic environments and oil source bed genesis, *Am. Assoc. Petroleum Geologists Bull.* **64**:1179–1209.

Dow, W. G., 1977. Kerogen studies and geological interpretations, *Jour. Geochem. Exploration* **7**:79–99.

Dole, L. J., and R. M. Garrels, 1985. What does percent organic carbon in sediments measure?, *Geo-Marine Letters* **5**:51–53.

Drummond, J. M., 1964. An appraisal of fracture porosity, *Bull. Canadian Petroleum Geology* **12**:226–245.

Ensminger, A., P. Albrecht, G. Ourisson, and B. Tissot, 1977. Evolution of polycyclic alkanes under the effect of burial (Early Toarcian shales, Paris basin), in *Advances in Organic Geochemistry 1975,* R. Campos and J. Goni, eds., Empresa Nacional Adaro de Investigaciones Mineras, Madrid, pp. 45–52.

Ernst, W. G., and S. E. Calvert, 1969. An experimental study of the recrystallization of porcelanite and its bearing on the origin of some bedded cherts, *Am. Jour. Sci.* **267-A**:114–133.

Espitalie, J., J. L. Laporte, M. Madec, F. Marquis, P. Leplat, J. Paulet, and A. Boutefeu, 1977. Méthode rapide de caractérisation des roches mères de leur potentiel pétrolier et de leur degré d'evolution, *Inst. Français Pétrole Rev.* **32**:23–42.

Farley, T., and M. L. Wilson, 1983. Geology of the Airox oil-saturated diatomite deposit, Santa Barbara County, California, in *Petroleum Generation and Occurrence in the Miocene Monterey Formation, California,* C. M. Isaacs and R. E. Garrison, eds., Pacific Section, Society of Economic Paleontologists and Mineralogists Publication 33, pp. 1–15.

French, R. W., 1940. Geothermal gradients in California oil wells, in *Drilling and Production Practice, 1939,* American Petroleum Institute, New York, pp. 653–658.

Garrison, R. E., 1975. *Neogene Diatomaceous Sedimentation in East Asia: A Review with Recommendations for Further Study,* United Nations Economic and Social Commission for Asia and the Pacific, Committee for Co-ordination of Joint Prospecting for Mineral Resources in Asian Offshore Areas, Technical Bulletin 9, pp. 57–69.

Garrison, R. E., and R. G. Douglas, eds., 1981. *The Monterey Formation and Related Siliceous Rocks of California,* Pacific Section, Society of Economic Paleontologists and Mineralogists Publication 15, 327p.

Garrison, R. E., M. Kastner, and D. H. Zenger, eds., 1984. *Dolomites of the Monterey Formation and Other Organic-rich Units,* Pacific Section, Society of Economic Paleontologists and Mineralogists Publication 41, 215p.

Gautier, D. L., and L. M. Pratt, 1986. Organic carbon accumulation and sulfur diagenesis in fine-grained Cretaceous rocks of the western interior of North America, in *USGS Research on Energy Resources—1986 Program and Abstracts,* L. M. H. Carter, ed., U.S. Geological Survey Circular 974, pp. 16–17.

Govean, F. M., and R. E. Garrison, 1981. Significance of laminated and massive diatomites in the upper part of the Monterey Formation, California, in *The Monterey Formation and Related Siliceous Rocks of California,* R. E. Garrison and R. G. Douglas, ed., Pacific Section, Society of Economic Paleontologists and Mineralogists Publication 15, pp. 181–198.

Graham, S. A., and L. A. Williams, 1985. Tectonic, depositional, and diagenetic history of Monterey Formation (Miocene), central San Joaquin basin, California, *Am. Assoc. Petroleum Geologists Bull.* **69:**385–411.

Hamilton, E. L., 1976. Variations of density and porosity with depth in deep-sea sediments, *Jour. Sed. Petrology* **46:**280–300.

Hammond, R. D., and J. R. Gaither, 1983. Anomalous seismic character—Bering Sea Shelf, *Geophysics* **48:**590–605.

Heasler, H. P., and R. C. Surdam, 1983. A thermally subsiding basin model for the maturation of hydrocarbons in the Pismo basin, California, in *Petroleum Generation and Occurrence in the Miocene Monterey Formation, California,* C. M. Isaacs and R. E. Garrison, eds., Pacific Section, Society of Economic Paleontologists and Mineralogists Publication 33, pp. 69–74.

Heasler, H. P., and R. C. Surdam, 1985. Thermal evolution of coastal California with application to hydrocarbon maturation, *Am. Assoc. Petroleum Geologists Bull.* **69:**1386–1400.

Hein, J. R., D. W., Scholl, J. A. Barron, M. G. Jones, and J. Miller, 1978. Diagenesis of Late Cenozoic diatomaceous deposits and formation of the bottom simulating reflector in the southern Bering Sea, *Sedimentology* **25:**155–181.

Ho, T. Y., M. A. Rogers, H. V. Drushel, and C. B. Koons, 1974. Evolution of sulfur compounds in crude oils, *Am. Assoc. Petroleum Geologists Bull.* **58:**2338–2348.

Howell, D. G., J. K. Crouch, H. G. Greene, D. S. McCulloch, and J. G. Vedder, 1980. Basin development along the late Mesozoic and Cainozoic California margin: A plate tectonic margin of subduction, oblique subduction and transform tectonics, in *Sedimentation in Oblique-slip Mobile Zones,* P. F. Ballance and H. G. Reading, eds., International Association of Sedimentologists Special Publication 4, pp. 43–62.

Huang, W., and W. G. Meinschein, 1976. Sterols as source indicators of organic materials in sediments, *Geochim. et Cosmochim. Acta* **40:**323–330.

Huang, W., and W. G. Meinschein, 1979. Sterols as ecological indicators, *Geochim. et Cosmochim. Acta* **43:**739–745.

Hunt, J. M., 1979. *Petroleum Geochemistry and Geology,* W. H. Freeman, San Francisco, 617p.

Iijima, A., and R. Tada, 1981. Silica diagenesis of Neogene diatomaceous and volcaniclastic sediments in northern Japan, *Sedimentology* **28**:185–200.

Ingle, J. C., Jr., 1980. Cenozoic paleobathymetry and depositional history of selected sequences within the southern California continental borderland, in *Studies in Marine Micropaleontology and Paleoecology,* W. V. Sliter, ed., Cushman Foundation for Foraminiferal Research Special Publication 19, pp. 163–195.

Ingle, J. C., Jr., 1981. Origin of Neogene diatomites around the North Pacific rim, in *The Monterey Formation and Related Siliceous Rocks of California,* R. E. Garrison and R. G. Douglas, eds., Pacific Section, Society of Economic Paleontologists and Mineralogists Publication 15, pp. 159–179.

Isaacs, C. M., 1981. Porosity reduction during diagenesis of the Monterey Formation, Santa Barbara coastal area, California, in *The Monterey Formation and Related Siliceous Rocks of California,* R. E. Garrison and R. G. Douglas, eds., Pacific Section, Society of Economic Paleontologists and Mineralogists Publication 15, pp. 257–271.

Isaacs, C. M., 1982. Influence of rock composition on kinetics of silica phase changes in the Monterey Formation, Santa Barbara area, California, *Geology* **10**:304–308.

Isaacs, C. M., 1984a. Disseminated dolomite in the Monterey Formation, Santa Maria and Santa Barbara areas, California, in *Dolomites of the Monterey Formation and Other Organic-rich Units,* R. E. Garrison, M. Kastner, and D. H. Zenger, eds., Pacific Section, Society of Economic Paleontologists and Mineralogists Publication 41, pp. 155–169.

Isaacs, C. M., 1984b. The Monterey—Key to Offshore California boom, *Oil and Gas Jour.* **82**(2):75–81.

Isaacs, C. M., 1985. Abundance versus rates of accumulation in fine-grained strata of the Miocene Santa Barbara basin, California, *Geo-Marine Letters* **5**:25–30.

Isaacs, C. M., 1987. Sources and deposition of organic matter in the Monterey Formation, south-central coastal basins of California, U.S.A., in *Exploration for Heavy Crude Oil and Bitumen,* R. F. Meyer, ed., American Association of Petroleum Geologists, Studies in Geology 23 (in press), Tulsa, Okla.

Isaacs, C. M., and R. E. Garrison, eds., 1983. *Petroleum Generation and Occurrence in the Miocene Monterey Formation, California,* Pacific Section, Society of Economic Paleontologists and Mineralogists Publication 33, 228p.

Isaacs, C. M., and L. B. Magoon, 1984. *Thermal Indicators of Organic Matter in the Sisquoc and Monterey Formations, Santa Maria Basin, California,* Abstracts, Society of Economic Paleontologists and Mineralogists, Annual Midyear Meeting, August 10–13, 1984, San Jose, California, p. 40.

Isaacs, C. M., K. A. Pisciotto, and R. E. Garrison, 1983. Facies and diagenesis of the Miocene Monterey Formation, California: A summary, in *Siliceous Deposits of the Pacific Region,* A. Iijima, J. R. Hein, and R. Siever, eds., Elsevier, New York, pp. 247–282.

Jones, J. B., and E. R. Segnit, 1971. The nature of opal I. Nomenclature and constituent phases, *Geol. Soc. Australia Jour.* **18**:57–67.

Jones, J. B., and E. R. Segnit, 1972. Genesis of cristobalite and tridymite at low temperatures, *Geol. Soc. Australia Jour.* **18**:419–422.

Jones, J. B., and E. R. Segnit, 1975. Nomenclature and the structure of natural disordered (opaline) silica, *Contr. Mineralogy and Petrology* **51**:231–234.

Kablanow, R. I., and R. C. Surdam, 1983. Diagenesis and hydrocarbon generation in the Monterey Formation, Huasna basin, California, in *Petroleum Generation and Occurrence in the Miocene Monterey Formation, California,* C. M. Isaacs and R. E. Garrison, eds., Pacific Section, Society of Economic Paleontologists and Mineralogists Publication 33, pp. 53–68. (Reprinted in R. C. Surdam (ed.), 1984. Stratigraphic, Tectonic, Thermal, and Diagenetic Histories of the Monterey Formation,

Pismo and Huasna Basin, California, *Society of Economic Paleontologists and Mineralogists Guidebook No. 2,* pp. 53-74.

Kastner, M., J. B. Keene, and J. M. Gieskes, 1977. Diagenesis of siliceous oozes—I. Chemical controls on the rate of opal-A to opal-CT transformation—an experimental study, *Geochim. et Cosmochim. Acta* **41**:1041-1059.

Katz, B. J., and L. W. Elrod, 1983. Organic geochemistry of DSDP Site 467, offshore California, Middle Miocene to Pliocene strata, *Geochim. et Cosmochim. Acta* **47**:389-396.

Keller, M. A., 1984. *Silica Diagenesis and Lithostratigraphy of the Miocene Monterey Formation of the Northwestern Ventura Basin, California, Including Biostratigraphy, Pyrolysis Results, Chemical Analyses, and a Preliminary Temperature Zonation of the Opal-CT Zone,* U.S. Geological Survey Open-File Report 84-368, 85p.

Keller, M. A., and C. M. Isaacs, 1985. An evaluation of temperature scales for silica diagenesis in diatomaceous sequences including a new approach based on the Miocene Monterey Formation, California, *Geo-Marine Letters* **5**:31-35.

King, J. D., and G. E. Claypool, 1983. Biological marker compounds and implications for generation and migration of petroleum in rocks of the Point Conception deep-stratigraphic test well, OCS-Cal 78-164 No. 1, offshore California, in *Petroleum Generation and Occurrence in the Miocene Monterey Formation, California,* C. M. Isaacs and R. E. Garrison, eds., Pacific Section, Society of Economic Paleontologists and Mineralogists Publication 33, pp. 191-200.

Kruge, M. A., 1983. Diagenesis of Miocene biogenic sediments in Lost Hills oil field, San Joaquin basin, California, in *Petroleum Generation and Occurrence in the Miocene Monterey Formation, California,* C. M. Isaacs and R. E. Garrison, eds., Pacific Section, Society of Economic Paleontologists and Mineralogists Publication 33, pp. 39-51.

Kruge, M. A., 1984. Comparison of diagenetic indicators in the Miocene Monterey Formation in Lost Hills oil field, San Joaquin basin, California, Abstracts, Society of Economic Paleontologists and Mineralogists, Annual Midyear Meeting, August 10-13, 1984, San Jose, California, p. 46.

Lagoe, M. B., 1984. Paleogeography of Monterey Formation, Cuyama Basin, California, *Am. Assoc. Petroleum Geologists Bull.* **68**:610-627.

Lagoe, M. B., 1985. Depositional environments in the Monterey Formation, Cuyama Basin, California, *Geol. Soc. America Bull.* **96**:1296-1312.

LeClaire, J. P., and K. R. Kelts, 1982. Calcium carbonate and organic carbon stratigraphy of late Quaternary laminated and homogeneous diatom oozes from the Guaymas Slope, HPC Site 480, Gulf of California, in J. R. Curray, D. G. Moore, et al., *Initial Reports of the Deep Sea Drilling Project,* vol. 64, U.S. Government Printing Office, Washington, D.C., pp. 1263-1275.

Lisitzin, A. P., 1972. *Sedimentation in the World Ocean,* Society of Economic Paleontologists and Mineralogists Special Publication 17, 218p.

MacDonald, G. H., 1956. Miocene of the Sechura Desert, Peru, *Soc. Geol. Peru Bol.* **30**:225-242.

Magoon, L. B., and C. M. Isaacs, 1983. Chemical characteristics of some crude oils from the Santa Maria basin, California, in *Petroleum Generation and Occurrence in the Miocene Monterey Formation, California,* C. M. Isaacs and R. E. Garrison, eds., Pacific Section, Society of Economic Paleontologists and Mineralogists Publication 33, pp. 201-211.

Malouta, D. N., D. S. Gorsline, and S. E. Thornton, 1981. Processes and rates of Recent (Holocene) basin filling in an active transform margin: Santa Monica Basin, California Continental Borderland, *Jour. Sed. Petrology* **51**:1077-1095.

McCulloh, T. H., 1979. Implications for petroleum appraisal, in *Geologic Studies of the Point Conception Deep Stratigraphic Test Well OCS-Cal 78-164 No. 1 Outer*

Continental Shelf Southern California, United States, H. E. Cook, ed., U.S. Geological Survey Open-File Report 79-1218, pp. 26–42.

McCulloh, T. H., and L. A. Beyer, 1979. Geothermal gradients, in *Geologic Studies of the Point Conception Deep Stratigraphic Test Well OCS-Cal 78-164 No. 1 Outer Continental Shelf Southern California, United States,* H. E. Cook, ed., U.S. Geological Survey Open-File Report 79-1218, pp. 43–48.

McGuire, M. D., J. R. Bowersox, and L. J. Earnest, 1983. Diagenetically enhanced entrapment of hydrocarbons—southeastern Lost Hills fractured shale pool, Kern County, California, in *Petroleum Generation and Occurrence in the Miocene Monterey Formation, California,* C. M. Isaacs and R. E. Garrison, eds., Pacific Section, Society of Economic Paleontologists and Mineralogists Publication 33, pp. 171–183.

Mertz, K. A., Jr., 1984*a.* Diagenetic aspects, Sandholdt member, Miocene Monterey Formation, Santa Lucia Mountains, California: Implications for depositional and burial environments, in *Dolomites of the Monterey Formation and Other Organic-rich Units,* R. E. Garrison, M. Kastner, and D. H. Zenger, eds., Pacific Section, Society of Economic Paleontologists and Mineralogists Publication 41, pp. 49–73.

Mertz, K. A., Jr., 1984*b.* Origin and depositional history of the Sandholdt Member, Miocene Monterey Formation, Santa Lucia Range, California, Ph.D. dissertation, University of California, Santa Cruz, 295p.

Milner, C. W. D., 1982. Geochemical analyses of sedimentary organic matter and interpretation of maturation and source potential, in *How to Assess Maturation and Paleotemperatures,* Society of Economic Paleontologists and Mineralogists Short Course 7, pp. 217–252.

Milner, C. W. D., M. A. Rogers, and C. R. Evans, 1977. Petroleum transformations in reservoirs, *Jour. Geochem. Exploration* **7**:101–153.

Mitsui, K., and K. Taguchi, 1977. Silica mineral diagenesis in Neogene Tertiary shales in the Tempoku district, Hokkaido, Japan, *Jour. Sed. Petrology* **47**:158–167.

Mizutani, S., 1970. Silica minerals in the early stage of diagenesis, *Sedimentology* **15**:419–436.

Mizutani, S., 1977. Progressive ordering of cristobalitic silica in the early stage of diagenesis, *Contr. Mineralogy and Petrology* **61**:129–140.

Mulhern, M. E., J. C. Eacmen, Jr., and G. K. Lester, 1983. Geology and oil occurrence of displaced diatomite member, Monterey Formation—McKittrick oil field, in *Petroleum Generation and Occurrence in the Miocene Monterey Formation, California,* C. M. Isaacs and R. E. Garrison, eds., Pacific Section, Society of Economic Paleontologists and Mineralogists Publication 33, pp. 17–37.

Mulhern, M. E., J. E. Laing, J. E. Senecal, R. E. Widdicombe, C. Isselhardt, and J. R. Bowersox, 1985. Electrofacies identification of lithology and stratigraphic trap, southeast Lost Hills fractured shale pool, Kern County, California, *Am. Assoc. Petroleum Geologists Bull.* **69**:671.

Murata, K. J., I. Friedman, and M. Cremer, 1972. *Geochemistry of Diagenetic Dolomites in Miocene Marine Formations of California and Oregon,* U.S. Geological Survey Professional Paper 724-C, 12p.

Murata, K. J., I. Friedman, and J. D. Gleason, 1977. Oxygen isotope relations between diagenetic silica minerals in Monterey Shale, Temblor Range, California, *Am. Jour. Sci.* **277**:259–272.

Murata, K. J., I. Friedman, and B. M. Madsen, 1969. *Isotopic Composition of Diagenetic Carbonates in Marine Miocene Formations of California and Oregon,* U.S. Geological Survey Professional Paper 614-B, 24p.

Murata, K. J., and R. R. Larson, 1975. Diagenesis of Miocene siliceous shales, Temblor Range, California, *U.S. Geol. Survey Jour. Research* **3**:553–566.

Murata, K. J., and J. K. Nakata, 1974. Cristobalitic stage in the diagenesis of diatomaceous shale, *Science* **184**:567–568.

Oil and Gas Journal, 1981. Chevron unveils oil discovery off California, *Oil and Gas Jour.* **79**(46):56.

Oil and Gas Journal, 1984. Arco tests oil in Point Pedernales step-out, *Oil and Gas Jour.* **82**(44):32.

Orr, W. L., 1983. Comments on pyrolytic hydrocarbon yields in source-rock evaluation, in *Advances in Organic Geochemistry 1981,* M. Bjorøy, et al. eds., John Wiley & Sons, New York, pp. 775–787.

Orr, W. L., 1984*a*. *Geochemistry of Asphaltic Monterey Oils from the Santa Maria Basin and Santa Barbara Channel Area Offshore,* Division of Geochemistry Abstracts, American Chemical Society, 187th National Meeting.

Orr, W. L., 1984*b*. *Sulfur and Sulfur Isotope Ratios in Monterey Oils of the Santa Maria Basin and Santa Barbara Channel Area,* Abstracts, Society of Economic Paleontologists and Mineralogists, Annual Midyear Meeting, August 10–13, 1984, San Jose, California, p. 62.

Orr, W. L., in press. Kerogen/asphaltene/sulfur relationships in sulfur-rich Monterey oils, in *Advances in Organic Geochemistry 1986,* D. Leythaeuser, ed.

Palacas, J. G., D. E. Anders, and J. D. King, 1985. South Florida Basin—A prime example of carbonate source rocks of petroleum, in *Petroleum Geochemistry and Source Rock Potential of Carbonate Rocks,* J. G. Palacas, ed., American Association of Petroleum Geology, Studies in Geology 18, Tulsa, Okla. pp. 71–96.

Pao, G. A., 1977. Sedimentary history of California Continental Borderland basins as indicated by organic carbon content, M.S. Thesis, University of Southern California, Los Angeles, 112p.

Petersen, N. F., and P. J. Hickey, 1983. Evidence of early generation of oil from Miocene source rocks, California coastal basins, in *Petroleum Generation and Occurrence in the Miocene Monterey Formation, California,* C. M. Isaacs and R. E. Garrison, eds., Pacific Section, Society of Economic Mineralogists and Paleontologists Publication 33, p. 226.

Petersen, N. F., and P. J. Hickey, 1984. California Plio-Miocene oils: Evidence of early generation, in *Exploration for Heavy Crude Oil and Bitumen,* R. F. Meyer, ed., American Association of Petroleum Geologists Research Conference, October 28–November 2, Santa Maria, California, Preprints, vol. 2.

Petersen, N. F., and P. J. Hickey, 1987. California Plio-Miocene oils: Evidence of early generation, in *Exploration for Heavy Crude Oil and Bitumen,* R. F. Meyer, ed., American Association of Petroleum Geologists, Studies in Geology 23 (in press), Tulsa, Okla.

Philippi, G. T., 1965. On the depth, time and mechanism of petroleum generation, *Geochim. et Cosmochim. Acta* **29**:1021–1049.

Pisciotto, K. A., 1978. Basinal sedimentary facies and diagenetic aspects of the Monterey Shale, California, Ph.D dissertation, University of California, Santa Cruz, 450p.

Pisciotto, K. A., 1981. Diagenetic trends in the siliceous facies of the Monterey Shale in the Santa Maria region, California, *Sedimentology* **28**:547–571.

Pisciotto, K. A., and R. E. Garrison, 1981. Lithofacies and depositional environments of the Monterey Formation, California, in *The Monterey Formation and Related Siliceous Rocks of California,* R. E. Garrison and R. G. Douglas, eds., Pacific Section, Society of Economic Paleontologists and Mineralogists Publication 15, pp. 97–122.

Pitman, W. C., III, 1978. Relationship between eustacy and stratigraphic sequences of passive margins, *Geol. Soc. America. Bull.* **89**:1389–1403.

Powell, T. G., and D. M. McKirdy, 1973. The effect of source material, rock type and diagenesis on the *n*-alkane content of sediments, *Geochim. et Cosmochim. Acta* **37**:623–633.

Powell, T. G., and L. R. Snowdon, 1983. A composite hydrocarbon generation model implications for evaluation of basins for oil and gas. *Erdol und Kohle Erdgas Petrochemie* **36**:169–170.

Redwine, L. E., 1981. Hypothesis combining dilation, natural hydraulic fracturing, and dolomitization to explain petroleum reservoirs in Monterey Shale, Santa Maria area, California, *Am. Assoc. Petroleum Geologists Bull.* **65**:977. (Also published in *The Monterey Formation and Related Siliceous Rocks of California,* R. E. Garrison and R. G. Douglas, eds., Pacific Section, Society of Economic Paleontologists and Mineralogists Publication 15, pp. 221–248.)

Regan, L. J., Jr., and A. W. Hughes, 1949. Fractured reservoirs of Santa Maria district, California, *Am. Assoc. Petroleum Geologists Bull.* **33**:32–51.

Roehl, P. O., 1981. Dilation brecciation—Proposed mechanism of fracturing, petroleum expulsion, and dolomitization in Monterey Formation, California, *Am. Assoc. Petroleum Geologists Bull.* **65**:980–981. (Also published in *The Monterey Formation and Related Siliceous Rocks of California,* R. E. Garrison and R. G. Douglas, eds., Pacific Section, Society of Economic Paleontologists and Mineralogists Publication 15, pp. 285–315.)

Seifert, W. K., and J. M. Moldowan, 1978. Applications of steranes, terpanes and monoaromatics to the maturation, migration and source of crude oils, *Geochim. et Cosmochim. Acta* **42**:77–95.

Seifert, W. K., J. M. Moldowan, G. W. Smith, and E. V. Whitehead, 1978. First proof of structure of a C_{28}-pentacyclic triterpane in petroleum, *Nature* **271**:436–437.

Sofer, Z., 1984. Stable carbon isotope compositions of crude oils: application to source depositional environments and petroleum alteration, *Am. Assoc. Petroleum Geologists Bull.* **68**:31–49.

Staplin, F. L., 1969. Sedimentary organic matter, organic metamorphism, and oil and gas occurrence, *Bull. Canadian Petroleum Geology* **17**:47–66.

Stearns, D. W., and M. Friedman, 1972. Reservoirs in fractured rock, in *Stratigraphic Oil and Gas Fields: Classification, Exploration Methods, and Case Histories,* R. E. King, ed., American Association of Petroleum Geologists Memoir 16, pp. 82–106.

Stein, C. L., and R. J. Kirkpatrick, 1976. Experimental porcelanite recrystallization kinetics: A nucleation and growth model, *Jour. Sed. Petrology* **46**:430–435.

Summerhayes, C. P., 1981. Oceanographic controls on organic matter in the Miocene Monterey Formation, offshore California, in *The Monterey Formation and Related Siliceous Rocks of California,* R. E. Garrison and R. G. Douglas, eds., Pacific Section, Society of Economic Paleontologists and Mineralogists Publication 15, pp. 213–219.

Surdam, R. C., ed., 1984. *Stratigraphic, Tectonic, Thermal, and Diagenetic Histories of the Monterey Formation, Pismo and Huasna Basin, California,* Society of Economic Paleontologists and Mineralogists Guidebook No. 2, 94p.

Surdam, R. C., and K. O. Stanley, 1981. Diagenesis and migration of hydrocarbons in the Monterey Formation, Pismo syncline, California, in *The Monterey Formation and Related Siliceous Rocks of California,* R. E. Garrison and R. G. Douglas, eds., Pacific Section, Society of Economic Paleontologists and Mineralogists Publication 15, pp. 317–327. (Reprinted in R. C. Surdam, (ed.), 1984. Stratigraphic, tectonic, thermal, and diagenetic histories of the Monterey Formation, Pismo and Huasna Basin, California, *Society of Economic Paleontologists and Mineralogists Guidebook No. 2,* pp. 84–94.)

Taliaferro, N. L., 1933. The relation of volcanism to diatomaceous and associated siliceous sediments, *California Univ. Pubs. Geol. Sci.* **23**:1–56.

Taylor, J. C., 1976. *Geologic Appraisal of the Petroleum Potential of Offshore Southern California: The Borderland Compared to Onshore Coastal Basins,* U.S. Geological Survey Circular 730, 43p.

Tissot, B. P., and D. H. Welte, 1978. *Petroleum Formation and Occurrence,* Springer-Verlag, Berlin, 538p.

U.S. Geological Survey, 1974. *Proposed Plan of Development, Santa Ynez Unit, Santa Barbara Channel, Off California—Final Environment Statement,* U.S. Geological Survey Final Environmental Statement 74-20, 3 vols. (Partially reprinted as Geology and reservoir characteristics of the Santa Ynez Unit, Santa Barbara Channel, off California, in *Petroleum Generation and Occurrence in the Miocene Monterey Formation, California,* C. M. Isaacs and R. E. Garrison, eds., 1983. Pacific Section, Society of Economic Mineralogists and Paleontologists Publication 33, pp. 111–130.)

Vail, P. R., and J. Hardenbol, 1979. Sea-level changes during the Tertiary, *Oceanus* **22:**71–79.

Van Dorsselaer, A., P. Albrecht, and J. Connan, 1977. Changes in composition of polycyclic alkanes by thermal maturation (Yallourn lignite, Australia), in *Advances in Organic Geochemistry 1975,* R. Campos and J. Goni, eds., Empresa Nacional Adaro de Investigaciones Mineras, Madrid, pp. 53–59.

Walker, A. L., T. H. McCulloh, N. F. Petersen, and R. J. Stewart, 1983. Anomalously low reflectance of vitrinite in comparison with other petroleum source-rock maturation indices, from the Miocene Modelo Formation in the Los Angeles basin, California, in *Petroleum Generation and Occurrence in the Miocene Monterey Formation, California,* C. M. Isaacs and R. E. Garrison, eds., Pacific Section, Society of Economic Paleontologists and Mineralogists Publication 33, pp. 185–190.

Waples, D. W., 1980. Time and temperature in petroleum formation: Application of Lopatin's method to petroleum exploration, *Am. Assoc. Petroleum Geologists Bull.* **64:**916–926.

Waples, D. W., 1981. *Organic Geochemistry for Exploration Geologists,* Burgess, Minneapolis, 151p.

Welte, D. H., and D. W. Waples, 1973. Uber die bevorzugung geradzahliger *n*-alkane in sedimentgesteinen, *Naturwissenschaften* **60:**516–517.

Williams, B., 1985a. Access problems cool exploration off California, *Oil and Gas Jour.* **83**(2):65–69.

Williams, B., 1985b. Big finds spur push off California, *Oil and Gas Jour.* **83**(2):55–64.

Williams, L. A., 1984. Subtidal stromatolites in Monterey Formation and other organic-rich rocks as suggested source contributors to petroleum formation, *Am. Assoc. Petroleum Geologists Bull.* **68:**1879–1893.

Williams, L. A., and S. A. Graham, 1982. *Monterey Formation and Associated Coarse Clastic Rocks, Central San Joaquin Basin, California,* Pacific Section, Society of Economic Paleontologists and Mineralogists Publication 25, 95p.

Williams, L. A., and C. Reimers, 1983. Role of bacterial mats in oxygen-deficient marine basins and coastal upwelling regimes: Preliminary report, *Geology* **11:**267–269.

Wilson, H., and B. Williams, 1981. Potential for giant finds seen on OCS Sale 53 tracts, *Oil and Gas Jour.* **79**(23):50–53.

5

Petroleum Occurrence, Generation, and Accumulation in the Miocene Siliceous Deposits of Japan

Koichi Aoyagi

Japan National Oil Corporation
Tokyo, Japan

Azuma Iijima

University of Tokyo
Tokyo, Japan

ABSTRACT. Siliceous shales are generally found in formations of the Miocene Onnagawa provincial stage of Japan from north Hokkaido Island to northeast Honshu Island. These formations are correlative in age and lithology to the Daegock Formation in the Pohang area of eastern South Korea and the middle part of the Monterey Formation in California. The geologic age of these formations is late middle Miocene, approximately 10–12 Ma.

These deposits consist mainly of hard mudstone, siliceous shale, diatomaceous mudstone, and pyroclastic rock. Lenses of marlstone are found in places in the mudstone and shale. Micropaleontological assemblages indicate that these rocks were deposited at bathyal depths under stagnant water masses, which were affected by cold upwelling currents.

Major oil and gas fields in Japan are located in the Akita and Niigata areas of Honshu Island. The Onnagawa Formation in Akita has produced 5.4 million kl of crude oil (about 18% of the total production in Japan) and 0.8 billion m^3 of natural gas (3%). The well-known oil and gas fields producing from the Onnagawa Formation are Asahikawa, Fukubezawa, Kurokawa, Toyokawa, and Yabase. The Lower Teradomari Formation in Niigata, equivalent to the Onnagawa Formation, has produced 6.1 million kl of oil (approximately 21% of the total production in Japan) and 4 billion m^3 of gas (16%). The most notable oil and gas fields producing from the Lower Teradomari Formation are Besho, Higashiyama, Kubiki, and Niitsu.

Producing reservoirs in these oil and gas fields are volcanic rock, tuff, tuffaceous sandstone, and carbonate rock. Tuff and tuffaceous sandstone are the most common reservoir rocks, while fractured siliceous rocks, which are common in the Monterey Formation of California, are rare. The effective porosity of reservoirs, excluding volcanic rocks, ranges from 10% to 40%, and air permeability ranges from 5 md to 30 md. Salinity of the formation water ranges from 5,000 mg/l to 17,000 mg/l, which is much lower than that of the Monterey Formation. Crude oil has light to medium specific gravity, while that in the Monterey Formation has heavy to extremely heavy specific gravity.

Average contents of organic carbon, hydrocarbons, and amorphous kerogen in the source rocks of the Onnagawa Formation in Akita and the Lower Teradomari Formation in Niigata show the highest values as compared with other deposits in both areas. The ratio of the number of oil and gas fields may be determined from the difference in contents of amorphous kerogen between these two areas.

INTRODUCTION

Siliceous rocks such as chert, porcelanite, and diatomite found in the Miocene deposits from north Hokkaido Island and northeast Honshu Island to the Pohang area of Korea form a part of the circum-Pacific belt of Neogene siliceous deposits extending from the western margin of North America to Far East Asia. In places these rocks have high porosity and permeability mainly due to fracturing resulting from deformation. Fractured chert and porcelanite of the Miocene Monterey Formation in California are widely known as good reservoirs for many oil and gas fields in the area. The Miocene Onnagawa Formation of Akita and the Lower Teradomari Formation of Niigata in Japan are correlative with part of the Monterey Formation and locally contain siliceous rocks with the potential to form good reservoirs, although they have not been exploited up till now.

Here, we first describe the stratigraphy and paleontology of siliceous rocks found in the middle Miocene Onnagawa provincial stage from north Hokkaido and northeast Honshu of Japan to the Pohang area of South Korea. Next we describe hydrocarbon fields, reservoir characteristics, and fluid properties of the Onnagawa Formation in Akita and the Lower Teradomari Formation in Niigata and compare them with the same characteristics of the Monterey Formation. Generation, migration, and accumulation of petroleum in the Yabase oil field of Akita and in the Kubiki gas field of Niigata are discussed last.

MIOCENE SILICEOUS DEPOSITS IN JAPAN AND KOREA

Several stratigraphic sections were studied in Japan and Korea (Fig. 5–1). Time-stratigraphic correlations can be made between these Neogene–Quaternary units (Fig. 5–2). Siliceous shales are generally found in the formations of the middle Miocene Onnagawa provincial stage of Japan; these include the lower part of Wakkanai Formation in north Hokkaido, the Kikkonai Formation in southwest Hokkaido, the Daidohji Formation in Aomori, the Onnagawa Formation in Akita, the Kusanagi Formation in Yamagata, the Lower Teradomari Formation in Niigata, and the Daegock Formation in Pohang area of eastern South Korea (Ingle, 1975; JNGA, 1982).

These formations are composed mainly of hard mudstone, siliceous shale, diatomaceous mudstone, and acidic pyroclastic rock. Lenses of marlstone are found in places in the mudstone and shale. Typical diatomites and porcelanites are recognized only in southwest Hokkaido Island and in northwest Honshu Island (Iijima and Tada, 1981). The ratio of siliceous shale to hard mudstone

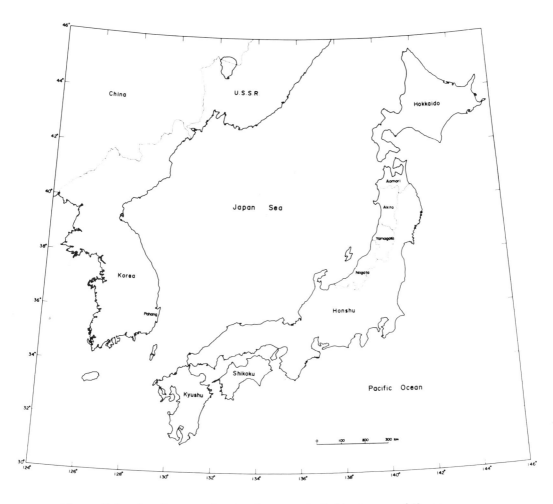

Figure 5-1.   Locality map showing the areas studied in Japan and Korea.

decreases to the south in Honshu, and stratified siliceous rocks are rare in the Lower Teradomari Formation of Niigata (Utada, 1972).

These siliceous deposits typically contain planktonic foraminifera such as *Globorotalia pseudopachyderma* and *Globigerina woodi;* benthonic foraminifera such as *Spirosigmoilinella compressa, Martinottiella communis,* and *Cyclammina japonica;* and diatoms such as *Denticulopsis hustedtii* and *Coscinodiscuss yabei* (Kim, 1965; Maiya, 1978; JNGA, 1982). These microfossil assemblages indicate that these rocks were deposited in bathyal, low-oxygen water masses, which were affected by cold ocean currents. The precise geologic ages of these deposits have not been determined. Planktonic foraminifera and diatom assemblages, however, suggest that these deposits are in large part of the late middle Miocene (approximately 10–12 Ma) and can be assigned to the planktonic foraminiferal N13–N15 zones of Blow (1969) (see Fig. 5–2). Therefore, these deposits correlate with the middle part of the Monterey Formation in California, which has been reported to be about 4.5–15 Ma (N9–N18 of Blow) by Addicott (1978).

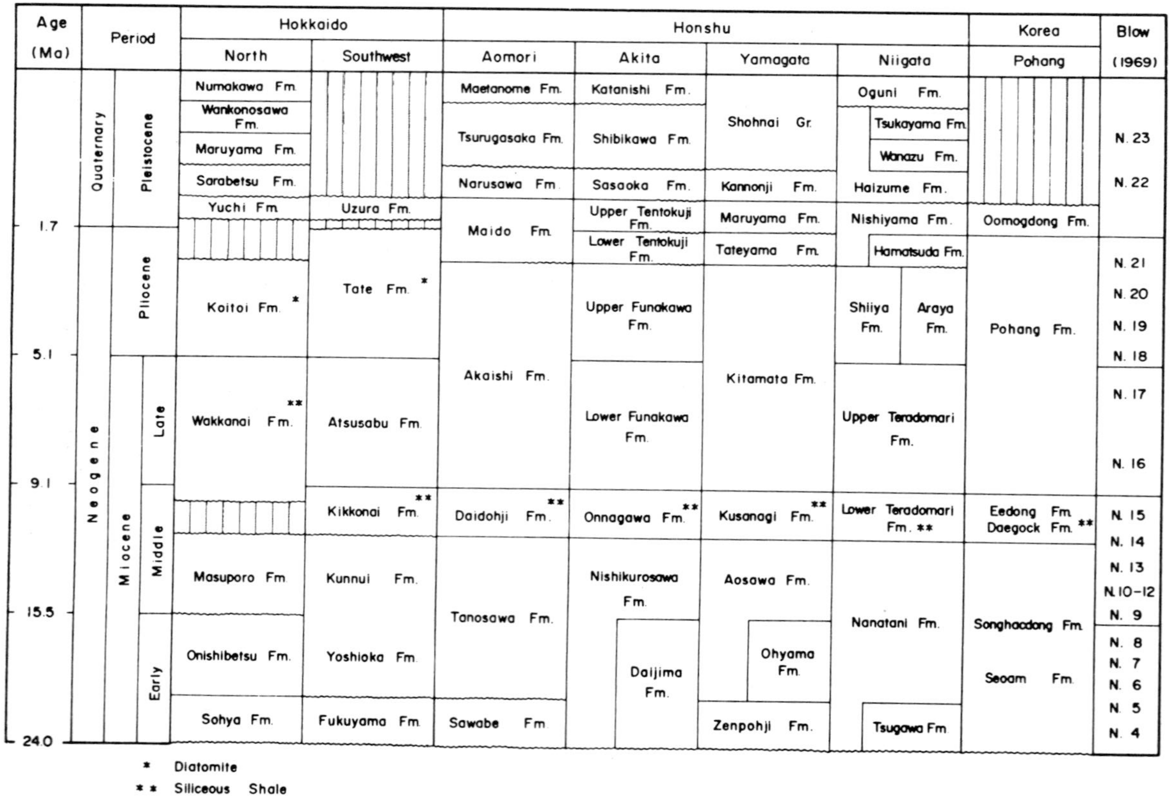

Figure 5-2. Geologic correlation of Neogene–Quaternary units in Japan and Korea. Vertical ruled areas are unconformities.

Hydrocarbon Fields in Japan

Major oil and gas fields in Japan are located in the area from central Hokkaido to northeast Honshu. The Akita and Niigata areas of Honshu Island are the most productive in Japan. Oil and gas have been produced from reservoirs of Miocene and Pliocene age. The cumulative production in Japan through the end of 1979 was 29.5 million kl of crude oil and 24.7 billion m³ of natural gas (JNGA, 1982). There is no commercial production of oil and gas in Korea, although exploration is receiving much attention.

Akita Area

In the Akita area, nineteen major oil and gas fields have been discovered. The cumulative production in the area through the end of 1979 was 12.0 million kl of crude oil and 1.6 billion m³ of natural gas (JNGA, 1982). The Onnagawa Formation has produced 5.4 million kl of oil (about 18% of the total production in Japan) and 0.8 billion m³ of gas (3%). The well-known oil and gas fields producing from the Onnagawa Formation are Asahikawa, Fukubezawa, Kurokawa, Toyokawa, and Yabase (Fig. 5-3). The hydrocarbon traps of these oil and gas fields are mainly anticlines and related faults.

The Yabase oil field is located to the west of Akita City and has been developed by the Teikoku Oil Company. The first wildcat in Yabase was drilled in 1810. Subsequently, 983 development wells were drilled. Kohya R-113, the deepest well in the field, has a total depth of 3,131 m. Yabase is the largest oil field in Japan, with cumulative production through the end of 1979 of 5.1 million kl of crude oil and 1.1 billion m³ of natural gas. The greatest annual production was 0.3 million kl of oil in 1959, and thereafter production gradually decreased to 0.02 million kl by 1979.

The trap in the Yabase oil field is a north-south elongate, symmetrical anticline paralleling the regional strike (Fig. 5-4). The structure is about 15 km long from north to south and 0.5 km wide from east to west (JAPT, 1973). The main reservoirs in the Yabase oil field range from the middle part of the Miocene Onnagawa Formation to the upper part of the Pliocene Lower Tentokuji Formation. Six oil- and gas-producing tuffaceous sandstones are found in the Onnagawa Formation and are called the VII to XII reservoirs. The average depth interval of these reservoirs ranges between 1,040 m and 1,750 m.

Niigata Area

In the Niigata area, twenty-four major oil and gas fields have been exploited. The cumulative production through the end of 1979 was 16.4 million kl of crude oil and 22.7 billion m³ of natural gas (JNGA, 1982). The Lower Teradomari Formation, equivalent to the Onnagawa Formation, produced 6.1 million kl of oil (approximately 21% of the total production in Japan) and 4 billion m³ of gas (16%). The most notable oil and gas fields producing from the Lower Teradomari Formation are Besho, Higashiyama, Kubiki, and Niitsu (Fig. 5-5). The hydrocarbon traps of these oil and gas fields are chiefly anticlines, domes, and related faults.

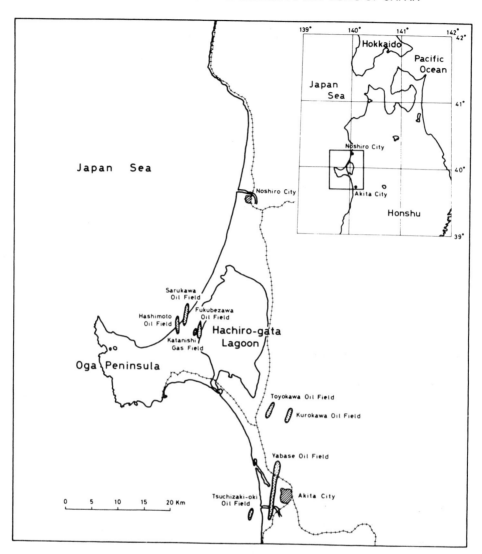

Figure 5–3. Locality map showing the major oil and gas fields producing from the Miocene Onnagawa Formation in Akita, Japan. (After Aoyagi and Iijima, 1983)

The Kubiki gas field is located northeast of Johetsu City (Fig. 5–5) and has been developed by the Teikoku Oil Company. The first wildcat in the field, Takada R-1, was drilled in 1951. Subsequently, 418 development wells were drilled. The cumulative production through the end of 1979 was 1.8 million kl of crude oil and 3.7 billion m^3 of natural gas (JNGA, 1982).

The Kubiki gas field is composed of three domal structures called Katamachi, Kuroi, and Meiji (Fig. 5–6). Each trap in the Kubiki gas field is a part of the complex dome structure (Figs. 5–6 and 5–7). The Katamachi structure is located in the highest structural position of the complex dome. The dip of each structure is less than 10°, and the structures are highly segmented by faults. The complex dome structure extends about 12 km from east to west and 11 km from north to south.

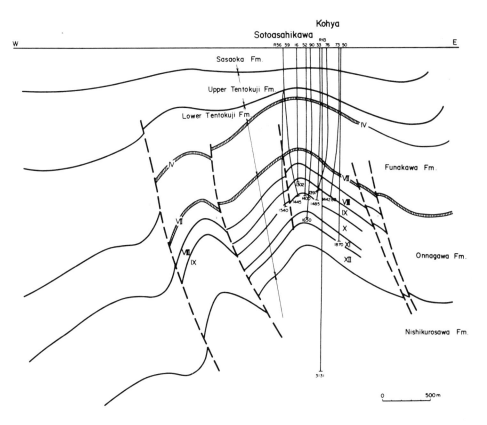

Figure 5-4. Geologic cross-section of the Yabase oil field in Akita, Japan. Roman numerals mark the oil- and gas-producing reservoirs. (After JNGA, 1982)

The main reservoirs in the Kubiki gas field range from the lower part of the Miocene Lower Teradomari Formation to the upper part of the Upper Teradomari Formation. Three oil- and gas-producing tuffaceous sandstone lenses are found in the Upper Teradomari Formation and are named B, I, and II reservoirs. Six gas-producing tuffaceous sandstones are recognized in the Lower Teradomari Formation and are called the III through VIII reservoirs. These reservoirs in the Lower Teradomari Formation are homogeneous in lithology and are found continuously throughout the area.

RESERVOIR CHARACTERISTICS
AND FLUID PROPERTIES

Producing reservoirs in the Onnagawa Formation of Akita and the Lower Teradomari Formation of Niigata are volcanic rock, tuff, tuffaceous sandstone, and carbonate rock. It is reported that 75% of total hydrocarbons in the Onnagawa Formation have been produced from tuff and tuffaceous sandstone, 19% from volcanic rock, and 6% from carbonate rock (JNGA, 1982). Volcanic reservoirs are productive in the Kurokawa oil field (liparitic volcanic breccia) and in the Kamihama oil field (liparite) of Akita. Carbonate rocks are found in places in the Onnagawa Formation (Aoyagi et al., 1970). Car-

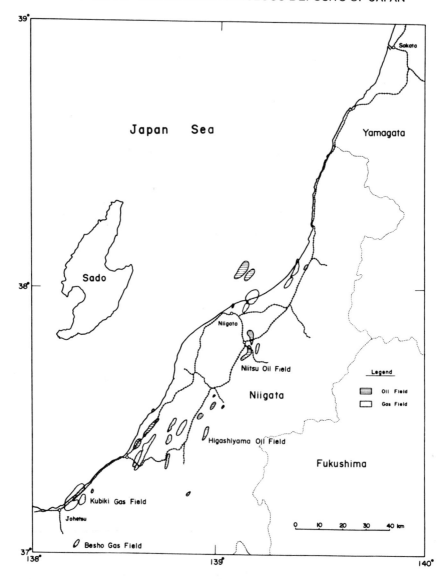

Figure 5-5. Locality map showing the major oil and gas fields, producing from the Miocene Lower Teradomari Formation in Niigata, Japan.

bonate reservoirs, however, are productive only in the Fukubezawa oil field of Akita (Takuma, 1969; Aoyagi, 1985). Tuff and tuffaceous sandstone have been the most common reservoirs found in the Onnagawa and Lower Teradomari Formations. All oil and gas fields in Akita were discovered in the areas where the abundance of tuff ranges between 40% and 60% of the stratigraphic thickness of the Onnagawa Formation (JNGA, 1982). Conversely, the most common reservoirs found in the Monterey Formation in California are siliceous rocks such as chert and porcelanite, along with locally important siliciclastic sandstone.

The effective porosity of reservoirs excluding volcanic rock in the Onnagawa Formation and sandstone in the Lower Teradomari Formation ranges

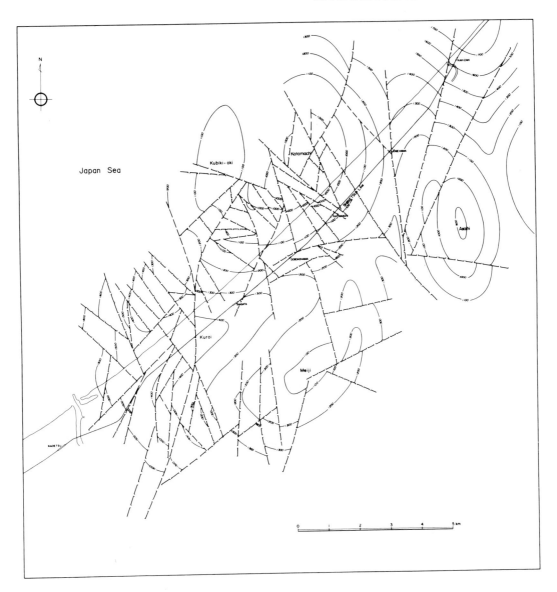

Figure 5-6. Subsurface structure map of the Kubiki gas field in Niigata, Japan. (After JNGA, 1982)

from 10% to 40%, and air permeability ranges from 10 md to 30 md (Tables 5-1 and 5-2). In contrast, volcanic reservoirs in the Kurokawa oil field in Akita and sandstone reservoirs in the Higashiyama and Niitsu oil fields in Niigata show a much higher porosity and permeability than any other type of reservoir.

The salinity of formation water in reservoirs of the Onnagawa and Lower Teradomari Formations is low, 5,000–17,000 mg/l. Formation water in the Niitsu oil field in Niigata shows extremely low salinity. According to the California Division of Oil and Gas (1974), the salinity of formation water in the Monterey Formation ranges from 10,000 mg/l to 20,000 mg/l, much higher than that in the Onnagawa and Lower Teradomari Formations.

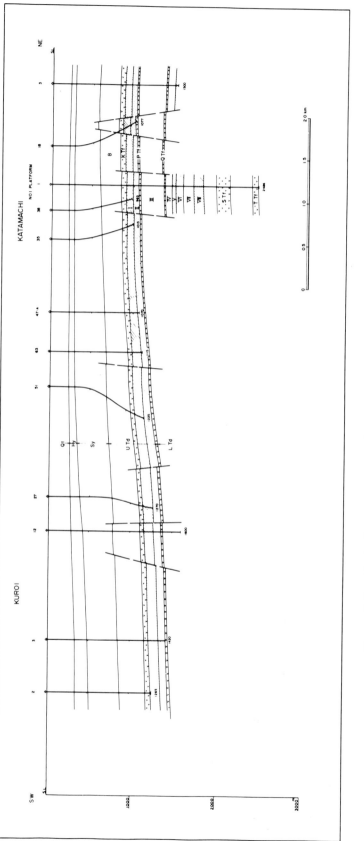

Figure 5-7. Geologic cross-section of the Kubiki gas field in Niigata, Japan. (After JNGA, 1982)

Table 5-1. Reservoir Characteristics of the Onnagawa Formation, Akita, Japan

Oil and Gas Fields	Trap	Reservoir	Depth (m)	Lithology	Area (1,000 m³)	Thickness (m)	Porosity (%)	Permeability (md)	Salinity (mg/l)
Sarukawa	Anticline fault	XII	1,460–1,480	Tuff	1,770	—	15–31	6–28	8,000–16,000
Fukubezawa	Anticline	XIII	1,265–1,335	Tuff	1,170	23	19–29	10	9,000
		XIV	1,130–1,390	Dolomite					
		XV	1,290–1,360	Dolomite					
Kurokawa	Anticline	I	255–275	Liparitic tuff	770	10	40	80	17,000
		II	295–315	Liparitic tuff					
		III	315–355	Liparitic tuff					
Toyokawa	Anticline	IV	134–149	Tuffaceous sandstone	570	—	—	—	9,500
		V	194–209	Tuffaceous sandstone					
		VI	254–269	Tuffaceous sandstone					
		VII	320–340	Tuffaceous sandstone					
		VII	1,044–1,114	Tuffaceous sandstone					
Yabase	Anticline fault	VIII	1,244–1,344	Tuffaceous sandstone	30–3,380	126	20–40	25–30	10,050–16,700
		IX	1,354–1,479	Tuffaceous sandstone					
		X	1,484–1,584	Tuffaceous sandstone					
		XI	1,634–1,684	Tuffaceous sandstone					
		XII	1,684–1,754	Tuffaceous sandstone					
Michikawa	Anticline	—	205–225	Tuffaceous sandstone	40	—	—	—	—
Asahikawa	Anticline	III	365–385	Liparite	220	10	—	—	—
Tsuchizaki-oki	Anticline fault	X	1,395–1,455	Tuff	300	32	15–30	5	5,000–11,500
		XIII	1,555–1,570	Tuff					
Kamihama	Anticline fault	I	217–417	Liparite	140	—	—	—	12,800

Source: After Aoyagi and Iijima, 1983.

Table 5-2. Reservoir Characteristics of the Lower Teradomari Formation, Niigata, Japan

Oil and Gas Fields	Trap	Reservoir	Depth (m)	Lithology	Area (1,000 m²)	Thickness (m)	Porosity (%)	Permeability (md)	Salinity (mg/l)
Higashiyama	Anticline	E	339–359	Sandstone	810	27	25–27	300–1,500	—
		F	639–689	Sandstone					
Katamachi	Anticline fault	III	1,035–1,315	Tuff					
		IV	1,350–1,405	Tuff					
		V	1,435–1,465	Tuff					
		VI	1,475–1,565	Tuff	640–6,100	109	10–25	—	5,000–11,000
		VII	1,565–1,685	Tuff					
		VIII	1,685–1,805	Tuff					
		STf	1,885–1,965	Tuff					
Kuroi	Anticline fault	III	1,447–1,592	Tuff					
		IV	1,622–1,672	Tuff					
		V	1,692–1,732	Tuff	60–5,600	54	15–25	—	5,000–8,000
		VI	1,742–1,822	Tuff					
		VII	1,822–1,942	Tuff					
Meiji	Anticline	III	1,116–1,296	Tuff	200–2,600	23	20	—	6,500
Niitsu	Anticline thinning	IIIa	452–562	Sandstone	870	15	30–40	200	120
		IIIb	697–843	Sandstone					
Besho	Anticline	IIIg	860–1,050	Tuffaceous sandstone	—	12	17–20	—	6,000–9,000

Source: After Japan Natural Gas Association, 1982.

Specific gravity (15/4°C) of crude oil produced from the Onnagawa Formation can be classified into three groups: (1) medium (0.830–0.904, API 39–24 at 60/60°F), (2) heavy (0.904–0.966, 25–15), and (3) extremely heavy (0.966+, 15–) oil (Table 5-3). Medium oil is the most abundant in the formation. Crude oil produced from the Lower Teradomari Formation normally shows a much lower specific gravity (0.834 on the average) than that from the Onnagawa Formation (0.901 on the average) and is also classified into three groups: (1) light (0.830–, 39+), medium, and heavy oil (Table 5-4). Light oil is the most common in the formation. The degree of degradation of oil by the invasion of meteoric water is determined by the ratio of n-alkanes/naphthenes (Tables 5-3 and 5-4). The specific gravity of oil typically reflects the degree of water degradation. The contents of sulphur and paraffin wax in the oil are usually low. The average content of sulphur (0.09%) and paraffin wax (0.64%) in the Lower Teradomari Formation are still lower than those (0.49% and 1.79%) in the Onnagawa Formation. Yield value of gasoline in oil produced from the Lower Teradomari Formation is much higher than that from the Onnagawa Formation.

In contrast, the API specific gravity of crude oil produced from the Monterey Formation in California is typically lower than 24, ranging from heavy to extremely heavy oil (California Division of Oil and Gas, 1974). Sulphur content in the formation ranges from 0.7% to 1.0% and is almost the same as in the Onnagawa Formation. Paraffin wax content in the Monterey Formation ranges from 0.4% to 0.7% and is much lower than that found in the Onnagawa and Lower Teradomari formations. The yield value of gasoline in crude oil from the Monterey Formation is extremely low and closely resembles that in the heavy and extremely heavy oil from the Onnagawa and Lower Teradomari formations.

Organic Matter in Source Rocks

Argillaceous rocks from each Quaternary and Neogene formation in the Akita and Niigata areas were analyzed for contents of organic carbon, hydrocarbons, and amorphous kerogen in the insoluble organic matter (Table 5-5). The highest average total organic carbon (TOC) contents occur in the petroleum source rocks from the Onnagawa and Lower Teradomari formations, which indicate that these formations are the best target horizons for exploration in the Akita and Niigata areas. In contrast, rock-eval analysis reveals a consistent and extraordinarily high organic carbon richness in the Monterey Formation at the Lost Hills oil field in California (Kruge, 1983); TOC values range between 1.43% and 10.23%, with a mean of 4.06%. The TOC values for eleven outcrop samples from the Daegock Formation in Korea range from 0.46% to 2.47% and average 1.44% (Chap. 6).

The average content of hydrocarbons in the source rocks is usually controlled by the quantity and quality of organic matter supplied into the basin, the paleotemperature history of the buried organic matter, and the mechanism of hydrocarbon migration. Therefore, it is reasonable to consider that the measured content of hydrocarbons alone may not correlate with the quality of the source rocks. It is also true, however, that the average content of hy-

Table 5-3. Physical and Chemical Properties of Crude Oil Produced from the Onnagawa Formation, Akita, Japan

Oil and Gas Fields	Well Number	Depth (m)	Specific Gravity (15/4°C)	Water De-gradation	Sulphur (%)	Paraffin Wax (%)	Yield Value (%) Gasoline	Yield Value (%) Heavy Oil
Fukubezawa	SK-6	1,300	0.841	−	0.29	2.21	37	44
Toyokawa	Mixture of 120 wells	350	0.990	+ +	0.80	0.39	3	77
Urayama	?	250–350	0.945	+ +	0.65	0.75	0	78
Kurokawa	Mixture of 40 wells	350	0.937	+ +	0.42	0.81	3	77
Kita-akita	Mixture of 9 wells	1,384–1,711	0.845	−	0.22	2.82	38	40
Sotoasahikawa	Mixture of 11 wells	1,194–1,840	0.866	−	0.45	2.84	30	49
Koya	Mixture of 5 wells	1,023–1,462	0.883	−	0.42	3.16	31	51
Yabase	Mixture of 3 wells	1,298–1,583	0.856	−	0.29	2.91	31	48
Omonogawa	Mixture of 8 wells	1,192–1,562	0.841	−	0.24	2.46	38	39
Araya	Mixture of 17 wells	1,135–1,500	0.850	−	0.17	2.53	34	43
Michikawa	C-1	200	0.973	+ +	0.74	0.57	0	89
Niida	R-11	950	0.928	+	0.88	1.42	10	70
Toyoyuwa	R-3	880	0.912	+	0.87	1.12	11	68
Kamihama	R-25	460–530	0.944	+ +	0.42	1.04	2	76

Source: After Aoyagi and Iijima, 1983.

Notes: + + means strong degradation of oil by invasion of meteoric water; + means weak degradation; − means no degradation.

Table 5-4. Physical and Chemical Properties of Crude Oil Produced from the Lower Teradomari Formation, Niigata, Japan

Oil and Gas Fields	Well Number	Depth (m)	Specific Gravity (15/4°C)	Water De-gradation	Sulphur (%)	Paraffin Wax (%)	Yield Value (%)	
							Gasoline	Heavy Oil
Minami-aga	Mixture of 4 wells	2,130–2,320	0.827	−	0.14	2.11	35	39
Minami-aga	Mixture of 5 wells	2,030–2,270	0.817	−	0.18	1.82	39	37
Fujikawa	SK-16	3,000	0.773	−	0.02	0.02	76	8
Betsuyama	?	1,550	0.839	?	0.06	?	40	27
Nagamine	?	850	0.863	?	0.10	?	37	35
Katamachi	Mixture	1,100–1,200	0.904	+	0.13	0.61	12	57
Higashi-kuroi	Mixture of 3 wells	1,150–1,540	0.807	−	0.04	0.32	74	14
Meiji	?	1,260	0.814	+	0.02	0.00	79	5
Meiji	R-20	1,040	0.934	−	0.19	0.17	0	70
Betsusho	AB-5	1,970	0.750	−	0.01	0.03	96	0
Maki	?	?	0.824	?	0.05	?	56	16
Gohtsu	?	1,083	0.854	?	0.09	?	36	30

Note: + means weak degradation of oil by invasion of meteoric water; − means no degradation.

Table 5-5. Average Content of Organic Carbon, Hydrocarbon, and Amorphous Kerogen in Insoluble Organic Matter in Argillaceous Rocks of Each Formation in Akita and Niigata Areas, Japan

Age	Akita Area				Niigata Area			
	Formation	Organic Carbon (%)	Hydrocarbon (ppm)	Amorphous Kerogen (%)	Formation	Organic Carbon (%)	Hydrocarbon (ppm)	Amorphous Kerogen (%)
Early Pleistocene	Sasaoka	0.57	67	37.5	Hiazume	0.70	112	16.0
Pliocene	Upper Tentokuji	0.86	106	70.5	Nishiyama	0.78	114	25.9
	Lower Tentokuji	0.86	106	81.6				
Late Miocene	Funakawa	1.12	157	87.6	Shiiya	0.79	122	34.5
Middle Miocene	Onnagawa	1.73	300	91.2	Teradomari	1.09	270	76.8
	Nishikurosawa	0.86	209	83.6	Nanatani	0.82	280	73.8

Source: After Japan Natural Gas Association, 1982.

drocarbons in argillaceous rocks of the Onnagawa and Lower Teradomari formations is much higher than that of any other formation in either area.

The average content of amorphous (sapropelic) kerogen in the insoluble organic matter in the Onnagawa and Lower Teradomari formations also shows the highest values relative to all other formations in both areas. Miocene deposits in Akita show higher contents of kerogen than those in Niigata, indicating that the Miocene source rocks in Akita tend to produce oil rather than gas and explaining why the number of oil fields in Akita is much greater than in Niigata.

GENERATION, MIGRATION, AND ACCUMULATION OF PETROLEUM

Many theories have been proposed concerning the generation, migration, and accumulation of petroleum in the Neogene deposits of northeast Honshu, Japan. Earlier opinions were based mainly on the so-called early origin theory of petroleum that proposed that generation occurred during early diagenesis (the proto-petroleum theory by Brooks, 1936). The following discussion on the generation, migration, and accumulation of petroleum at the Yabase oil field in Akita and the Kubiki gas field in Niigata is based on the late origin hypothesis of petroleum generation, which is suggested to have occurred during late diagenesis (the kerogen theory of Abelson, 1963).

A restored geologic cross-section, along with depth/temperature relationships was constructed for the Yabase oil field in Akita as conditions appeared at the end of the late Miocene Funakawa stage (see Fig. 5–8). The Yabase anticline was a part of the basin structure formed before and during the Funakawa stage. Aiba (1977) considered that the main reservoirs (VIII–IX reservoirs) of the Onnagawa Formation at the end of this stage were buried to approximately 1,200 m depth and reached a temperature of about 70°C, which was not a high enough temperature to generate oil. He also suggested that if the paleotemperature had been higher, any oil generated would have migrated to higher positions in the basin, and this would have resulted in sparse accumulation of oil in the Yabase anticline, which was formed in the center of the basin at a later time. Konno (1964) reported that the migration and accumulation of oil into the anticlinally folded Onnagawa Formation of the Yabase oil field occurred during deformation that took place during the Pliocene Lower Tentokuji stage. Aiba supported this idea based on the fact that the VIII–IX reservoirs of the Onnagawa Formation reached burial depths of 1,500–1,650 m at the end of the Lower Tentokuji stage, with estimated paleotemperatures of 87–94°C, which are sufficient to generate considerable amounts of oil.

Large amounts of gas accumulated in the III–VII reservoirs of the Lower Teradomari Formation in the Katamachi structure of the Kubiki gas field, while gas is found only in the III reservoir in the Meiji structure. These two structures are adjacent to one another at the Kubiki gas field and have almost the same quality of source and reservoir rocks. Aiba (1963) studied the tectonic development of these two stuctures and concluded that the Katamachi struc-

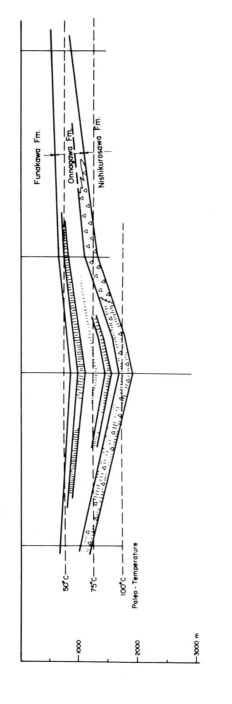

Figure 5–8. Restored geologic cross-section and paleotemperature/depth relationships in the Yabase oil field at the end of the late Miocene Funakawa stage. (After JNGA, 1982).

ture has been located at a higher structural position in the Kubiki area since the end of the Miocene Lower Teradomari stage, while the Meiji structure developed, forming a hydrocarbon trap, in the Plio-Pleistocene Nishiyama stage. From this conclusion, he further considered that the III reservoir of the Lower Teradomari Formation was buried to 1,300 m depth and reached 60°C at the end of Pliocene Shiiya stage, which was not a high enough temperature to generate gas. At the same stage, the IV reservoir was buried to a depth of 1,700 m and reached a paleotemperature of 75°C, which is sufficient to generate gas. At the end of Plio-Pleistocene Nishiyama stage, the IV–VII reservoirs were buried to 2,000–2,500 m and reached 85–100°C, which is too high to generate gas. In the Kubiki gas field, therefore, accumulation of natural gas would have occurred at approximately 1,400 m of burial depth at a temperature of 65–85°C during the Pliocene Shiiya and Plio-Pleistocene Nishiyama stages.

CONCLUSION

Our main conclusions follow:

1. Siliceous deposits in Japan and Korea belong to the late middle Miocene (approximately 10–12 Ma) and can be correlated with the middle part of the Monterey Formation in California.
2. Siliceous shales are found in the middle Miocene Onnagawa Formation of Akita, the Lower Teradomari Formation of Niigata, and equivalent formations of each area in Japan and Korea.
3. Major oil and gas fields in Japan are located in Akita and Niigata areas of Honshu Island. Tuff and tuffaceous sandstone are the most common reservoirs found in the Onnagawa Formation in Akita and the Lower Teradomari Formation in Niigata, while siliceous rocks such as chert and porcelanite are common reservoirs in the Monterey Formation, along with locally important siliciclastic sandstone.
4. Salinity of the formation water in the Monterey Formation ranges from ten to twenty times greater than that in the Onnagawa and Lower Teradomari formations.
5. The specific gravity of crude oil produced from the Onnagawa Formation is normally of the medium range; that from the Lower Teradomari Formation, the light range; and that from the Monterey Formation, the heavy to extremely heavy range.
6. The average TOC content is greatest in the source rocks of the Onnagawa Formation in Akita and the Lower Teradomari Formation in Niigata relative to other deposits in the areas. TOC in the Monterey Formation ranges from three to four times greater than that in the Onnagawa and Lower Teradomari formations.

ACKNOWLEDGMENTS

The writers express their sincere appreciation to Japan National Oil Corporation (JNOC) for permission to publish this chapter. Physical and chemical properties of crude oil produced from the Onnagawa Formation in Akita and the Lower Teradomari Formation in Niigata were provided by Mr. Keisaku Kato of Japan Petroleum Exploration Company (JAPEX). Ms. Toshie Takamasa of JAPEX and Fumie Tada of JNOC drafted the figures and tables and typed the manuscript. Dr. James R. Hein of the U.S. Geological Survey read the manuscript and offered important comments to improve it. We thank them very much.

REFERENCES

Abelson, P. H., 1963. *Organic Geochemistry and the Formation of Petroleum,* Proceedings of the 6th World Petroleum Congress, pp. 397–407.

Addicott, W. O., 1978. *Neogene Biostratigraphy of Selected Areas in the California Coast Ranges,* U.S. Geological Survey Open File Report 78-446, 109p.

Aiba, J., 1963. Geological study of Kubiki gas field, *Japanese Assoc. Petroleum Technology Jour.* **28**:43–53 (in Japanese).

Aiba, J., 1977. Geohistorical consideration to the primary migration of petroleum, *Japanese Assoc. Petroleum Technology Jour.* **42**:117–128 (in Japanese).

Aoyagi, K., 1985. Origin of the carbonate reservoir rocks in Akita, northeast Honshu, Japan, in *Carbonate Petroleum Reservoirs,* P. O. Roehl and P. W. Choquette, eds., Springer-Verlag, New York.

Aoyagi, K., and A. Iijima, 1983. Reservoir characteristics and petroleum migration in the Miocene Onnagawa Formation of Akita, Japan, in *Petroleum Generation and Occurrence in the Miocene Monterey Formation, California,* C. M. Isaacs and R. E. Garrison, eds., Pacific Section, Society of Economic Paleontologists and Mineralogists, Los Angeles, pp. 75–84.

Aoyagi, K., T. Sato, and T. Kazama, 1970. Distribution and origin of the Neogene carbonate rocks in the Akita oil field, Japan, *Japanese Assoc. Petroleum Technology Jour.* **35**:67–76 (in Japanese).

Blow, W. H., 1969. *Late Middle Eocene to Recent Planktonic Foraminiferal Biostratigraphy,* Proceedings of the First International Conference on Planktonic Microfossils, Geneva, pp. 199–421.

Brooks, B. T., 1936. Origin of petroleum, chemical and geochemical aspects, *Am. Assoc. Petroleum Geologists Bull.* **58**:3–33.

California Division of Oil and Gas, 1974. *California Oil and Gas Fields (2),* Report No. TR 12, Sacramento.

Iijima, A., and R. Tada, 1981. Silica diagenesis of Neogene diatomaceous and volcaniclastic sediments in northern Japan, *Sedimentology* **28**:185–200.

Ingle, J. C., Jr., 1975. Summary of Late Paleogene-Neogene Insular Stratigraphy, Paleobathymetry, and Correlations, Philippine Sea and Sea of Japan Region, in *Initial Reports of the Deep Sea Drilling Project Leg 31,* D. E. Karig, J. C. Ingle, Jr., et al., U.S. Government Printing Office, Washington, D.C., pp. 837–855.

Japanese Association of Petroleum Technologists (JAPT), 1973. *Technology in Oilmining Industry of Japan,* Tokyo, 430p (in Japanese).

Japan Natural Gas Association (JNGA), 1982. *Oil and Natural Gas Resources in Japan,* Tokyo, 455p (in Japanese).

Kim, B. K., 1965. The stratigraphic and paleontologic studies on the Tertiary (Miocene) of the Pohang area, Korea, *Seoul Univ. Jour. Sci. Tech.,* ser. 15, pp. 32–121.

Konno, T., 1964. Time of oil accumulation in Akita Plain oil fields, Akita Prefecture, *Japanese Assoc. Petroleum Technology Jour.* **29**:315–328 (in Japanese).

Kruge, M. A., 1983. Diagenesis of Miocene biogenic sediments in Lost Hills oil field, San Joaquin basin, California, in *Petroleum Generation and Occurrence in the Miocene Monterey Formation, California,* C. M. Isaacs and R. E. Garrison, eds., Pacific

Section, Society of Economic Paleontologists and Mineralogists, Los Angeles, pp. 39-51.

Maiya, S., 1978. Late Cenozoic planktonic foraminiferal biostratigraphy of the oil field region of northeast Japan, in *Cenozoic Geology of Japan,* K. Fujita, ed., Professor Nobuo Ikebe Memorial Volume, Osaka, pp. 35-60 (in Japanese).

Takuma, T., 1969. Exploration of Fukubezawa oil field, *Jour. Japanese Petroleum Inst.* **12**:43-48 (in Japanese).

Utada, M., 1972. Diagenesis of the Neogene argillaceous rocks in Japan, *Jour. Marine Geology* **1**:1-11 (in Japanese).

6

Concentration of Uranium in Marine Siliceous Rocks

James R. Hein, Lisa A. Morgenson, and Rosemary E. Sliney

U.S. Geological Survey
Menlo Park, California

ABSTRACT. Concentrations of uranium three to eight times above the crustal average occur in circum-Pacific marine diatomite-porcelanite sequences. The average uranium content of the rocks decreases with increasing diagenesis—that is, from diatomite to porcelanite to chert. Uranium is correlated with organic matter and secondarily with biogenic silica, but these correlations are commonly masked by the presence of other constituents. The variability in uranium contents is influenced by the relative amounts of organic matter, detrital minerals, authigenic minerals, biogenic silica, and the degree of diagenesis. The series of events leading to uranium enrichment begins with the deposition of organic-matter-rich biosiliceous sediments in continental margin basins. Organic matter and biogenic silica fixed uranium from seawater during deposition and early diagenesis. Probable mechanisms include adsorption of U^{6+} and reduction of U^{6+} to relatively insoluble U^{4+} by H_2S and organic matter. Bacterial degradation of organic matter released the adsorbed uranium, which was then adsorbed predominantly by biogenic silica. During silica diagenesis uranium was again released. The uranium released during this final stage may migrate to adjacent sandstone host rocks, where economic concentrations may develop. Thus, the siliceous deposits may be considered as source rocks for uranium deposits.

INTRODUCTION

The occurrence of isolated high concentrations of uranium in marine siliceous rocks has been known for many decades (Walker et al., 1956; Troxel et al., 1957; Osterwald, 1965; Finch, 1967). Durham (in press) completed the first systematic study of the distribution of uranium and thorium in a marine siliceous unit, the Miocene Monterey Formation of California. Durham found that on the average the Monterey Formation contains five to six times the average crustal abundance of uranium and reported a maximum concentration of about 2,000 ppm for a diatomite. He suggested that the uranium is associated with organic matter and that some uranium might also be adsorbed on diatom frustules.

Here, we report the uranium and thorium concentrations in fine-grained marine siliceous rocks from formations of the circum-Pacific and from modern offshore analogues. We include several analyses from fresh water siliceous deposits for comparison. Based on these data we propose mechanisms for the concentration and mobilization of uranium in marine siliceous rocks.

We use the silica polymorph terminology of Jones and Segnit (1971) and the textural terminology of Bramlette (1946). Silica is deposited on the seafloor as opal-A (X-ray amorphous biogenic silica) tests and frustules of Radiolaria, diatoms, silicoflagellates, and spines of sponges. Through diagenesis, the siliceous ooze transforms texturally into diatomite or radiolarian earth, then to porcelanite and finally to chert. These textural transformations are accompanied by mineralogical transformations where opal-A → opal-CT → quartz. Opal-CT is a disordered, interlayered phase of cristobalite and tridymite. In places, the mineralogical transformations lag behind or come before the textural transformations, producing, for example, rocks such as quartz porcelanite or opal-CT chert.

It should be noted that although marine siliceous rocks are significantly enriched in uranium over the crustal average, they are not usually rich enough in this element to be economic targets. However, because of the diagenetic history of these rocks, the contained uranium may be mobilized and redeposited in favorable adjacent sedimentary rocks where additional concentration may occur. Thus, marine siliceous rocks can be considered potential source rocks for economic uranium deposits.

METHODS

Uranium and thorium were determined on 130 samples of siliceous rocks by delayed neutron activation analysis (DN) and major oxides by X-ray spectroscopy (XRF). FeO was determined by wet chemistry. Most thorium results are maximum values only. Carbon was converted to CO_2 by combustion, and total CO_2 was determined by titration using a Coulometrics, Inc. CO_2 coulometer. Inorganic carbon was converted to CO_2 by acid treatment, and the amount of CO_2 was again determined by titration using a coulometer. Organic carbon was determined by difference.

DEPOSITS STUDIED

The uranium and thorium contents of thirty-eight northeast equatorial Pacific siliceous ooze samples were presented by Piper et al. (1979). In addition to the average of Piper et al.'s data listed in Table 6-1, we present six additional analyses including analysis of the siliceous microfossils isolated from the sediment. Sediments range from siliceous ooze to siliceous mud with various amounts of admixed detrital minerals, volcanic debris, authigenic min-

(*Text continues on page 147*)

Table 6-1. Location and the Uranium, Thorium, and Organic Carbon Contents of Siliceous Rocks and Sediments

Sample Number	Lithology	Latitude	Longitude	U (ppm)	Th (ppm)	Th/U	Organic Carbon (wt. %)	C_{org}/U	Age	Remarks
Northeast Equatorial Pacific										
46-1-9-12A	Glass-bearing clayey siliceous ooze	9°20.7'N	150°50.7'W	2.32	11	4.74	—	—	Quaternary	5,160 m
46-1-9-12B	Siliceous microfossils (>44μm)	"	"	1.8	22	12.2	—	—	Quaternary	Water depth
52-42-4-7A	Siliceous mud	11°15.5'N	139°03.3'W	2.13	12	5.63	—	—	Late	4,871 m
52-42-4-7B	Siliceous microfossils (>44μm)	"	"	<2.5	<24	—	—	—	Quaternary	Water depth
48-19-22-26A	Glass-bearing siliceous mud	8°16.5'N	151°07.3'W	1.67	11.3	6.7	—	—	Quaternary	5,043 m
48-19-22-26B	Siliceous microfossils (>44μm)	"	"	<4.0	<40	—	—	—	Quaternary	Water depth
Domes A, B, C	Siliceous ooze to siliceous clay. Average of 38 samples from Piper.			2.05(0.30)	13.12(2.33)	6.40	—	—		
Bering Sea and Northwest Pacific										
19-184-7-1-110-112	Silt- and clay-bearing diatom ooze	53°42.64'N	170°55.39'W	2.31	<5.5	<2.38	0.5	0.22	late Pliocene	Umnak
19-184-10-2-118-120	Diatom ooze	"	"	2.48	6.6	2.66	0.5	0.20	" "	Plateau
19-184-17-2-86-88	Silt-bearing, clay-rich diatom ooze	"	"	2.01	7.8	3.88	0.3	0.15	late Miocene	1,910 m
19-185-6-3-95-97	Silt-bearing, clay-rich diatom ooze	54°25.73'N	169°14.59'W	1.43	<5.5	<3.85	0.4	0.28	early Pleistocene	2,110 m
19-188-2-1-120-124	Silt-, clay-, and spicule-bearing diatom ooze	53°45.21'N	178°39.56'E	2.56	<9.1	<3.55	0.5	0.20	late Pleistocene	Bowers Ridge
19-188-8-6-145-147	Diatom ooze	"	"	1.5	<7.5	<5.00	0.5	0.33	early Pleistocene	2,649 m
19-188-15-2-134-136	Silt- and clay-bearing diatom ooze	"	"	<0.59	<5.0	<8.47	0.3	>0.51	late Miocene	"
19-190-1-1-48-50	Diatom ooze	55°33.55'N	171°38.42'E	1.47	<5.6	<3.81	0.3	0.20	late Pleistocene	Aleutian Basin
19-190-13-1105-108	Silt- and clay-bearing diatom ooze	"	"	2.17	<6.4	<2.95	0.5	0.23	early Pliocene	3,875 m
19-192-4-3-130-132	Silt-, clay-, and carbonate-bearing diatom ooze	53°00.57'N	164°42.81'E	1.65	7.4	4.48	0.3	0.18	middle Pleistocene	Meiji Guyot

Sample	Lithology	Lat (N)	Long (W)						Age	Depth/Notes
19-192-14-3-40-42	Silt- and clay-rich diatom ooze	ʺ	ʺ	2.51	<6.4	<2.55	0.5	0.20	early Pliocene	3,014 m
19-192-20-1100-104	Silt-bearing, clay-rich diatom ooze	ʺ	ʺ	3.14	<5.9	<1.88	0.4	0.13	late Miocene	ʺ
Average				2.11(0.55)	<6.65(1.19)	<3.15	0.4(0.09)	0.19		
Southern California Continental Borderland: Monterey Formation										
L2-78-SC-29	Diatomaceous mudstone	38°54.7'N	119°28.2'W	19.8	<19	<0.96	6.29	0.32	Relizian	575 m
L2-78-SC-123	ʺ	32°21.8'N	118°24.7'W	41.6	<28	<0.67	5.02	0.12	early Relizian	720 m
L2-78-SC-134	ʺ	32°19.4'N	118°52.4'W	17.5	<16	<0.91	16.17	0.92	late Relizian	482 m
L2-78-SC-158	limestone	32°30.2'N	119°19.1'W	9.36	<10	<1.07	4.73	0.51	early Mohnian	340 m
L2-78-SC-179	mudstone	32°32.9'N	119°37.2'W	7.17	<11	<1.53	6.36	0.89	late Relizian	563 m
L2-78-SC-184	ʺ	32°31.4'N	119°41.2'W	20.0	<16	<0.80	5.83	0.29	Relizian	1,100 m
L2-78-SC-332	ʺ	33°50.2'N	119°53.0'W	24.2	<15	<0.62	11.40	0.47	early Mohnian	270 m
Average				19.95(11.32)	<16(6)	<0.80	7.97(4.25)	0.40		
Gulf of California										
A-5KC-10	Diatomaceous mud	26°43.4'N	110°07.0'W	6.32	<6.7	<1.06	3.58	0.57	late Neogene	705 m
A-5KC-30	ʺ	ʺ	ʺ	6.48	<5.8	<0.90	3.45	0.53	ʺ	Laminated
A-5KC-130	ʺ	ʺ	ʺ	6.63	7.7	1.16	3.23	0.49	ʺ	H$_2$S smell
B-28KC-85	ʺ	26°42.5'N	111°24.5'W	6.46	<7.7	<1.19	4.59	0.71	ʺ	712 m
B-28KC-150	ʺ	ʺ	ʺ	8.22	<10	<1.22	3.98	0.48	ʺ	Laminated
B-28KC-155	ʺ	ʺ	ʺ	7.74	<7.9	<1.02	4.82	0.62	ʺ	
E-10KC-80	ʺ	27°52.2'N	111°39.7'W	8.19	<9.1	<1.11	4.63	0.57	ʺ	644 m
E-10KC-105	ʺ	ʺ	ʺ	9.91	<8.8	<0.89	4.45	0.45	ʺ	H$_2$S smell
E-10KC-135	ʺ	ʺ	ʺ	7.11	<7.6	<1.07	4.31	0.61	ʺ	
E-10KC-155	ʺ	ʺ	ʺ	7.71	<9.2	<1.19	4.12	0.53	ʺ	
Average				7.48(1.12)	<8.05(1.25)	<1.08	4.12(0.54)	0.55		
Northern California: Monterey Formation										
277-1-1B	Diatomite	36°38'N	121°48'W	5.08	<6.5	<1.28	0.34	0.07	Miocene	Near Carmel
277-1-1D	ʺ	ʺ	ʺ	10.1	<7.6	<0.75	0.35	0.03	ʺ	ʺ
277-1-1E	ʺ	ʺ	ʺ	15.6	<8.2	<0.53	0.29	0.02	ʺ	ʺ
277-1-1F	ʺ	ʺ	ʺ	9.22	<9.4	<1.02	0.30	0.03	ʺ	ʺ
J71	Laminated chert-porcelanite	37°45'N	111°2'W	2.39	<3.8	<1.59	—	—	ʺ	Berkeley Hills
Average 4 diatomites				10.0(4.33)	<7.93(1.21)	<0.79	0.32(0.03)	0.03		

(continued)

141

Table 6-1. (Continued)

Sample Number	Lithology	Latitude	Longitude	U (ppm)	Th (ppm)	Th/U	Organic Carbon (wt. %)	C_{org}/U	Age	Remarks
Average	76 outcrop samples of Monterey Fm. siliceous rocks from Durham			12.31(13.69)	<8.99(4.87)	<0.73	—	—		
Average	16 drill core samples of Monterey Fm. siliceous rocks from Durham			13.54(6.88)	<7.26(3.10)	<0.54	6.36(3.71)	0.47		
Baja California, Mexico										
H6-1C	Diatomite	31°05'N	115°05'W	5.64	<9.3	<1.65	0.30	0.05	Miocene–	Near San Felipe
H6-1D	”	”	”	5.31	8.4	1.58	0.23	0.04	Pliocene	”
H6-2A	”	”	”	6.21	<10	<1.61	0.15	0.02	boundary	”
H6-2B	”	”	”	6.50	<9.1	<1.40	0.16	0.02	”	”
H6-2E	”	”	”	7.63	<12	<1.57	0.16	0.02	”	”
H6-2D	”	”	”	3.94	<4.9	<0.64	0.20	0.05	”	”
H6-1A	”	”	”	5.89	<5.2	<0.88	0.24	0.04	”	”
H6-1E	”	”	”	4.76	<4.8	<1.01	0.21	0.04	”	”
H6-1F	”	”	”	4.09	7.8	1.91	0.24	0.06	”	”
1179-1-1A	Cherty porcelanite	24°20'N	111°02'W	2.23	<4.2	<1.56	—	—	Miocene	S. Baja
1179-1-1B	Porcelanite	”		3.19	<4.7	<1.57	—	—	”	California
Average	9 diatomites			5.55(1.18)	<7.94(2.52)	<1.43	0.21(0.05)	0.04		
Average	9 diatomites + 2 porcelanites			5.04(1.58)	<7.31(2.66)	<1.45	—	—		
Ecuador										
979-13-1A	Laminated chert, black	2°10'S	79°53'W	<0.23	<2.2	—	0.10	>0.43	Cretaceous	Guayaquil
979-13-2C	Chert (from bedded chert sequence)	”	”	0.80	2.6	<3.25	0.06	0.06	Cretaceous	Guayaquil
979-14-1A	Calcareous diatomite, white	2°23'S	80°28'W	3.36	<3.3	<0.98	0.21	0.06	late early	
979-14-1B	Calcareous brown laminated diatomite	”	”	4.39	<4.3	<0.98	0.27	0.06	Miocene or early middle Miocene	
979-14-2	Calcareous diatomite	”	”	3.07	<3.2	<1.04	0.27	0.09	”	
979-15-1	Laminated black chert	1°55'S	80°35'W	1.41	<3.1	<2.20	0.03	0.02	Cretaceous(?)	
Average	Cretaceous cherts			1.11(0.43)	<2.63(0.45)	<2.37	0.06(0.04)	0.05		
Average	Miocene diatomites			3.61(0.69)	<3.60(0.61)	<1.00	0.25(0.03)	0.07		

	Description	Lat.	Long.						Age	Notes
Costa Rica										
979-4-1BI	Fresh water diatomite	10°57'N	84°19.5'W	5.61	<5.8	<1.03	0.57	0.10	Pleistocene	Near Turru-caras Nicoya Fm.
979-4-1C	Calcareous, ash-rich, fresh water diatomite	"	"	11.5	<7.1	<0.62	0.23	0.02	"	Nicoya Fm.
979-4-1A	Ash-rich fresh water diatomite	"	"	3.51	<6.0	<1.71	0.34	0.10	"	"
979-4-1BII	Fresh water diatomite, calcareous	"	"	8.44	<8.5	<1.01	0.36	0.04	"	"
Average				7.27(3.47)	<6.85(1.24)	<0.94	0.38(0.14)	0.05		
Peru										
979-18-1A	Ash-rich porcelanite	14°20'S	75°45'W	6.04	17.7	2.93	0.13	0.02	early Pliocene	Pisco Fm.
979-18-1B	Diatomite	"	"	5.42	14.4	2.65	0.61	0.11	" "	"
979-18-2B	"	14°18'S	"	4.69	16.9	3.60	0.25	0.05	Pliocene	"
979-18-2C	"	"	"	4.13	11.0	2.66	0.27	0.07	"	"
979-18-3	"	14°20'S	75°40'W	5.78	<8.6	<1.49	0.60	0.10	early Pliocene	"
979-18-4A	Calcareous, ash-rich porcelanite	13°40'S	76°15'W	3.40	8.17	2.40	0.05	0.01	" "	"
979-18-4B	Diatomite	"	"	49.8	<30	<0.60	0.47	0.01	" "	"
979-18-4C	"	"	"	19.2	<14	<0.73	0.28	0.01	" "	"
979-14-4D	Calcareous diatomite	"	"	14.0	<15	<1.07	0.19	0.01	" "	"
979-18-4E	Laminated, halite, and ash-rich diatomite	"	"	2.67	9.9	3.71	0.08	0.03	" "	"
Average				11.51(14.44)	<14.57(6.37)	<1.13	0.29(0.20)	0.03		
New Zealand										
283-6-2A	Diatomite	45°04.75'S	170°53.5'E	1.19	2.8	2.35	0.05	0.04	early Tertiary	Oamaru Fm.
283-6-2BI	Porcelanite	"	"	0.930	7.67	8.25	0.06	0.06	" "	S. Island
283-6-2BII	Black chert rim on 2BI	"	"	1.29	<4.1	<3.18	0.15	0.12	" "	Affected by heat of near-by dike
283-6-2C	Porcelanite	"	"	0.963	5.04	5.23	0.19	0.20	" "	
283-6-2D	Porcelanite	"	"	1.14	10.0	8.77	0.14	0.12	" "	
283-6-1AI	Calcareous diatomite	"	"	1.39	3.3	2.37	0.11	0.08	late Eocene	Oamaru Fm.
283-6-1AII	Calcareous diatomite	"	"	1.64	3.5	2.13	0.18	0.11	" "	"
283-6-3B	Diatomaceous lime-stone	45°05.8'S	170°52.75'E	0.31	3.5	11.29	0.16	0.52		
Average	8(U), 7(Th)			1.11(0.40)	5.12(2.72)	4.61	0.13(0.05)	0.12		

(*continued*)

143

Table 6-1. (Continued)

Sample Number	Lithology	Latitude	Longitude	U (ppm)	Th (ppm)	Th/U	Organic Carbon (wt. %)	C_{org}/U	Age	Remarks
Japan										
881-23-1AI	Black quartz chert nodule	39°54.8′N	139°45′E	0.32	<2.0	<6.25	0.23	0.72	late Miocene	Oga Peninsula
881-23-1AII	Quartz porcelanite rim	"	"	0.46	<2.7	<5.87	0.04	0.09	"	Onnagawa Fm.
881-23-1B	Opal-CT procelanite	"	"	7.23	<6.6	<0.91	1.50	0.21	"	"
881-23-2A	Black opal-CT and tri-dymite chert nodule	"	"	1.55	<2.4	<1.55	0.80	0.52	"	"
881-23-2B	Diatomite	39°57.5′N	139°46.75′E	11.8	<11	<0.93	2.71	0.23	"	"
881-23-3	Black opal-CT and tri-dymite chert	"	"	3.32	<3.6	<1.08	1.86	0.56	"	"
Average	Opal-A and opal-CT rocks			5.98(4.55)	<5.90(3.83)	<0.99	1.72(0.79)	0.29		
Average	Quartz rocks			0.39(0.10)	<2.35(0.49)	<6.03	0.14(0.13)	0.36		
Korea									early middle	
981-15-1A	Diatomite	36°13′N	129°22′E	12.0	<8	<0.67	0.60	0.05	Miocene	Yeohill Group,
981-15-1B	"	"	"	7.3	13.4	1.84	0.91	0.12	"	near
981-15-2	Quartz porcelanite	36°11′N	129°21′E	6.7	12.4	1.85	0.98	0.15	"	Pohang
981-16-1A	Middle of dolomite nodule	36°03′N	129°23′E	0.73	<2	<2.74	—	—	"	"
981-16-1B	Near bottom of dolomite nodule	"	"	0.80	<3	<3.75	—	—	"	"
981-16-1B2	Bottom of dolomite nodule, rim	"	"	1.37	<3	<2.19	—	—	"	"
981-16-1C1	Top of dolomite nodule, rim	"	"	3.33	<5	<1.50	—	—	"	"
981-16-1C2	Near top of dolomite nodule	"	"	0.84	<4	<4.76	—	—	"	"
981-16-1DI	Quartz porcelanite	"	"	6.4	7.8	1.22	1.67	0.26	"	"
981-16-1DII	" "	"	"	12.8	<7	<0.55	2.47	0.19	"	"
981-16-1E	" "	"	"	3.37	7.3	2.17	2.13	0.63	"	"
981-16-2	Diatomite	36°10′N	129°22′E	5.0	14.7	2.94	0.46	0.09	"	"
981-16-3	Quartz porcelanite	36°09′N	129°19′E	8.0	14.0	1.75	2.37	0.30	"	"
981-16-4A	Argillaceous opal-CT porcelanite	36°06′N	129°20′E	4.65	<9	<1.94	2.03	0.44	"	"

Sample	Description	Latitude	Longitude						Age	Location
981-16-4B	Opal-CT porcelanite	"	"	8.5	<10	<1.18	0.71	0.08	"	"
981-16-5	"	36°04'N	129°21'E	2.54	<6	<2.36	1.52	0.60	"	"
Average	11 diatomites and porcelanites			7.02(3.24)	<9.96(3.12)	<1.42	1.44(0.74)	0.21		
Average	5 samples through a large dolomite nodule			1.41(1.10)	<3.40(1.14)	<2.98	—	—		
Alaska										
YD-4K-173-B	Chert	59°51.33'N	139°18.83'W	0.32	4.2	13.13	—	—	Late Cretaceous	SE Alaska
SB-3K-45B	"	57°21.78'N	134°56.92'W	1.33	6.0	4.51	—	—	"	"
YB-3K-293-D	"	59°21.45'N	138°45.16'W	1.70	<3.3	<1.91	—	—	"	"
79-SK-247C	"	57°33.38'N	135°51.38'W	0.51	<2.4	<4.71	—	—	"	"
79-SK-311C	"	57°37.18'N	135°54.92'W	0.66	<2.6	<3.94	—	—	"	"
Average				0.90(0.59)	<3.70(1.47)	<4.11	—	—		
California: Franciscan Complex										
384-28-2	Red chert	36°36'N	121°30'W	0.221	1.19	5.38	—	—	Late Jurassic	Diablo Range
384-28-8A	Red chert	"	"	0.237	1.22	5.15	—	—	"	"
484-12-1B	Green siliceous argillite	37°31'N	121°24'W	1.42	9.62	6.77	—	—	"	"
484-13-1G	Green chert	"	"	0.487	1.15	2.36	—	—	"	"
484-13-1K	Red chert	"	"	0.221	1.59	7.19	—	—	"	"
484-13-1U	Brown siliceous argillite	"	"	0.981	6.44	6.56	—	—	"	"
484-20-2C	Mottled red-green chert	"	"	0.564	1.47	2.61	—	—	"	"
484-20-2J	Red chert	"	"	0.479	1.30	2.71	—	—	"	"
484-20-2O	Gray chert, contact with Mn ore	"	"	0.933	0.426	0.46	—	—	"	"
Average	7 cherts			0.45(0.26)	1.19(0.37)	2.64	—	—		
Average	2 siliceous argillites			1.20(0.31)	8.03(2.25)	6.69	—	—		
Average	All 9			0.62(0.41)	2.71(3.13)	4.37	—	—		
Costa Rica: Nicoya Complex										
880-22-1C	Black chert	10°26'N	85°48'W	<0.50	0.827	>1.65	—	—	late Valanginian/ Hauterivian	Punta Salinas
880-23-4	Red chert	10°36'N	85°37'W	<0.50	2.03	>4.06	—	—	Early Cretaceous	Sardinal
880-23-7A1	Banded black and red chert	10°29'N	85°42'W	0.671	3.75	5.59	—	—	Turonian or Coniacian	El Frances
880-23-7AII	Manganiferous chert	"	"	<0.50	1.34	>2.68	—	—	"	"

(continued)

145

Table 6-1. *(Continued)*

Sample Number	Lithology	Latitude	Longitude	U (ppm)	Th (ppm)	Th/U	Organic Carbon (wt. %)	C_{org}/U	Age	Remarks
880-24-1AII	White porcelanite	10°20'N	85°50'W	<0.50	0.172	>0.34	—	—	late early Eocene	Cartegena
880-24-2D	Pale brown chert	"	"	<0.50	0.317	>0.63	—	—	middle Eocene	"
880-24-3B	Argillaceous yellow jasper	"	"	<0.50	<0.10	—	—	—	Albian/Cenomanian	Hatillo
880-24-3C	Siliceous siltstone	"	"	0.549	0.771	1.40	—	—	Coniacian	"
880-28-1D	Red tuffaceous chert	8°23'N	83°18'W	1.60	9.21	5.76	—	—	Cretaceous	Osa Peninsula
880-29-3B	Red chert	8°32'N	83°14'W	<0.50	0.416	>0.83	—	—	Cretaceous	Golfito
980-1-1C	Red chert	9°23'N	84°10'W	0.988	<0.10	<0.10	—	—	late early Eocene	Quapos
5-23-2-78-1	Red and yellow jasper	9°32'N	84°35'W	<0.50	0.298	>0.60	—	—	late Turonian to Santonian	Judas
5-23-2-78-2	White chert	"	"	<0.50	0.547	>1.09	—	—	"	"
5-23-2-78-3	Yellow jasper	"	"	<0.50	<0.10	—	—	—	"	"
879-30-1A	Red chert	10°24'N	85°50'W	<0.50	<0.10	—	—	—	Berriasian or Valanginian	Punta Salinas
Average				<0.62(0.30)	<1.34(2.39)	—	—	—		

Sources: Domes A, B, C average is from Piper et al., 1979. Average for Monterey Fm. rocks calculated from data provided by Durham, in press. Dredged samples from the Southern California Continental Borderland were provided by J. G. Vedder, U.S. Geological Survey, and core samples from the Gulf of California were provided by H. Schrader and E. K. Asbury, Oregon State University. Cherts from Alaska were provided by S. M. Karl, U.S. Geological Survey. Age dates for Baja California, Ecuador, Peru, and Korea were provided by John Barron, those for the Costa Rica diatomites by J. P. Bradbury and those for Costa Rica chert and porcelanite by Gerta Keller and C. D. Blome, all of the U.S. Geological Survey.

Notes: Dash means not available. Numbers in parentheses are standard deviations of the averages. The >44 μm size fractions listed for the northeast equatorial Pacific contain >99% siliceous microfossils, mostly radiolarians.

erals, and biogenic debris (Hein et al., 1979). Sediments were deposited at abyssal depths with little calcium carbonate and organic carbon. Oxic bottom waters exist over the entire area.

Bering Sea samples are from Deep Sea Drilling Project Leg 19 and consist of diatom ooze to diatomaceous mud with various amounts of detrital minerals (Hein et al., 1978; Creager et al., 1973). Calcium carbonate is absent or occurs in minor amounts, and organic carbon occurs in moderate amounts (Table 6-1). Bottom waters are oxic and a surface-sediment oxidizing layer occurs. Samples were collected from depth within cores where reducing conditions prevail.

Samples from dredge hauls from the southern California continental borderland belong to the Miocene Monterey Formation, which crops out over extensive areas of California. Bramlette (1946) described the siliceous rocks of the Monterey Formation in detail. The seven samples we studied were recovered from offshore and are composed of opal-A, calcite, and various amounts of apatite, pyrite, and detrital minerals. Rocks were deposited in continental margin basins primarily within the oxygen-minimum zone where anaerobic conditions prevailed (Bramlette, 1946; Ingle, 1973). The advantage of studying samples dredged from the marine environment rather than outcrop samples is that weathering and oxidation have not significantly altered the original composition of the rocks as is demonstrated by the high contents of organic matter compared with outcrop samples of the Monterey Formation. Core samples likewise would better preserve original composition.

Core samples of Gulf of California diatomaceous muds are laminated, smelled of H_2S when recovered, and were taken from within the oxygen-minimum zone. Cores were from the continental slopes adjacent to the Carmen and Guaymas basins. Organic matter is abundant and calcium carbonate is minor.

Outcrop samples of the Miocene Monterey Formation are from near Carmel and Berkeley in northern California. The diatomite analyzed contains opal-A, opal-CT, calcite, and detrital minerals, whereas the chert-porcelanite contains quartz. The average of seventy-six samples listed in Table 6-1, which were analyzed by Durham (in press), are from outcrops, and the average of sixteen are from drill cores. Comparison of outcrop samples with drill core and marine samples indicates that 94-95% of the organic matter is oxidized or otherwise removed from outcrop samples of the Monterey Formation, although the average uranium content of each group is about the same.

Diatomite was collected from near San Felipe in the northeast part of Baja California, and porcelanite came from the southern part of the peninsula. Diatomite consists of opal-A, calcite, and detrital minerals. Organic carbon contents are low. The San Felipe diatomite is most commonly laminated or thin bedded. It was deposited in a near-shore basin with a well-developed oxygen-minimum zone (Boehm, 1982). Sediments were deposited at upper-middle bathyal depths, 500-1,500 m (Boehm, 1982).

Cretaceous cherts from Ecuador are part of a rhythmically bedded sequence of calcite-rich quartz cherts that occur within the city limits of Guayaquil. Diatomite occurs west of Guayaquil as part of the Villingota member of the Tosagua Formation. Diatomite consists of calcite, opal-A, and detrital minerals. Organic carbon is minor. The original siliceous sediments were deposited at upper-middle bathyal depths, 1,500-2,000 m (Kristin McDougall, personal communication, 1980), in continental margin basins.

Fresh water diatomite from the Nicoya Formation in central Costa Rica is included for comparison with the marine diatomites. Rocks consist of opal-A, calcite, detrital minerals, and volcanic glass.

Diatomite and porcelanite from Peru are from the Pisco Formation immediately north and southeast of the town of Pisco. During the early Pliocene, these sediments were deposited in restricted to open-shelf and upper-slope basins (J. A. Barron and Kristin McDougall, personal communication, 1980). Sediments represent a low-oxygen facies. Rocks are composed of opal-A, sulfate minerals, calcite, apatite and halite in some places, and detrital minerals. Rocks contain low to moderate amounts of organic carbon.

Siliceous rocks from the south island of New Zealand are from the Oamaru Formation. The first five rocks listed in Table 6–1 were affected by the heat of a nearby volcanic dike and show advanced diagenetic effects. These rocks are composed of opal-A, opal-CT, quartz, heulandite, and detrital minerals.

Rocks from Japan are part of the Onnagawa Formation on the Oga Peninsula (Honda, 1978; Kano, 1979; Iijima and Tada, 1981; Tada and Iijima, 1982). Some of the rocks contain late-stage weathering products such as tridymite. The opal-CT porcelanite and the diatomite are typical of the relatively unaltered facies, which probably has an average uranium content of about 10 ppm. Four rocks represent minor diagenetic facies. Organic carbon is low to moderate and calcite is minor or not present.

Siliceous rocks from Korea are from the Yeonill Group near Pohang on the east coast. Also, a series of samples from a large dolomite nodule greater than 1 m long and 0.75 m wide were analyzed. In places, nodules are abundant in the diatomite and porcelanite. Rocks contain 40–70% siliceous microfossils, 30–60% detrital minerals, and minor pyrite, glauconite, fish debris, and terrestrial plant material (Garrison et al., 1979). Water depth was possibly 1,000–2,000 m. Laminated rocks and phosphorites are scarce or absent.

Chert from southeast Alaska occurs in rhythmically bedded sequences of chert-shale (Karl, 1982). These chert sections occur as blocks in mélange units. The chert is predominantly quartz.

Chert from the Franciscan Complex is from the Diablo Range in northern California (Chap. 9). The rhythmically bedded chert-shale sequence is intercalated with sandstone. Cherts are predominantly quartz.

Chert from the Costa Rica Nicoya Complex is also in rhythmically bedded chert-shale sequences but is enclosed in basalt rather than sandstone (Hein et al., 1983a). Chert is predominantly quartz.

RESULTS

URANIUM AND THORIUM CONTENTS

The highest uranium contents measured are 41.6 ppm and 49.8 ppm respectively for a sample from the Monterey Formation and one from the Pisco Formation of Peru (see Table 6–1). Durham (in press) reported a maximum value of about 2,000 ppm for the Monterey Formation. The highest average uranium concentrations are for the Monterey Formation offshore (19.95 ppm), onshore (10–13.54 ppm), and the Pisco Formation (11.51 ppm). These are enrichments of four to eight times over the crustal average of 2.5 ppm uranium. Gulf of California, Costa Rica diatomite, and Korean deposits are all enriched about three times over the crustal average; Baja California and Japan deposits are enriched about two and a half times; whereas other opal-A- and opal-CT-rich deposits are near the crustal average. Quartz cherts are all significantly impoverished in uranium compared to the crustal average.

The limited number of absolute values for thorium limits conclusions regarding thorium distribution. The highest thorium contents measured are 22 ppm and 17.7 ppm respectively for isolated siliceous microfossils from the northeast equatorial Pacific and a porcelanite from Peru. The average for Peru and for the equatorial Pacific are about the same as for average shale (12 ppm; Adams and Weaver, 1958); all others are significantly below the average for shale. The apparent concentration of thorium in the siliceous-microfossil fraction of equatorial Pacific siliceous deposits is curious because the concentration of thorium is extremely low in seawater and thorium is not likely to be extracted from seawater by the plankton along with the silica. Enrichment must be post- or syndepositional adsorption onto the opaline silica.

Uranium and thorium contents decrease with increasing diagenesis—that is, from diatomite to porcelanite to chert (Table 6-1; Fig. 6-1). Any single rock sample, however, may have an anomalously high or low concentration, depending on the uranium content and relative proportion of detrital, volcanic, authigenic, and biogenic phases present and on the diagenetic history. This result is consistent with previous studies that show that most other elements as well are lost or diluted by SiO_2 as ooze transforms to chert (Hein et al., 1981, 1983b; Brueckner and Snyder, 1985).

Th/U varies from less than 0.7 to 6.4. Nine out of the fifteen groups of samples studied show ratios of less than 2, possibly indicating extraction of the uranium from seawater (Adams and Weaver, 1958). The equatorial Pacific

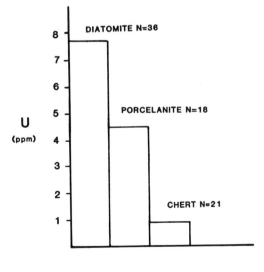

LITHOLOGY

Figure 6-1.   Histogram of the average uranium content for diatomites, porcelanites, and cherts listed in Table 6-1.

siliceous sediments show a ratio typical of continental shales (Adam and Weaver, 1958), whereas the ratios for chert are typically intermediate between seawater and shale values.

ORGANIC CARBON CONTENT

Organic carbon contents are difficult to interpret because our results suggest that outcrop samples have lost significant amounts of their original organic carbon, probably through oxidation. Thus, only marine and drill core samples show a significant relationship between uranium and organic carbon. It is unknown how much the oxidation of organic carbon at the outcrop affects the C/U ratio. For the Monterey Formation, the ratio changes from 0.40 and 0.47 for submarine outcrops and drill core samples, respectively, to 0.03 for subaerial outcrop samples.

For the marine and drill core samples, the Gulf of California and Monterey Formation show similar C/U ratios, 0.40–0.55, whereas the Bering Sea samples contain more uranium relative to organic carbon, C/U = 0.19. These all fall within the range listed for marine samples by Baturin (1973), whereas for samples taken from outcrops only the samples from Japan and Korea have C/U ratios that fall within the range listed by Baturin.

POTASSIUM-URANIUM RATIOS

Potassium is largely contributed by the detrital mineral phases, and anomalously low values of the K/U ratio indicate enrichment of uranium over that contributed by a typical or average detrital suite. The average K/U ratio of the dissolved load carried by rivers is 3,300 (Bloch, 1980), and that listed simply as rivers by MacDougall (1977) is 8,000. The ratios for samples analyzed here range from 35 to 5,800, all well below the ratio presented by MacDougall. Out of sixty-two rocks analyzed, only four had ratios greater than 3,600—all from Peru—and four are within the range 3,000 to 3,600—two from Korea, and two from Peru. All samples from Baja California (2,277 average), Gulf of California (1,909 average), and Korea (1,842 average) have values smaller than the 3,300 detrital ratio, whereas Monterey Formation samples have ratios much smaller, 270 and 912 for offshore and onshore rocks, respectively. Peru rocks are mixed with some equal to, some larger, and some smaller than the detrital ratio.

STATISTICAL STUDIES

Correlation coefficient matrices were constructed for all the major oxides and loss on ignition (LOI) (Table 6–2) as well as U, Th, and organic carbon contents (see Table 6–1). A matrix was constructed for samples from each geographic area, for various combinations of locations, and for all samples combined (Table 6–3). Chemical data for the cherts and Bering Sea samples are not available. In addition, uranium was plotted on scatter diagrams against organic carbon, SiO_2 (Fig. 6–2, on page 156), and Th.

(*Text continues on page 157*)

Table 6-2A. Major Oxides in Weight-Percent of Siliceous Rocks and Sediments Selected from Table 6-1

Sample	SiO_2	Al_2O_3	Fe_2O_3*	MgO	CaO	Na_2O	K_2O	TiO_2	P_2O_5	MnO	LOI†	Total
Monterey Formation, Southern California Continental Borderland												
L2-78-SC-29	38.9	7.92	2.84	2.21	15.3	2.45	0.90	0.38	2.07	0.02	24.3	97.29
L2-78-SC-123	47.2	2.86	1.44	1.16	14.9	2.71	0.39	0.15	0.25	<0.02	26.9	97.96
L2-78-SC-134	42.4	6.19	3.43	2.00	3.79	2.69	0.90	0.45	1.36	0.03	34.7	97.94
L2-78-SC-158	4.73	0.76	0.11	0.59	46.3	0.51	0.04	<0.02	0.26	<0.02	44.0	97.30
L2-78-SC-179	43.0	4.21	1.89	2.85	13.5	2.49	0.65	0.30	0.64	<0.02	28.5	98.03
L2-78-SC-184	41.5	1.45	1.0	0.83	20.4	1.88	0.18	0.13	0.50	<0.02	30.6	98.47
L2-78-SC-332	32.0	3.08	0.92	0.98	20.9	1.50	0.43	0.15	0.69	<0.02	37.7	98.35
Gulf of California												
A-5KC-10	51.1	11.3	3.77	2.56	2.02	5.25	2.15	0.50	0.24	0.03	19.4	98.32
A-5KC-30	52.1	11.2	3.89	2.41	3.11	4.62	2.15	0.50	0.22	0.03	18.0	98.23
A-5KC-130	51.7	11.7	3.98	2.52	3.45	3.67	2.28	0.54	0.27	0.03	18.8	98.94
B-28 KC-85	55.4	6.55	2.27	2.40	1.31	5.26	1.12	0.29	0.36	<0.02	23.0	97.96
B-28 KC-150	53.5	6.98	2.43	2.38	2.96	4.96	1.17	0.32	0.26	<0.02	23.6	98.56
B-28KC-155	51.4	8.94	2.92	2.59	3.69	4.61	1.52	0.40	0.26	0.02	22.4	98.75
E-10KC-80	54.1	7.90	2.50	2.24	1.16	4.95	1.55	0.34	0.22	<0.02	23.5	98.46
E-10KC-105	57.3	8.19	2.63	2.14	1.40	4.62	1.60	0.36	0.23	<0.02	20.6	99.07
E-10KC-135	55.3	8.00	2.53	2.24	1.13	4.92	1.58	0.35	0.24	<0.02	22.3	98.59
E-10KC-155	55.7	7.95	2.51	2.26	1.04	5.32	1.53	0.35	0.23	<0.02	21.7	98.59
Monterey Formation, Carmel												
277-1-1B	79.9	5.21	2.41	0.71	0.67	0.96	0.87	0.26	0.13	<0.02	7.74	98.86
277-1-1D	59.9	9.74	3.50	1.34	4.76	3.85	1.48	0.49	0.37	<0.02	14.5	99.93
277-1-1E	63.1	5.49	1.73	0.58	10.6	1.91	0.88	0.26	0.24	<0.02	14.7	99.49
277-1-1F	82.6	3.64	1.93	0.51	0.29	0.66	0.60	0.18	0.06	<0.02	7.87	98.34
Baja California												
H6-1C	59.9	8.06	3.29	1.54	8.68	2.96	1.73	0.44	0.26	0.02	10.5	97.38
H6-1D	53.8	8.19	3.54	1.65	13.0	2.29	1.81	0.48	0.29	0.03	14.2	99.28
H6-2A	68.1	7.56	2.81	1.43	6.09	1.18	1.52	0.36	0.21	<0.02	9.06	98.32
H6-2B	60.8	8.35	3.30	1.77	9.76	1.04	1.74	0.43	0.28	0.03	11.4	98.90

(continued)

151

Table 6-2A (Continued)

Sample	SiO$_2$	Al$_2$O$_3$	Fe$_2$O$_3$*	MgO	CaO	Na$_2$O	K$_2$O	TiO$_2$	P$_2$O$_5$	MnO	LOI†	Total
H6-2E	77.6	4.58	1.91	0.84	4.00	0.72	0.99	0.25	0.18	<0.02	7.12	98.19
H6-2D	50.0	5.26	2.11	1.32	10.9	4.68	0.77	0.29	0.21	<0.02	23.8	99.34
H6-1A	60.9	8.60	3.40	1.67	8.93	1.43	1.75	0.45	0.26	0.02	12.0	99.41
H6-1E	61.5	7.10	2.92	1.44	10.1	2.16	1.57	0.37	0.29	<0.02	12.2	99.65
H6-1F	61.6	6.71	2.79	1.28	7.69	3.80	1.46	0.37	0.24	<0.02	13.4	99.34
Ecuador												
979-14-1A	51.4	11.1	3.51	0.95	12.5	0.66	0.46	0.43	0.33	<0.02	18.1	99.44
979-14-1B	64.5	9.59	3.28	0.80	5.63	1.14	0.43	0.39	0.25	<0.02	14.6	100.61
979-14-2	42.5	10.9	4.15	0.90	17.2	0.67	0.45	0.41	0.31	<0.02	22.5	99.99
Costa Rica												
979-4-1BI	62.0	11.2	7.42	0.69	0.86	0.40	0.58	0.54	0.16	<0.02	15.2	99.05
979-4-1C	63.7	16.3	2.65	0.55	0.90	0.52	0.52	0.65	0.07	<0.02	13.5	99.36
979-4-1A	64.3	12.5	5.15	0.67	2.10	0.83	0.36	0.55	0.07	<0.02	13.0	99.53
979-4-1BII	60.9	11.8	8.70	0.70	0.78	0.33	0.52	0.57	0.15	<0.02	13.8	98.25
New Zealand												
283-6-2A	53.1	21.5	2.96	1.07	6.61	3.85	0.28	2.67	0.38	<0.02	7.59	100.01
283-6-2BI	76.0	8.00	1.97	0.90	1.06	0.50	1.31	0.47	<0.05	<0.02	8.96	99.17
283-6-2BII	82.1	4.97	1.11	0.46	1.04	0.45	0.85	0.29	0.11	<0.02	6.87	98.25
283-6-2C	76.4	7.87	1.88	1.07	1.20	0.49	1.53	0.40	<0.05	<0.02	8.35	99.19
283-6-2D	63.5	15.3	3.79	0.95	3.18	1.61	3.97	0.72	0.09	<0.02	6.27	99.31
283-6-1AI	45.1	12.7	7.84	2.57	10.6	1.11	0.47	1.53	0.26	0.05	18.0	100.23
283-6-1AII	37.9	9.84	4.79	1.99	17.8	0.35	0.68	1.04	0.26	0.04	25.5	100.19
283-6-3B	11.0	2.49	0.94	0.94	45.0	0.35	0.44	0.15	0.13	<0.02	38.6	100.04
Japan												
881-23-1AI	96.8	0.76	0.11	<0.10	0.40	0.15	0.06	<0.02	<0.05	<0.02	1.43	99.71
881-23-1AII	95.8	0.79	0.11	<0.10	0.13	<0.15	0.13	0.03	<0.05	<0.02	1.48	98.47
881-23-1B	84.9	4.67	0.51	0.57	<0.02	0.18	0.60	0.16	0.08	<0.02	6.68	98.35
881-23-2A	89.2	1.13	0.37	<0.10	<0.02	0.20	0.16	0.03	0.08	<0.02	7.32	98.49
881-23-2B	78.2	2.65	1.26	0.30	0.03	0.25	0.39	0.09	<0.05	<0.02	15.1	98.27
881-23-3	84.5	2.34	1.12	0.21	0.06	0.24	0.47	0.1	<0.05	<0.02	9.32	98.36

Korea

Sample	SiO₂	Al₂O₃	Fe₂O₃	FeO	MgO	CaO	Na₂O	K₂O	TiO₂	P₂O₅	MnO	BaO	LOI	Total
981-15-1A	61.3	15.0	6.52		1.00	0.39	1.22	2.23	0.60		0.18	<0.02	9.97	98.41
981-15-1B	70.2	13.4	2.26		0.65	0.17	1.22	2.10	0.59		<0.05	<0.02	8.47	99.06
981-15-2	67.2	14.0	2.74		0.93	0.15	1.0	2.09	0.58		0.07	<0.02	9.93	98.69
981-16-1DI	80.7	8.17	2.06		0.36	<0.02	0.44	1.24	0.29		<0.05	<0.02	6.09	99.35
981-16-1DII	66.6	13.5	3.28		0.54	0.04	0.66	1.72	0.49		0.06	<0.02	13.0	99.89
981-16-1E	78.3	8.83	1.59		0.38	0.05	0.62	1.46	0.33		0.06	<0.02	7.83	99.45
981-16-2	71.0	10.6	2.80		0.77	0.09	0.89	1.47	0.46		<0.05	<0.02	9.72	97.80
981-16-3	59.0	14.6	5.17		1.39	0.49	1.09	2.26	0.60		0.06	0.02	14.1	98.78
981-16-4A	76.2	8.28	1.69		0.50	0.04	0.46	1.18	0.34		0.11	<0.02	8.98	97.78
981-16-4B	75.7	10.7	1.60		0.64	0.03	0.44	1.46	0.48		<0.05	<0.02	7.97	99.02
981-16-5	83.0	5.46	1.10		0.37	0.1	0.44	0.93	0.21		0.05	<0.02	6.69	98.35

Table 6-2B. Major Oxides in Weight-Percent of Siliceous Rocks and Sediments Selected from Table 6-1

Sample	SiO₂	Al₂O₃	Fe₂O₃	FeO	MgO	CaO	Na₂O	K₂O	TiO₂	P₂O₅	MnO	BaO	LOI†	Total
Peru														
979-18-1A	66.3	13.7	1.73	0.25	1.2	0.86	2.8	2.79	0.33	<0.1	0.04	0.09	9.04	99.13
979-18-1B	61.1	13.5	3.25	0.02	2.3	0.80	2.8	2.16	0.58	<0.1	<0.02	0.05	12.09	98.65
979-18-2B	64.7	14.5	2.27	0.48	1.0	2.32	3.1	3.28	0.45	0.2	<0.02	0.10	5.94	98.34
979-18-2C	61.6	10.4	2.76	0.04	2.6	1.08	3.5	1.70	0.42	0.4	<0.02	0.06	14.10	98.66
979-18-3	61.1	9.41	2.96	0.07	1.5	5.28	2.0	1.39	0.48	2.2	<0.02	0.04	11.90	98.33
979-18-4A	56.6	13.7	4.76	0.14	1.7	4.81	3.4	2.10	0.56	0.2	0.05	0.09	11.34	99.45
979-18-4B	71.6	8.13	2.19	0.20	1.0	2.00	1.7	1.17	0.34	0.72	<0.02	0.05	9.46	98.56
979-18-4C	67.3	10.7	3.77	0.15	1.2	1.55	2.6	1.98	0.46	0.56	<0.02	0.06	8.86	99.19
979-18-4D	61.4	8.54	2.70	0.13	1.3	6.87	2.2	1.74	0.36	2.9	<0.02	0.08	10.36	98.58
979-18-4E	57.4	7.77	2.66	0.04	1.2	2.29	7.0	1.49	0.29	0.67	0.27	0.08	15.84	97.00

Notes for Tables 6-2A and 6-2B:
Analyses performed at U.S. Geological Survey analytical laboratories. Analysts: R. Bies, M. Coughlin, S. Danahey, L. Espos, B. Keaten, S. Lasater, M. Malcolm, H. T. Millard, J. Storey, J. Taggart, and R. B. Vaughn.
*Total iron reported as Fe₂O₃.   †LOI (Loss on Ignition) measured at 900°C.

Table 6–3. Correlation Coefficient Matrices for Chemical Data from the Four Geographic Locations Containing the Most Samples and Most Complete Set of Analyses

Gulf of California

	U	C_{org}	SiO_2	Al_2O_3	Fe_2O_3	MgO	CaO	Na_2O	K_2O	TiO_2	P_2O_5
C_{org}	.500										
SiO_2	.590	.493									
Al_2O_3	−.467	−.772	−.710								
Fe_2O_3	−.520	−.815	−.742	.987							
MgO	−.640	−.353	−.896	.549	.602						
CaO	−.229	−.405	−.775	.533	.600	.747					
Na_2O	−.008	.414	.342	−.554	−.562	−.255	−.637				
K_2O	−.408	−.771	−.575	.977	.945	.375	.373	−.542			
TiO_2	−.473	−.797	−.726	.996	.992	.580	.586	−.599	.964		
P_2O_5	−.355	.204	.068	−.347	−.253	.307	.019	.086	−.435	−.304	
LOI	.367	.788	.408	−.900	−.904	−.309	−.371	.486	−.908	−.895	.290

Baja California

	U	C_{org}	SiO_2	Al_2O_3	Fe_2O_3	MgO	CaO	Na_2O	K_2O	TiO_2	P_2O_5
C_{org}	−.445										
SiO_2	.764	−.444									
Al_2O_3	.009	.355	−.316								
Fe_2O_3	−.050	.461	−.378	.974							
MgO	−.182	.283	−.600	.916	.892						
CaO	−.582	.365	−.910	.442	.544	.688					
Na_2O	−.894	.503	−.703	−.245	−.175	−.040	.432				
K_2O	.113	.371	−.119	.943	.958	.770	.327	−.357			
TiO_2	−.088	.514	−.444	.951	.992	.887	.591	−.103	.924		
P_2O_5	−.272	.423	−.516	.770	.852	.805	.742	−.005	.793	.835	
LOI	−.775	.154	−.835	−.214	−.176	.138	.638	.813	−.431	−.103	.037

Peru

	U	Th	C_org	SiO₂	Al₂O₃	Fe₂O₃	FeO	MgO	CaO	Na₂O	K₂O	TiO₂	P₂O₅	BaO
Th	**.857**													
C_org	.301	.347												
SiO₂	**.775**	**.941**	.312											
Al₂O₃	−.450	.546	−.104	−.067										
Fe₂O₃	−.220	−.759	−.106	−.506	.176									
FeO	.122	.627	−.227	.456	.476	−.359								
MgO	−.405	−.350	2.50	−.431	.180	.321	−.606							
CaO	−.063	−.618	−.109	−.395	−.305	.291	−.072	−.207						
Na₂O	−.465	−.516	−.533	−.576	−.157	.042	−.235	.029	−.196					
K₂O	−.442	.808	−.295	.054	**.866**	−.146	**.728**	−.136	−.274	−.033				
TiO₂	−.309	−.155	.380	−.308	.581	**.712**	−.122	.513	.058	−.311	.209			
P₂O₅	.029	−.335	.337	−.091	−.524	−.215	−.300	−.118	**.784**	−.354	−.385	−.214		
BaO	−.380	.197	**−.835**	−.222	.458	−.071	.611	−.355	.087	.357	**.696**	−.210	−.304	
LOI	−.305	−.727	−.040	**−.633**	−.478	.196	**−.865**	.543	.008	.617	−.625	−.099	.071	−.325

Korea

	U	Th	C_org	SiO₂	Al₂O₃	Fe₂O₃	MgO	CaO	Na₂O	K₂O	TiO₂	P₂O₅
Th	.529											
C_org	−.035	−.490										
SiO₂	**−.698**	**−.803**	.043									
Al₂O₃	**.767**	.764	−.156	**−.941**								
Fe₂O₃	**.685**	.624	−.084	**−.880**	**.771**							
MgO	.412	.745	−.136	**−.889**	**.779**	**.789**						
CaO	.346	.459	.000	−.772	.612	**.848**	**.872**					
Na₂O	.404	**.846**	−.337	**−.814**	**.826**	.722	.744	.733				
K₂O	**.619**	.642	−.156	**−.909**	**.961**	.768	.811	.731	**.906**			
TiO₂	**.669**	**.839**	−.305	**−.903**	**.971**	.695	.806	.600	**.848**	**.947**		
P₂O₅	.442	.289	−.628	−.368	.345	.617	.247	.364	.474	.339	.370	
LOI	.581	.693	.346	**−.860**	.734	.656	.733	.544	.501	**.649**	**.662**	−.046

Note: Correlations at greater than 95% confidence level are boldfaced.

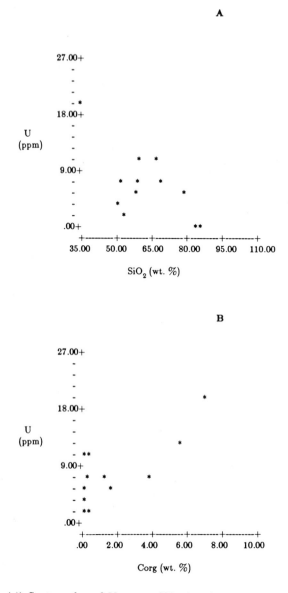

Figure 6-2. (*A*) Scatter plot of U versus SiO$_2$ for the averages from twelve geographic areas (see Tables 6–1 and 6–2). The highest average U and lowest average SiO$_2$ point represents a calcite-rich end member, California continental borderland, whereas the lowest average U and highest average SiO$_2$ point (two points together) represents the SiO$_2$-rich chert end member, the Franciscan and Nicoya complexes. (*B*) Scatter plot of U versus organic carbon for the averages from twelve geographic areas (see Tables 6–1 and 6–2) including the average listed for Durham's (in press) Monterey Formation data. Averages that fall below 1.5% organic carbon (outcrop samples) show a random distribution relative to U, whereas averages for the drill core and offshore groups, organic carbon >1.5%, show a positive linear relationship between U and organic carbon.

A positive correlation exists between uranium and thorium in the two areas where enough absolute values of thorium are available, Peru and the California Franciscan cherts (Table 6-3). Uranium does not correlate with organic carbon at the 95% confidence level for any geographic area, although some high degree of positive correlation exists for the Gulf of California and the Bering Sea samples. A positive correlation exists between U and SiO_2 for samples from the Gulf of California, Baja California, and Peru, but they are negatively correlated for rocks from Korea. A positive correlation exists between uranium and the group of oxides representative dominantly of detrital minerals (Al, Fe, K, Ti) for Korean rocks. Most other positive correlations are between oxides representative of detrital minerals or between elements (CaO, MgO, LOI) of the carbonate fraction. Various combinations of geographic areas produce positive correlations between U and SiO_2, organic carbon, and P_2O_5 and negative correlations with detrital oxides.

DISCUSSION

DISTRIBUTION OF MARINE DIATOMITE AND BASIN DEVELOPMENT

Marine diatomites are known from the entire circum-Pacific region and are especially extensive in Peru, California, Siberia, Japan, and Korea (Garrison, 1975; Chap. 7; Chap. 2). In addition, many near-shore regions contain large deposits of diatomite—most notably, the Peru shelf, Gulf of California, Bering Sea, and Sea of Japan. The best studied formations include the Monterey Formation of California and the Onnagawa and Funakawa formations of Japan.

The development of circum-Pacific Neogene basins is described by Ingle (1973, 1981), Garrison (1975), and Orr (1972). They showed that subsidence began in the Oligocene and was accompanied by deposition of continental and shallow marine clastic sediments. In middle and late Miocene time, rapid subsidence produced silled basins cut off from terrigenous input, thus allowing for the main biosiliceous or diatomaceous depositional phase (Ingle, 1981). Basins were filled in the Pliocene and Pleistocene when diatomaceous sections were capped by rapidly advancing wedges of coarse clastic sediment.

A combination of favorable climatic and tectonic events caused the synchronous development of Neogene diatomaceous deposits in the circum-Pacific (Orr, 1972; Ingle, 1973, 1981). Expansion of the Antarctic ice cap during the middle Miocene increased oceanic and atmospheric circulation, causing prolific diatom productivity (Ingle, 1981). Synchronous development of Oligocene and late Miocene tectonic basins was the result of an increased rate of spreading at the East Pacific Rise and possible readjustment of lithospheric plates.

SEDIMENTATION

Diatomaceous sediments deposited in the continental margin silled basins are commonly laminated because anoxic conditions prevailed. Well-developed oxygen minima produced anoxic conditions below sill depth (Ingle, 1981). Little or no oxygen allowed for the preservation of both abundant marine-sapropelic and terrestrial-humic types of organic matter. The sapropelic organic matter developed into the petroleum deposits common to many of the Neogene diatomaceous sections, whereas the humic organic matter was the major substrate for adsorption of uranium from seawater (see the next section). The Korean diatomaceous deposits were deposited under oxic conditions (Garrison et al., 1979) and contain relatively abundant humic material because deposition took place in near-shore basins that received significant terrigenous and associated organic debris.

The Neogene diatomaceous deposits span the range from diatomaceous siltstone and mudstone to nearly pure diatomite. These deposits contain various amounts of detrital minerals represented chemically by Si, Al, Fe, Ti, and K and in places also by Mg, Na, Ca, and P (see Tables 6–2 and 6–3); biogenic debris including calcareous fossils (Ca, Mg, LOI), siliceous fossils (Si), and fish debris (P, Ca); organic carbon (C, LOI); and authigenic minerals, pyrite (Fe), phosphorite (P, Ca), dolomite (Ca, Mg, LOI), and glauconite (Fe, K, Si, Al). Previous studies indicate that uranium concentrates in several of these phases including organic matter, apatite (fish debris and phosphorite), detrital heavy minerals such as zircon, and as we show here, also siliceous microfossils (see also Durham, in press).

URANIUM ENRICHMENT

The most likely source of additional uranium is seawater, and the proposed primary mechanism of extraction involves incorporation in humic organic matter. A correlation between uranium and organic carbon has been noted in many studies of offshore deposits where uranium is concentrated (e.g., Baturin et al., 1971; Dorta and Rona, 1971; Hein et al., 1982; Brumsack and Gieskes, 1983) and is suggested by our statistical data for the Bering Sea and Gulf of California deposits (see Table 6–3 and Fig. 6–2B). The oxidation of organic matter in outcrop samples and later diagenesis of the rocks precludes maintenance of this relationship. The lack of a strong correlation between uranium and P_2O_5 suggests that phosphatic material, which commonly contains abundant uranium (Altschuler et al., 1958; Goldberg, 1965; Nash et al., 1981), is not the host for the bulk of the uranium, although locally phosphate appears to hold a small part of the total uranium, perhaps up to 10%.

The type of organic matter present can influence the amount of uranium that will be concentrated. Sapropelic organic matter, derived largely from algal and other marine plant and animal remains, is not as effective in concentrating uranium as humic matter, derived from terrestrial cellulose plant material (Swanson, 1960, 1961; Vine, 1962). Petrographic study of Miocene siliceous rocks shows that terrestrial plant debris is ubiquitous, occurs in varying amounts, and is usually less abundant than sapropelic organic matter.

The early sequence of events in the depositional basin included inorganic and bacterially mediated processes. The extraction of uranium from seawater proceeded under anaerobic conditions with the reduction of dissolved U^{6+} to the less soluble U^{4+}. H_2S produced by bacterial sulfate reduction, strongest in the surficial sediments (Brumsack and Gieskes, 1983), speeded the reduction of U^{6+} (Nash et al., 1981). The fixation of U^{4+} was probably dominantly on humic organic matter but also partly on sapropelic organic matter and biogenic silica. Organic matter may also fix U^{6+} by forming complexes that are later reduced to U^{4+} by the organic matter and H_2S. Pyrite is observed in many of the sections studied and results from the reaction of H_2S with iron.

As bacteria decomposed the organic matter in the zone of sulfate reduction and later, after deeper burial, in the zone of carbonate reduction, some uranium was released from the organic matter (mobilized) and was at least partly readsorbed on other particles. We suggest that the host for the displaced uranium was opal-A, biogenic silica. This is the most reactive phase in the sediments next to organic matter and has an open-framework structure capable of admitting uranium ions (see Zielinski, 1980, 1982). Smectite may also adsorb some uranium in deposits rich with this mineral (MacDougall, 1977; Nash et al., 1981). Transfer of uranium from organic matter to opal-A or to pore waters also may occur as organic matter was oxidized by exposure to oxic conditions during uplift.

The evidence for a U-SiO_2 association is twofold. First, SiO_2 and U show positive correlation coefficients in some of the deposits studied (see Table 6-3). Second, diatoms from diatomites containing large amounts of uranium appear brighter than they should be under the scanning electron microscope using back-scattered X-rays. This information indiates that some element of heavy atomic weight is associated with opaline silica. The brighter appearance is evenly distributed throughout the diatom frustules present in the rock.

DIAGENESIS

Mobilization of uranium accompanied silica diagenesis. Our chemical data show that uranium content decreases from diatomites through porcelanites to quartz chert, where it is uniformly low, 1 ± 1 ppm U (see Fig. 6-1). During diagenesis opal-A (containing uranium) transformed by solution and reprecipitation to opal-CT and finally to quartz; porosity was reduced and compaction of the sediment occurred (see Isaacs, 1981a, b). In addition, both reactions, opal-A $\rightarrow$ opal-CT and opal-CT $\rightarrow$ quartz are dehydration reactions that produced the waters necessary for the transport of the uranium and other elements known to be released from the silica during dissolution (Hein et al., 1983b; Brueckner and Snyder, 1985). Each successive silica polymorph formed has a structure less capable of accommodating the large uranium ion.

The nature of silica diagenesis guarantees that the uranium originally deposited with the amorphous silica and organic matter will eventually be mobilized through organic matter degradation and through solution and precipitation of more crystalline silica polymorphs. If the redox conditions and lithologic characteristics of adjacent sedimentary rocks are appropriate, then concentration of uranium in these adjacent rocks is possible. The lithologic succession of the depositional basins (described earlier) offers excellent possibilities for secondary traps of uranium. The diatomaceous sections are both underlain and overlain by continental to shallow marine siltstone and sandstone. Epigenetic uranium deposits are known to occur in Tertiary sandstones adjacent to and within the Monterey Formation of California (Dickinson, 1982). We suggest that areas adjacent to large outcroppings of sedimentary siliceous rocks, especially those that have undergone at least moderate diagenesis, are good places to look for concentrations of uranium. Rocks from the Pisco Formation in Peru have not undergone extensive diagenesis, and porcelanite is minor. This is also true of the San Felipe area in Baja California. In contrast, the Korean deposits contain much porcelanite but few chert beds, whereas the Monterey Formation of California contains extensive porcelanite and chert.

Variations in the amount and distribution of uranium in the studied formations are produced by variations in the original composition of the sediment and the geochemical environment in bottom sediments of the depositional basin. For example, uranium in the Korean deposits may be hosted in large part by detrital minerals, as is indicated by the correlation of U with the detrital elements Al, Fe, K, and Ti. This is a reasonable assumption for the Korea deposits because the source rocks for the continental margin basins that accumulated biosiliceous debris contained high concentrations of uranium (Gabelman, 1982). As another example, the redox conditions of bottom waters in basins where siliceous sediments are deposited influence the rate of accumulation of uranium if suitable substrates are available. Thus, the oxic surface sediment of the Bering Sea accumulates only 28 μg cm^{-2} 10^3 yr^{-1} uranium, whereas the more reducing surface sediment of the Gulf of California accumulates 530 μg cm^{-2} 10^3 yr^{-1} uranium (Veeh, 1967; Yamada and Tsunogai, 1983/1984).

CONCLUSION

Uranium occurs in amounts above the crustal average in all circum-Pacific sedimentary siliceous sequences. The following is the most likely sequence of events to explain this enrichment.

1. Deposition of organic-matter-rich biosiliceous sediments occurred in continental margin basins.
2. Primarily the humic organic matter and secondarily the sapropelic organic matter and biogenic silica fixed and concentrated uranium from seawater during sediment deposition and very early diagenesis. Probable mechanisms include adsorption of U^{6+} and reduction of U^{6+} to relatively insoluble U^{4+} by H_2S and organic matter.
3. Further bacterial and chemical degradation of the organic matter released some uranium that was then predominantly adsorbed onto biogenic silica.
4. Even later degradation or oxidation of residual organic matter and transformation of biogenic silica into opal-CT and then into quartz again released adsorbed uranium and other elements.

The uranium released at steps 3 and 4 may have migrated to adjacent sandstone host rocks, where economic concentrations of uranium may develop.

ACKNOWLEDGMENTS

We thank Dave Durham, U.S. Geological Survey, for helpful discussions and for providing a preprint of his paper. John N. Rosholt and Robert A.

Zielinski, both of the U.S. Geological Survey, provided valuable insights and helpful reviews. Marlene Noble, U.S. Geological Survey, aided in the production and assessment of the statistical data.

REFERENCES

Adams, J. A. S., and C. E. Weaver, 1958. Thorium-to-uranium ratios as indicators of sedimentary processes: Example of concept of geochemical facies, *Am. Assoc. Petroleum Geologists Bull.* **42**:387–430.

Altschuler, Z. S., R. S. Clarke, Jr., and E. J. Young, 1958. *Geochemistry of Uranium in Apatite and Phosphorite,* U.S. Geological Survey Professional Paper, 314-D, 90p.

Baturin, G. N., 1973. Uranium in the modern marine sedimentary cycle, *Geokhimiya* **9**:1362–1372. (Translated in *Geochemistry Internat.* **10**(5):1031–1041.)

Baturin, G. N., A. V. Kochenov, and Yu. M. Senin, 1971. Uranium concentration in recent ocean sediments in zones of rising currents, *Geokhimiya* **4**:456–462. (Translated in *Geochemistry Internat.* **8**(2):281–286.)

Bloch, S., 1980. Some factors controlling the concentration of uranium in the world ocean; *Geochim. et Cosmochim. Acta* **44**:373–377.

Boehm, M. C. F., 1982. Biostratigraphy, lithostratigraphy, and paleoenvironments of the Miocene-Pliocene San Felipe marine sequence, Baja California Norte, Mexico, Ph.D. dissertation, Stanford University, 326p.

Bramlette, M. N., 1946. *The Monterey Formation of California and the Origin of Its Siliceous Rocks,* U.S. Geological Survey Professional Paper, 212, 57p.

Brueckner, H. K., and W. S. Snyder, 1985. Chemical and Sr-isotopic variations during diagenesis of Miocene siliceous sediments of the Monterey Formation, California, *Jour. Sed. Petrology* **55**:553–568.

Brumsack, H. J., and J. M. Gieskes, 1983. Interstitial water trace-metal chemistry of laminated sediments from the Gulf of California, Mexico, *Marine Chemistry* **14**:89–106.

Creager, J. S., D. W. Scholl, et al., 1973. *Initial Reports of the Deep Sea Drilling Project,* vol. 19, U.S. Govt. Printing Office, Washington, D.C., 913p.

Dickinson, K. A., 1982. *Epigenetic Uranium Deposits in Tertiary Sedimentary Rocks in Ventura County, California: A Preliminary Report,* U.S. Geological Survey Open-File Report 82-818B, 26p.

Dorta, C. C., and E. Rona, 1971. Geochemistry of uranium in the Cariaco Trench, *Bull. Marine Sci.* **21**(3):754–765.

Durham, D. L. (in press). Uranium in the Monterey Formation of California, *U.S. Geol. Survey Bull.*

Finch, W. I., 1967. *Geology of Epigenetic Uranium Deposits in Sandstone in the United States,* U.S. Geological Survey Professional Paper 538, 121p.

Gabelman, J. W., 1982. *Uranium on the Oceanic Side of the Circum-Pacific Mobile Belt,* Transactions of the 3rd Circum-Pacific Energy and Mineral Resources Conference, Honolulu, Hawaii, pp. 487–493.

Garrison, R. E., 1975. Neogene diatomaceous sedimentation in East Asia: A review with recommendations for further study, United Nations ESCAP, CCOP Technical Bulletin 9, pp. 57–69.

Garrison, R. E., L. E. Mack, Y. G. Lee, and H. Y. Chun, 1979. Petrology, sedimentology and diagenesis of Miocene diatomaceous and opal-CT mudstones in the Pohang area, Korea, *Geol. Soc. Korea Jour.* **15**(3):229–251.

Goldberg, E. D., 1965. Minor constituents in seawater, in *Chemical Oceanography,* vol. 1, J. P. Riley and G. Skirroco, eds., Academic Press, New York, pp. 163–195.

Hein, J. R., D. W. Scholl, J. A. Barron, M. G. Jones, and J. Miller, 1978. Diagenesis of late Cenozoic diatomaceous deposits and formation of the bottom simulating reflector in the southern Bering Sea, *Sedimentology* **25**:155–181.

Hein, J. R., C. R. Ross, E. Alexander, and H.-W. Yeh, 1979. Mineralogy and diagenesis of surface sediments from DOMES areas A, B, and C, in *Marine Geology and Oceanography of the Pacific Manganese Nodule Province,* J. L. Bischoff and D. Z. Piper, eds., Plenum, New York, pp. 365–396.

Hein, J. R., T. L. Vallier, and M. A. Allan, 1981. Chert petrology and geochemistry, mid-Pacific mountains and Hess Rise, Deep Sea Drilling Project Leg 62, in J. Thiede, T. L. Vallier, et al., *Initial Reports of the Deep Sea Drilling Project,* vol. 62, Washington, D.C., U.S. Govt. Printing Office, pp. 711–748.

Hein, J. R., R. A. Koski, and L. A. Morgenson, 1982. Uranium and thorium enrichment in rocks from the base of DSDP Hole 465A, Hess Rise, central north Pacific, *Chem. Geology* **36:**237–251.

Hein, J. R., E. P. Kuijpers, P. Denyer, and R. E. Sliney, 1983*a.* Petrology and geochemistry of Cretaceous and Paleogene cherts from western Costa Rica, in *Siliceous Deposits in the Pacific Region,* A. Iijima, J. R. Hein, and R. Siever, eds., Elsevier, Amsterdam, pp. 143–174.

Hein, J. R., C. Sancetta, and L. A. Morgenson, 1983*b.* Petrology and geochemistry of silicified upper Miocene chalk, Costa Rica rift, Deep Sea Drilling Project Leg 69, in *Initial Reports of the Deep Sea Drilling Project,* vol. 69, J. R. Cann, M. G. Langseth, J. Honnorez, R. P. Von Herzen, and S. M. White, Washington, D.C., U.S. Govt. Printing Office, pp. 395–422.

Honda, S., 1978. Composition of the so-called hard shale of the Onnagawa formation of Miocene age, *Geol. Soc. Japan Mem.* **15:**103–118.

Iijima, A., and R. Tada, 1981. Silica diagenesis of Neogene diatomaceous and volcaniclastic sdiments in northern Japan, *Sedimentology* **28:**185–200.

Ingle, J. C., 1973. Summary comments on Neogene biostratigraphy, physical stratigraphy, and paleo-oceanography in the marginal northeastern Pacific ocean, in L. D. Kulm, R. von Huene et al., *Initial Reports of the Deep Sea Drilling Project,* vol. 18, Washington, D.C., U.S. Govt. Printing Office, pp. 949–960.

Ingle, J. C., 1981. Origin of Neogene diatomites around the north Pacific rim, in *The Monterey Formation and Related Siliceous Rocks of California,* R. E. Garrison and R. G. Douglas, eds., Pacific Section, Society of Economic Paleontologists and Mineralogists, Special Publication 15, pp. 159–179.

Isaacs, C. M., 1981*a.* Outline of diagenesis in the Monterey Formation examined laterally along the Santa Barbara coast, California, in *Guide to the Monterey Formation in the California Coastal Area, Ventura to San Luis Obispo,* C. M. Isaacs, ed., Pacific Section, American Association of Petroleum Geologists, vol. 52, pp. 25–38.

Isaacs, C. M., 1981*b.* Porosity reduction during diagenesis of the Monterey Formation, Santa Barbara Coastal Area, California, in *The Monterey Formation and Related Siliceous Rocks of California,* R. E. Garrison and R. G. Douglas, eds., Pacific Section, Society of Economic Paleontologists and Mineralogists, Publication 15, pp. 257–271.

Jones, J. B., and E. R. Segnit, 1971. The nature of opal nomenclature and constituent phases, *Geol. Soc. Australia Jour.* **18:**57–68.

Kano, K., 1979. Deposition and diagenesis of siliceous sediments of the Onnagawa Formation, *Tohoku Univ. Sci. Repts.* **30**(3):59–73.

Karl, S. M., 1982. Geochemical and depositional environments of upper Mesozoic radiolarian cherts from the northeastern Pacific rim and from Pacific DSDP cores, Ph.D. dissertation, Stanford University, 245p.

MacDougall, J. D., 1977. Uranium in marine basalts: Concentration, distribution and implications, *Earth and Planetary Sci. Letters* **35:**65–70.

Nash, J. T., H. C. Granger, and S. S. Adams, 1981. Geology and concepts of genesis of important types of uranium deposits, *Econ. Geology* **75:**63–116.

Orr, W. N., 1972. Pacific Northwest siliceous phytoplankton, *Palaeogeography, Palaeoclimatology, Palaecology* **12:**95–114.

Osterwald, F. W., 1965. *Structural Control of Uranium-Bearing Vein Deposits and Districts in the Conterminous United States,* U.S. Geological Survey Professional Paper, 455-G, pp. 121–146.

Piper, D. Z., K. Leong, and W. F. Cannon, 1979. Manganese nodule and surface sediment compositions: DOMES sites A, B, and C, in *Marine Geology and Oceanography of the Pacific Manganese Nodule Province,* J. L. Bischoff and D. Z. Piper, eds., Plenum, New York, pp. 437–473.

Swanson, V. E., 1960. *Oil Yield and Uranium Content of Black Shales,* U.S. Geological Survey Professional Paper 365-A, 44p.

Swanson, V. E., 1961. *Geology and Geochemistry of Uranium in Marine Black Shales— A Review,* U.S. Geological Survey Professional Paper 356-C, 46p.

Tada, R., and A. Iijima, 1982. Petrology and diagenetic changes of Neogene siliceous rocks in northern Japan, *Jour. Sed. Petrology* 53:911–930.

Troxel, B. W., M. C. Stinson, and C. W. Chesterman, 1957. Uranium, in *Mineral Commodities of California,* L. A. Wright, ed., California Division of Mines Bulletin 176, pp. 669–687.

Veeh, H. H., 1967. Deposition of uranium from the ocean, *Earth and Planetary Sci. Letters,* 3:145–150.

Vine, J. D., 1962. *Geology of Uranium in Coaly Carbonaceous Rocks,* U.S. Geological Survey Professional Paper 356-D, 55p.

Walker, G. W., T. G. Lovering, and H. G. Stephens, 1956. Radioactive deposits in California, *California Div. Mines and Geology Spec. Rept.* **49,** 38p.

Yamada, M., and S. Tsunogai, 1983/1984. Postdepositional enrichment of uranium in sediment from the Bering Sea, *Marine Geology* 54:263–276.

Zielinski, R. A., 1980. Uranium in secondary silica: A possible exploration guide, *Econ. Geology* 75:592–602.

Zielinski, R. A., 1982. Uraniferous opal, Virgin Valley, Nevada: Conditions of formation and implications for uranium exploration, *Jour. Geochem. Expl.* 16:197–216.

7

DIATOMITE: ENVIRONMENTAL AND GEOLOGIC FACTORS AFFECTING ITS DISTRIBUTION

John A. Barron

U.S. Geological Survey
Menlo Park, California

Diatomite is a light-colored, porous, lightweight sedimentary rock that is composed almost entirely of the shells or frustules of diatoms. Diatoms are microscopic single-celled algae that possess ornate, boxlike frustules of opaline silica ($SiO_2.nH_2O$). Diatoms live in virtually all aqueous environments that are exposed to light; consequently, there are both marine and nonmarine diatomites.

Low density and high porosity is imparted to diatomite by the diatom frustules, which are typically perforated by numerous holes, the combined area of which may constitute 10–30% of the frustule (Lewin and Guillard, 1963). Dry unconsolidated diatomite has a bulk specific gravity between 0.12 g/cm^3 and 0.25 g/cm^3 or less than half that of water, whereas the specific gravity of the opaline silica of diatom frustules is about twice that of water (Durham, 1973; Clark, 1978). Lohman, in Bramlette (1946), estimated that a cubic inch of diatomite from the Monterey Formation of California may contain as many as 21 million diatom frustules.

The term *diatomite* is usually reserved for material of commercial quality, implying few impurities such as terrigenous mineral grains, calcium carbonate, or volcanic ash. Diatomites diagenetically alter to porcelanite or opal-CT chert that in turn transforms to quartz chert, wherein the opal-A (amorphous-opaline silica) of the diatom frustules converts first to opal-CT (disordered cristobalite-tridymite) and then to quartz. The delicate structure of the diatom frustule is destroyed during the crystallization of opal-CT. Rocks containing diatoms as well as terrigenous material are referred to as diatomaceous shale, mudstone, or siltstone. Commercial-grade diatomite contains 70–90% SiO_2, 2–10% Al_2O_3, and variable but small amounts of Fe_2O_3, FeO, TiO_2,

P_2O_5, CaO, MgO, Na_2O, and K_2O (Cressman, 1962; Cummins, 1960). Geologists, however, often use the term *diatomite* for any soft punky rock in which diatoms are conspicuous. Other terms for diatomite include *kieselguhr, infusorial earth,* and *tripoli.*

COMMERCIAL ASPECTS

Diatomite was used as a building material as early as 432 A.D. when the Roman Emperor Justinian I used a natural block to construct the dome of Hagia Sofia Church in Constantinople (Calvert, 1930). Presently, between three hundred and five hundred uses have been acknowledged for diatomite. These uses fall into ten main categories: (1) filters, (2) mineral filler, (3) insulating material, (4) fine abrasives, (5) absorbents, (6) catalysts, (7) sources of reactive silica, (8), structural materials (mainly lightweight aggregate), (9) pozzolan, and (10) conditioners or anticaking agents (Clark, 1978). The predominant use for diatomite in the United States is as a filtering agent (Meisinger, 1975). Most uses are dependent on the aggregate effect of the microscopically complex and chemically inert diatom frustules (Durham, 1973).

Aside from its light weight and porosity, other characteristics of diatomite make it suitable for industrial uses. Diatomite has a low thermal conductivity and a melting point that ranges between 1,400° and 1,750°C, although certain impurities can result in a considerably lower melting point (Durham, 1973). The opaline silica of diatomite is nearly chemically inert and is soluble only in hydrofluoric acid and strongly alkaline solutions, so diatomite is especially useful as a filler (Durham, 1973).

Diatomite occurs in massive, laminated, lenticular, or tabular beds that range in thickness from a few centimeters to tens of meters. Modern methods of mining diatomite typically utilize an open pit from which material is removed by ripping and scraping by bulldozers (Clark, 1978). Underground mining was once extensively practiced but is rare today. Deposits are thoroughly studied and individual strata are classified according to their most appropriate use. Waste material is removed to dumps, but commercial-grade material is segregated according to its determined use and transported to the mill (Clark, 1978). Processing techniques vary but typically involve crushing and/or screening, drying, and classifying. Calcining in kilns at temperatures of 980–1,200°C is sometimes done to reduce the surface area of the particles and to render most impurities insoluble (Clark, 1978).

In 1976, 631,000 short tons of commercial diatomite valued at $55 million were produced in the United States. About 60% of that total came from California, principally from marine deposits of late Miocene age near Lompoc in Santa Barbara County (Clark, 1978). The United States led world production in 1971, followed by the USSR, Denmark, France, West Germany, and Italy (West, 1971).

Most of the production in the United States is divided between the Johns-Manville Corporation, which operates a large quarry and plant near Lompoc, California, and the Dicalite Division of Great Lakes Carbon Corporation, which has operations at Lompoc and Walteria, California; Terrebonne, Oregon; and Basalt, Nevada (Leppla, 1953). The United States' current reserves will supply the nation's needs for about one hundred years (Clark, 1978).

The prospects of finding additional large minable diatomite deposits are limited. A major cost in diatomite production is shipping, and major deposits in the immediate vicinity of markets in North America and Europe have long been known (Calvert, 1930).

Diatoms

Diatomites are rather unique sedimentary rocks that form only under specific environmental and geologic conditions. To determine these conditions, it is necessary to understand the nature of diatoms and the oceanic (or limnologic) factors that affect their distribution.

Diatoms are assigned to the golden brown algae, class Bacillariophyceae. They possess an external, boxlike shell or frustule that consists of two overlapping opaline-silica valves. Diatoms range in size from 1 μm to 1,000 μm (1 mm), but the majority of species is found in the 10 μm to 100 μm size range.

Various modes of benthic and planktonic lifestyles have been adopted by diatoms. Benthic diatoms are typically rare in deep-sea sediment because living diatoms are restricted to the photic zone (100 m or shallower). Marine planktonic diatoms are either associated with shelf areas of continents or are completely oceanic in their distribution. A group of marine diatoms that is intermediate between benthic and planktonic diatoms is the tychopelagic (or opportunistically planktonic) diatoms. These forms are commonly found in the near-shore plankton but apparently spend most of their life on the seafloor. Both planktonic and benthic diatoms are also present in lakes, but benthic diatoms dominate in other nonmarine environments such as streams and soils.

Only between 1% and 10% of the diatom frustules produced in the photic zone of the ocean actually reach the bottom sediment (Lisitzin, 1972; Calvert, 1974). After death, the organic coating covering the diatom cell wall deteriorates (Lewin, 1961), and the opaline-silica frustule begins to dissolve because of the undersaturated state of silica in seawater. Preservation of delicate diatom frustules in diatomites apparently is due to the incorporation of diatom frustules into the fecal pellets of copepods and other zooplankton, which speeds their transport to the seafloor and provides some protection from dissolution in the water column (Schrader, 1971).

Phosphorus, nitrate, and silica are the basic nutrients required for diatom growth (Calvert, 1974; Tappan, 1980). Because diatoms are overwhelmingly photosynthetic autotrophs, light is also normally required for growth. The abundance of diatoms in the Pacific and other oceans closely parallels the nitrate, phosphate, and silica concentrations in the surface waters (Lisitzin, 1972; Calvert, 1974). These nutrients are most abundant in regions of upwelling where deeper waters richer in nutrients are brought to the surface by wind or current dispersal of surface waters (Lisitzin, 1972).

Silica is present in solution in natural waters in the form of monomeric orthosilicic acid $Si(OH)_4$ (Stumm and Morgan, 1970). Open water in the oceans and lakes is always undersaturated with silica (Krauskopf, 1956; Wollast, 1974). Calvert (1974) cites numerous laboratory studies that show that silica is a fundamental constituent of the diatom cell wall and an essential requirement for cell division. Lack of silica in the culture medium leads to decreased rates of synthesis of nucleic acids, proteins, carbohydrates, chlorophyll and lower rates of oxygen evolution, CO_2 fixation, and phosphorus uptake.

DISTRIBUTION OF DIATOMACEOUS SEDIMENT

MODERN MARINE DISTRIBUTION

Areas of high diatom production correspond closely with areas of upwelling, which contain high surface water concentrations of nutrients (Fig. 7–1) (Lisitzin, 1972; Heath, 1974). Phosphates, nitrates, and silica are depleted from surface waters by biologic productivity, and renewed supplies from deeper waters are necessary to sustain high levels of biologic productivity. Processes of upwelling bring deeper waters, and consequently these nutrients, to the surface in regions with diverging surface currents and in regions along continents where offshore winds disperse surface waters farther out to sea. Coastal areas affected by eastern boundary currents, such as California, Peru, and southwest Africa, are especially prone to upwelling caused by wind dispersal of surface waters. In colder areas of the ocean where surface temperatures do not differ markedly from temperatures of deeper waters (a weak thermocline), nutrients entrained in deep waters can also rise to the surface and allow high diatom productivity.

Within the oceans there are three major belts where diatomaceous sediment is being deposited: (1) a southern belt circling the globe between 45° and 65°S; (2) a northern belt within the Pacific including the Sea of Okhotsk, Sea of

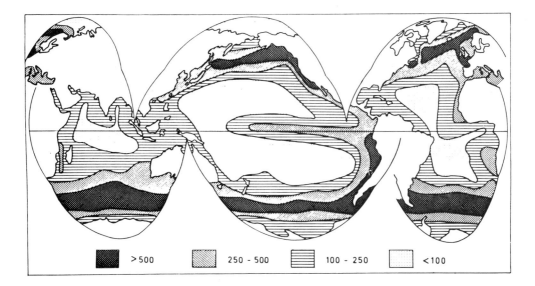

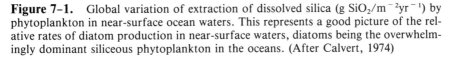

Figure 7–1.   Global variation of extraction of dissolved silica (g $SiO_2/m^{-2}yr^{-1}$) by phytoplankton in near-surface ocean waters. This represents a good picture of the relative rates of diatom production in near-surface waters, diatoms being the overwhelmingly dominant siliceous phytoplankton in the oceans. (After Calvert, 1974)

Japan, and Bering Sea; and (3) an equatorial belt that is well defined in the Pacific and Indian oceans (Fig. 7-2) and less well defined in the Atlantic (Lisitzin, 1972). A comparison of Figures 7-1 and 7-2 shows the effects of dilution of diatomaceous sediments by terrigenous material near the continents—for example, off the west coast of South America.

Heath (1974) emphasized that much of the annual global deposition of biogenic silica occurs in bays, estuaries, and other near-shore areas, where its presence is masked by rapidly accumulating terrigenous material. As evidence, Heath noted that biogenic opal is presently accumulating at a rate of 50 g/cm^2 1,000 yr in the Cascadia Basin off central Oregon within an area of strong upwelling and high biological productivity but that its concentrations in the sediment are commonly less than 5%. As much as 85-90% of the opaline silica entering the geologic record may be laid down in estuaries and restricted near-shore basins where it is masked by dilution from detrital particles (Heath, 1974). Thus, accumulation of relatively pure and commercially useful diatomaceous sediment in the ocean requires relatively low rates of influx of terrigenous materials such as are found in deep-sea basins and in outer continental basins (Lisitzin, 1972; Ingle, 1981).

Within the deep sea, biogenic carbonate (calcareous nannoplankton and foraminifers) also accumulates rapidly in the highly productive equatorial regions, so siliceous ooze in these regions is more typically found below 4,800-5,500 m water depth or below the calcium carbonate compensation depth (CCD), where CaCO$_3$ is not deposited on the seafloor because it is removed by solution within the water column (Heath, 1974).

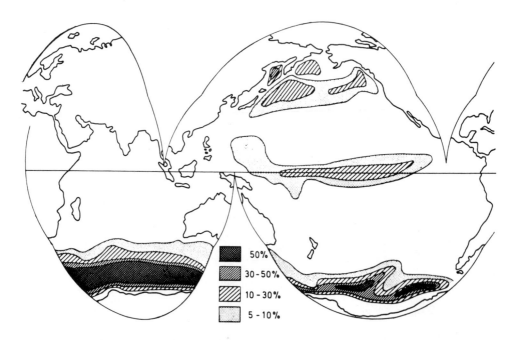

■	50%
▨	30-50%
▧	10-30%
▢	5-10%

Figure 7-2.   Distribution and concentration of biogenous opal in surface sediments of the Pacific and Indian oceans on a CaCO$_3$-free basis (Calvert, 1974). Diatoms are the dominant opaline microfossil in high-latitude areas, whereas radiolarians dominate (by weight-percent) in the tropics (Lisitzin, 1972).

The southern belt of high diatomaceous sediment accumulation is characterized by its large width and high productivity (Figs. 7-1 and 7-2). Over three-quarters of the world oceans' biogenic silica accumulates there (Lisitzin, 1972). Sediment containing greater than 10% amorphous silica occupies a belt that is 900-2,000 km wide, with its northern boundary coinciding with the Antarctic convergence (Lisitzin, 1972). Diatom ooze is found south of the Antarctic Circle and appears on the Antarctic shelf in a number of places (Lisitzin, 1972).

Lower biogenic silica concentrations and a discontinuous distribution distinguish the northern belts of diatomaceous sediment from the southern belt (see Fig. 7-2). Biogenic silica concentrations within this northern belt do not commonly exceed 10-20% and only rarely reach 30% (Lisitzin, 1972). Sediment of the Bering Sea and Sea of Okhotsk, however, contain substantially higher biogenic silica contents (up to 37% in the Bering Sea and up to 56% in the Sea of Okhotsk) (Lisitzin, 1972).

In equatorial regions biogenic carbonate is a major sedimentary component. Biosiliceous ooze accumulates on the seafloor only at depths greater than the CCD, where carbonate is dissolved and biosiliceous material is no longer diluted with carbonate. Equatorial belts of biosiliceous sediment typically lie within 10° of the equator where nutrient concentrations are high due to upwelling and are best developed in the Pacific (Lisitzin, 1972).

Two additional small areas of marine diatomaceous sediment deposition are noteworthy. Sediment of the Gulf of California contains biogenic silica contents up to 65% (Calvert, 1966), and sediment near the mouth of the Orange River off the coast of southwest Africa contains contents greater than 50% (Lisitzin, 1972). Both regions are affected by eastern boundary currents where strong offshore winds cause intense upwelling during a substantial part of the year.

The abundance of biosiliceous sediment in the Pacific and its contrasting rarity in the Atlantic is due to differences in the circulation of deep waters within the two oceans. The Atlantic has two types of deep waters, North Atlantic deep water and Antarctic bottom water; the Pacific, however, receives only Antarctic bottom water. As a result, the Atlantic loses silica-rich deep water in exchange for silica-poor surface water from the other oceans. The Pacific, conversely, gains silica-rich deep water from the other oceans and loses surface waters that have largely been stripped of silica by diatoms and radiolarians (Berger, 1970).

GEOLOGIC DISTRIBUTION
OF MARINE DEPOSITS

As Heath (1974) pointed out, marine diatomites must have been genetically related with areas of upwelling since at least the Cretaceous (>66 m.y. B.P.), when diatoms first became significant in marine sediment. Lithified diatomaceous deposits, however, are also affected by diagenesis, which results in the destruction of the opaline silica of the diatom frustule and reduction in the porosity and increase in the density of the rock, two of the physical properties that make diatomite commercially valuable (Isaacs, 1981). With burial and increased temperature, the opal of the diatom frustule is recrystallized, and the intricate structure of the diatom frustule is destroyed (Calvert, 1974; Hein et al., 1978; Isaacs et al., 1983). This recrystallization of biogenic opal and the formation of porcelanite and chert have been well documented both in marine cores (Calvert, 1971; Hein et al., 1978) and in onshore deposits such as the Monterey Formation of California (Bramlette, 1946; Murata et al., 1977; Pisciotto, 1981; Isaacs et al., 1983). These studies show that rock properties change markedly and abruptly first at about 50°C (transition of biogenic silica as opal-A to opal-CT) and again at about 80°C (transition of opal-CT to quartz). The depth of burial at which these transformations occur is dependent on the thermal gradient of the particular region, but it is typically between 600 m and 1,500 m depth (Pisciotto, 1981; Isaacs et al., 1983). Thus, in models of the distribution of marine diatomites through time, one must take into account the fact that diatomites are not preserved where they have experienced either deep burial or high temperatures.

Leinen (1979) measured the accumulation rates through time of biogenous opal in Cenozoic equatorial Pacific sediment. She noted that the middle Eocene and late Miocene were times of maximum opal accumulation. The onshore distribution of marine diatomites reflects this conclusion in that both middle Eocene and upper Miocene deposits are widespread (see Chap. 2).

The late early to late Miocene Monterey Formation of California is perhaps the most well known of all marine diatomaceous units. It is widely exposed throughout the Coast Ranges of California, extending nearly 800 km (500 mi) from Point Arena north of San Francisco to San Onofre in San Diego County. At places, the Monterey Formation is more than 2,000 m thick (Murata and Larson, 1975; Isaacs, 1983), with the greatest thicknesses occurring in southern California. Rocks of the Monterey Formation are typified by varying amounts of biogenic silica, carbonate, detrital material, and volcanic ash (Bramlette, 1946; Isaacs, 1983). Rocks greatly enriched in one component at the expense of the others are an exception. Although the Monterey Formation ranges as old as the late early Miocene, thick, pure diatomites are characteristically of late Miocene age (Bramlette, 1946; Isaacs, 1983). Near Lompoc, California the Manville Corporation operates the largest diatomite quarry in the world (Durham, 1973). Over 200 m of upper Miocene diatomites of the upper part of the Monterey Formation are mined there.

Diatomaceous deposits and genetically related porcelanites and cherts equivalent in age to the Monterey Formation are widespread in middle Miocene through lowermost Pliocene basinal sequences around the margin of the north Pacific Ocean, including the Bering Sea, Kamchatka, Japan, Korea, and the Sea of Japan (Garrison, 1975; Ingle, 1981). The Onnagawa and Funakawa formations of Japan are well-described analogs of the Monterey Formation.

Upper Miocene diatomaceous sediments are also reported from Chile (Frenguelli, 1949), Peru (Mertz, 1966), Algeria (Gersonde, 1980), Spain (Gersonde, 1980), Italy (Schrader, 1975; Burckle, 1978), and the Central Paratethys in Eastern Europe (Reháková, 1977). The name tripoli for diatomite comes from a diatomaceous deposit near Tripoli, Libya, and is perhaps best known for the latest Miocene diatomites within the lower part of the Messinian stage in Italy.

Middle Miocene diatomaceous sediments are described from most of the same localities as upper Miocene diatomites as well as from Maryland and Virginia and other selected localities along the Atlantic coastal plain of the

United States (Abbott, 1978), Trinidad (Lohman, 1974), and Java (Reinhold, 1937). Middle Miocene diatomaceous sediments may in fact be more widespread than late Miocene diatomaceous sediments in onshore deposits because sea level was relatively high during the middle Miocene and receding during the late Miocene (Vail and Hardenbol, 1979). Pelagic sediments such as diatomites should be more widespread during transgressive periods than regressive periods.

Middle and upper Eocene diatomaceous rocks are widespread in California (the Kreyenhagen Formation) (Hanna, 1931), the Barbados and other Caribbean Islands (Sanfilippo and Riedel, 1974), and in both the eastern and western USSR (Glezer, 1966; Jousé, 1978). Rocks containing middle Eocene diatoms are also present in Israel (Ehrlich and Moshkovitz, 1982). The upper Eocene Oamaru Formation of New Zealand and the lower Eocene Mohler Formation of Denmark represent other well-known Eocene diatomaceous deposits. Within the North Atlantic, Horizon A, an extensive sequence of biosiliceous cherts and porcelanites, ranges in age from late early Eocene to latest middle Eocene (Tucholke, 1979). A review of sediment data in the initial reports of the Deep Sea Drilling Project (Barron, unpublished data) also shows that middle Eocene diatomaceous sediment is more widespread than either upper or lower Eocene diatomaceous sediment in the Atlantic.

Late Cretaceous diatomaceous rocks are present in California (Moreno Shale), along the eastern slopes of the Ural Mountains, in northwest Siberia, near Gdynia in Poland, and on the Kurile Islands in the northwest Pacific (Jousé, 1978). Rocks containing Paleocene diatoms occur along the eastern slopes of the Urals and in the central Volga region of the USSR. Oligocene diatomites are found in southern Baja California, Mexico; in the southeastern USSR; in the Central Paratethys of Eastern Europe; and in Barbados (Glezer, 1966; Reháková, 1977; and Jousé, 1978).

MODERN NONMARINE DISTRIBUTION

Nonmarine diatoms have the same nutrient requirements as marine diatoms (i.e., phosphate, nitrate, silica, etc.), and they are found living in virtually all environments that combine moisture with sunlight (Patrick, 1948), including lakes, ponds, streams, rivers, springs, and soils. Nonmarine diatoms are found aerially attached on moss, trunks of trees, damp stones, and leaves (Patrick, 1948). Nonmarine environments are much more variable than marine environments in terms of temperature, salinity, pH, nutrients, and water current.

Planktonic, benthic, and epiphytic (attached) diatoms are present in nonmarine environments, although planktonic diatoms are most typical of quiet water such as lakes and ponds. The dominant diatoms of rivers and streams are often pennate benthic species.

Nonmarine diatomaceous sediment is typically lacustrine in origin. Like the marine setting, a relatively stable environment with little terrigenous input is necessary for the accumulation of relatively pure nonmarine diatomaceous sediment. In addition, nonalkaline conditions are necessary for the preservation of diatomaceous sediment because the solubility of silica increases abruptly at a pH greater than 9 (Krauskopf, 1959). In the eastern United States and Canada, modern nonmarine diatomaceous sediment is actively mined both from the shoreline and the bottoms of modern lakes and bogs (Eardley-Wilmot, 1928; Calvert, 1930).

GEOLOGIC DISTRIBUTION OF
NONMARINE DIATOMITES

Preservation of nonmarine diatomites through time requires protection from subaerial erosion, as may occur in a stable basin of deposition. Packaging of soft diatomaceous sediment between more resistant units such as sandstones or volcanic tuffs or flows also helps to protect them from erosion. In addition, the absence of silica-starved and/or alkaline-rich pore waters is necessary for the preservation of the opaline shells of diatoms. For example, Lohman (1960) noted that the Upper Cenozoic Furnace Creek Formation of southern California contains lacustrine claystones and mudstones that are locally enriched in sodium and calcium borates. No diatoms are preserved in these claystones and mudstones, although interbedded fresh water limestones do contain some diatoms. Diatoms in the relatively impermeable limestones were presumably protected from exposure to alkaline pore waters (Lohman, 1960).

Nonmarine diatoms occur in rocks as old as late Eocene (Lohman and Andrews, 1968), but most nonmarine diatomites are late Tertiary or Quaternary in age. Nonmarine diatomites are widespread in the western United States, especially in northeastern California, northern Nevada, eastern Oregon, southwestern Idaho, and central Washington (Eardley-Wilmot, 1928; Calvert, 1930). Almost all these deposits are associated with Tertiary and (or) Quaternary volcanic rocks. In British Columbia, Tertiary nonmarine diatomites are present in the Quesnel and Fraser River valleys. Notable deposits of nonmarine diatomites are also present in Australia, New Zealand, Bolivia, Peru, Ecuador, Chile, Scotland, France, Germany, Czechoslovakia, Sweden, Italy, the USSR, the Rift Valley area in East Africa, and in the Transvaal area of South Africa. An extensive review of these deposits is provided by Eardley-Wilmot (1928), Calvert (1930), and Taliaferro (1933).

ASSOCIATION WITH VOLCANISM

Early workers recognized an association of diatomaceous rocks with volcanism and volcanic rocks and argued that volcanism must have supplied the silica necessary for diatom growth (Taliaferro, 1933; Bramlette, 1946). Taliaferro cited numerous examples of the association of diatomaceous sediment and volcanic rocks both in marine and nonmarine environments throughout the world. He concluded that during the Tertiary of California, altered ash was the chief source of silica for the rapid and continued growth of diatoms and other siliceous organisms that contributed to the Kreyenhagen and Monterey formations.

In his classic paper on the Monterey Formation of California, Bramlette (1946) came to much the same conclusion, although he also suggested that selective concentration of diatoms by current drifting was also responsible for thick deposits of diatomite and diatomaceous rocks. Bramlette added associations of volcanic rocks and biosiliceous sediment found in north Africa, central China, Ecuador, and in deep-sea cores from the North Atlantic to the extensive list of associated volcanic and diatomaceous rocks compiled by Taliaferro (1933). Bramlette argued that loss of silica is one of the earliest and quantitatively most important effects of the alteration of vitric pyroclastic rocks.

MARINE ENVIRONMENTS

It is now known, however, that marine diatom production occurs in regions of upwelling regardless of the presence or absence of volcanism (Lisitzin, 1972; Calvert, 1974; Heath, 1974). Upwelling is needed to bring phosphorous, nitrate, and silica to the surface where they can be utilized by diatoms (Lisitzin, 1972; Calvert, 1974; Heath, 1974). Consequently, Heath argued that massive injection of volcanic silica into the ocean system should lead to thicker deposits of biosiliceous sediment beneath the biologically most productive areas rather than near volcanic sources.

Nevertheless, biosiliceous cherts do appear to be more common in volcanically active regions (Heath, 1974). Heath suggested that Calvert's (1966) studies on the Gulf of California might explain this relationship. Tectonism in the Gulf of California associated with divergence and transform faulting along the boundary between the Pacific and North American plates has generated a series of closed basins, most of which are shielded from coarse terrigenous debris. These basins form the locus of deposition of modern diatomaceous sediment in the area. The tectonism responsible for these basins is associated with late Cenozoic volcanism, so mixtures of volcanic ash and diatomite are found in the closed basins.

It is interesting to note that relatively common volcanic rocks in the late early and early middle Miocene of California (Bramlette, 1946) were deposited during a period of active tectonism after the subduction of the Farallon Plate. Deposition of the Monterey Formation began at this time in numerous coastal basins that had become isolated from the influx of terrigenous material (Ingle, 1981).

The association of volcanic rocks and marine diatomites most likely reflects the active tectonism needed to produce a series of basins arranged so that the bulk of detrital material being shed from the continent is ponded in the more in-shore basins. The outer basins, therefore, are free to accumulate relatively pure pelagic sediment. Upwelling produces the conditions necessary to make diatomaceous ooze dominate such pelagic sediment.

NONMARINE ENVIRONMENTS

In the nonmarine setting the association of diatomites with volcanic rocks may be more direct. Cleveland (1966) noted that lacustrine diatomite typically is found in volcanic terranes. He argued that old drainage systems may be dammed by lava flows and that new basins may be created atop the flows. Cleveland assumed that large amounts of silica would be supplied to associated lakes both by silica-rich hydrothermal solutions and by chemical breakdown of volcanic ash. Silica, however, is rarely a limiting nutrient for diatom growth in lakes (Paasche, 1980), and diatoms thrive in numerous lakes not associated with volcanism.

Lacustrine deposits are more likely to be preserved from erosion if they are interbedded between relatively resistant volcanic flows and ashes. In addition, volcanic ash may retard dissolution of biogenic-opaline silica (Riedel, 1959), especially in a relatively closed system such as a lake. Krauskopf (1959) argued that cations released by altering ash might reduce the solubility of amorphous silica, and MacKenzie et al. (1967) suggested that pyroclastic-rich deposits probably are low in certain clay minerals that otherwise act as a sink for dissolved silica in pore waters. Lewin (1961) observed that opal solution rates were reduced by the presence of cations such as Al, Fe, and Ti.

The proportion of detrital silicate minerals that are depleted in silica by intense chemical weathering is likely to be lower in volcanic environments, where most minerals are relatively young. Johnson (1976) argued that anomalously poor preservation of opaline silica in eastern tropical Pacific sediment off southern Mexico and Guatemala was caused by a high input rate of chemically weathered terrigenous silicates. He stated that unstable silicate minerals that have low silicon/aluminum ratios may readily react with silica released from microfossils dissolving in sediment to form other silicate minerals such as sepiolite, talc, or smectite. The formation of such silicate minerals in sediment acts to lower the interstitial silica concentration and increases the tendency for siliceous microfossils to dissolve. If Johnson's arguments are true, youthful environments associated with volcanism should produce a lower proportion of such silica-reactive detrital minerals and should, therefore, be more favorable to the preservation of diatoms.

CONCLUSION

Commercial-grade diatomites result from environmental conditions that favor the growth of diatoms; depositional conditions that eliminate or reduce the input of terrigenous, volcanic, and biogenic carbonate materials; and a geologic history that has allowed little diagenesis or erosion.

In marine environments, high diatom productivity is associated with upwelling where nutrients such as phosphorus, nitrate, and silica are brought to the surface where they can be utilized by diatoms. The association of marine diatomites with regions of upwelling has existed since at least the Cretaceous (>66 m.y. B.P.) when diatoms first became abundant. In the deep Pacific, diatomaceous ooze is found in regions of high biologic productivity north of 40°N, between 45° and 65°S, and along the equator at water depths below the CCD, where biogenic carbonate has been dissolved. Along ocean margins, diatomites commonly occur in upwelling environments within basins that have been isolated from continued influx of terrigenous materials by active tectonism.

In the nonmarine setting, diatomites occur in lacustrine environments that are rich in nutrients for diatom growth, are not excessively alkaline, and do not have a steady influx of terrigenous material. Nonmarine diatomites range as old as late Eocene and are commonly associated with volcanic rocks. Interbedding of nonmarine diatomaceous sediment between relatively resistant volcanic tuffs and flows can help prevent to erosion of nonmarine diatomites.

Volcanism may also enhance the likelihood of preservation of diatoms in nearby lacustrine sediment either directly or indirectly by the introduction of a high proportion of relatively stable silicate minerals.

In both marine and nonmarine rocks, increasing depth of burial and high temperature result in the destruction of the delicate diatom frustule during the transformation of amorphous opaline silica (opal-A) to disordered cristobalite-tridymite (opal-CT). The low density and high porosity, which make diatomites commercially valuable, are lost during this transformation.

Thus, commercially minable diatomites imply an environment rich in nutrients for diatom growth (phosphorus, nitrate, and silica), a depositional setting that eliminates most contaminants, and the lack of exposure to deep burial or high temperature. The abundance of upper Miocene marine diatomites in California and elsewhere around the Pacific attests to these conditions, as does the abundance of Upper Cenozoic and Quaternary nonmarine diatomites in lacustrine basins of the Great Basin of the western United States.

ACKNOWLEDGMENTS

I thank J. Platt Bradbury, James Hein, and Caroline Isaacs of the U.S. Geological Survey, and Jack G. Baldauf of the Ocean Drilling Program for their helpful discussions. This manuscript benefited from the reviews of James Hein, Caroline Isaacs, and J. Platt Bradbury.

REFERENCES

Abbott, W. H., 1978. Correlation and zonation of Miocene strata along the Atlantic margin of North America using diatoms and silicoflagellates, *Marine Micropaleo.* 3:15–34.

Berger, W. H., 1970. Biogenous deep-sea sediments—Fractionation by deep-sea circulation, *Geol. Soc. America Bull.* 81(5):1385–1401.

Bramlette, M. N., 1946. *The Monterey Formation of California and the Origin of Its Siliceous Rocks,* U.S. Geological Survey Professional Paper 212, 57p.

Burckle, L. H., 1978. Diatom biostratigraphy of Unit 2 (Tripoli) of the neostratotype Messinian, *Riv. Italiana Paleontologia* 84(4):1037–1050.

Calvert, R., 1930. *Diatomaceous Earth,* American Chemical Society Monograph Series No. 52, Chemical Catalog Company, Inc., New York, 251p.

Calvert, S. E., 1966. Accumulation of diatomaceous silica in the sediments of the Gulf of California, *Geol. Soc. America Bull.* 77(6):569–596.

Calvert, S. E., 1971. Nature of silica phases in deep sea cherts of the North Atlantic, *Nature* 234:133–134.

Calvert, S. E., 1974. *Deposition and Diagenesis of Silica in Marine Sediments,* Special Publications of the International Association of Sedimentology No. 1, pp. 273–299.

Clark, W. B., 1978. Diatomite industry in California, *California Geology* 31(1):3–9.

Cleveland, G. B., 1966. Diatomite in mineral and water resources of California, *California Div. Mines and Geology Bull.* 191:151–158.

Cressman, E. R., 1962. Nondetrital siliceous sediments, in *Data of Geochemistry,* 6th ed. U.S. Geological Survey Professional Paper 440-T, pp. T1–T23.

Cummins, A. B., 1960. Diatomite, in *Industrial Minerals and Rocks,* 3rd ed. American Institute of Mining, Metallurgical, and Petroleum Engineers, New York, pp. 303–319.

Durham, D. L., 1973. *Diatomite,* U.S. Geological Survey Professional Paper 820, pp. 191–195.

Eardley-Wilmot, V. L., 1928. *Diatomite, Its Occurrence, Preparation, and Uses,* Mines Branch, Canada Department of Mines, Publication 691, 182p.

Ehrlich, A., and S. Moshkovitz, 1982. On the occurrence of Eocene marine diatoms in Israel, *Acta Geolog. Acad. Scientiarum Hungaricae* 25(1–2):23–37.

Frenguelli, J., 1949. Diatomeas fosiles de los yacimientos chilenos de Tiltil y Mejillones, Darwinia, *Revista del Inst. de Botanica Darwinion, Acad. Nac. Ciencias Exactas, Fisicas y Naturales de Buenos Aires* 9:97–157.

Garrison, R. E., 1975. *IV Neogene Diatomaceous Sedimentation in East Asia: A Review with Recommendations for Further Study,* United Nations Economic and Social Commission for Asia and the Pacific, Committee for Coordination of Joint Prospecting for Mineral Resources in Asian Offshore Areas, Technical Bulletin 9, pp. 57–69.

Gersonde, R., 1980. Paläoökologische und biostratigraphische auswertug von diatomeenassozciationen aus dem Messinium des Caltanisseta-Beckens (Sizilien) und einiger vergleichs profile in So-Spanien, NW-Algerien und auf Kreta, Ph.D. dissertation, Christian-Albrechts-Universitat, Zu Kiel (W. Germany). 393p.

Glezer, Z. I., 1966. Silicoflagellatophyceae, in *Cryptogamic Plants of the U.S.S.R.,* vol. 7, M. M. Gollerbakh, ed., Akad. Nauk SSSR, V. A. Komarova Bot. Inst. (translated from Russian by Israel Program for Scientific Translations Ltd., Jerusalem, 1970), pp. 1–363.

Hanna, G. D., 1931. *Diatoms and Silicoflagellates of the Kreyenhagen Shale,* California Division of Mines, 27th Report of the State Mineralogist, pp. 187–201.

Heath, G. R., 1974. Dissolved silica and deep-sea sediments, in *Studies in Paleo-Oceanography,* W. W. Hay, ed., Society of Economic Paleontologists and Mineralogists Special Publication 20, pp. 77–93.

Hein, J. R., D. W. Scholl, J. A. Barron, M. C. Jones, and J. Miller, 1978. Diagenesis of late Cenozoic diatomaceous deposits and formation of the bottom simulating reflector in the southern Bering Sea, *Sedimentology* 25(2):155–181.

Ingle, J. C., Jr., 1981. Origin of Neogene diatomites around the North Pacific rim, in *The Monterey Formation and Related Siliceous Rocks of California,* R. E. Garrison and R. G. Douglas, eds., Pacific Section, Society of Economic Paleontologists and Mineralogists, Los Angeles, pp. 159–179.

Isaacs, C. M., 1981. Porosity reduction during diagenesis of the Monterey Formation, Santa Barbara coastal area, Califronia, in *The Monterey Formation and Related Siliceous Rocks of California,* R. E. Garrison and R. G. Douglas, eds., Pacific Section, Society of Economic Paleontologists and Mineralogists, Los Angeles, pp. 257–271.

Isaacs, C. M., 1983. Compositional variation and sequence in the Monterey Formation, Santa Barbara coastal area, California, in *Cenozoic Marine Sedimentation, Pacific Margin, U.S.A.,* D. K. Larue and R. J. Steel, eds., Pacific Section, Society of Economic Paleontologists and Mineralogists Special Publication pp. 117–132.

Isaacs, C. M., K. A. Pisciotto, and R. E. Garrison, 1983. Facies and diagenesis of the Miocene Monterey Formation, California: A summary, in *Siliceous Deposits in the Pacific Region,* A. Iijima, J. R. Hein, and R. Siever, eds., Elsevier, Amsterdam, pp. 247–282.

Johnson, T. C., 1976. Controls on the preservation of biogenic opal in sediments of the eastern tropical Pacific, *Science* 192:887–890.

Jousé, A. P., 1978. Diatom biostratigraphy on the generic level, *Micropaleontology* 24(3):316–326.

Krauskopf, K. B., 1956. Dissolution and precipitation of silica at low temperatures, *Geochim. et Cosmochim. Acta* 10(1):1–26.

Krauskopf, K. B., 1959. The geochemistry of silica in sedimentary environments, in

Silica in Sediments, H. Andrew Ireland, ed., Society of Economic Paleontologists and Mineralogists Special Publication 7, pp. 4–19.

Leinen, M. A., 1979. Biogenic silica accumulation in the central equatorial Pacific and its implications for Cenozoic paleoceanography, *Geol. Soc. America Bull.* **90**(Part II):1310–1376.

Leppla, P. W., 1953. Diatomite, *California Div. Mines Mineral Information Service* **6**(11):1–30.

Lewin, J. C., 1961. The dissolution of silica from diatom walls, *Geochim. et Cosmochim. Acta* **21**:182–198.

Lewin, J. C., and R. R. L. Guillard, 1963. Diatoms, *Ann. Rev. Microbiology* **17**:373–429.

Lisitzin, A., 1972. *Sedimentation in the World Ocean,* Society of Economic Paleontologists and Mineralogists Special Publication 17, 218p.

Lohman, K. E., 1960. The ubiquitous diatom—A brief survey of the present state of knowledge. *Am. Jour. Sci.* **258-A**:180–191.

Lohman, K. E., 1974. Lower middle Miocene marine diatoms from Trinidad, *Naturf. Gesell. Basel Verh.* **84**(1):326–360.

Lohman, K. E., and G. W. Andrews, 1968. *Late Eocene nonmarine diatoms from the Beaver Divide area, Fremont County, Wyoming,* U.S. Geological Survey Professional Paper 593-E, pp. E-1–E-26.

MacKenzie, F. T., R. M. Garrels, D. P. Bricker, and F. Bickley, 1967. Silica in sea water: Control by silica minerals, *Science* **155**:1404–1405.

Meisinger, A. C., 1975. *Diatomite,* U.S. Bureau of Mines, Commodity Data Summaries, pp. 50–51.

Mertz, D., 1966. Mikropaläotologische und sedimentologische Untersuchung der Pisco Formation Südperus, *Palaeontographica* **118**(b):1–51.

Murata, K. J., I. Friedman, and J. D. Gleason, 1977. Oxygen isotope relations between diagenetic silica minerals in Monterey Shale, Temblor Range, California, *Am. Jour. Sci.* **277**:259–272.

Murata, K. J., and R. R. Larson, 1975. Diagenesis of Miocene siliceous shales, Temblor range, California, *U.S. Geol. Survey Jour. Res.* **3**:553–566.

Paasche, E., 1980. Silicon, in *The Physiological Ecology of Phytoplankton, Studies in Ecology,* I. Morris, ed., University of California Press, Berkeley, pp. 259–284.

Patrick, R., 1948. Factors affecting the distribution of diatoms, *Bot. Rev.* **14**:473–524.

Pisciotto, K. A., 1981. Diagenetic trends in the siliceous facies of the Monterey Shale in the Santa Maria region, California, *Sedimentology* **28**:547–571.

Reháková, Zdeňka, 1977. Marine planktonic diatom zones of the Central Paratethys Miocene and their correlation, *Věstnik Ústředního Ústavu Geologického* (Czechoslovakia) **52**:147–158.

Reinhold, T., 1937. Fossil diatoms of the Neogene of Java and their zonal distribution, *Geologie en Mijnbouw* **12**(1):43–133.

Riedel, W. R., 1959. Siliceous organic remains in pelagic sediments, *Silica in Sediments,* Society of Economic Paleontologists and Mineralogists Special Publication 7, pp. 80–91.

Sanfilippo, A., and W. R. Riedel, 1974. *Radiolarian Occurrences in the Caribbean Region,* VII Caribbean Geological Conference, Guadeloupe, June–July, 1974, 31p.

Schrader, H. J., 1971. Fecal pellets: Role in sedimentation of pelagic diatoms, *Science* **174**:55–57.

Schrader, H. J., 1975. *Correlation of the Neostratotype of the Messinian with Pacific and Indian Ocean Deep-sea Drilling Sections Based on Marine Planktonic Diatoms,* Abstract, VI Congress of the Regional Committee on Mediterranean Neogene Stratigraphy, Bratislava, pp. 403–405.

Stumm, W., and J. J. Morgan, 1970. *Aquatic Chemistry,* Wiley-Interscience, New York, 583p.

Taliaferro, N. L., 1933. The relation of volcanism to diatomaceous and associated siliceous sediments, *California Univ. Pubs. Geol. Sci.* **23**(1):1–56.

Tappan, H., 1980. *The Paleobiology of Plant Protists,* W. H. Freeman San Francisco, 1028p.

Tucholke, B. E., 1979. Relationships between acoustic stratigraphy and lithostratigraphy in the western North Atlantic Basin, in *Initial Reports of the Deep Sea Drilling Project,* Vol. 43, B. E. Tucholke and P. R. Vogt, eds., U.S. Government Printing Office, Washington, D.C., pp. 827–841.

Vail, P. R., and J. Hardenbol, 1979. Sea-level changes during the Tertiary, *Oceanus* **22**(3):71–79.

West, J. M., 1971. Diatomite, in *Metals, Minerals, and Fuels,* vols. 1 and 2, U.S. Bureau of Mines, Minerals Yearbook, 1969, Washington, D.C., pp. 483–485.

Wollast, R., 1974. The silica problem, in *The Sea,* vol. 5, E. D. Goldberg, ed., Wiley-Interscience, New York, pp. 359–392.

PART III

BEDDED CHERT SEQUENCES

8

Origin of Manganese Nodules in the Jurassic Siliceous Rocks of the Inuyama District, Central Japan

Ryo Matsumoto

University of Tokyo
Tokyo, Japan

ABSTRACT. Middle Jurassic radiolarian siliceous shale and bedded chert of the Inuyama district, central Japan, yield abundant manganese nodules at a particular horizon. The nodules are composed mainly of spherulitic rhodochrosite with subordinate apatite. Spherules are 0.2 mm to 1.6 mm in diameter. Carbon and oxygen isotope ratios of rhodochrosite are $-5.63‰$ to $-9.32‰$ Peedee belemnite (PDB) and $+0.47‰$ to $-1.85‰$ PDB, respectively. Isotopic compositions suggest precipitation of rhodochrosite at $12–23°C$ from interstitial water having $-0.5‰$ to $-3‰$ $\delta^{18}O$ standard mean ocean water (SMOW) and under the influence of methane fermentation. Judging from the minor element concentrations and the rare-earth element (REE) patterns through a manganese nodule and surrounding host rocks, Mn contained in the nodules is considered to have been contained originally in the host sediment probably as hydrogenous manganese that later migrated and concentrated into a zone of nodules during burial diagenesis.

Introduction

Bedded manganese deposits are widespread in Mesozoic and Paleozoic formations and their metamorphic equivalents of the Chichibu Geosyncline, central Japan. According to the historical review by Hirowatari (1980), there were 1,045 manganese mines in the Mesozoic and Paleozoic strata in Japan. However, most of these mines had been worked on only a small scale and were closed by the end of the 1960s. Manganese deposits in the Chichibu Belt usually occur as bands, lenses, or nodules in a zone commonly less than 1 m thick stratigraphically. The bedded manganese deposits are frequently associated with bedded chert and in some places are directly underlain by one to a few meters of massive chert. In places, manganese deposits are spatially related with basaltic pillow lava, basic tuff, and tuff breccia, so the genetic relationship between the formation of manganese deposits and submarine volcanisms has often been emphasized (e.g., Yoshimura, 1952; Watanabe, 1957). However, the development of radiolarian biostratigraphy has revealed that manganese deposits and basic volcanic rocks are not necessarily of the same age; for example, manganese deposits of the Yumiyama Mine, about 25 km north of Kyoto, are considered to have formed in the Jurassic (Imoto et al., 1982), whereas the ages of the basic volcanic rocks in this area are Early to Middle Permian and Middle to Late Triassic (Shimizu, 1972).

Many studies have been completed on the occurrence and origin of bedded manganese deposits in the Chichibu Belt, particularly during the 1950s and 1960s. Genetic models of the bedded manganese deposits are represented by two contrasting theses: (1) the epigenetic theory of Yoshimura (1952) and (2) the syngenetic theory of Watanabe (1957). Yoshimura explained the successive precipitation of various manganese minerals as being the result of the evolution of ore-forming fluid in connection with magma differentiation. He considered that manganese deposits are of metasomatic origin. Watanabe attached importance to the constant stratigraphic localization of a large number of manganese deposits in the Ashio district, about 100 km north of Tokyo, and considered that bedded manganese deposits are syngenetic submarine exhalative or submarine hydrothermal deposits. Mesozoic and Paleozoic formations in the Chichibu Belt are in places extensively metamorphosed and tectonically deformed. In such places, it is difficult to know the original constituents and to reconstruct the original structures and textures of the manganese deposits and their relationships to surrounding rocks. In fact, in the Ashio district, various manganese skarn minerals are observed within the contract aureoles of later granitic intrusions (Watanabe, 1957). The secondary modification of manganese deposits is probably the most important reason why the genesis of bedded manganese deposits in the Chichibu Belt has not been fully understood.

Manganese deposits in the Inuyama district occur as megascopic nodules in siliceous shale and bedded chert. The nodules tend to concentrate at a particular stratigraphic horizon of about 10–20 m thick to form a nodule zone. Inuyama nodular manganese deposits are small in scale and not important as a manganese resource, although they offer important information about the genesis of the Chichibu Belt manganese deposits. Inuyama nodules are composed principally of spherulitic rhodochrosite; the associated chert and shale do not show any indications of regional or contact metamorphism, so Inuyama nodules may maintain the original mineralogic composition and textures. Moreover, the radiolarian biostratigraphy of Inuyama chert has been well investigated (Yao et al., 1980), and the transition of the lithologies with geologic age has been well documented; the sedimentation rate of chert and shale has also been determined (Matsuda et al., 1980). These data are necessary to discuss the origin of chert-hosted manganese deposits.

Here, a typical manganese nodule and the related shale and chert in the Inuyama district are described first from a geochemical point of view, and the chemical composition and carbon and oxygen isotopic compositions of rhodochrosite and dolomite are given. Second, the process of initial accumulation of manganese and the formative process of rhodochrosite nodules are discussed in comparison with modern deep-sea sediment. Finally, occurrence and genesis of the Inuyama nodules are compared with other chert-hosted manganese deposits in Japan.

Methods

Fresh samples of chert, shale, and manganese and dolomite nodules were collected from exposures along the Kiso River (Figs. 8-1 and 8-2). Rocks were crushed by tungsten-carbide mill, pulverized in an agate mortar, and analysed by an X-ray diffractometer (XRD) to determine constituent minerals. One gram of the pulverized sample was mixed with anhydrous lithium borate

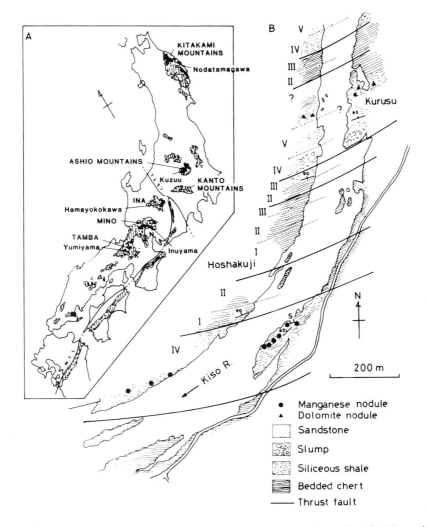

Figure 8-1. (*A*) map showing the localities of manganese mines (dots) in Mesozoic and Paleozoic formations. N = Nogoya, K = Kyoto. Hatched areas are the Mesozoic and Paleozoic formations, and solid lines are the Median Tectonic Line (MTL) and the Itoigawa–Shizuoka Tectonic Line (ISTL). (*B*) Geologic map of the Inuyama district along the Kiso River. I, Middle Triassic; II, Upper Triassic; III, Lower Jurassic; IV, Middle Jurassic, V, Upper Jurassic (I through V after Yao et al., 1980).

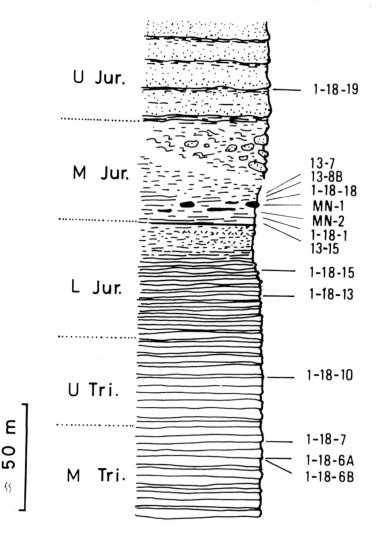

Figure 8-2. Schematic columnar section of the Triassic to Jurassic formations in the Inuyama district. Lines indicate the locations of samples. Rock types are described in Figure 8-1.

and fused to make bead samples to determine the ten major elements Si, Ti, Al, Fe, Mn, Mg, Ca, Na, K, and P, using an X-ray fluorescence spectrometer (XRF). Another 5 g of the sample was pressed without a binder into a disk to determine the nine minor elements Ba, Cr, Cu, Ni, Rb, Sr, V, Zn, and Zr, using XRF. Analytical conditions and procedures of data processing were after Matsumoto and Urabe (1980). One hundred milligrams of pulverized sample was sealed in polyethylene film and irradiated for neutron activation analysis in a nuclear reactor. Thermal neutron flux was 1×10^{12} n/cm²sec, and irradiation time was 12–24 hr. After shorter-lived nuclides had decayed out, gamma ray spectra were measured with a Ge(Li) detector, and the concentration of the seven REEs La, Ce, Sm, Eu, Tb, Yb, and Lu were determined.

Ca, Mg, Mn, and Fe contents of rhodochrosite were analyzed with an X-ray microanalyzer JCXA-733 with the specimen current of $10^{-8}\mu A$ on periclase. Pulverized samples of manganese and dolomite nodules were dissolved in 100% phosphoric acid at 25°C to determine the carbon and oxygen isotope ratios of carbonates. Two weeks of reaction time was needed for rhodochrosite and four days for dolomite to get 100% CO_2 from these carbonates. The manganese nodule contains a few to 15 weight-percent apatite, which dissolves easily in phosphoric acid, but the presence of apatite did not change the $\delta^{18}O$ values of CO_2 from rhodochrosite. This is probably due to the strong bonding energy of the P-O bond. CO_2 gas was purified in a preparation line, then $^{44}CO_2$, $^{45}CO_2$, and $^{46}CO_2$ were measured with a Finnigan-Mat Delta E mass spectrometer. Standard deviations of the measurements were 0.02 ‰ for $\delta^{45/44}$ and 0.04 ‰ for $\delta^{46/44}$.

Geologic Setting

The Inuyama district, about 30 km north of Nagoya in central Japan, is located geologically in the inner tectonic zone of southwest Japan, where folded and faulted formations of the Mesozoic and Paleozoic Chichibu Geosyncline occur (see Fig. 8–1). This district is characterized by the westward-plunging Sakahogi Syncline and many thrust faults (Kondo and Adachi, 1975; Yamazaki, 1977). Bedded chert, siliceous shale, sandstone, and slump deposits crop out repeatedly in 100–250 m thick thrust sheets along the Kiso River. The section shown in Figure 8–1 dips 60–90° northwest to north-northwest and occupies the southern part of the syncline. According to Yao et al. (1980), this section includes Middle Triassic to Upper Jurassic rocks (I to IV in Fig. 8–1). The widths of the outcrops of these formations are about 280 m, but rocks are extensively folded to form homoclinal structures, so the true thickness of the section is estimated to be half to two-thirds of the width of outcrops (see Fig. 8–2). The sedimentation rate of the Inuyama chert-shale sequence has been calculated to be 2.8 m/m.y. based on radiolarian biostratigraphy (Matsuda et al., 1980).

Middle and Upper Triassic bedded chert is made up of rhythmic alternation of a 3–5 cm thick chert layers and a few millimeters thick shale partings, whereas Lower Jurassic bedded chert is an alternation of 2–3 cm thick chert layers with a few millimeters thick shale partings. Both the Triassic and Jurassic bedded cherts are composed principally of radiolarian tests and, in lesser amounts, sponge spicules. Cherts are usually red to reddish brown in color except where leached along cracks and joints. Light gray to light brown tuffaceous(?) shale occurs in the upper part of the Lower Jurassic section (see Fig. 8–2). The Middle Jurassic section includes red to brown siliceous shale, argillaceous bedded chert, black shale with sandstone layers a few centimeters thick, and sandstone/mudstone slump deposits. Siliceous shale/bedded chert and black shale/slump deposits occur in the different thrust sheets, so the relationships between these two facies are not clear. Manganese nodules occur in the lower part of the Middle Jurassic red siliceous shale and chert section. Red argillaceous chert on the east bank of the Kiso River near the sluice gate (S in Fig. 8–1B) yields abundant manganese nodules that concentrate in a 7–10 m thick zone. The abundance of manganese nodules in the nodule zone is estimated roughly to be 4–6 volume-percent of the section based on the field observations. Red siliceous shale on the west bank also contains manganese nodules, though sporadically; the abundance is probably about 1 volume-percent. Sandstone intercalations in black shale commonly exhibit convolute laminae, cross-stratification, and graded bedding. The Late Jurassic section is made up of sandstone turbidites a few decimeters to 10 m thick that are characterized by granule-sized intraclasts of black shale. Red to gray shale with sporadic chert lenses and layers near Kurusu yields abundant dolomite nodules. The geologic age of this shale is not known, although it is probably Early to Middle Jurassic, judging from the similarity of lithology.

Progressive change in lithology from Triassic and Lower Jurassic bedded chert through Middle Jurassic siliceous shale, black shale with sandstone and slumps to Upper Jurassic thick turbidite sandstone clearly demonstrates a relative increasing contribution of terrigenous clastics with geologic age. It is worth noting that manganese nodules and probably dolomite nodules occur in the transitional zone between the dominantly biogenic section and the dominantly terrigenous section (see Fig. 8–2).

RESULTS

OCCURRENCE OF MANGANESE AND DOLOMITE NODULES

Manganese nodules in the Inuyama district are flattened parallel to the bedding plane (Fig. 8–3). The thicknesses range from 3 cm to 22 cm, being mostly around 15 cm, and the lengths are 12 cm to more than 160 cm. Nodules are commonly chocolate-brown to black in color on weathered surfaces due to oxidation of rhodochrosite and are light brown to light gray on fresh surfaces. Manganese nodules in bedded chert occur frequently in shale partings rather than chert layers. In some places, nodules cut laminations in the host shale and overgrow lithologic boundaries between chert and shale. Chert and shale layers curve around the nodule and in places are traceable into the nodule. Manganese nodules are commonly cut by numerous black veins and stringers nearly perpendicular to the bedding (Fig. 8–4). Black veins and stringers are filled with X-ray amorphous supergene manganese oxides.

Fine spherulitic aggregates of rhodochrosite occur (see Fig. 8–4). Rhodochrosite spherules are 0.2–1.6 mm in diameter and exhibit various shapes such as dumbbell, fan, rod, and spherule (Fig. 8–5). The former three forms are probably precursors to spherules. These incipient spherules are common in the margins of the nodule, whereas the central part is composed mostly of closely packed spherules. Rhodochrosite spherules commonly include well-preserved radiolarian tests (see Fig. 8–5); delicate structures of radiolarian tests are observed in spherules, but these tests in the matrix between spherules have been dissolved and deformed; only large tests, more resistent to dissolution, are observed in the matrix. Most radiolarian tests in the matrix are recognized only as 3–250 μ long white spots and flattened spherules (see Fig. 8–5). Occurrence and textures of the Inuyama manganese nodules strongly suggest growth in the soft sediment prior to the deformation and dissolution of siliceous skeletons.

Figure 8-3. (*A*) Manganese nodule in the Middle Jurassic red siliceous shale on the west bank of the Kiso River. The length of the pencil is 14 cm. (*B*) Manganese nodule in the Middle Jurassic argillaceous bedded chert near sluice gate (S in Fig. 8-1) on the east bank of the Kiso River. The nodule is set off by minor faults oblique to the bedding plane. The length of the hammer is 32 cm.

Dolomite nodules are 5–40 cm thick and 25–250 cm long and are composed of 65–80 weight-percent dolomite and less than 20 weight-percent quartz, feldspars, and clay minerals. Apatite was not detected. In thin section, dolomite nodules exhibit a mosaic texture; fine subhedral and anhedral grains of dolomite, mostly 30–50 μ across, are closely packed.

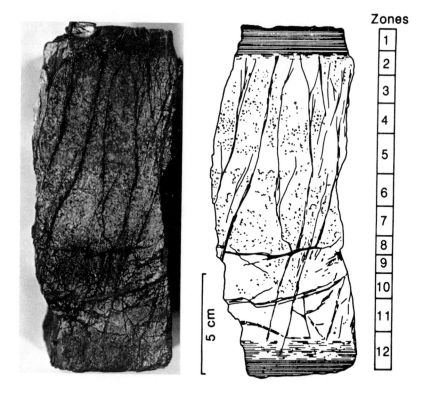

Figure 8–4. Cross-section of manganese nodule Mn-1, collected near sluice gate (S in Fig. 8–1). The approximately 1 cm thick dark layer at the uppermost part is the transition zone between the manganese nodule and the host shale. Dendritic black stringers, filled with manganese oxides, were probably formed during weathering. White spots, about 1 mm in diameter, are spherulitic rhodochrosite.

BULK MINERALOGY AND CHEMISTRY OF MANGANESE NODULE AND HOST ROCKS

To reveal the zonal structure of manganese nodules, a 1 cm × 1 cm × 17 cm column was cut from a typical manganese nodule, Mn-1, then the column was split into twelve pieces (Mn-1-1 to Mn-1-12). Each piece, 0.8–2 cm thick, represents an analyzed zone of the nodule (see Fig. 8–4). The mineralogy and bulk chemistry of each zone were determined by XRD and XRF. The manganese nodule consists dominantly of rhodochrosite with subordinate amounts of apatite, quartz, feldspar, illite, and chlorite; trace amounts of calcite are rarely observed. The highest Mn content is 48 weight-percent MnO in the center of the nodule, which corresponds to 78 weight-percent rhodochrosite (Table 8–1). The top and bottom layers of the nodule equal 6–30 weight-percent MnO, which corresponds to 10–49 weight-percent rhodochrosite, respectively. P is concentrated in the central part (5–8 weight-percent P_2O_5) compared with the margin (0.1–0.5 weight-percent P_2O_5). Apatite contents calculated from

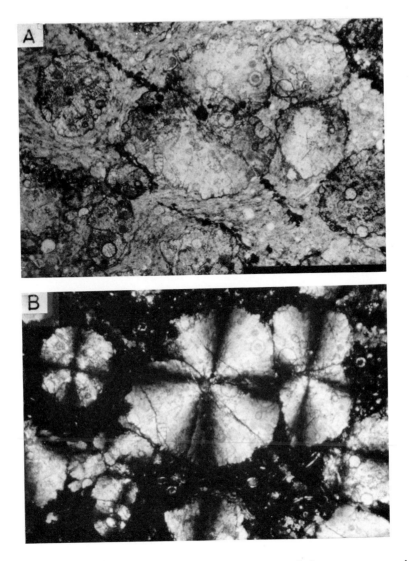

Figure 8-5. (*A*) Photomicrographs of the outer zone of the manganese nodule Mn-1. Rhodochrosite spherules, about 0.54-1.15 mm in diameter, include well-preserved tests of radiolarians, whereas the matrix contains deformed and partly dissolved tests. Matrix clay is deformed around spherules probably because of compaction and/or growth of spherules. Scale bar is 1 mm. (*B*) Cross-nicols.

bulk chemistry range from 15 weight-percent in the center to 0.2 weight-percent in the margin. This finding suggests a genetic relationship between apatite and rhodochrosite. The host shale contains quartz, feldspar, illite, and chlorite; rhodochrosite and apatite were not detected. Small amounts of apatite were rarely observed in the shale parting of Middle Triassic bedded chert. Phosphate had been reported frequently from Neogene siliceous sediment (Pisciotto and Garrison, 1981; Hosoyamada, 1982) and was derived from biogenic components.

Table 8–1. Chemical Composition of Manganese Nodules and Associated Rocks in the Inuyama District, Central Japan

Sample	1-18-1	1-18-6A	1-18-6B	1-18-7	1-18-10	1-18-13	1-18-15	1-18-18	1-18-19
Age	M.Jur.	M.Tr.	M.Tr.	M.Tr.	L.Tr.	E.Jur.	E.Jur.	M.Jur.	L.Jur.
Lithology	Sil.Sh.	Bed.Ch.	Sh.Part.	Bed.Ch.	Bed.Ch.	Bed.Ch.	Bed.Ch.	Blk.Ms.	Gry.Ms.
SiO_2(%)	86.60	92.74	40.20	94.43	92.58	93.89	96.25	66.92	65.56
TiO_2	0.23	0.13	0.72	0.12	0.13	0.09	0.07	0.64	0.80
Al_2O_3	6.19	2.90	16.90	2.60	2.99	2.19	1.72	14.93	18.86
Fe_2O_3	2.68	1.46	7.05	1.18	1.36	1.61	0.58	5.07	4.46
MnO	0.42	0.063	0.11	0.056	0.090	0.14	0.015	0.066	0.037
MgO	1.43	0.65	2.41	0.56	0.64	0.58	0.25	1.51	1.64
CaO	0.20	0.07	12.71	0.08	0.06	0.12	0.11	0.81	0.41
Na_2O	0.74	0.0	1.16	0.25	0.26	0.80	0.55	1.94	2.04
K_2O	1.10	0.87	5.56	0.72	0.90	0.65	0.42	2.78	4.50
P_2O_5	0.03	0.02	8.15	0.02	0.02	0.04	0.03	0.03	0.0
Total	99.62	98.90	94.97	100.02	99.03	100.11	100.00	94.70	98.31
Mn/Fe	0.17	0.048	0.017	0.052	0.073	0.096	0.029	0.014	0.009
Na_2O/K_2O	0.67	0.0	0.21	0.35	0.29	1.23	1.31	0.70	0.45
Ba (ppm)	160	200	590	170	200	160	130	460	570
Cr	5	0	66	1	4	1	0	44	65
Cu	20	25	10	30	24	52	35	18	45
Ni	25	25	60	25	24	30	12	30	30
Rb	60	45	160	35	45	30	18	140	220
Sr	50	22	290	20	25	25	40	150	120
V	23	15	70	15	15	10	10	80	100
Zn	55	40	90	32	35	35	15	80	84
Zr	60	25	120	25	25	25	25	190	205
La (ppm)	12.4	4.0	70.2		7.0	8.1	6.9	43.5	36.9
Ce	37.0	8.9	107.0		15.0	25.0	23.0	85.0	64.0
Sm	2.29	0.70	10.9		1.26	2.02	1.83	7.23	4.69
Eu	0.53	0.20	2.54		0.30	0.55	0.45	1.07	0.89
Tb	0.35	0.09	1.74		0.16	0.44	0.26	0.76	0.63
Yb	1.54	0.63	12.5		0.62	1.18	0.64	3.51	4.11
Lu	0.27	0.10	1.65		0.05		0.01	0.71	0.43
Ce/Ce*	1.45	1.09	0.77		1.06	1.52	1.52	0.98	0.92
La/Yb	8.05	6.35	5.62		11.29	6.86	10.78	12.39	8.98

Notes: Ce/Ce* = Cerium anomaly: > 1 is a negative anomaly; < 1 is a positive anomaly. Ce* is interpolated from La and Sm abundances on the REE pattern diagrams.

Key: Jur. = Jurassic; Tr. = Triassic; E. = Early; M. = Middle; L. = Late. Sil.Sh. = siliceous shale; Bed.Ch. = bedded chert; Sh.Part. = shale parting in chert-shale sequence; Blk.Ms. = black mudstone; Gry.Ms. = gray mudstone; Mn Nod. = manganese nodule.

Siliceous shale from the zone of nodules contains 0.11–0.42 weight-percent MnO, whereas the Middle Jurassic red and black shale devoid of manganese nodules contains only 0.07 weight-percent MnO. Thus, the host shale of the nodule zone is relatively enriched with manganese. The weighted average of the manganese content of the Middle Jurassic shale is 0.19 weight-percent. In contrast to manganese, the iron content of the manganese nodule is low (0–0.43 weight-percent Fe_2O_3) compared with black shale (5.07 weight-percent) and red shale (2.68 weight-percent) of the same age.

The sodium-oxide content of the host shale and the margin (zones 1 and 12 of Fig. 8–4) and the center (zones 2 to 11) of the manganese nodule are similar to each other, 0.27–0.88, 0.41–0.47, and 0.24–0.33 weight-percent, respectively (see Table 8–1). However, potassium-oxide content differs greatly between the host shale and the margin and inner zones of the nodule (Table 8–1). Consequently, the ratio Na_2O/K_2O decreases from the center (24.0) to the margin (0.59–0.84). Considering the mineral composition of the manganese

13-7 M.Jur. Sil.Sh.	13-8C M.Jur. Sil.Sh.	13-15 M.Jur. Bed.Ch.	Mn-1-1 M.Jur. MnNod.	Mn-1-2 M.Jur. MnNod.	Mn-1-4 M.Jur. MnNod.	Mn-1-6 M.Jur. MnNod.	Mn-1-9 M.Jur. MnNod.	Mn-1-11 M.Jur. MnNod.	Mn-1-12 M.Jur. MnNod.	Mn-2 M.Jur. MnNod.
74.30	80.17	82.24	81.20	23.17	10.08	8.92	13.23	16.46	47.29	
0.43	0.32	0.27	0.20	0.05	0.03	0.03	0.05	0.06	0.13	
12.51	10.65	7.57	5.10	0.10	0.0	0.0	0.20	0.43	2.51	
4.06	2.62	3.52	2.68	0.74	0.12	0.11	0.40	0.80	1.79	
0.07	0.11	0.29	6.17	41.28	43.62	47.93	32.63	46.70	30.23	
1.20	1.11	1.13	1.31	1.19	0.78	0.90	0.88	1.29	1.31	
0.27	0.20	0.19	1.13	6.18	9.54	11.79	17.59	5.81	2.71	
0.88	0.65	0.27	0.47	0.33	0.33	0.24	0.33	0.29	0.41	
2.72	2.00	1.25	0.79	0.09	0.04	0.01	0.08	0.15	0.49	
0.0	0.0	0.0	0.08	1.43	3.80	4.89	7.97	1.14	0.51	
96.44	97.83	96.73	99.13	74.56	68.34	74.82	73.36	73.13	87.38	
0.019	0.046	0.091	2.55	61.75	402.39	482.35	90.44	64.62	18.70	
0.32	0.33	0.22	0.59	3.67	8.25	24.0	4.13	1.93	0.84	
290	245	220	320	290	6	25	110	450	390	
43	35	36	10	0	0	5	0	0	4	
30	20	50	45	10	20	5	30	65	30	
38	46	30	25	4	0	0	0	5	10	
135	118	70	35	0	0	0	0	0	5	
110	100	100	40	30	20	20	60	30	30	
65	47	40	25	15	0	0	2	55	30	
90	80	88	80	35	25	25	30	40	45	
110	76	58	40	0	0	0	0	0	10	
					18.5				13.2	9.9
					37.0				52.0	21.0
					2.79				4.69	2.02
					0.26				1.00	0.45
					0.35				0.72	0.33
					1.13				3.58	1.12
					0.83					0.32
					1.02				1.72	1.01
					16.37				3.69	8.84

nodules and host shale, potassium must be contained mainly in illite and/or feldspar and sodium in feldspar. Therefore, a drastic change in the sodium-to-potassium ratio strongly suggests that illite in the nodule was preferentially replaced by rhodochrosite during the growth of the nodule.

The Ba content of the analyzed manganese nodule and host rocks of the Inuyama district does not exceed 590 ppm (see Table 8-1), which is below the average value of terrigenous clastic sediment (Matsumoto and Iijima, 1983). The contents of Cu, Ni, and V are comparable to those of average shale. The manganese nodule notably lacks these heavy metals.

Abundances of seven REEs were determined on eleven samples from the Inuyama district including the manganese nodule, shale, and chert. The results are plotted as chondrite-normalized patterns (Fig. 8-6). Samples analyzed here are commonly enriched in light REEs relative to heavy REEs; chondrite-normalized values of La and Yb are between 10 and 185, and 2.5 and 50, respectively. Positive cerium anomalies are observed in four out of eleven

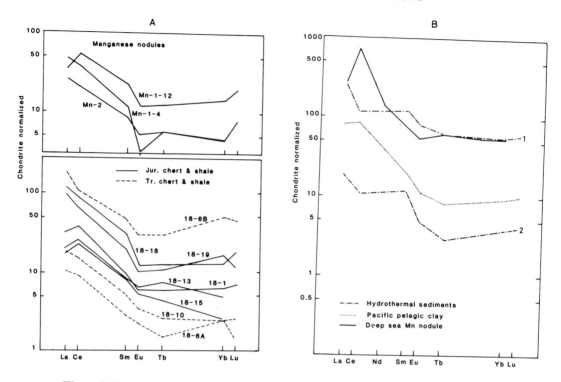

Figure 8-6. Chondrite-normalized REE patterns of the Inuyama nodule, chert, shale, and modern deep-sea sediments and manganese nodules. (*A*) Mn-1-4, Mn-1-12, Mn-2: Inuyama manganese nodules; 18-1: Middle Jurassic siliceous shale; 18-13: Early Jurassic bedded chert; 18-15: Early Jurassic bedded chert; 18-18: Middle Jurassic black shale; 18-19: Late Jurassic gray shale; 18-16A: Middle Triassic bedded chert; 18-6B: shale parting in Middle Triassic bedded chert; 18-10: Late Triassic bedded chert. (*B*) 1, Hydrothermal sediment near the East Pacific Rise (KH 70-2-9); 2, hydrothermal sediment from Costa Rica Rift (DSDP Site 504). (Data on the hydrothermal sediments and pelagic clay are from Matsumoto et al., 1985; and on the manganese nodule, from Barrett, 1981.

samples analyzed. They are the margin of the manganese nodule (sample Mn-1-12), Middle Jurassic siliceous shale (1-18-1) that bears manganese nodules and Early Jurassic cherts (1-18-13, 1-18-15). Positive cerium anomalies may be genetically related to manganese nodules. A weak negative cerium anomaly is recognized exclusively in the Middle Triassic chert. The other six samples show neither a positive nor a negative cerium anomaly.

CHEMICAL COMPOSITION OF
RHODOCHROSITE
AND DOLOMITE

The chemical composition of rhodochrosite was determined at ten to twenty spots in each of the twelve splits of the typical manganese nodule by means of an x-ray microanalyzer and the mole-percentages of Mn, Fe, Ca, and Mg were calculated from these data. X-ray microanalysis of dolomite was made on forty-two spots of the core of the dolomite nodule. The composition of rhodochrosite ranges between 82.0 and 97.5 mole-percent $MnCO_3$, between 1.0 and 15.0 mole-percent $CaCO_3$, and between 1.5 and 5 mole-percent $MgCO_3$ (Fig. 8-7). Fe content is always below 0.1 mole-percent, so Inuyama rhodochrosite is named a calcian rhodochrosite and represented as $Mn_{0.82-0.98}Ca_{0.01-0.15}Mg_{0.02-0.05}CO_3$. Compositional zoning of Mn and Ca within the manganese nodule is well developed (Fig. 8-8), although mean mole-percentages of $MgCO_3$ mostly fall between 2.5 and 3.5 (Table 8-2). Mean Ca and Mn contents in outer zones (zones 1, 2, 3, 9, 10, 11, and 12) lie between 8 and 11 mole-percent and 86.0 and 88.5 mole-percent, respectively, whereas in the inner zones (zones 4, 5, 7, and 8), they are between 3 and 5.5 mole-percent and 91 and 94.5 mole-percent, respectively. Rhodochrosite from zone 6 shows a slightly different composition from other inner zones; it shifts somewhat back toward the composition of outer zone rhodochrosite. These patterns indicate that the manganese nodule, Mn-1, began to grow from two centers, zones 4 and 7, and that at the growth stage of zone 6, the two incipient smaller manganese nodules were combined and became one larger nodule, and then continued to grow toward zones 1 and 12.

The chemical composition of the dolomite in the dolomite nodule (No. 1-18-22) ranges mostly between 54 and 58 mole-percent $CaCO_3$, 38 and 44 mole-percent $MgCO_3$, and 2 and 4 mole-percent $MnCO_3$ (Fig. 8-7). Fe content does not exceed 0.1 mole-percent. Inuyama dolomite is a calcian-manganiferous dolomite. Manganoan dolomite is not as common as ferroan dolomite in ma-

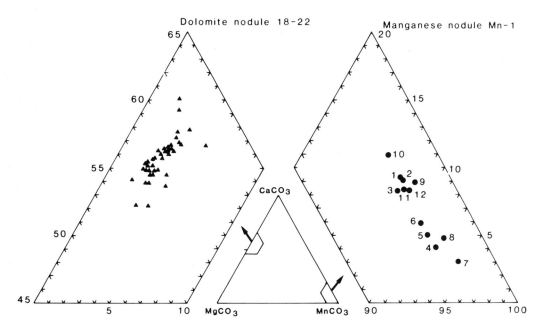

Figure 8-7. Chemical composition of dolomite and rhodochrosite as expressed in mole-percent. Fe contents of dolomite and rhodochrosite are always below 0.1 mole-percent $FeCO_3$. Numbers in the right diagram indicate zones of the manganese nodule shown in Figure 8-4.

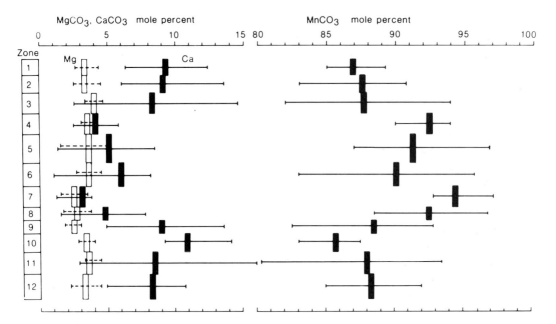

Figure 8–8.   Compositional zoning of manganese nodule, Mn-1. Broken and solid lines indicate the ranges of the concentration of each component and open and filled rectangles the mean value. Ca and Mn contents change in relation to each other, showing W-shaped patterns of variation.

Table 8–2.   Chemical Composition and Isotopic Ratio
of Rhodochrosite and Dolomite

Zone	Ca	Mg	Mn	$\delta^{13}C$	$\delta^{18}O$
	(Mean value, mole %)			(‰ PDB)	(‰ PDB)
Manganese Nodule, Mn-1					
1	9.3	3.3	87.4	−5.85	0.00
2	9.1	3.3	87.6	−7.12	−0.32
3	8.3	4.0	87.7	−8.59	−0.80
4	4.1	3.5	92.5		
5	5.1	3.6	91.3	−8.86	−0.81
6	6	3.6	90.1	−8.59	−1.85
7	3.1	2.5	94.4		
8	4.8	2.7	92.5	−9.32	−1.14
9	9.0	2.5	88.5	−7.93	−0.57
10	10.9	3.4	85.7	−7.26	−1.70
11	8.4	3.6	88.0	−6.25	−0.46
12	8.3	3.3	88.4	−5.63	+0.47
Dolomite Nodule, 1-18-22					
Core	55.7	41.3	3.0	−13.81	−4.64
Rim				−13.45	−5.01

Notes: The widths of the zones are shown in Figure 8–8. $FeCO_3$ content is always less than 0.1 mole %.

rine sediment, so Inuyama dolomite is considered to have formed in an environment with extraordinarily high Mn activity as well as high Ca and Mg activities.

Isotopic Composition of Rhodochrosite and Dolomite

$\delta^{13}C$ of rhodochrosite in nodule Mn-1 ranges between $-5.63\permil$ and $-9.32\permil$ PDB (Table 8–2). $\delta^{13}C$ values increase from around $-9\permil$ in the inner part to -8.5 to $-5.5\permil$ in the outer part (Fig. 8–9). Rhodochrosite from zone 6, however, has a little heavier carbon compared with neighboring zones. Rhodochrosite from the Inuyama nodule on the west bank of the Kiso River has -4.78 to $-7.32\permil$ $\delta^{13}C$ (Minoura et al., 1983), which is similar to the values reported here. $\delta^{18}O$ of rhodochrosite falls within a relatively narrow range between -1.85 and $+0.47\permil$ PDB. The heaviest value appears in zone 12; the lightest value, in zone 6.

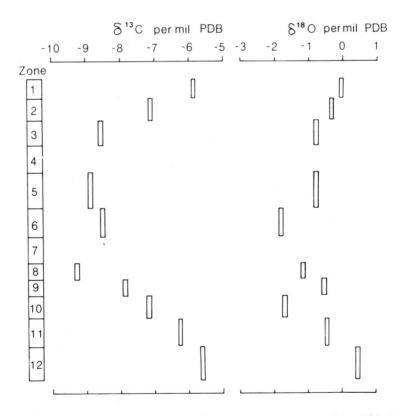

Figure 8–9. Variations of $\delta^{13}C$ and $\delta^{18}O$ in the manganese nodule. $\delta^{13}C$ shows a similar W-shaped pattern to that of the $CaCO_3$ content. $\delta^{18}O$ in the inner part (zones 3 through 10) seems to show a W-shaped pattern, somewhat similar to $MnCO_3$, molepercent.

$\delta^{13}C$ and $\delta^{18}O$ of dolomite are -13.45 to -13.81% PDB, and -4.64 to -5.01%, respectively (Table 8-2). The nodule margin has slightly heavier carbon and slightly lighter oxygen than the inner zone. The different carbon and oxygen isotopic compositions between rhodochrosite and dolomite suggest that these carbonates formed at different stages of diagenesis.

DISCUSSION

FORMATION OF MANGANESE NODULES

The chemical composition of authigenic carbonates strongly reflects the chemistry of the interstitial water (e.g., Tsusue, 1970; Matsumoto and Iijima, 1981; Lancelot and Ewing, 1972). Therefore, the compositional zoning of the Inuyama manganese nodule suggests an increase in the activity of Ca^{++} relative to Mn^{++} of the interstitial water in the course of nodular growth. Relative enrichment of Ca^{++} is favorable to the formation of dolomite and calcite relative to rhodochrosite. This finding may suggest that Inuyama rhodochrosite formed prior to dolomite. Although the compositional zoning is clearly recognized in the nodule (see Fig. 8-8), such zonal structure was not always detected within a single rhodochrosite spherule (Fig. 8-10); dumbbell-shaped aggregates have a reverse zoning with a Ca-rich core and Ca-poor rim. This is probably due to a fluctuation in the Ca/Mn ratio of the interstitial water during diagenesis; that is, the activity ratio did not change monotonously but fluctuated. A wide range of compositions observed in a single zone (see Fig. 8-8) also suggests fluctuation in the Ca/Mn ratio.

In general, the $\delta^{13}C$ composition of diagenetic carbonate minerals from marine sediments decreases from 0% to -30% PDB at relatively shallow depths of burial, then increases to 0% to $+10\%$ PDB under deep burial (Curtis, 1977; Irwin et al., 1977; Pisciotto, 1981; Matsumoto and Matsuhisa, 1985). Variation of $\delta^{13}C$ with depth has been interpreted as the result of oxidation and sulfate reduction of organic matter at shallow burial and fermentation and equilibration with methane at deep burial. The growth stage of the Inuyama nodule characterized by an increasing $\delta^{13}C$ from -9% to -5% corresponds to the early stage of fermentation. Curtis (1977) considered that the fermentation zone would occur between 10 m and 1,000 m subbottom in marine sediment. In fact, at Deep Sea Drilling Project Sites 438, 439, and 584 on the deep-sea terrace near the Japan Trench, the fermentation zone does not appear until greater than 100 m subbottom (Matsumoto and Matsuhisa, 1985). $\delta^{13}C$ of dolomite also shows a small increase during nodule growth, suggesting dolomite formation in the zone of bacterial fermentation.

$\delta^{18}O$ of rhodochrosite in the core of the nodule tends to decrease from -1% to -2% PDB (Fig. 8-9). This variation is considered to reflect an increase of temperature of formation and/or a decrease of $\delta^{18}O$ of the interstitial water. $\delta^{18}O$ of the interstitial water of marine sediment commonly shows a gradual decrease with depth, though fluctuating widely, and this is usually interpreted as the result of reaction of the interstitial water with clay minerals and volcanic glass (Lawrence et al., 1975). In the Neogene siliceous sediment at Deep Sea Drilling Project Site 584, $\delta^{18}O$ of the interstitial water decreases at a rate of 0.26% per 100 m (Matsuhisa and Matsumoto, 1985). Provided that the tem-

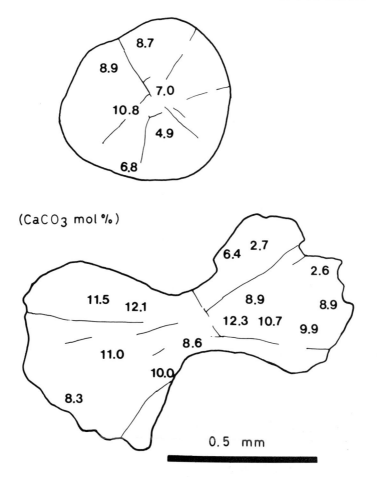

Figure 8-10.   Variation of Ca content within single rhodochrosite spherules revealed by microprobe analysis. Both spherules are from the outer zone (see Fig. 8-4) of the nodule Mn-1.

perature of the bottom water was 4-12°C, that $\delta^{18}O$ of the bottom water was 0‰ SMOW, that the geothermal gradient was 10-25°C/km, and that $\delta^{18}O$ of the interstitial water decreased at the rate of 2-3‰/km, the evolution of the interstitial water during burial would fall within the range represented by the hatched area and arrows in Figure 8-11. Because $\delta^{18}O$ of rhodochrosite and dolomite are +0.5 to −2.0‰ and −4.6 to −5.0‰, respectively, the interstitial waters required to have precipitated rhodochrosite and dolomite are −0.5 to −3.0‰ $\delta^{18}O$ SMOW at 12-23°C and −3.0 to −6.0‰ $\delta^{18}O$ SMOW at 25-40°C, respectively. The possible areas of the interstitial waters are shown by the shaded areas in Figure 8-11. This means that rhodochrosite was formed at a relatively shallow depth of burial prior to the formation of dolomite, which is consistent with the sequence estimated from compositional zoning within the manganese nodule. Burial diagenesis at the temperature range of 12° to 40°C roughly corresponds to the fermentation zone of organic matter diagenesis. The increase of $\delta^{18}O$ of rhodochrosite at the margin of the nodule does not likely mean an inverse evolution of the interstitial water chemistry but a decrease of

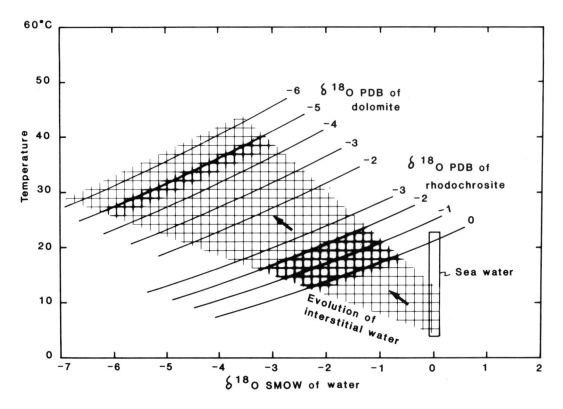

Figure 8-11. Solid lines show the relationship between $\delta^{18}O$ (SMOW) and temperature of the interstitial water and $\delta^{18}O$ (PDB) of dolomite and rhodochrosite. Crosshatched area shows the evolution of the interstitial water during burial diagenesis. Shaded parts indicate the conditions of the interstitial water necessary to precipitate Inuyama rhodochrosite and dolomite. (Fractionation factors for rhodochrosite and dolomite were estimated using the data and diagrams prepared by Friedman and O'Neil, 1977; O'Neil, 1977.

temperature because the chemical composition and $\delta^{13}C$ do not show a similar inverse pattern of variation (see Figs. 8-8 and 8-9). A decrease in temperature during burial suggests a drastic change of geothermal gradient of the sedimentary basin and/or uplift and erosion.

Interstitial water of marine sediment is expected to have high Mg and Ca contents at the time of deposition (Matsumoto and Matsuhisa, 1985); therefore, Mg and Ca carbonates (dolomite and calcite) might be expected to form prior to Mn and Fe carbonates (rhodochrosite and siderite) (Matsumoto, 1978, 1983). In the Inuyama district, however, rhodochrosite formed prior to dolomite, suggesting that the initial concentration of manganese was high in the Middle Jurassic siliceous sediment.

ORIGIN OF MANGANESE

Hydrothermal deposits from the East Pacific Rise and the Costa Rica Rift show strong negative cerium anomalies, whereas Pacific pelagic clay does not show a negative, but in places a slightly positive, cerium anomaly (see Fig.

8–6*B*). A negative cerium anomaly is probably indicative of submarine hydrothermal activity (Matsumoto et al., 1985). REE patterns and trace element concentrations of the Inuyama chert, shale, and manganese nodules are not favorable to a submarine exhalative origin of the manganese nodules. In fact, volcanic rocks of the Middle Jurassic have not been found in or around the Inuyama district. In contrast to the hydrothermal deposits, modern deep-sea manganese nodules, which are considered as typical hydrogenous products, commonly have a strong positive cerium anomaly (see Fig. 8–6*B*). Positive cerium anomalies observed in the Inuyama manganese nodule and related rocks strongly suggest that manganese in the nodules originated from hydrogenous manganese.

Manganese deposits make up about 4–6 volume-percent of the nodule zone, and shale and chert make up the remaining 94–96%. The thickness of the nodule zone is one-fifth to one-eighth of the total thickness of the Middle Jurassic shale. Supposing that Mn in manganese nodules was originally distributed homogeneously in the Middle Jurassic siliceous rocks, then the original content of manganese is calculated as $(0.04–0.06) \times 40 \times (1/5–1/8) + 0.19 = 0.39–0.67$ weight-percent MnO, of which 40% and 0.19% are the average MnO content of the manganese nodules and the Middle Jurassic sediment, respectively. The original content of manganese can be determined from the rate of sedimentation of the host rock (Matsumoto et al., 1985), by making several assumptions. The rate of sedimentation of the Middle Jurassic sediment is estimated to be about 3 m/m.y. based on paleontologic dating (Matsuda et al., 1980). The thickness reduction due to compaction during burial is estimated to be at least 60% using the porosity and bulk density data of Deep Sea Drilling Project cores of similar lithology (Scientific Party, 1980). Thus, the sedimentation rate corrected for compaction was at least 5 m/m.y. According to Matsumoto et al. (1985), Mn content and sedimentation rate have an inverse relationship, which is interpreted as the result of dilution of constantly accumulating hydrogenous manganese chiefly by terrigenous and biogenic components. A sedimentation rate of 5 m/m.y. corresponds to 0.35–0.75 weight-percent MnO (Matsumoto et al., 1985). Within the limit of error this value is similar to the value of 0.39–0.67 weight-percent calculated for the original Mn content of Middle Jurassic shale.

The preceding discussion leads to the following conclusions about the origin of manganese: (1) Mn in the manganese nodules was originally contained in the host shale probably as manganese oxyhydroxide deposited through a hydrogenous process. (2) Hydrogenous manganese was reduced in the sediment, which raised the Mn activity at relatively shallow depths of burial to form Mn carbonate. (3) Present Mn contents of host shale and chert are considered to be about one-half the original concentration due to secondary migration and localization of manganese during diagenesis. In fact, in places, late Cenozoic deep-sea mud with high Mn contents contains nodular and disseminated rhodochrosite as reported from several Deep Sea Drilling Project sites, 184 through 192 and 436 and 487 (Hein et al., 1979; Scientific Party, 1980; Wada et al., 1982). The rhodochrosite is considered to have resulted from the secondary migration of manganese in the host mud. For the formation of manganese deposits during diagenesis, it is crucial to accumulate a large amount of manganese at the time of deposition. Slowly deposited bedded chert and shale are favorable to the accumulation of enough hydrogenous manganese. This is the important point of the close association of manganese deposits and bedded chert.

Several reasons why the Inuyama manganese nodules were formed preferentially in the Middle Jurassic sediment that is stratigraphically located between a pelagic-biogenic section (chert-shale of Middle Triassic to Early Jurassic age) and a near-shore terrigenous section (mudstone and sandstone of Late Jurassic age) include the following. First, concentration of apatite, which probably originated from siliceous organisms, kept the microenvironment of the Middle Jurassic shale at relatively high pH conditions. Second, much CO_2 gas used in carbonate formation was generated through the decay of abundant organic materials such as plant debris; Jurassic sediment commonly contains terrestrial plant debris. Finally, dilution by terrigenous mud and sand was not great, so enough hydrogenous manganese accumulated to form rhodochrosite.

COMPARISON WITH OTHER JAPANESE MANGANESE DEPOSITS

DISTRIBUTION OF CHERT-HOSTED MANGANESE DEPOSITS IN JAPAN

Bedded and nodular manganese deposits of Mesozoic and Paleozoic formations are in most places closely associated with bedded chert and siliceous shale, suggesting a genetic relationship between manganese deposits and chert. Chert-hosted manganese deposits tend to concentrate at several areas such as the northern Kitakami, Kanto, and Ashio mountains and the Ina, Mino, and Tamba districts (see Fig. 8–1). The Nodatamagawa mine of the northern Kitakami Mountains was one of the biggest and most typical chert-hosted manganese deposits in Japan. This mine had been intensively metamorphosed by intrusions of Cretaceous granitic rocks; host rocks consist of hornfels and metachert. The manganese ores are made up of metamorphic minerals such as hausmannite, jacobsite, tephroite, and rhodonite and are underlain by massive chert. Some manganese deposits within the contact aureoles of granitic intrusions in the Ashio Mountains show an occurrence similar to the Nodatamagawa mine, but weakly or nonmetamorphosed sections in the district are made up of rhodochrosite microspherules as are the Inuyama manganese nodules. Manganese deposits of the Yumiyama mine of the Tamba district, which has suffered low-grade metamorphism of prehnite-pumpellyite facies, dominantly consist of rhodochrosite with subordinate jacobsite, alabandite, and several manganese oxides (Otsuka, 1983).

TEMPORAL COMPARISON

Researchers had believed that the Chichibu Geosyncline was made up of Paleozoic formations, but recently Triassic and even Jurassic chert and shale have been found at many locations in the Chichibu Belt. Geologic ages of manganese deposits have not been fully investigated except for a few areas.

Yumiyama manganese deposits formed during Early to Middle Jurassic (Imoto et al., 1982), but some other deposits in the Tamba district are associated with Triassic to Jurassic chert (Isozaki and Matsuda, 1982; Imoto, 1984). Judging from the geology and stratigraphy of unmetamorphosed formations of adjacent regions, manganese deposits of the Nodatamagawa mine is considered to be of Triassic to Early Jurassic age (Koike et al., 1971; Koike et al., 1974; Minoura et al., 1981; Sashida et al., 1982); manganese deposits of the Ashio Mountains occur in Spathian to Carnian (Early to Late Triassic) bedded chert (Koike et al., 1971; Kakuwa and Iijima, 1979). Thus, manganese deposits of the Chichibu Geosyncline seem to occur in sections of Late(?) Triassic to Middle Jurassic age, although there are still a large number of manganese deposits of unknown age.

GENETIC COMPARISON

Nodular manganese deposits of the Inuyama district are very small in scale compared with minable bedded manganese deposits. However, they have some important points in common with the more typical manganese deposits of the Chichibu Belt as stated in the previous parts. Therefore, the genetic model of the Inuyama nodules may be applicable to the larger chert-hosted manganese deposits.

Manganese deposits of the Yumiyama mine of the Tamba district are an intermediate type between Inuyama nodules and typical metamorphosed manganese deposits, being composed dominantly of rhodochrosite and underlain by thick massive chert and overlain by tuffaceous shale and thin-bedded chert. REE patterns of the Yumiyama manganese deposits and the host chert do not show a negative cerium anomaly but rather a slightly positive one (Fig. 8–12), suggesting that a hydrothermal contribution was not an important source of manganese. $\delta^{18}O$ of rhodochrosite of the Yumiyama manganese deposits are around $-9\%_{00}$ PDB, which corresponds to the precipitation (or recrystallization) at about 30–45°C, according to Figure 8–11. There is thus the possibility that manganese deposits of the Yumiyama mine formed by a process similar to that of Inuyama manganese nodules.

Compaction-corrected rates of sedimentation of some Triassic and Jurassic cherts and shales in the Chichibu Belt are estimated to be about 5–7 m/m.y. (Tanaka, 1980; Yao et al., 1980; Yao, 1982; Isozaki and Matsuda, 1980, 1982; Sashida et al., 1982; Igo and Koike, 1983), whereas the manganese content is mostly between 0.1 weight-percent and 0.3 weight-percent MnO. This is about half to one-third the amount estimated from the relationship between the sedimentation rate and Mn content of modern sediments. Provided that the relationship for the modern sediment is applicable to the ancient sedimentary rocks, the difference between the observed and the estimated manganese content is suggested to have been caused by the loss of some of the original hydrogenous manganese. The lost manganese is considered to have formed manganese deposits in chert-shale sections of the Chichibu Belt. Triassic and Jurassic manganese deposits are not concentrated at a distinct stratigraphic horizon and are not always associated with volcanic rocks. These facts support the diagenetic model of the genesis of manganese deposits.

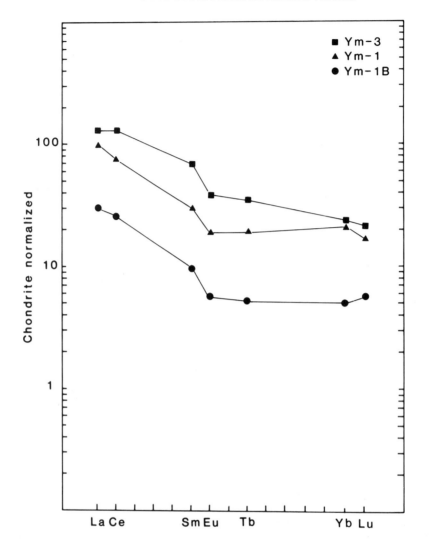

Figure 8-12. Chondrite normalized REE patterns of the bedded manganese deposits and associated rocks of the Yumiyama mine. All three samples show not a negative cerium anomaly but a slight positive one. Ym-3, Early Jurassic bedded chert; Ym-1, bedded manganese deposits; Ym-1B, bedded manganese deposits.

CONCLUSION

1. Manganese nodules of the Inuyama district occur exclusively in the Middle Jurassic argillaceous chert and siliceous shale.
2. Manganese nodules are composed principally of spherulitic rhodochrosite with minor but significant amounts of apatite.
3. Inuyama rhodochrosite is expressed as $Mn_{0.82-0.98}Ca_{0.01-0.15}-Mg_{0.02-0.05}CO_3$.
4. Carbon and oxygen isotopic composition of rhodochrosite are -5.63 to $-9.32‰$ PDB and $+0.47$ to $-1.85‰$ PDB, respectively.

5. REE patterns of Inuyama manganese nodules and host siliceous rocks do not show a negative cerium anomaly but a slightly positive cerium anomaly or a smooth pattern.
6. The temperature of rhodochrosite formation estimated from oxygen isotopes is 12–23°C.
7. Rhodochrosite in the Inuyama manganese nodules was formed from hydrogenous manganese originally contained in the host sediment. This manganese was reduced and migrated in the sediments during early diagenesis and eventually precipitated as rhodochrosite to form a horizon of manganese nodules.

ACKNOWLEDGMENTS

The author expresses his gratitude to Dr. Y. Minai (Department of Chemistry, University of Tokyo), who measured the REE concentration of the Inuyama and Yumiyama samples. He also thanks Dr. J. R. Hein (U.S. Geological Survey), Professor A. Iijima, and Mr. Y. Kakuwa (University of Tokyo) for many helpful suggestions for improving this chapter. Instrumental neutron activation analysis (INAA) was performed at a nuclear reactor of the Rikkyo University and Isotope Center of the University of Tokyo. X-ray microanalysis of rhodochrosite and dolomite was done at the Ocean Research Institute of the University of Tokyo. This research was financially supported by grants-in-aid from the Ito Science Foundation and the Ministry of Education and Culture (No. 58420015 and No. 59740394).

REFERENCES

Barrett, T. J., 1981. Chemistry and mineralogy of Jurassic bedded chert overlying ophiolites in the north Apennines, Italy, *Chem. Geology* **34**:289–317.

Curtis, C. D., 1977. Sedimentary geochemistry: Environments and processes dominated by involvement of aqueous phases, *Royal Soc. London Philos. Trans.* **A286**:353–372.

Friedman, I., and J. R. O'Neil, 1977. *Compilation of Stable Isotope Fractionation Factors of Geochemical Interest,* U.S. Geological Survey Professional Paper 440-KK, pp. 1–12.

Hein, J. R., J. O'Neil, and M. G. Jones, 1979. Origin of authigenic carbonates in sediment from the deep Bering sea, *Sedimentology* **26**:681–705.

Hirowatari, F., 1980. *Historical Review of the Studies and Geological Surveys of the Bedded Manganese Ore Deposits in Japan,* Japanese Association of Mining, Petrology, and Economic Geology Journal Special Publication No. 2, pp. 151–164.

Hosoyamada, K., 1982. Geology, Petrology, and Geochemistry of the Neogene Siliceous Sediments in the Oga Peninsula, Akita Prefecture, Japan, Master's thesis, Geological Institute, University of Tokyo, pp. 1–112.

Igo, H., and Koike, T., 1983. Conodont biostratigraphy of cherts in the Japanese Islands, in *Siliceous Deposits in the Pacific Region,* A. Iijima, J. R. Hein, and R. Siever, eds., Elsevier, Amsterdam, pp. 175–191.

Imoto, N., 1984. Stratigraphy and structure of Mesozoic-Paleozoic system in the Tamba belt, in *DESK Reports,* K. Nakazawa, ed., University of Kyoto Press, pp. 7–15.

Imoto, N., A. Tamaki, T. Tanabe, and H. Ishiga, 1982. An age determination on the basis of radiolarian biostratigraphy of a bedded manganese deposit at the Yumiyama

Mine in the Tamba district, southwest Japan, *Proceedings of the First Japanese Radiolarian Symposium,* News of Osaka Micropaleontology, Special Volume 5, pp. 227–235.

Irwin, H., C. D. Curtis, and M. Coleman, 1977. Isotopic evidence for source of diagenetic carbonates formed during burial of organic-rich sediments, *Nature* **296**:209–213.

Isozaki, Y., and T. Matsuda, 1980. Age of the Tamba Group along the Hozugawa "Anticline," western hills of Kyoto, southwest Japan, *Osaka City Univ. Jour. Geosciences* **23**:115–134.

Isozaki, Y., and T. Matsuda, 1982. Middle and Late Triassic Conodonts from bedded chert sequences in the Mino-Tamba belt, southwest Japan, *Osaka City Univ. Jour. Geosciences* **25**:103–136.

Kakuwa, Y., and A. Iijima, 1979. *On the Geology and Bedded Chert of the Triassic System in the Kuzuu District,* Abstract, 86th Annual Meeting of the Geological Society of Japan (Akita), p. 206.

Koike, T., H. Igo, S. Takizawa, T. Kinoshita, 1971. Contribution to the geological history of the Japanese Islands by the conodont biostratigraphy II, *Jour. Geol. Soc. Japan* **77**:165–168.

Koike, T., H. Igo, and T. Kinoshita, 1974. Unconformity between Permian Nabeyama Formation and Triassic Adoyama Formation in the Kuzuu district and its geological significance, *Jour. Geol. Soc. Japan* **80**:293–306.

Kondo, N., and M. Adachi, 1975. Mesozoic strata of the area north of Inuyama, with special reference to the Sakahogi conglomerate, *Jour. Geol. Soc. Japan* **81**:373–386.

Lancelot, Y., and J. I. Ewing, 1972. Correlation of natural gas zonation and carbonate diagenesis in Tertiary sediments from the northwest Atlantic, in C. D. Hollister, J. I. Ewing, et al., *Initial Reports of the Deep Sea Drilling Project,* vol. 11, U.S. Government Printing Office, Washington, D.C., pp. 791–799.

Lawrence, J. R., J. M. Gieskes, and W. S. Broecsker, 1975. Oxygen isotope and cation composition of DSDP pore water and the alteration of Layer II basalt, *Earth and Planetary Sci. Letters* **27**:1–10.

Matsuda, T., Y. Isozaki, and A. Yao, 1980. *Stratigraphic relation of Triassic-Jurassic System in the Inuyama District of the Mino Belt,* Abstract, 87th Annual Meeting of the Geological Society of Japan (Matsue), p. 107.

Matsuhisa, Y., and R. Matsumoto, 1985. Oxygen isotope ratios of the interstitial water from the Nankai trough and Japan trench, Leg 87, in D. Karig, H. Kagami, W. T. Coulbourn, et al. *Initial Reports of the Deep Sea Drilling Project,* vol. 87, U.S. Government Printing Office, Washington, D.C., pp. 853–856.

Matsumoto, R., 1978. Occurrence and origin of authigenic Ca-Mg-Fe carbonates and carbonate rocks in the Paleogene coalfield regions in Japan, *Tokyo Univ. Fac. Sci. Jour.,* sec. II, **19**:335–367.

Matsumoto, R., 1983. Mineralogy and geochemistry of carbonate diagenesis of the Pliocene and Pleistocene hemipelagic mud on the Blake Outer Ridge, Site 533, Leg 76, in R. E. Sheridan, F. M. Gradstein, et al., *Initial Reports of the Deep Sea Drilling Project,* vol. 76, U.S. Government Printing Office, Washington, D.C., pp. 411–427.

Matsumoto, R., and A. Iijima, 1981. Origin and diagenetic evolution of Ca-Mg-Fe carbonates in some coalfields in Japan, *Sedimentology* **28**:239–257.

Matsumoto, R., and A. Iijima, 1983. Chemical sedimentology of some Permo-Jurassic and Tertiary bedded cherts in central Honshu, Japan, in *Siliceous Deposits in the Pacific Region,* A. Iijima, J. R. Hein, and R. Siever, eds., Elsevier, Amsterdam, pp. 175–191.

Matsumoto, R., and Y. Matsuhisa, 1985. Chemistry, carbon and oxygen isotope compositions, and origin of deep sea carbonates at Sites 438, 439, and 584: Inner slope of the Japan Trench, in D. Karig, H. Kagami, W. T. Coulbourn, et al., *Initial Reports of the Deep Sea Drilling Project,* vol. 87, U.S. Government Printing Office, Washington, D.C., pp. 669–678.

Matsumoto, R., and T. Urabe, 1980. An automatic analysis of major elements in silicate rocks with X-ray fluorescence spectrometer using fused disc samples, *Japanese Assoc. Mineralogists, Petrologists and Econ. Geologists Jour.* **76**:111–121.

Matsumoto, R., Y. Minai, and A. Iijima, 1985. Manganese content, cerium anomaly, and rate of sedimentation as aids of characterization and classification of deep sea sediments, in *Formation of Ocean Margins,* N. Nasu, K. Kobayashi, and H. Kagami, eds., Terra Scientific Publishers, Tokyo, pp. 913–939.

Minoura, K., S. Endo, and H. Suzuki, 1981. *Rikuchu Group Near Omoto of the Northern Kitakami Mountains,* Abstract, 88th Annual Meeting of the Geological Society of Japan, Tokyo, p. 141.

Minoura, K., M. Nakaya, and A. Takemura, 1983. Origin of manganese carbonate ore in Mino belt, *Marine Sciences Monthly* **15**:426–432.

O'Neil, J. R., 1977. Stable isotopes in mineralogy, *Phy. Chem. Minerals* **2**:105–123.

Otsuka, F., 1983. Bedded manganese deposits of the Yumiyama Mine in the Tamba district, Master's thesis, Geological Institute, University of Tokyo, pp. 1–30.

Pisciotto, K. A., 1981. Review of secondary carbonates in the Monterey Formation, California, in *The Monterey Formation and Related Siliceous Rocks of California,* R. E. Garrison and R. G. Douglas, eds., Society of Economic Paleontologists and Mineralogists Speical Publication 15, pp. 273–283.

Pisciotto, K. A., and R. E. Garrison, 1981. Lithofacies and depositional environments of the Monterey Formation, California, in *The Monterey Formation and Related Siliceous Rocks of California,* R. E. Garrison and R. G. Douglas, eds., Society of Economic Paleontologists and Mineralogists Special Publication, pp. 97–122.

Sashida, K., H. Igo, S. Takizawa, K. Hisada, and T. Shibata, 1982. On the Jurassic radiolarian assemblages in the Kanto district, *Proceedings of the First Japanese Radiolarian Symposium* (Osaka), pp. 51–66.

Scientific Party, 1980. Site 436, Japan Trench Outer Rise, Leg 56, in M. Langseth, H. Okada, et al. *Initial Reports of the Deep Sea Drilling Project,* vol. 56/57, part 1, U.S. Government Printing Office, Washington, D.C., pp. 399–446.

Shimizu, D., 1972. Horizons and occurrence of Permian and Triassic greenstone formations of the Tamba belt, southwest Japan, *Jour. Geol. Soc. Japan* **85**:391–399.

Tanaka, T., 1980. Kanoashi Group, an olistostrome, in the Nichihara area, Shimane Prefecture, *Jour. Geol. Soc. Japan* **86**:613–628.

Tsusue, A., 1970. The coprecipitation of calcium with rhodochrosite at elevated temperature, in *Volcanism and Ore Genesis,* T. Tatsumi, ed., University of Tokyo Press, Tokyo, pp. 119–142.

Wada, H., N. Niitsuma, K. Nagasawa, and H. Okada, 1982. Deep sea carbonates nodules from the middle America Trench area off Mexico, Deep Sea Drilling Project, Leg 66, in J. S. Watkins, J. C. Moore, et al., *Initial Reports of the Deep Sea Drilling Project,* vol. 66, U.S. Government Printing Office, Washington, D.C., pp. 453–474.

Watanabe, T., 1957. Genesis of bedded manganese deposits and cupriferous pyrite deposits in Japan, *Mining Geology* **7**:87–97.

Yamazaki, K., 1977. Geology of the Inuyama district, Aichi and Gifu Prefectures, Master's thesis, Geological Institute, University of Tokyo, pp. 1–115.

Yao, A., 1982. Middle Triassic to Early Jurassic radiolarians from Inuyama area, central Japan, *Osaka City Univ. Jour. Geosciences* **25**:53–70.

Yao, A., T. Matsuda, and Y. Isozaki, 1980. Triassic and Jurassic radiolarians from the Inuyama area, central Japan, *Osaka City Univ. Jour. Geosciences* **23**:135–154.

Yoshimura, T., 1952. Some problems on the manganese ore deposits in Japan, *Mining Geology* **2**:197–205.

9

Chert-Hosted Manganese Deposits in Sedimentary Sequences of the Franciscan Complex, Diablo Range, California

James R. Hein and **Randolph A. Koski**

U.S. Geological Survey
Menlo Park, California

Hsueh-Wen Yeh

University of Hawaii, Honolulu

ABSTRACT. Manganese deposits in the Franciscan Complex of the Diablo Range in the central California Coast Ranges occur as conformable lenses within bedded radiolarian chert-argillite sequences that are, in turn, intercalated within thicker sections of sandstone and shale. The field relationships, composition, and petrographic and isotopic characteristics of the Ladd and Buckeye deposits indicate that the manganese was concentrated by diagenetic reconstitution of siliceous and hemipelagic sediment during burial.

The ore lenses are Mn-rich and Fe-poor assemblages that consist largely of rhodochrosite, manganese silicates, opal-CT, and quartz. Although multiple sets of quartz-rich veins crosscut the red and green thin-bedded chert that hosts the manganese mineralization, no Fe- or Mn-rich feeder system is evident. Highly negative δ-13 carbon values of rhodochrosite samples indicate that CO_2 originated from oxidation of methane; less negative values result from mixing of methanogenic carbon and CO_2 derived from bacterial degradation of organic matter. δ-18 oxygen values for rhodochrosite samples indicate temperatures of formation in the range 20° to 100°C.

Massive chert beds adjacent to the manganese lenses formed from silica released when siliceous host rocks were partly replaced by carbonate. The oxidation of methane prior to carbonate precipitation may have been accomplished by Mn and Fe oxyhydroxides and oxides deposited with the sediment. The mobilization of manganese from biogenic and terrigenous sources in the sediment column into discrete horizons and the fractionation of manganese from iron reflect the presence of oxidation reduction boundaries and gradients in the sediment column. Fluids derived from silica dehydration reactions in the transformation of opal-A to quartz were involved in the transportation of principal components. Their sedimentary and geochemical attributes suggest that the deposits formed in a deep-water environment in a zone of oceanic upwelling at or near a continental margin.

Introduction

More than four hundred manganese deposits occur within the Franciscan Complex located in the Coast Ranges of California (Fig. 9-1; Trask, 1950). The manganese occurs in conformable lenses within bedded chert-argillite sequences that, in turn, form lenticular bodies in sandstone or shale sections. Greenstone, basalt, or more silicic volcanic rocks may or may not be present. Individual deposits are low tonnage (a few hundred to several thousand tons) and low to high grade (25–50% Mn). Ores were mined primarily during the two world wars.

The Ladd–Buckeye district in the Diablo Range east of San Francisco produced 63,000 tons of manganese ore, which is the largest quantity of manganese produced in California. We studied two deposits in this district in detail. The compositional and lithological characteristics of the Ladd and Buckeye deposits are similar to most of the manganese deposits in the Franciscan Complex (Trask, 1950). Our objectives are to describe the geologic setting, geochemical characteristics, and lithologic associations of two chert-hosted manganese deposits in the Franciscan Complex, to infer a depositional environment, and to develop a genetic model.

In the first half of this century, geologists interpreted manganese ores of the Franciscan Complex as volcanogenic-sedimentary deposits based on field observations (Taliaferro and Hudson, 1943; Trask, 1950; Hewett, 1966). Recent workers have interpreted the deposits to be hydrothermal and to have formed at an oceanic spreading axis (Snyder, 1978; Crerar et al., 1982; Chyi et al., 1984). We present field, petrographic, geochemical, and isotopic data that indicate the Ladd and Buckeye deposits formed by diagenetic processes at depth in an unlithified sedimentary section in a deep basin near a continental margin.

Review: Evolution of Ideas

The evolution of thought regarding the origin of chert-hosted manganese deposits is tied to the development of ideas regarding formation of the bedded chert-argillite host rock. Until the late 1960s most workers considered bedded chert to be a chemical precipitate, the silica being derived from submarine hotsprings or from weathering of associated volcanic rocks (e.g., Davis, 1918; Bailey et al., 1964). Stanaway et al. (1978) considered the entire rock suite, including chert, shale, and manganese, to be products of submarine volcanic exhalations. In this model, the rhythmic bedding in chert-argillite sequences results from diagenetic segregation of silica from clay within a silica gel. The most elegant presentation of ideas for an inorganic origin was given by Bailey et al. (1964). Many later workers emulated this hypothesis despite field and petrographic studies that showed that an origin for chert by inorganic precipitation was untenable (e.g., Huebner, 1967; Stanaway et al., 1978). Subsequent work (Garrison, 1974; Hein et al., 1978) has shown that bedded cherts are not related genetically to the commonly associated volcanic rocks and that the source of the silica is biogenic debris (radiolarians, diatoms, and sponge spicules). Rhythmically bedded sequences can result from turbidite deposition,

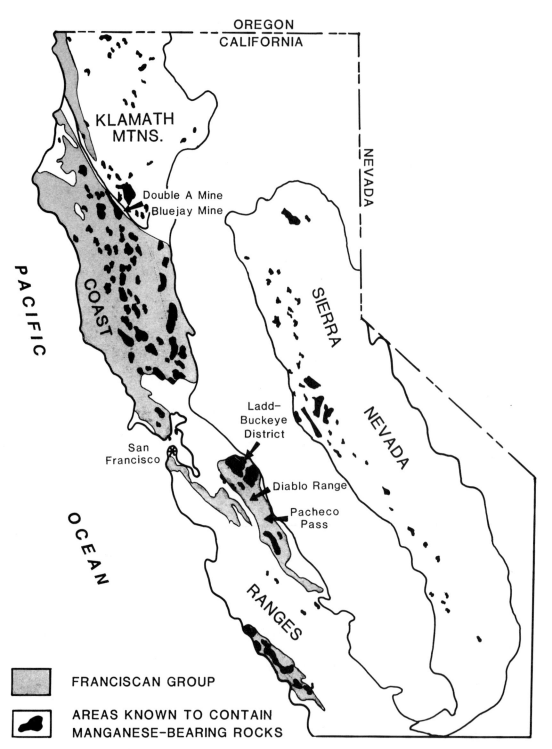

Figure 9-1. The distribution of manganese deposits in northern and central California. Most manganese deposits are chert hosted, and those located in the western part of the Sierra Nevada are high-grade metamorphic equivalents to those of the Franciscan Complex.

bottom currents, and/or productivity cycles of plankton in surface waters (McBride and Folk, 1979; Jenkyns and Winterer, 1982; Hein and Karl, 1983).

Similarly, suggestions for the origin of the manganese associated with bedded chert sections also called on precipitation from submarine hydrothermal exhalations (Shatskiy, 1954; Reed, 1960; Kuypers and Denyer, 1979; Watanabe et al., 1970). Although many of the chert-hosted manganese deposits in California, Japan, and New Zealand are associated with thick sequences of sandstone in which volcanic rocks are relatively minor or absent, recent workers have postulated a midocean spreading ridge, volcanic-exhalative origin for the manganese (Snyder, 1978; Crerar et al., 1982; Chyi et al., 1984). Manganese deposits within bedded chert of ophiolite sequences such as the Nicoya Complex, Costa Rica, are associated with basalt; these deposits appear to be genetically related to thermal springs on the paleoseafloor (Kuypers and Denyer, 1979).

The regional geologic setting for deposition of bedded chert and associated manganese deposits has long been in dispute. Some early workers argued for a deep-sea, open-ocean environment equivalent to modern radiolarian ooze belts (Chamberlain, 1914; Molengraaff, 1916, 1922); others recognized that deposition occurred in a continental margin environment or doubted the likelihood of abyssal deposits being preserved in the geologic record (Murray and Renard, 1891; Taliaferro and Hudson, 1943; Tromp, 1948). This controversy was enhanced by the recovery of abyssal cherts during the Deep Sea Drilling Project. These abyssal cherts were proposed as analogs to the bedded chert found in orogenic belts. Careful comparisons, however, showed that the cherts of orogenic belts and cherts in the abyssal open ocean have little in common (Jenkyns and Winterer, 1982; Hein and Karl, 1983) and that the orogenic-belt cherts are near-shore, deep-to-shallow water deposits (Price, 1977; Hallam, 1976; Robertson, 1981; Barrett, 1982; Hein et al., 1983a).

FRANCISCAN COMPLEX

REGIONAL FRAMEWORK AND LITHOLOGIC ASSOCIATIONS

The Franciscan Complex of the California Coast Ranges (Fig. 9–1) has been divided into three principal stratigraphic belts: (1) Coastal, (2) Central, and (3) Eastern, or Yolla Bolly (Blake and Jones, 1974, 1981). The westernmost, or Coastal, belt consists of Upper Cretaceous through Miocene sandstone, mudstone, and conglomerate. Rocks of the Upper Jurassic and Cretaceous Central belt form a tectonic mélange consisting of sandstone, chert, and argillite plus knockers of blueschist, eclogite, and limestone. Upper Jurassic and Lower Cretaceous rocks of the Yolla Bolly belt consist of metaclastic rocks, radiolarian metachert, and sills and flows of metabasalt (Blake et al., 1982). The chert-rich stratigraphy of the Ladd–Buckeye area in the Diablo Range of the central Coast Ranges is equivalent to the middle unit of the Yolla Bolly belt.

The Franciscan Complex is in structural contact with the overlying Coast Range ophiolite and Great Valley sequence along the Coast Range thrust. The Franciscan Complex and Great Valley sequence have typically been interpreted as trench and forearc deposits, respectively, deposited during eastward subduction and development of the Klamath–Sierran arc complex at the western margin of North America during Late Jurassic and Cretaceous time. Recently, the stratigraphy of the Franciscan Complex has been further subdivided to distinguish rock units representing subduction or trench-complex deposits from rocks derived by lateral crustal movement from more distant oceanic regions (Blake et al., 1985).

Chert makes up less than 0.5% of the entire Franciscan Complex (Bailey et al., 1964), and manganese deposits make up a small fraction of the chert sections. Chert occurs as blocks in mélange in the Coastal belt, as blocks or continuous stratigraphic sequences in the Central belt, and is intercalated with quartzofeldspathic sandstone in the Yolla Bolly belt (Blake and Jones, 1981). Rhythmically bedded chert-argillite (ribbon chert) is typical of the Central and Yolla Bolly belts; sections 40–80 m thick are common, and sections up to 300 m thick occur in the Ladd–Buckeye area. A common lithologic sequence is chert-argillite interbedded with or overlain by graywacke or shale; less frequently, chert-argillite is interbedded with or underlain by sandstone or volcanic rocks of basaltic to andesitic composition. Thick sections of bedded chert-argillite and sandstone are especially prominent in the Pacheco Pass area (Blake and Jones, 1974) and in the Ladd–Buckeye area of the Diablo Range (Trask, 1950; Raymond, 1973a, 1974).

Manganese deposits typically occur within the bedded chert-argillite sections adjacent to green, gray, or white chert (see Fig. 9–2 for typical stratigraphic sections). Invariably, a layer of thick-bedded chert will occur immediately below or above the manganese lens. The thick-bedded cherts are a hallmark of this type of manganese deposit and are found in sections in California, New Zealand, Japan, and other places. The thick-bedded cherts are actually amalgamated thin beds of chert in which the intercalated argillites were removed, replaced, or never deposited. With increased diagenesis and metamorphism, the chert becomes more massive, but all stages in the evolution can be seen in different sections. The bulk of the chert sections are thin-bedded red, red-brown, and green chert with minor beds of black and gray chert; shale beds are green, gray, and red-brown. In places, single beds are mottled red and green chert, or red chert grades into green chert laterally within a single bed. Red is the original color and green is produced by iron reduction during diagenesis. Most commonly, individual chert beds are less than 10 cm thick, and shale beds are less than 4 cm thick. Thicker shale beds, to 15 cm, may occur more frequently near manganese lenses.

Lithologic associations typical of the Yolla Bolly terrane occur in the stratigraphic section at the Buckeye mine. Above the faulted base of the section, conglomerate is overlain successively by intercalated graywacke/chert-argillite (argillite dominated), chert-argillite (chert dominated), a manganese lens, chert-argillite, another manganese lens, chert-argillite, graywacke, and chert-argillite (see Fig. 9–2). The sedimentary rocks in the Ladd–Buckeye district have been subjected to high pressure/low temperature metamorphism with at least the incipient development of blueschist-facies assemblages (Ernst, 1971; Raymond, 1973a, b). Contacts between different lithologies are sedimentary, although the 200–3,500 m thick section may represent two individual thrust packets. Total thickness of the chert-argillite is 100 m. Several thin intercalated tuff beds at the Ladd mine are of intermediate-silica composition. Soft-sediment deformation of the chert-argillite turbidites is common, and sandstone dikes are rare.

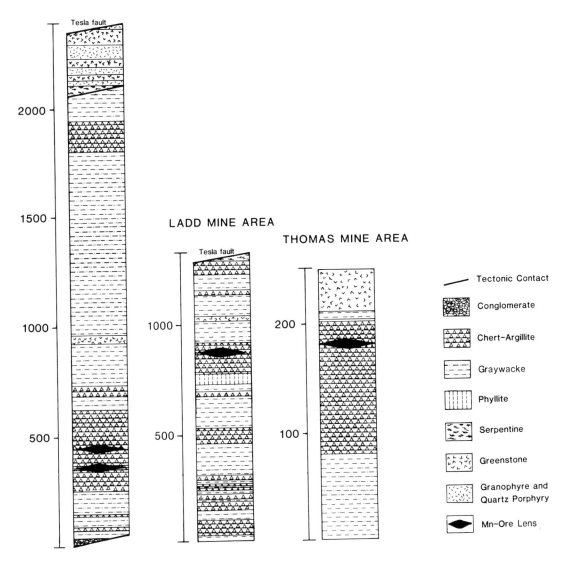

Figure 9–2. Stratigraphic columns of the Franciscan Complex in areas representative of most manganese deposits. Note the change in the meter scale from the Ladd–Buckeye sections to the Thomas Section. (Modified from Trask, 1950).

Manganese lenses in the Franciscan Complex are conformable, stratiform, and stratabound within the chert and are most commonly disc shaped. In the Ladd–Buckeye district, the ratio of the maximum to minimum diameter for twelve deposits ranges from 1.1–3, and the ratio of the maximum diameter to maximum thickness ranges from 13–43 (Trask, 1950). The dimensions of the two largest ore bodies are 245 m × 110 m × 11 m (Ladd east ore bed) and 67 m × 61 m × 4 m (Buckeye north bed). The primary ore mineral for most Franciscan deposits is rhodochrosite or mixed rhodochrosite and manganese silicates (Trask, 1950). Some ore bodies are banded gray and pink rhodochrosite. The ore bodies are commonly stratified with chert, secondary silica, and/or manganese silicates, but some deposits are massive.* Boundaries of ore bodies may be sharp, but the adjacent cherts to several tens of meters commonly contain rhombs or spherules of disseminated rhodochrosite. Furthermore, several centimeters of laminated silica-rhodochrosite-manganese silicates occur along the contact of some deposits. Many deposits are oxidized during weathering to depths of 1–15 m (Trask, 1950).

PETROGRAPHY AND MINERALOGY, LADD–BUCKEYE DISTRICT

Rocks from the Ladd and Buckeye mines include metamorphosed conglomerate, sandstone, chert, argillaceous chert, siliceous argillite, argillite, pyroclastic beds, and manganese ore. Sandstone interbedded with the chert-argillite sections is poorly sorted, angular to subrounded, feldspathic graywacke. The source terrane consists of volcanic, plutonic, and sedimentary rocks. Although the original clastic texture is preserved, the graywackes exhibit varying degrees of recrystallization and development of secondary-mineral assemblages. The larger clasts include altered plagioclase crystals, single and polygranular quartz grains, volcanic rock fragments, and less abundant grains of quartzite, chert, shale, opaques, amphibole, biotite, and calcite. Much of the plagioclase is replaced by albite or the blueschist facies assemblage albite + lawsonite ± jadeitic pyroxene, but the latter two phases are not abundant. White mica, illite, chlorite, stilpnomelane, and calcite replace plagioclase, lithic fragments, and groundmass phases.

Chert color and texture vary considerably, from red densely packed radiolarian chert (originally a radiolarian sand) to green chert consisting of microcrystalline aggregates of quartz and ghosts of radiolarians. All gradations occur between these end members, but green chert always shows a more advanced degree of diagenesis than red or brown chert. Red chert is apparently primary, indicating an oxidizing depositional environment; when both colors are present, green is commonly localized along veins and fractures. The color is due to the oxidation state of the iron. Red chert averages 1.93% Fe_2O_3 and 0.24% FeO, whereas green chert averages 0.56% Fe_2O_3 and 0.56% FeO. MnO is also more abundant in red chert (0.27%) than in green chert (0.06%). The same relationships apply to the argillite.

Detrital plagioclase and quartz grains, fragments of volcanic rock, and sponge spicules are rare components of chert. The argillaceous matrix of most chert samples is riddled with minute (5–15 μ) blue-green needlelike crystals. X-ray diffraction analysis indicates a sodic (?) pyroxene phase. Raymond (1973a) reported fine-grained lawsonite, blue amphibole (?), and white mica in metachert from the northeast Diablo Range. Secondary minerals include chlorite, smectite, hematite, calcite, and rhodochrosite. About 15% of the chert beds contain abundant illite showing mass extinction. Radiolarian tests are predominantly filled with quartz and rarely with clay minerals, chalcedony, calcite, and rhodochrosite. Rhodochrosite rhombs and spherules occur in chert

---

*For convenience, we use *rhodochrostone* for this sedimentary rock composed dominantly of rhodochrosite but mixed with quartz and other minerals. In the chemical and isotopic analyses, *rhodochrostone* refers to analysis of the bulk rock and *rhodochrosite* to the separated mineral. *Rhodochrostone* is used in the same context as *dolostone*.

within 50 m of the ore bodies and are commonly oxidized. The spherules originated as carbonate infilling of radiolarian tests that recrystallized to form the rhombs. Laminations and graded bedding are common and are defined by the number of radiolarians and the amount of iron oxide. Burrowing or fluid-escape structures are evident in a few beds. Deformation of the chert beds is indicated by deformed veins, vein breccia, strained quartz, microbrecciation, microfaults, and squashed and aligned radiolarians. Squashed radiolarians are most common near the ore body, especially in the hanging-wall chert. Bedding-parallel stylolites have removed up to 35% of some beds, as indicated by reconstruction of partly dissolved crosscut veins. The quartz crystallinity (Murata and Norman, 1976) in seventy-one of seventy-three chert and argillite rocks varies between the narrow range of 6 and 7. The other two values are 8 and 9. This suggests that the rocks have been subjected to low-grade metamorphism. In contrast, Deep Sea Drilling Project cherts have values less than 4 (Hein and Yeh, 1981, 1983) and plutonic quartz has a value 10 (Murata and Norman, 1976).

Argillaceous chert and siliceous argillite are arbitrarily defined by the relative amounts of clay minerals, iron oxide, and SiO_2. The cherts and more argillaceous rocks have similar characteristics, but clay minerals, sponge spicules, and hematite are more abundant, and radiolarians are less abundant in the latter. However, in some of the less siliceous rocks, radiolarians form a grain-supported texture. Chlorite and illite dominate the clay-mineral assemblage; smectite is minor. Barite is rare and one siliceous-shale bed contains sursassite, a manganese aluminosilicate. Sursassite also occurs in the Alps in pumpellyite-actinolite-grade manganese ores associated with siliceous sedimentary rocks (Peters et al., 1980).

Red and green argillite beds are composed largely of the clay minerals illite and chlorite with rare smectite. Plagioclase is dominant in some beds, and quartz is present in all. Hematite is more abundant in the red argillite. Argillites contain many more sponge spicules relative to radiolarians than do the more siliceous beds. Beds are massive to laminated, the laminae being defined by the proportion of siliceous microfossils and the amount of iron oxides. Iron oxides are usually more abundant than in more siliceous rocks. Rhodochrosite is rare: in one argillite bed, half of a large rhodochrosite rhomb fills a radiolarian test and shows sharp crystal faces, whereas the other half extends into and replaces the argillite and exhibits ragged edges.

The Ladd and Buckeye manganese deposits range in mineral composition from pure primary rhodochrosite + manganese silicate to mixtures of these minerals and chert to mixtures of secondary oxides. The complete list of manganese minerals is presented in Table 9-1. Based on XRD and petrographic analysis, the dominant primary manganese mineral is rhodochrosite. Braunite and bementite are abundant in some samples studied by us, and hausmannite is reported from ore samples from the Buckeye mine (Huebner, 1967). Less abundant primary manganese minerals include kutnohorite, manganese calcite, pennantite, and serandite. According to Huebner (1967), hausmannite and braunite result form decarbonation of rhodochrosite in the presence of quartz and high oxygen fugacity during incipient blueschist metamorphism of the deposits. In addition to hausmannite and braunite, sursassite (found in this study) and santaclarite (found by Erd and Ohashi, 1984) probably formed during metamorphism.

Table 9–1. Manganese Minerals Identified at the Ladd and Buckeye Deposits

Mineral	Formula	Abundant	Not abundant	Rare
Rhodochrosite	$MnCO_3$	x		
Kutnohorite	$Ca(Mn,Mg)(CO_3)_2$		x	
Mn-calcite	$(Ca,Mn)CO_3$		x	
Braunite	$3Mn_2O_3 \cdot MnSiO_3$	x		
Bementite	$Mn_7Si_6O_{15}OH_8$	x		
Pennantite	$(Mn,Al)_3(Si,Al)_2O_5(OH)_4$		x	
Serandite	$(Mn,Ca)_2NaH(Si_3O_9)$		x	
Sursassite	$Mn_5Al_4Si_5O_{21} \cdot 3H_2O$			x
Santaclarite[a]	$CaMn_4[Si_5O_{14}(OH)](OH) \cdot H_2O$			x
Hausmannite[b]	Mn_3O_4	x		
δ-MnO_2	δ-MnO_2	x		
Birnessite	$Na_4Mn_{14}O_{27} \cdot 9H_2O$	x		
Pyrolusite	MnO_2	x		
Manganite	$\gamma MnOOH$	x		
Nsutite	γMnO_2			x
Todorokite	(Na,Ca,K,Mn^{2+}) $(Mn^{4+},Mn^{2+}Mg)_6$ $O_{12} \cdot 3H_2O$			x
Cryptomelane	$K_{1-2}Mn_8O_{16} \cdot xH_2O$			x

[a]Erd and Ohashi, 1984.
[b]Huebner, 1967.

The dominant secondary manganese minerals (Table 9–1), formed during supergene oxidation of the deposits, are δ-MnO_2, manganite, pyrolusite, and birnessite; much less abundant are nsutite, todorokite, and cryptomelane. δ-MnO_2 was identified by two characteristic X-ray diffractions near 2.40 and 1.42 Å (Burns and Burns, 1979).

Nonmanganese minerals that occur in the manganese deposits include opal-CT (disordered cristobalite-tridymite; Jones and Segnit, 1971), quartz, chlorite, plagioclase, smectite, amphibole, K-feldspar, and barite. The occurrence of opal-CT is noteworthy because it is rare in pre-Cretaceous rocks. It is also the early diagenetic product of the transformation of biogenic opaline silica (opal-A) to quartz (Hein et al., 1978). The opal-CT occurs only with the manganese and not in any of the surrounding rocks, indicating that the opal-A to opal-CT to quartz transformations were halted during the metastable opal-CT stage by the formation of rhodochrosite and manganese silicates. This places the timing of primary manganese deposition at a specific known diagenetic stage because the physiochemical conditions of the silica-polymorph transformations are well known (see Discussion). This association also suggests that metamorphism did not significantly affect either the primary rhodochrosite or the opal-CT that it enclosed.

At least three vein sets crosscut all rock types. Bedding-parallel veins formed prior to other vein sets. Vein minerals, in order of decreasing abundance, include quartz, phyllosilicates (illite, chlorite, vermiculite, stilpnomelane), rhodochrosite, manganese oxides, calcite, hematite, zeolites, albite, and barite.

Aragonite, identified in a single quartz-rich vein, may be a product of blue-schist facies metamorphism.

Vein thicknesses range from less than a millimeter to centimeters. Quartz is dominant in all three sets of veins and is either crowded with fluid inclusions (milky) or is clear. All of the vein sets contain variable numbers of small (<30 μ) fluid-dominated inclusions. The tiny vapor bubble suggests entrapment of dilute, low-temperature fluid.

GEOCHEMISTRY

Chert and argillite samples were crushed to millimeter- and centimeter-sized grains and hand picked to obtain samples free of surface weathering, veins, and other contaminants. The hand-picked samples were analyzed by X-ray fluorescence spectroscopy (XRF) for major oxides, emission spectroscopy (ICP) for minor and trace elements, and neutron activation analysis (INAA) for trace and rare-earth elements (REE) (Tables 9–2 and 9–3). Al, Ca, Co, Cr, Fe, K, Mg, Mn, Na, P, Pb, Ti, and Zn were analyzed by two of the three techniques. Manganese contents analyzed by XRF and ICP were very close, and the XRF values were used. The amounts of other elements were comparable between the techniques except for Cr and Zn, which in some samples have significantly different values.

The average chert and argillite have SiO_2 and Al_2O_3 contents of 94.39% and 58.13% and 1.71% and 16%, respectively (Table 9–2). In the lithologic progression, chert, argillaceous chert, siliceous argillite, argillite, all major, minor, and trace elements progressively increase in abundance, except for SiO_2, which decreases, and Mn, which is higher in rocks of intermediate SiO_2 content. Fe_2O_3 and FeO increase markedly in argillaceous rocks. The few rocks we call argillaceous chert have more MnO relative to Fe_2O_3 and more Fe_2O_3 relative to Al_2O_3 than the other rock types analyzed (Table 9–2). Larger Fe/Mn ratios and smaller Fe/Al ratios characterize the rock series from chert to argillite (Table 9–2). High SiO_2 is especially characteristic of chert, whereas high Al_2O_3, Fe_2O_3, Na_2O, K_2O, Cr, Th, and Zr are characteristic of argillite. In addition, argillite is relatively enriched in Cu, reflecting a biogenic component.

The average MnO content of rhodochrostone is 34.6% (51.6% $MnCO_3$) and for Mn-oxide ores 49.5%; the maximum values are 54.7% (88.7% $MnCO_3$) and 73.4%, respectively. On the average, the rhodochrostone is characterized by high amounts of MnO, CaO, MgO, volatiles (LOI), Zn, low amounts of all other major oxides, Zr, and Th, and the lowest Fe/Mn and Al/Al + Fe + Mn ratios. In contrast, the average oxide ore is characterized by high amounts of MnO, P_2O_5, Ba, Co, Cu, V, Zn, U, and with especially high Ni and Sr. On the average, the oxidation of rhodochrosite decreases Ca and volatiles and increases Al_2O_3, TiO_2, Fe_2O_3, Na_2O, Co, Cr, K_2O, P_2O_5, MnO, Ba, Cu, Ni, Sr, V, Zn, and Zr. Analyses of the inner rhodochrosite core and the 6 cm thick oxidized rim of a single boulder showed the same trend, except that Li and MgO were also depleted during oxidation. In addition, all the REE (except Nd) are more abundant in the oxidized ore (see Table 9–3).

Manganese ores and other rock types are easily discriminated on the SiO_2 - Al_2O_3 × 10 - (Fe_2O_3 + MnO) × 10 ternary diagram (see Fig. 9–3). Other

Table 9–2. Major (weight-percent) and Minor (ppm) Element Chemistry for Different Lithologies in the Ladd-Buckeye District

Rock Type	Average Chert (35)*	Average Argillaceous Chert (4)	Average Siliceous Argillite (7)	Average Argillite (7)	Average Rhodochrostone (5)	Average Oxide Ore (9)	Average Ore (14)
SiO_2 (wt%)	94.39	84.65	73.76	58.13	38.54	28.89	32.33
Al_2O_3	1.71	4.22	9.11	16.0	0.97	3.02	2.29
TiO_2	0.07	0.23	0.53	0.87	0.04	0.17	0.12
Fe_2O_3	0.67	2.54	4.23	5.81	0.74	2.30	1.74
FeO	0.48	1.16	1.20	2.49	—	—	—
MgO	0.59	1.37	2.33	3.21	3.05	2.21	2.45
CaO	0.12	0.25	0.41	0.89	2.47	1.35	1.75
Na_2O	0.28	0.60	1.12	1.52	0.18	0.79	0.57
K_2O	0.34	1.04	2.70	4.08	0.02	0.26	0.17
P_2O_5	0.05	0.05	0.12	0.35	0.05	0.25	0.18
MnO	0.21	1.29	1.05	0.27	34.62	49.49	44.18
LOI	0.72	2.21	3.29	6.0	19.82	11.61	14.55
Total	99.63	99.61	99.85	99.62	100.5	100.29	100.33
As (ppm)	—	—	—	—	26.7	72.2	60.8
Ba	214	240	518	870	165	2,311	1,545
Co	8.0	10.3	24.7	27.8	12.7	44	33.1
Cr	10.6	21.5	61.3	89.4	3.9	15.0	11.1
Cu	44.0	49.0	103.0	130.0	26.0	193	133
Li	12.9	17.8	24.0	36.3	18.8	25.3	23.0
Ni	22.4	35.8	54.0	105.0	188.4	394.3	320.8
Sr	17.8	12.3	26.4	67.6	51.4	787.3	524.5
V	20.4	82.3	214.4	128.3	193.4	238.2	222.2
Y	6.1	8.5	19.3	37.4	6.0	19.8	14.9
Zn	24.8	36.8	78.6	105.4	286.8	378.4	345.7
Si/Si+Al+Fe	0.96	0.89	0.80	0.66	0.95	0.81	0.86
Fe/Al	0.91	1.2	0.81	0.69	1.02	1.01	1.01
Al/Al+Fe+Mn	0.48	0.38	0.51	0.58	0.02	0.04	0.03
Fe+Mn Fe/Mn	5.13	2.68	4.81	27.76	0.02	0.042	0.036

*Numbers in parentheses are number of samples average is based on.

LOI = loss on ignition at 900°C. Total iron is listed as Fe_2O_3 for the manganese ores. Other elements scanned, but below the limits of detection (listed in the parentheses in ppm), include: Ag (4); Cd (4); Mo (4), except four oxide ores showed 30, 7, 492, and 10 ppm, a rhodochrostone 8 ppm, and two argillites 8 and 5 ppm; Pb (8), except three oxide ores showed 59, 22, and 83 ppm, a rhodochrostone 9 ppm, four argillites 9, 36, 14, and 15 ppm, and four cherts 21, 32, 40, and 10 ppm. Elements and oxides below the limits of detection were arbitrarily halved and used in the averages: Al_2O_3 (0.10%) one chert; Fe_2O_3 (0.40%) one chert; TiO_2 (0.02%) six cherts; TiO_2 (0.04%) three oxide ores, three rhodochrostones; CaO (0.02%) six cherts; Na_2O (0.15%) eight cherts; K_2O (0.04%) one oxide ore, three rhodochrostones, one chert; P_2O_5 (0.05%) half of the cherts and argillaceous cherts, one siliceous argillite; P_2O_5 (0.10%) three oxide ores and three rhodochrostones; MnO (0.02%) seven cherts; Co (2) two cherts; Cr (2) 2 cherts; Cu (2) one chert, one rhodochrostone; Li (4) seven cherts; Ni (4) two cherts; Sr (4) one chert; Y (4) half the cherts, one oxide ore, three rhodochrostones; Zn (8) two cherts. As for rhodochrostone is based on three values, for oxide ore on nine values. One As value for argillite is 30 ppm and one for chert is <20 ppm; other samples were not analyzed for As. One anomalously high Y value (197 ppm) was left out of the chert average, which is therefore based on thirty-four values. Analyses performed at U.S. Geological Survey analytical laboratories. Analysts: J. L. Seely, P. H. Briggs, W. Updegrove, D. Shepard, J. Cornell, J. E. Taggart, K. Stewart, and L. Espos.

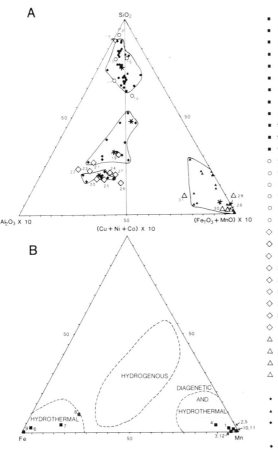

EXPLANATION

■ 1 Average Ladd–Buckeye Mn-Oxide Ore

■ 2 Average Ladd–Buckeye Mn-Carbonate Ore

■ 3 Average New Zealand South Island Mn Ore

■ 4 Average New Zealand North Island Mn Ore

■ 5 Costa Rica Mn Ore

■ 6 Costa Rica Fe Ore

■ 7 Cyprus Umbers

■ 8 East Pacific Rise Metalliferous Sediment

■ 9 Afar Rift Fe Beds

■ 10 Afar Rift Massive Mn Beds

■ 11 Afar Rift Porous Mn Beds

■ 12 Afar Rift Powdery Mn Beds

○ 13 DSDP Leg 62 Chert

○ 14 DSDP Leg 69 Chert

○ 15 Average New Zealand South Island Chert

○ 16 Average New Zealand North Island Chert

○ 17 Average Nicoya Complex Chert

○ 18 Average Nicoya Complex Cherts and Jaspers

○ 19 Average Nicoya Complex Shale

◇ 20 Average Pacific Pelagic Clay

◇ 21 Offshore Japan Hemipelagic Clay

◇ 22 Average Terrigenous Shale

◇ 23 Average New Zealand South Island Argillite

◇ 24 Average New Zealand North Island Argillite

◇ 25 East-central Pacific Siliceous Pelagic Clay

◇ 26 Northwest Pacific Pelagic Clay

◇ 27 Pacific Zeolitic Pelagic Clay Site 164

△ 28 Average Nicoya Complex Mn Ore

△ 29 Average New Zealand South Island Mn Ore

△ 30 Average New Zealand North Island Mn Ore

△ 31 East Pacific Rise Metalliferous Sediment

• Upper Field: Ladd Buckeye Chert, ✳Average

▲ Lower Right Field: Ladd-Buckeye Mn Ores, ✳Average

• Middle Field: Ladd Buckeye Argillaceous Chert, ✳Average
    and Siliceous Argillite, ✳Average

• Lower Field: Ladd Buckeye Argillite, ✳Average

Figure 9–3. Ternary diagrams. (*A*) SiO_2-$Al_2O_3 \times 10$-$(Fe_2O_3 + MnO) \times 10$ for various rock types in the Ladd–Buckeye district of the Franciscan Complex. Other rocks are shown for comparison. (*B*) Mn-Fe-$(Cu + Ni + CO) \times 10$ plot of average Ladd–Buckeye ores. Various hydrothermal and diagenetic Fe and Mn deposits are shown for comparison. [Data for New Zealand rocks are from Hein (unpublished data); for Costa Rica rocks from Hein et al., 1983*a*; for Cyprus umbers from Robertson and Hudson, 1973; for East Pacific Rise metalliferous sediment from Bostrom and Peterson, 1969; for Afar rocks from Bonatti et al., 1972*a*; for DSDP Leg 62 rocks from Hein et al., 1981; for DSDP Leg 69 rocks from Hein et al., 1983*b*; for hemipelagic clay from offshore Japan from Matsumoto and Iijima, 1983; for pelagic clays from Hein and Vanek, 1981, Bischoff et al., 1979, Pimm, 1973, and Couture, 1977; for average terrigenous shale from Pettijohn, 1975]

data are displayed for comparison. New Zealand chert falls within the field of Franciscan Complex chert, but Nicoya Complex chert falls just outside the field. The argillite interbedded with the chert falls within a small field that is bounded by average terrigenous shale and pelagic clay. The Ladd–Buckeye, New Zealand, and Nicoya Complex ores all have similar average values (see Fig. 9–3).

On the $(Cu + Ni + Co) \times 10$ - Fe - Mn ternary diagram of Bonatti et al. (1972*b*), all argillites, manganese ores and all but two cherts plot within the

Table 9–3. Trace and Rare Earth Elements (in ppm), Ladd–Buckeye District, California

Element	Sample Number						
	384-28-2	*384-28-4A*	*384-28-6A*	*384-28-8A*	*384-28-8F*	*384-28-8G*	*484-12-1B*
Cs	0.99	0.04	0.25	1.2	0.63	0.03	6.2
Rb	21	—	<2.5	21	3.2	—	140
Sb	0.33	11	0.31	0.17	2.7	2.1	0.29
Sc	2.5	3.9	0.41	2.8	3.3	0.11	20
Th	1.2	0.82	0.14	1.2	0.93	<0.05	9.6
U	0.22	0.98	2.8	0.27	2.6	2.5	1.4
Zr	17	<22	0.71	21	<36	0.43	130
La	4.1	3.8	1.5	4.2	6.0	0.91	33
Ce	7.7	11	2.1	6.8	8.1	0.15	55
Nd	2.9	4.4	1.1	2.5	4.3	1.2	24
Sm	0.54	1.1	0.31	0.57	1.1	0.26	4.9
Eu	0.11	0.27	0.06	0.12	0.28	0.05	1.0
Gd	0.42	1.1	0.33	0.52	1.2	0.25	4.9
Tb	0.08	0.18	0.05	0.09	0.23	0.04	0.68
Tm	0.06	0.09	0.04	0.06	0.17	0.04	0.40
Yb	0.42	0.62	0.26	0.37	1.3	0.31	2.5
Lu	0.07	0.11	0.04	0.06	0.21	0.5	0.38
Hf	0.50	0.34	0.08	0.54	0.48	0.19	3.8
Ta	0.13	0.06	0.01	0.15	0.07	—	1.2
Lithology	Red chert	Black Mn-oxide ore	Rhodochrostone	Red chert	Mn-oxide	Siliecous Mn-oxide ore	Green siliceous argillite

— means not detected.

Analyses performed at U.S. Geological Survey analytical laboratories. Analysts: D. M. McKown, J. Budahn, and R. Knight.

hydrothermal and diagenetic field of oceanic manganese deposits (Fig. 9–3). Chert values span the range from the Fe apex to the Mn apex, but are more common near the Fe apex. All argillites occur near the Fe apex.

ISOTOPIC COMPOSITION OF RHODOCHROSITE

Seven purified rhodochrosite samples from the Ladd and Buckeye mines yielded δ-^{13}C (PDB) values between −17 per mil and −54 per mil (Hodgson, 1966; Yeh et al., 1985); and one sample from the Double A mine in the northern Coast Ranges was −39.4 per mil (Hodgson, 1966). The more negative values could have been produced only if the CO_2 that formed the $MnCO_3$ was derived from the oxidation of early diagenetic methane, which can have δ-^{13}C values of about −50 to −90 per mil (Claypool et al., 1973). Such methane is produced by anaerobic respiration of bacteria using CO_2 as an electron ac-

Sample Number						
484-13-1G	*484-13-1K*	*484-13-1U*	*484-20-2C*	*484-20-2I*	*484-20-2J*	*484-20-2O*
0.67	1.0	4.0	0.76	12	1.3	0.30
14	20	74	13	170	19	10
0.10	0.39	0.45	0.10	1.1	0.13	0.04
1.8	3.6	16	5.9	31	4.0	1.6
1.2	1.6	6.4	1.5	10	1.3	0.43
0.49	0.22	0.98	0.56	1.9	0.48	0.93
15	32	98	26	150	21	< 16
3.8	12	25	6.8	29	4.5	0.88
6.9	15	43	17	64	8.8	1.4
3.6	11	22	9.0	29	4.3	0.72
0.82	2.4	4.3	2.1	5.3	0.88	0.15
0.15	0.50	0.82	0.47	1.0	0.16	0.03
0.75	2.2	3.5	2.1	3.4	0.69	0.18
0.12	0.33	0.51	0.31	0.63	0.10	0.03
0.08	—	0.30	0.16	0.47	0.07	0.03
0.47	1.0	1.9	1.0	3.1	0.48	0.23
0.07	0.16	0.29	0.16	0.49	0.08	0.04
0.47	0.65	2.9	0.43	4.6	0.62	0.21
0.13	0.16	0.81	0.08	1.2	0.16	0.04
Green chert	Red chert	Brown siliceous argillite	Mottled red-green chert	Red argillite	Red chert	Pale gray chert

ceptor. The δ-^{13}C values less negative than about -25 per mil could have resulted from CO_2 produced by metabolic oxidation of organic matter during bacterial reduction of sulfate or from CO_2 produced early in the carbonate reduction stage (Claypool, 1974).

The sequence of diagenetic stages that relate to the bacterial use of organic matter are (1) oxic and suboxic reduction of O_2, manganese oxides, nitrate, and iron oxides (Froelich et al., 1979); (2) anoxic sulfate reduction, which produces CO_2 and H_2S; and (3) anoxic carbonate reduction, which produces methane and CO_2. Oxidation of the methane produced in the carbonate reduction stage can take place if methane diffuses or bubbles up into the other zones (Hathaway and Degens, 1969; Claypool, 1974). The δ-^{13}C values (in per mil) of CO_2 produced in these stages are about -25, -25, and -20 to $+15$, respectively (Claypool et al., 1973; Irwin et al., 1977). The δ-^{13}C of CO_2 from oxidized methane is -45 to -90 per mil. The carbonate minerals that form from the CO_2 would have a δ-^{13}C value about 1 per mil heavier than the total dissolved CO_2 per se, due to fractionation. Mixing of CO_2 can result in carbonates with δ-^{13}C values between about $+20$ and -80, although the isotopically lightest value of which we are aware is -60 per mil (Hathaway and Degens, 1969). However, δ-^{13}C values less than about -25 per mil must be partly derived from CO_2 produced by the oxidation of methane.

The δ-^{18}O (SMOW) composition of eight rhodochrosite samples is $+19.5$–$+26.4$ per mil (Hodgson, 1966; Yeh et al., 1985), which indicates temperatures of formation of 20–100° C, assuming a δ-^{18}O of 0 per mil and -3 per mil, respectively, for the water of formation (Yeh et al., 1985). An oxidized rim, composed of nsutite and pennantite, of a rhodochrosite boulder gives a δ-^{13}O value of $+5.5$, yielding a temperature of formation of 110° C; this manganiferous material formed later, apparently at a higher temperature than the rhodochrosite.

Because isotopic exchange of carbon could not have taken place, these isotopic measurements indicate that the primary carbonate-rich ore formed after methane production at depth in the sediment column and, assuming no oxygen exchange, at low (≤ 100°C) temperatures. A temperature of <80°C is indicated by the opal-CT mineralogy and a temperature of <50°C by the stability range for the oxidation of methane. In addition, the rhodochrosite has not altered (reequilibrated) during subsequent lower blueschist facies (~ 150°C and 6–8 kb; M. C. Clarke, personal communication, 1985) metamorphism, and the exchange of δ-^{13}C has not been significant.

DISCUSSION

The occurrence and lithologic association of manganese deposits and their textural, mineralogic, and isotopic characteristics indicate that rhodochrosite-rich deposits in chert of the Franciscan Complex formed by diagenetic processes related to microbial activity at depth in the sedimentary column. However, this interpretation requires that several characteristics of the deposits and the conditions of formation need to be explained. We discuss the origin of the massive chert beds that occur adjacent to most ore bodies, the depth and timing of formation of the rhodochrosite, the source of the manganese, and the depositional and tectonic environment of the sediment and associated ore.

MASSIVE CHERT BEDS

It has been suggested previously that the massive chert beds adjacent to manganese deposits in the Franciscan Complex formed from hydrothermal silica deposited by the same system that provided the manganese (Taliaferro and Hudson, 1943; Snyder, 1978). Alternatively, we suggest that the massive chert beds formed by the addition of silica that was released when the host rock was replaced by rhodochrosite. Replacement textures (radiolarian tests, vein selvages) are evident in and near the manganese lenses. If replacement of the host rock was concurrent with the opal-A to opal-CT or opal-CT to quartz transformation, the excess water evolved during these dehydration reactions and compaction could have transported soluble elements some distance from the site of replacement.

It should be noted that some massive chert beds in the Franciscan Complex are not associated with manganese ore deposits (B. Murchey, personal communication, 1983). These beds, however, appear to represent chemically unstable zones in which siliceous deposits accumulating over many millions of years underwent dissolution and reprecipitation while the sediment was unlithified or semilithified. This type of stratigraphic hiatus was not observed in the sections studied in the Ladd–Buckeye area (B. Murchey, personal communication, 1985).

TIMING AND DEPTH OF RHODOCHROSITE FORMATION

In a diagenetic model, the timing and depth of rhodochrosite formation are constrained by the temperature of formation as determined by the oxygen isotopic compositions, the location of the zone of organic matter degradation from which the rhodochrosite carbon was derived as determined by the carbon isotopic composition, and the replacement textures of rhodochrosite and silica polymorphs. The oxygen isotopic composition indicates formation at a temperature between 20° and 100°C (Yeh et al., 1985). The thick section of sandstone enclosing the chert and manganese probably represents a rapidly deposited, deep-water, continental margin sedimentary facies (Blake et al., 1982). Geothermal gradients for an active continental margin could produce temperatures of 20–100°C at burial depths of 20–1,500 m; using sedimentation rates of 20–200m/m.y. would give 0.23–75 m.y. as the amount of time elapsed from the beginning of sedimentation to rhodochrosite deposition (data from Deep Sea Drilling Project Initial Reports for legs 5, 19, 64, 65).

δ-^{13}C values indicate that the rhodochrosite formed from the oxidation of bacterially produced methane. Some methane may also have been derived abiogenically from deeper stratigraphic levels by thermocatalytic reactions. The oxidation of methane occurs relatively late in the diagenesis of the sediment following completion or near completion of sulfate reduction. Sulfate reduction may be complete by burial to a depth of 10–25 m. Rapid rates of sedimentation would shorten the residence time of the organic matter in the zone of sulfate reduction. After sulfate reduction, carbonate reduction and methane production occur at subbottom depths of about 10–1,000 m or more in continental margin deposits (Lancelot and Ewing, 1972; Claypool, 1974; Irwin et al., 1977; Hein et al., 1979; Pisciotto and Mahoney, 1981). Subsequent to methane production, methane oxidation may occur at any time and at any stratigraphic level where the appropriate redox conditions prevail. Except at the seawater-sediment interface, the sediment above the zone of methane production was probably reducing and could not have supplied oxygen to oxidize the methane. We suggest that manganese and iron oxyhydroxides or oxides deposited with the sediment acted as an oxidant for the methane via a reaction such as $2MnOOH + 2CH_4 + 2H_2O \rightarrow 2MnCO_3 + 7H_2$. The hydrogen would either be used in bacterial metabolic processes or combined with other phases, such as nitrogen, to produce ammonia. Iron and manganese oxides have considerable capacity for oxidizing organic matter (Reeburgh, 1983), but little is known about this process. In slowly deposited pelagic sediments, manganese and iron are reduced before sulfate (Froelich et al., 1979), but in a rapidly deposited continental margin upwelling facies, much iron and manganese should have escaped early oxidation by rapid burial. Even though anaerobic-methane oxidation can occur in the sulfate reduction zone (Reeburgh and Heggie, 1977; Barnes and Goldberg, 1976), metal sulfide rather than carbonate would precipitate. Marine pore waters below several centimeters' depth have been shown to be saturated with respect to $MnCO_3$ (Pedersen and Price, 1982; Sawlan and Murray, 1983).

Formation of rhodochrosite predated the transformation of opal-CT to quartz. The silica polymorph transformations are dependent on temperature, time, host sediment composition, and chemistry of pore waters (Kastner et al., 1977; Iijima et al., 1978; Hein et al., 1978; Isaacs, 1982). Temperature is the most important factor in carbonate-poor continental margin deposits. Likely temperatures and depths of burial for this silica transformation are 45–90°C and 200–1,000 m, respectively (Murata et al., 1977; Hein et al., 1978; Pisciotto, 1981).

SOURCE OF THE MANGANESE AND MANGANESE-IRON FRACTIONATION

Manganese in the primary rhodochrosite ore was deposited with the radiolarian-rich and clay-rich beds in the form of manganese oxide or manganese oxyhydroxide. The ultimate source of the manganese is uncertain, but it may have come from hydrothermal discharge, seafloor weathering of volcanic rocks, or terrigenous organic and inorganic compounds. The paucity of volcanic rocks in many sections hosting manganese deposits in the Franciscan Complex suggests that manganese from an immediate volcanogenic source (hydrothermal or halmyrolytic) is unlikely; however, hydrothermal circulation and transportation within a sediment-covered rift zone analogous to the Guaymas Basin in the Gulf of California cannot be discounted.

Manganese is a more abundant cation in terrestrially dominated organic matter (humic material) than calcium or iron (Suess, 1979). Humic material was no doubt deposited with the hemipelagic argillites and terrigenous sandstones. In addition, radiolarian ooze has a larger Mn/Fe ratio and larger absolute amount of manganese than any other sediment type (Stanton, 1972, p. 455). If the manganese in the two lenses at the Buckeye mine were redistributed vertically through the 600 m thick chert-argillite sequence, then the present average MnO content of 0.26% in the sediment would originally have been about 0.40–0.50%. This figure is comparable to the MnO content of radiolarian ooze and continental margin deposits associated with an oxidation reduction boundary (see Chap. 8). Trask (1950) and Watanabe et al. (1970) noted a proportionality between the thickness of the chert sections and the thickness of the manganese lenses, implying that the chert-argillite may be the source of the manganese.

We suggest that the lack of significant primary (biogenic) carbonate and

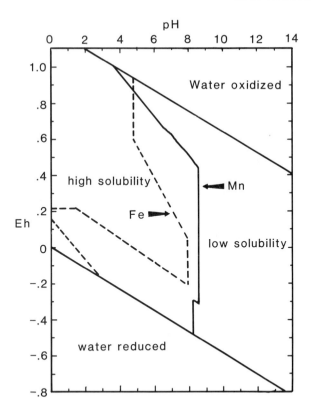

Figure 9-4 Comparative solubility of manganese and iron in system H_2O-Mn-Fe-CO_2-S-H_2O at 25°C and 1 atm. Total CO_2 species activity 2,000 mg/l as HCO_3^-; total sulfer species activity 2,000 mg/l as SO_4^{-2}. The boundaries for both Fe and Mn are shown for activities of 10 mol/l. (Adapted from Hem, 1972)

minor amount of volcanic ash in the enclosing sedimentary strata reduced the availability of calcium and magnesium for the formation of calcite and dolomite. Such carbonates are common in many continental margin deposits (Claypool, 1974).

It is apparent in Table 9-2 that extreme fractionation of manganese and iron exists in the ore deposits (Fe/Mn = 0.04) relative to chert (5.1) and argillite (27.8). The abundant pervasive iron in the host rocks suggests that both iron and manganese were deposited with the sediment and that the fractionation occurred during diagenesis. Over a wide range of Eh and pH in natural aqueous systems, manganese is more soluble than iron (see Fig. 9-4), and this difference in solubility provides a mechanism for fractionation (Krauskopf, 1957; Hem, 1972). It is well known that manganese has much greater mobility under reducing conditions in marine and lacustrine sediments (e.g., Lynn and Bonatti, 1965; Pedersen and Price, 1982); manganese reduction and mobilization occur before iron reduction (Sawlan and Murray, 1983). The reducing environment of the organic-rich sediment permitted mobilization of manganese, while iron remained fixed, a situation that is favored in hemipelagic sediments. For example, the pore waters of hemipelagic deposits of offshore Mexico contain iron at levels an order of magnitude less than manganese. The manganese shows regions of production (reduction) or consumption (oxidation) separated by zones of diffusion (Sawlan and Murray, 1983). This type of separation on a larger scale (tens of meters) could partly explain the segregation of manganese into discrete bodies or lenses. The transportation and deposition of manganese carbonate were also controlled by porosity, permeability, grain size, and host-sediment composition.

TECTONIC AND SEDIMENTARY ENVIRONMENT OF DEPOSITION

Several features indicate the tectonic-sedimentary environment of formation of these manganese ore deposits: the thick sections of rapidly deposited turbidite graywacke sandstone, the moderately thick sections of less rapidly deposited interbedded chert-argillite, the abundant manganese and iron deposited with chert-argillite sediments, the paucity of volcanic rocks in the sections studied and in most other manganese-bearing sections in the Franciscan Complex, and the diagenetic processes that affected the deposits. Prior to manganese deposition, a considerable volume of sandstone was deposited in a basin near a continental margin. Gradational sedimentary contacts of the sandstone with the overlying chert-argillite section indicate that the terrigenous source was gradually shut off, possibly by tectonic movements (strike-slip faulting; downwarping), by changes in the adjacent on-land drainage basins, or by a eustatic rise in sea-level. The radiolarian chert-argillite section indicates that oceanic upwelling occurred above the same basin and produced abundant plankton accumulations that were redeposited by bottom and turbidity currents. These organic-rich deposits were in turn intercalated with layers of hemipelagic clay that also contain radiolarians and other debris. These siliceous deposits are not equivalent in texture, mode of formation, or lithologic associations to the radiolarian siliceous oozes that occur today north and south of the equator (Jenkyns and Winterer, 1982; Hein and Karl, 1983).

The diagenetic processes described here, especially the generation of methane by bacterial degradation of organic matter, are typical of continental margin deposits, not deep-sea deposits. We propose that the following sequence of events combined to form manganese deposits in the Franciscan sediment pile. The siliceous deposits underwent a dehydration reaction and compaction as the opal-A (biogenic silica) transformed to opal-CT at about 30–50°C after several hundred meters of burial. A second dehydration reaction and compaction episode occurred as opal-CT transformed to quartz at about 80°C and 700 m of burial. During early diagenesis, bacterial degradation of the organic carbon residing in the sediment resulted in the production of CO_2 and CH_4. After the time of the opal-A to opal-CT transformation, the CH_4 diffused upward into overlying sediment and was oxidized to CO_2. The increased alkalinity and presence of dissolved manganese led to precipitation of $MnCO_3$; some CO_2 in the carbonate was derived from the earlier stages of organic matter degradation. The fluids produced by the silica dehydration reactions and from the compaction of the sediment provided a means to transport manganese, CH_4, and CO_2 under conditions of low Eh within the sediment column.

Although terrigenous and biogenic sources for manganese have already been considered, some manganese and iron in these siliceous deposits may have been derived from a relatively distant oceanic spreading center. Because the amount of iron and manganese is not greatly increased over average hemipelagic siliceous deposits and few volcanic rocks are present in the sections, we speculate that such a source was not closer than 50–100 km. Certainly, if a spreading center were nearby, the rate of sediment deposition would be much greater than the rate of spreading.

Possible tectonic stratigraphic settings that are modern analogs to the Franciscan Complex described here include: (1) forearc and back-arc basins such as those flanking the Mariana Island Arc and (2) rifted continental margins with narrow ocean basins such as the Gulf of California.

CONCLUSIONS

1. Chert-hosted manganese deposits in the Franciscan Complex formed by complex diagenetic processes operating at depth in the sedimentary column.
2. The ore deposits formed at a temperature of about 20–100°C and at burial depths of 400 ± 250 m.
3. The source of the carbon for the primary rhodochrosite ore was the oxidation of methane produced by bacterial fermentation processes in organic-rich sediments and the carbon dioxide produced during either the sulfate reduction or early carbonate-reduction stages.
4. The immediate source of the manganese was from within the chert-argillite sediments per se and was ultimately derived from relatively distant continental and (or) volcanogenic sources.
5. Massive chert beds adjacent to the ore bodies formed by addition of silica derived from the replacement of chert-argillite by the rhodochrosite.
6. Lower blueschist facies metamorphism had little or no effect on the carbon-isotopic composition of the primary rhodochrosite and possibly little effect on the oxygen-isotopic composition.
7. The stratigraphy and diagenetic processes suggest deposition of the sediments at a continental margin in a region of oceanic upwelling.
8. Lithologic associations, stratigraphy, and geochemistry suggest that the sediments were deposited in a newly formed ocean basin, back-arc or forearc basin, or rifted continental margin.
9. The long-noted disparity between the composition of primary orogenic belt manganese ores (carbonates and silicates) compared with present-day oceanic deposits (oxides) can be understood in terms of the mechanisms of manganese deposition: seafloor hydrothermal and hydrogenous/diagenetic mechanisms for modern deposits and diagenetic processes for the orogenic belt deposits.

ACKNOWLEDGMENTS

We thank the following people for help in the field and for technical assistance: Lisa Morgenson, Rosemary Sliney, Robin Bouse, Janet Whitlock, Phyllis Swenson, and Tasha Hein. M. C. Blake and George Claypool of the

U.S. Geological Survey provided helpful reviews of this chapter. We were given access to the Buckeye mine by Manuel Gonzalez and to the Ladd mine by Robert Connolly.

REFERENCES

Bailey, E. H., W. P. Irwin, and D. L. Jones, 1964. Franciscan and related rocks, *California Div. Mines and Geology Bull.* **183**:1–177.

Barnes, R. O., and E. D. Goldberg, 1976. Methane production and consumption in anoxic marine sediments, *Geology* **4**:297–300.

Barrett, T. J., 1982. Stratigraphy and sedimentology of Jurassic bedded chert overlying ophiolites in the north Apennines, Italy, *Sedimentology* **29**:353–373.

Bischoff, J. L., G. R. Heath, and M. Leinen, 1979. Geochemistry of deep-sea sediments from the Pacific manganese nodule province: Domes Sites A, B, and C, in *Marine Geology and Oceanography of the Pacific Manganese Nodule Province*, J. L. Bischoff and D. Z. Piper, eds., Plenum Press, New York, pp. 397–436.

Blake, M. C. and D. L. Jones, 1974. *Origin of Franciscan Melanges in Northern California,* Society of Economic Paleontologists and Mineralogists Special Publication No. 19, pp. 345–355.

Blake, M. C. and D. L. Jones, 1981. The Franciscan assemblage and related rocks in Northern California: A reinterpretation, in *The Geotectonic Development of California,* W. G. Ernst ed., Prentice-Hall, Englewood Cliffs, N. J., pp. 307–328.

Blake, M. C., A. S. Jayko, and D. G. Howell, 1982. Sedimentation, metamorphism, and tectonic accretion of the Franciscan assemblage of northern California, in *Trench-Foreare Geology*, J. K. Legget, ed., Geological Society of London Special Publication No. 10, pp. 433–438.

Blake, M. C., A. S. Jayko and R. J. McLaughlin, 1985. Tectonostratigraphic terranes of the northern Coast Ranges, California, in *Tectonostratigraphic Terranes of the Circum-Pacific Region,* D. G. Howell, ed., Vol. 1, Circum-Pacific Council for Energy and Mineral Resources, Earth Science Series, pp. 159–170.

Bonatti, E., D. E. Fisher, O. Joensuu, H. S. Rydell, and M. Beyth, 1972a. Iron-manganese-barium deposits from the northern Afar Rift (Ethiopia), *Econ. Geology* **67**:717–730.

Bonatti, E., T. Kraemer, and H. S. Rydell, 1972b. Classification and genesis of submarine iron-manganese deposits, in *Ferromanganese Deposits on the Ocean Floor,* D. R. Horn, ed., Conference on International Decade of Ocean Exploration, Columbia University, pp. 159–166.

Bostrom, K., and M. N. A. Peterson, 1969. The origin of aluminum-poor ferromanganoan sediments in areas of high heat flow on the East Pacific Rise, *Marine Geology* **7**:427–447.

Burns, R. G., and V. M. Burns, 1979. Manganese oxides, in *Marine Minerals*, R. G. Burns, ed., Mineralogical Society of America Short Course Notes 6, 1–46.

Chamberlain, T. C., 1914. Diastrophism and the formative process. Volume: The testimony of the deep-sea deposits, *Jour. Geology* **22**:131–144.

Chyi, M. S., D. A. Crerar, R. W. Carlson, and R. F. Stallard, 1984. Hydrothermal Mn-deposits of the Franciscan Assemblage, II. Isotope and trace element geochemistry, and implications for hydrothermal convection at spreading centers, *Earth and Planetary Sci. Letters* **73**:31–45.

Claypool, G. E., 1974. Anoxic diagenesis and bacterial methane production in deep-sea sediments, Ph.D. dissertation, University of California, Los Angeles, 276p.

Claypool, G. E., B. J. Presley, and I. R. Kaplan, 1973. Gas analyses in sediment samples from legs 10, 11, 13, 14, 15, 18, and 19, in J. S. Creager, D. W. Scholl et al., *Initial Reports of the Deep-Sea Drilling Project* Vol. 19, U.S. Govt. Printing Office, Washington, D.C., pp. 879–884.

Couture, R. A., 1977. Composition and origin of palygorskite-rich and montmorillonite-rich zeolite-containing sediments from the Pacific Ocean; *Chem. Geology* **19**:113–130.

Crerar, C. A., J. Namson, M. S. Chyi, L. Williams, and M. D. Feigenson, 1982. Manganiferous cherts of the Franciscan Assemblage, I. General geology, ancient and modern analogues, and implications for hydrothermal convection at oceanic spreading centers, *Econ. Geology* **77**:519–540.

Davis, E. F., 1918. The radiolarian cherts of the Franciscan group, *Califiornia Univ. Dept. Geology Bull.* **2**(3):235–432.

Erd, R. C., and Y. Ohashi, 1984. Santaclarite, a new calcium-manganese silicate hydrate from California, *Am. Mineralogist* **69**:200–206.

Ernst, W. G., 1971. Petrologic reconnaissance of Franciscan metagraywackes from the Diablo Range, central California Coast Ranges, *Jour. Petrology* **12**:413–437.

Froelich, P. N., G. P. Klinkhammer, M. L. Bender, N. A. Luedtke, G. R. Heath, D. Cullen, P. Dauphin, D. Hammond, B. Hartman, and V. Maynard, 1979. Early oxidation of organic matter in pelagic sediments of the eastern equatorial Atlantic: Suboxic diagenesis, *Geochim. et Cosmochim. Acta* **43**:1075–1090.

Garrison, R. E., 1974. Radiolarian cherts, pelagic limestones, and igneous rocks in eugeosynclinal assemblages, in *Pelagic sediments: On Land and Under the Sea*, K. J. Hsu and A. C. Jenkyns, eds., International Assocation of Sedimentologists Special Publication No. 1, pp. 367–399.

Hallam, A., 1976. Geology and plate tectonics interpretation of the sediments of the Mesozoic radiolarite-ophiolite complex in the Neyriz region, south Iran, *Geol. Soc. America Bull.* **87**:47–52.

Hathaway, J. C., and E. T. Degens, 1969. Methane-derived marine carbonates of Pleistocene Age, *Science* **165**:690–692.

Hein, J. R., and S. M. Karl, 1983. Comparisons between open-ocean and continental margin chert sequences, in *Siliceous Deposits in the Pacific Region*, A. Iijima, J. R. Hein, and R. Siever, eds., Elsevier, Amsterdam, pp. 25–44.

Hein, J. R., and E. Vanek, 1981. Origin and alteration of volcanic ash and pelagic brown clay, Leg 62, north-central Pacific, in J. Thiede, T. L. Vallier et al., *Initial Reports of the Deep Sea Drilling Project* Vol. 62, U.S. Govt. Printing Office, Washington, D.C., pp. 559–569.

Hein, J. R., and H. W. Yeh, 1981. Oxygen-isotopic composition of chert from the mid-Pacific mountains and Hess Rise, Leg 62, in J. Thiede, T. L. Vallier, et al., *Initial Reports of the Deep Sea Drilling Project* Vol. 62, U.S. Govt. Printing Office, Washington, D.C., pp. 749–758.

Hein, J. R. and H. W. Yeh, 1983. Oxygen-isotope composition of secondary silica phases, Costa Rica Rift, Leg 69, in J. R. Cann, M. G. Langseth, J. Honnorez, R. P. Von Herzen, and S. M. White, *Initial Reports of the Deep Sea Drilling Project,* Vol. 69, U.S. Govt. Printing Office, Washington, D.C., pp. 423–429.

Hein, J. R., D. W. Scholl, J. A. Barron, M. G. Jones, and J. Miller, 1978. Diagenesis of Late Cenozoic diatomaceous deposits and formation of the bottom simulating reflector in the southern Bering Sea, *Sedimentology* **25**:155–181.

Hein, J. R., J. R. O'Neil, and M. G. Jones, 1979. Origin of authigenic carbonates in sediment from the Bering Sea, *Sedimentology* **26**:681–705.

Hein, J. R., T. L. Vallier, and M. A. Allan, 1981. Chert petrology and geochemistry, mid-Pacific mountains and Hess Rise, Leg 62, in J. Thiele, T. L. Vallier, et al., *Initial Reports of the Deep Sea Drilling Project* Vol. 62, U.S. Govt. Printing Office, Washington, D.C., pp. 711–748.

Hein, J. R., E. P. Kuypers, P. Denyer, and R. E. Sliney, 1983*a*. Petrology and geochemistry of Cretaceous and Paleogene cherts from western Costa Rica, in *Siliceous Deposits in the Pacific Region*, A. Iijima, J. R. Hein, and R. Siever, eds., Elsevier, Amsterdam, pp. 143–174.

Hein, J. R., C. Sancetta, and L. A. Morgenson, 1983*b*. Petrology and geochemistry of silicified upper Miocene chalk, Costa Rica Rift, Leg 69, in J. R. Cann, M. G. Langseth, J. Honnorez, R. P. Von Herzen, S. M. White, *Initial Reports of the Deep Sea Drilling Project* Vol. 69, U.S. Govt. Printing Office, Washington, D.C., pp. 395–422.

Hem, J. D., 1972. Chemical factors that influence the availability of iron and manganese in aqueous systems, *Geol. Soc. America Bull.* **83**:443–450.

Hewett, D. F., 1966. Stratified deposits of the oxides and carbonates of manganese, *Econ. Geology* **69**(3):431–461.

Hodgson, W. A., 1966. Carbon and oxygen isotope ratios in diagenetic carbonates from marine sediments, *Geochim. et Cosmochim. Acta* **30**:1223–1233.

Huebner, J. S., 1967. Stability relations of minerals in the system Mn-Si-C-O, Ph.D. dissertation, Johns Hopkins University, 278p.

Iijima, A., Y. Kakuwa, K. Yamazaki, and Y. Yanagimoto, 1978. Shallow-sea organic origin of the Triassic bedded chert in central Japan, *Univ. Tokyo Fac. Sci. Jour. Sec. II*, **19**:369–400.

Irwin, H., C. Curtis, and M. Coleman, 1977. Isotopic evidence of diagenetic carbonates formed during burial of organic-rich sediments, *Nature* **269**(5625):209–213.

Isaacs, C. M., 1982. Influences of rock composition on kinetics of silica phase changes in the Monterey Formation, Santa Barbara area, California, *Geology* **10**:304–308.

Jenkyns, H. C., and E. L. Winterer, 1982. Palaeoceanography of Mesozoic ribbon radiolarites, *Earth and Plaetary Sci. Letters* **60**:351–375.

Jones, J. B., and E. R. Segnit, 1971. The nature of opal nomenclature and constituent phases, *Jour. Geol. Soc. Australia* **18**(1):57–68.

Kastner, M., J. B. Keene, and J. M. Gieskes, 1977. Diagenesis of siliceous oozes I. Chemical controls on the rate of opal-A to opal-CT transformations—An experimental study, *Geochim. et Cosmochim. Act* **41**:1041–1051.

Krauskopf, K. B., 1957. Separation of manganese from iron in sedimentary processes, *Geochim. et Cosmochim. Acta* **12**:61–84.

Kuypers, E. P., and P. Denyer, 1979. Volcanic exhalative manganese deposits in the Nicoya Ophiolite Complex, Costa Rica, *Econ. Geology* **74**:672–678.

Lancelot, Y., and J. I. Ewing, 1972. Correlation of natural gas zonation and carbonate diagenesis in Tertiary sediments from the north-west Atlantic, in C. D. Hollister, J. I. Ewing et al., *Initial Reports of the Deep Sea Drilling Project,* Vol. 11, U.S. Govt. Printing Office, Washington, D.C., pp. 791–799.

Lynn, D., and E. Bonatti, 1965. Mobility of manganese in diagenesis of deep-sea sediments, *Marine Geology* **3**:457–474.

Matsumoto, R., and A. Iijima, 1983. Chemical sedimentology of some Permo-Jurassic and Tertiary bedded cherts in central Honshu, Japan, in *Siliceous Deposits in the Pacific Region*, A. Iijima, J. R. Hein, and R. Siever eds., Elsevier, Amsterdam, pp. 175–191.

McBride, E. F., and R. L. Folk, 1979. Features and origin of Italian Jurassic radiolarites deposited on continental crust, *Jour. Sed. Petrology* **49**(3):837–868.

Molengraaff, G. A. F., 1916. On the occurrence of nodules of manganese in Mesozoic deep-sea deposits from Borneo, Timor and Rotti, their significance and mode of formation, *Proc. Acad. Sci. Amsterdam* **18**:415–430.

Molengraaff, G. A. F., 1922. On manganese nodules in Mesozoic Deep-Sea deposits of Dutch Timor, *Proc. Acad. Sci. Amsterdam* **23**:997–1012.

Murata, K. J., and M. B. Norman, 1976. An index of crystallinity of quartz, *Amer. Jour. Sci.* **276**:1120–1130.

Murata, K. J., I. Friedman, and J. D. Gleason, 1977. Oxygen isotope relations between diagenetic silica minerals in Monterey Shale, Temblor Range, California, *Amer. Jour. Sci.* **277**:259–272.

Murray, J, and A. F. Renard, 1981. Deep Sea Deposits in *Rept. Sci. Results of Voyage of H.M.S. Challenger*, C. W. Thompson, eds., Her Majesty's Stationery Office, London, 525p.

Pedersen, T. F., and N. B. Price, 1982. The geochemistry of manganese carbonate in Panama Basin sediments, *Geochim. et Cosmochim. Acta.* **46**:59–68.

Peters, Tj., V. Trommsdorff, and J. Sommerauer, 1980. Progressive metamorphism of manganese carbonates and cherts in the Alps, in *Geology and Geochemistry of Manganese*, vol. 1, I. M. Varentsov and Gy. Grasselly, eds., E. Schweizerbart'sche Verlagsbuchhandlung (Nagele u. Obermiller), Stuttgart, pp. 271–283.

Pettijohn, F. J., 1975. *Sedimentary Rocks*, 3rd ed., Harper & Row, New York, 628p.

Pimm, A. C., 1973. Trace element determinations compared with X-ray diffraction results of brown clay in the Central Pacific, in E. L. Winterer, J. I. Ewing et al., *Initial Reports of the Deep Sea Drilling Project*, Vol. 17, U.S. Govt. Printing Office, Washington, D.C., pp. 511–513.

Pisciotto, K. A., 1981. Distribution, thermal histories, isotopic compositions and reflection characteristics of siliceous rocks recovered by the Deep Sea Drilling Project, in *The Deep Sea Drilling Project: A Decade of Progress*, J. E. Warne, R. G. Douglas, and E. L. Winterer, eds., Society of Economic Paleontologists and Mineralogists Special Publication No. 32, pp. 129–148.

Pisciotto, K. A., and J. J. Mahoney, 1981. Isotopic survey of diagenetic carbonates, Leg 63, in R. S. Yeats, B. U. Haq et al., *Initial Reports of the Deep Sea Drilling Project* Vol. 63, U.S. Govt. Printing Office, Washington, D.C., pp. 595–609.

Price, I., 1977. Facies distinction and interpretation of primary cherts in a Mesozoic Continental Margin succession, Othris, Greece, *Sed. Geology* **18**:321–335.

Raymond, L. A., 1973a. Franciscan geology of the Mt. Oso area, California, Ph.D. dissertation, University of California, Davis, 185p.

Raymond, L. A., 1973b. Tesla-Ortigalita fault, Coast Range thrust fault, and Franciscan metamorphism, northeastern Diablo Range, California, *Geol. Soc. America Bull.* **84**:3547–3562.

Raymond, L. A., 1974. Possible modern analogs for rocks of the Franciscan, Mount Oso area, California, *Geology* **2**:143–146.

Reeburgh, W. S., 1983. Rates of biogeochemical processes in anoxic sediments, in G. W. Wetherill, A. L. Albee, and F. G. Stehli, eds., *Annual Review of Earth and Planetary Sciences* Vol. 11, Annual Reviews, Inc., Palo Alto, California, pp. 269–298.

Reeburgh, W. S., and D. T. Heggie, 1977. Microbial methane consumption reactions and their effect on methane distributions in freshwater and marine environments, *Limnology and Oceanography* **22**:1–9.

Reed, J. J., 1960. Manganese ore in New Zealand, *New Zealand Jour. Geology and Geophysics* **3**(3):344–354.

Robertson, A. H. F., 1981. Metallogenesis on a Mesozoic passive continental margin, Antalya Complex, Southwest Turkey, *Earth and Planetary Sci. Letters* **54**:323–345.

Robertson, A. H. F., and J. D. Hudson, 1973. Cyprus umbers: Chemical precipitates on a Tethyan Ocean ridge, *Earth and Planetary Sci. Letters* **18**:93–101.

Sawlan, J. J., and J. W. Murray, 1983. Trace metal remobilization in the interstitial waters of red clay and hemipelagic marine sediments, *Earth and Planetary Sci. Letters* **64**:213–230.

Shatskiy, N. S., 1954. The metallogeny of manganese, paper 1. Volcanogenic-sedimentary manganiferous formations, *Internat. Geology Rev.* **6**(6):1030–1056.

Snyder, W. S., 1978. Manganese deposited by submarine hot springs in chert-greenstone complexes, western United States, *Geology* **6**:741–744.

Stanaway, K. J., H. W. Kobe, and J. Sekula, 1978. Manganese deposits and the associated rocks of Northland and Auckland, New Zealand, *New Zealand Jour. Geology and Geophysics* **21**:21–32.

Stanton, R. L., 1972. *Ore Petrology*, McGraw-Hill, New York, 713p.

Suess, E., 1979. Mineral phases formed in anoxic sediments by microbial decompositon of organic matter, *Geochim. et Cosmochim. Acta.* **43**:339–352.

Taliaferro, N. L., and F. S. Hudson, 1943. Genesis of the manganese deposits of the Coast Ranges of California, in *Manganese in California*, O. P. Jenkins, ed., California Division of Mines Bull. 125, p. 217–275.

Trask, P. D., 1950. Manganese Deposits of California, California Division of Mines Bull. 152, 378p.

Tromp, S. W., 1948. Shallow-water origin of radiolarites in southern Turkey, *Jour. Geology* **56**(5):492–494.

Watanabe, T., S. Yui, and A. Kato, 1970. Bedded manganese deposits in Japan, a review, in *Volcanism and Ore Genesis*, T. Tatsumi, ed., University of Tokyo Press, Tokyo, pp. 119–142.

Yeh, H. W., J. R. Hein, and R. A. Koski, 1985. *Stable- isotope Study of Volcanogenic- and Sedimentary-Manganese Deposits*, U.S. Geological Survey Open File Report 85–662, 16p.

10

IRON ORES DERIVED BY ENRICHMENT OF BANDED IRON-FORMATION

R. C. Morris

Division of Mineralogy and Geochemistry
CSIRO Australia

ABSTRACT. The major in situ banded iron-formation (BIF) derived iron ores of the world have formed, either entirely or initially, by supergene enrichment. The process involved metasomatic replacement of gangue by hydrous iron oxides in gravity-controlled hydraulic systems resembling small artesian basins. Ore formed initially at various depths under the influence of large electrochemical cells in zones such as faults that favored fluid access and extended laterally and upward in the BIF as iron was added from the now-eroded outcrop extension. Slow isostatic uplift probably kept pace with erosion and enabled large ore bodies to form over periods of tens to hundreds of millions of years.

The supergene process first produced significant iron enrichment at depth in exposed BIF throughout the world at about 2,000 ± 200 Ma. This enrichment resulted from an increase of oxygen in the atmosphere, which also coincided with the end of major worldwide deposition of BIF. Ores have formed subsequently wherever erosion exposed suitable structural features to the particular conditions of climate, topography, and tectonic stability required for the slow process.

Continuing erosion probably destroyed many of the early-formed deposits. However, some were preserved by burial and variously metamorphosed. Some deposits may have been involved in several cycles. Rising temperatures formed increasing amounts of secondary, characteristically microplaty, hematite from the goethite. Where reducing components such as organic matter were present, minor magnetite also formed.

In some buried deposits, igneous intrusives caused further recrystallization. Ores derived in this way are characterized by high levels of magnetite, but the deposits are typically small compared with the hematite ores. Erosion has now exposed many of these metamorphosed ores to renewed supergene processes. Oxidation, leaching, and precipitation have further modified their textures. In many re-exposed deposits preferential leaching of the residual goethite has resulted in significant upgrading of hematite-goethite ores to nearly pure hematite concentrations.

Unmetamorphosed ore bodies are characterized by abundant hydrous iron oxides. These deposits show a wide variety of features that are dependent on their initial mineralogy, subsequent leaching, and exposure above the water table. Only the most mature of these contain significant secondary hematite at depth.

Ore bodies subjected to weathering for extended periods are capped by ferricrete formed by repeated solution and deposition of iron in the vadose zone, a process that destroys the original BIF textures preserved in the metasomatic or metamorphosed metasomatic ore. The contrasting textures resulting from the two different supergene processes are easily distinguished.

INTRODUCTION

Despite the importance of the mining of iron ore to the growth of civilization over the past three thousand years, virtually no consensus has been achieved on the genesis of the wide variety of iron concentrations in sedimentary, igneous, and metamorphic rocks. The model presented in this chapter is an attempt to rationalize the genetic background of one of the most important of these groups: the iron ores derived by enrichment of the banded siliceous rocks, rocks whose anomalous iron content gave rise to the term *banded iron-formation* (BIF).

Iron ore is probably one of the most loosely defined terms in economic geology, used for such a wide variety of materials that it is often difficult to understand precisely what is meant by the term. For example, many use *iron ore* and *iron formation* interchangeably even though the vast bulk of iron formation is unlikely to be exploited as ore in the foreseeable future.

As an economic term, *iron ore* is best restricted to rocks that could be exploited commercially for their iron content, although commercial exploitation does not necessarily imply direct monetary profit. Social and political necessity or previously established infrastructure may allow the use of normally uneconomic concentrations as ore in some countries.

In this chapter *iron ore* is specifically applied to material of economic significance whose elemental iron content is greater than 50% as a result of natural enrichment of BIF (jaspillite, ferruginous quartzite, banded ironstone, itabirite, taconite, etc.). Such enriched BIF ores form the main reserves of cheaply exploitable iron in Africa, Australia, India, South America, and the USSR. The once large deposits of the United States were depleted by the industrial demands of World War II, forcing development of techniques to exploit BIF (taconite) as ore, a problem that will increasingly affect the immense production of the USSR.

In the broad sense, BIF-derived ores include not only the in situ BIF replacement types but also the eluvial and colluvial deposits such as the cangas of South America and their Hamersley (Western Australia) equivalents, the so-called scree ores. In addition, the Hamersley Iron Province contains large reserves of pisolitic geothitic ore (40–60% Fe) associated with Mesozoic to Tertiary drainage channels. These ores are generally accepted, though not proven, as chemical-biochemical precipitates from meandering rivers, possibly associated with heavily modified detrital accumulations from weathering of BIF. Ores of this type, known as Robe River Pisolites, are currently mined at Pannawonica in the Hamersley area.

This chapter is concerned only with the in situ BIF-derived ores. These can be divided broadly with two classes. The first class includes a wide range of ores, ranging from very friable yellow ochres to firmly indurated brown goethite-rich material, generally showing residual BIF features such as banding. Because they lack evidence of metamorphism, are related to present erosion surfaces, and contain abundant hydrous iron oxides, this group of hematite-goethite ores is generally accepted as supergene.

The second class is dominated by the high-grade hematite-rich ores whose origin has attracted much debate. These are commonly hard at the surface but vary greatly below outcrop and may grade to friable blue dust ores. *This group is characterized by the presence of abundant secondary microplaty hematite.* The immense size of some of these deposits (Mt. Whaleback, Western Australia, $>1,500 \times 10^6$ tonnes; N4E deposit, Carajas, Brazil, $>1,300 \times 10^6$ tonnes) makes them the largest and most concentrated secondary accumulations of any single metalliferous element in the Earth's crust. A subgroup of this class includes small deposits of magnetite-rich ore, rarely exceeding a few million tonnes and generally associated with microplaty hematite ores. These magnetite ores are usually attributed to igneous or metamorphic activity.

History of Genetic Models

Evolution of Concepts

Most of the early genetic models originated from North and South American workers, and their hypotheses have tended to dominate the ideas on the origin of iron deposits. Although the USSR is the world's largest iron ore producer by far, and the relevant literature is apparently extensive, little of this information is available in English, apart from the brief accounts of the Kiev meeting (UNESCO, 1973) and the 1977 translation by Brown of Sokolov and Grigor'ev's (1974) work.

In Australia, the early contributions on iron ore were essentially limited to the small but complex Middleback Range deposits of South Australia, but important advances have been made since the 1970s in genetic modeling with the study of the Hamersley deposits.

Neither South Africa nor India have added significantly to the basic concepts, but the Liberian contributions through Berge et al. (1977), like the work of Ayres (1971) in Australia, were a landmark in the reporting of petrographic data.

Mann (1953) provided a comprehensive summary of early North American hypotheses, and Guild (1953) supplied a shorter version for Brazil. These, together with data from the extensive lists of basic models compiled by Park (1959) and Morris (1985), have been used for the selective historical summary that follows.

One of the earliest milestones was the model of Van Hise and Bayley (1897) in which surface waters decomposed iron carbonates, carrying ferrous iron deep into the strata. This iron was reprecipitated at depth by a confluence with oxygen-bearing waters flowing directly from the surface. By 1911 Van Hise and Leith had developed the hypothesis that the high-grade hematite ores in the Marquette Range resulted from supergene alteration of the Negaunee Iron Formation and were later modified by metamorphism.

Meanwhile in Brazil, Harder and Chamberlain (1915) stressed syngenetic models. Having attributed BIF deposition to biogenic precipitation of iron interspersed with deposition of clastic quartz, they suggested that the high-grade ores represented concentrations of iron in areas starved of clastic impurities. This suggestion contrasted with Gathman's (1913) model of supergene leaching of silica and residual concentration of iron for the Brazilian deposits. With the development of chemical precipitation models for BIF genesis, the syngenetic models lost favor. These were revived in the form of sedimentary/diagenetic concentration models for the Hamersley ores by Haddon F. King (unpublished reports, 1972–1976) and by Schorscher (1975) and Schorscher and Guimaraes (1976) for the Brazilian deposits.

The early supergene and syngenetic models were followed by the controversial hypogene-hydrothermal models of Gruner (1926, 1930, 1937) for the Lake Superior ores and by that of Sanders (1933) for Brazil. These ideas were amplified by the U.S.-Brazilian team led by J. V. N. Dorr II (e.g., Guild, 1953; Dorr and Barbosa, 1963; Dorr, 1965), whose hydrothermal models for Brazilian ores were paralleled by Miles (1954) in South Australia and supported later by Gruss (1973), Sims (1973), and Berge et al. (1977) for African deposits. The detailed concepts of Dorr (1965) dominated the post–World War II literature, although Gross (1965, 1967, 1968) in Canada, MacLeod (1966, 1973) and Campana (1966) in Australia, and particularly James et al. (1968) in the United States revived interest in supergene processes.

Kornilov (1970), from the USSR, was among the first to renew the supergene-metamorphic model, but many of his interpretations appear dubious in the light of present knowledge. Gershoig (1971) and others (unnamed) were credited by Sokolov and Grigor'ev (1974) with the suggestion that the rich ores of the Krivoy Rog that formed in a Proterozoic weathering crust were then metamorphosed to magnetite and "specularite" ores, and further enriched and oxidized within a Phanerozoic weathering crust. The more complex model of Belevtsev (1973) for the same area involved primary, metamorphic, and later supergene enrichment.

Gair (1973, 1975) reintroduced the 1911 Van Hise–Leith model for specific Superior deposits in the United States, a concept supported later by Cannon (1976). Cannon, however, attributed associated magnetite deposits entirely to metamorphically derived hydrothermal fluids. Morris (1980, 1983a, 1985) added further support for supergene and supergene-metamorphic models in which initial supergene enrichment occurred in large electrochemical-hydrodynamic cells (Morris et al., 1980).

CLASSIFICATION OF MODELS

Although many workers have distinguished between the wide diversity of iron ore types and their different origins, much of the controversy surrounding genetic models has resulted from a tendency, particularly by those not directly involved, to oversimplify the diverse types to a single collective term, *iron ore*.

A review of the literature suggests that hypotheses for the genesis of iron ore from BIF can be classified into eleven basic models (Morris, 1985), which can be simplified further to three:

1. Syngenetic: with or without subsequent modification by diagenetic, supergene, or metamorphic processes;
2. Hypogene: metamorphic, igneous, or both;
3. Supergene: associated with present or past weathering surfaces, with or without subsequent metamorphic or weathering modifications.

SYNGENETIC MODELS

The basic syngenetic model requires that during deposition, small areas with sharp boundaries, ranging from tens of square meters to a few square kilometers, were centers of concentrated primary chemical precipitation of iron for long periods, while normal BIF was deposited in stratigraphic continuity in the surrounding areas. Such a concept is not easily related to known sedimentary processes, and no convincing evidence has been offered to demonstrate anomalous volumes of primary concentration of iron in the excellent exposures of the Hamersley BIF.

HYPOGENE MODELS

Gruner (1926, 1930, 1937) is probably the best known of the early hypogene protagonists. His basic model required oxidation and concentration of iron minerals by leaching of silica from BIF in hot magmatic water. In 1937 he used data from Yellowstone (National) Park in the United States as an example of the type of environment he envisaged for the extensive Mesabi (U.S.) ores. In this model, hot gases from igneous intrusives heated oxygenated groundwater which dissolved silica and oxidized the iron minerals. Enrichment also occurred by replacement of quartz by hematite.

Similar replacement of BIF matrix by hematite was integral to most of the later models such as those of Guild (1953), Miles (1954), Dorr (1965), and Sims (1973). The lack of apparent changes to the country rocks was explained, as in Dorr (1965), as the result of diffusion of supercritical fluids. These fluids selectively dissolved minute amounts of iron from the surrounding BIF and precipitated this iron at the ore sites. No satisfactory mechanism has been advanced to support the feasibility of these selective processes, but this fact does not necessarily invalidate the hypotheses (Dorr, 1965; Morris, 1985). However, supporting evidence such as conduits, hydrothermal minerals, or adequate magmatic sources have not been found associated with the major hematite or hematite-goethite deposits (James et al., 1968; Gair, 1975).

Nevertheless, there can be little doubt that hydrothermally affected deposits do exist. An excellent example is the Koolyanobbing mine about 350 km east of Perth, the capital of Western Australia. In this deposit, pegmatitelike segregations of bladed hematite, associated with magnetite and quartz, are present in pipelike bodies (Griffin, 1980). Similarly, massive magnetite segregation such as in the Marquette Range (United States) (Cannon, 1976); El Pao, Venezuela; Bomi Hills, Liberia (Gruss, 1973); and along dike margins in the Channar deposit of the Hamersleys attest to the introduction of reducing solutions and to recrystallization at moderate to high temperatures. These segregations are probably derived by magmatic modification of preexisting iron concentrations rather than by introduction of iron in solution (Morris, 1985); *direct* replacement of quartz by hematite is unlikely under hydrothermal conditions.

SUPERGENE MODELS

Hypotheses involving meteoric water have been described since about 1886, when Irving suggested a combination of in situ oxidation and precipitation of iron oxides from solution, from which Van Hise and his colleagues apparently drew inspiration in the following decades. But it was not until the 1960s that supergene models regained their early prominence.

In general, the hypotheses take two forms. The first is based entirely on residual enrichment of the primary iron minerals by removal of the BIF gangue in groundwater, presumably followed by settling and consolidation. The second form requires that the matrix be largely replaced by iron oxides, most commonly envisaged as the infilling of voids formed by solution of silica, but in more recent papers, by metasomatic—that is, pseudomorphous—replacement of the matrix.

The most influential earlier papers on supergene modeling are probably those of Dorr (1964), MacLeod (1966, 1973), and James et al. (1968). The latter drew attention, in particular, to two major objections to the meteoric models: (1) the removal of silica on a large scale and (2) the difficulty of circulation of groundwaters to depths often measured in kilometers. The room problem, or the what-happened-to-the-silica? question, is often repeated when investigators are discussing meteoric enrichment. As James et al. showed, massive solution of silica can be achieved theoretically in reasonable geologic time, and the necessary deep circulation can be attributed to artesian systems. A third major problem is that of the transport of ferrous iron and its precipitation at depth as ferric compounds. The Van Hise and Bayley (1897) model, in which oxygen-bearing water and a separate flow of ferrous iron-bearing water converged to precipitate iron oxides at depth, was probably the earliest suggested detailed mechanism. Even more complex mechanisms have been proposed, requiring pyramiding of special and unusual geologic conditions. However, most writers have tended to ignore the difficulties and simply used the more obvious signs of weathering, such as the oxidized mineral assemblage, the association of ores with present or past erosion surfaces, and the juxtaposition of the ores with the most logical source of oxidation potential, the atmosphere, to support a supergene origin. As a consequence, many models have included the concept of solution of iron in the vadose zone or below the water table, and its precipitation into voids left by solution of silica, at the water table. Progressive downward enrichment continues as the water table falls; deep ores develop by continued recycling and "represent the end products of a long continued process of physical breakdown by erosion and chemical concentration of iron" (MacLeod, 1973, p. 294). However, texture-destroying processes of this type are not compatible with the petrographic evidence of preservation of BIF textures in the ores (Morris, 1980), textures that are retained until modified or destroyed by surface weathering or by metamorphism. A recently proposed electrochemical mechanism (Morris et al.,

1980) may help overcome some of the difficulties encountered in previous supergene models.

General Conceptual Model for BIF-Derived Iron Ores

The Hamersley Iron Province is an excellent environment for BIF and ore studies since the detailed investigations of the extensive exposures by the Geological Survey of Western Australia (GSWA) (e.g., MacLeod, 1966; Trendall and Blockley, 1970; Trendall, 1983), the exploration and mining companies (e.g., *Economic Geology of Australia-Papua-New Guinea,* Australasian Institute of Mining and Metallurgy, 1975, Chapter 13), and CSIRO (e.g., Morris, 1980; Ewers and Morris, 1981) have provided a solid reference framework for additional research. The quality of preservation of the BIF in this unique type area limits the need for speculations engendered by poor exposure, complex folding, or high-grade metamorphism. The wide variety of metamorphosed and unmetamorphosed ores of this area were derived essentially from only three laterally continuous parent BIF units, the Dales Gorge and Joffre Members of the Brockman Iron Formation and the Marra Mamba Iron Formation. These unifying factors enabled the development and testing of a simple logical model for iron ore genesis (Morris, 1980, 1983*a,*), which has now been extended to include most of the BIF-derived iron ores of the world (Morris, 1985).

The model incorporates important elements of many genetic hypotheses although it is based essentially on supergene and supergene metamorphic processes. The parent BIF may be considered as cherts with syngenetic concentrations of iron, mainly as oxides, but only the richest of these siliceous rocks are iron ores in their own right. In Minas Gerais, Brazil, these normally refractory rocks have become extremely friable by silica leaching under heavy rainfall (Fig. 10–1), and their iron content can be concentrated simply and economically to supplement the direct-shipping enrichment ores.

However, the iron ores of most economic significance throughout the world are those initially formed by supergene metasomatic enrichment of BIF. Not only is the gross stratigraphy retained by the process, but also the microscopic features of the parent rocks are preserved by pseudomorphous replacement of the matrix minerals by hydrous iron oxides. These oxides eventually crystallized mainly as geothite.

Ore bodies not subjected to metamorphism are characterized by abundant hydrous iron oxides. These deposits show a wide variety of features that result from their initial mineralogy, subsequent leaching, and exposure above the water table. Only the most mature of these deposits contain significant secondary hematite at depth. Hematite-goethite deposits of this type form the major iron ore reserves of the Hamersley Iron Province.

Although continued erosion probably destroyed many of the earliest deposits, others were preserved by burial and were variously affected by meta-

Figure 10–1. Friable meta-BIF (itabirite), Caue mine, Minas Gerais. The iron oxides remain as a framework while the quartz grains, loosened by leaching under heavy rainfall, collect at the base of the bench face. Vertical striations are bucket teeth marks (photo by M. Kneeshaw).

morphism. Rising temperatures formed increasing amounts of secondary hematite in the goethite, producing a characteristic microplaty hematite texture. Where reducing components such as organic matter were present, minor magnetite also formed.

In some of these buried deposits, igneous intrusives caused further recrystallization. Ores derived in this way are characterized by large amounts of magnetite, but such deposits are usually small compared with the hematite ores.

Erosion has now exposed many of these variously metamorphosed ores to renewed supergene processes, and thus oxidation, leaching, and precipitation further modified their textures. In many re-exposed deposits, preferential leaching of residual goethite by groundwater resulted in significant upgrading of hematite-goethite ores to nearly pure hematite concentrations. Ores of this type form the basis for much of the iron ore export capacity of Brazil and Australia.

Ore bodies subjected to weathering for extended periods are capped by ferricrete formed by repeated solution and deposition of iron in the vadose zone, leading to the destruction of the original BIF textures preserved in the metasomatic or metamorphosed metasomatic ore. The contrasting textures resulting from the two different supergene processes are easily distinguished. The framework of this model is shown diagrammatically in Figure 10–2 and in more detail in Figure 10–3.

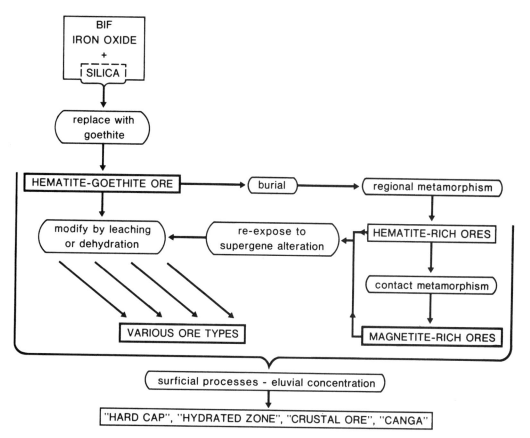

Figure 10-2.   Framework of the conceptual model for iron-enrichment ores in BIF.

FORMATION OF SUPERGENE
ORE FROM BIF

IRON-FORMATION AND BANDED IRON-
FORMATION DEFINITIONS

Iron-formation (IF), as defined by James (1954, pp. 239–240), "is a chemical sediment, typically thin-bedded or laminated, containing 15 percent or more iron of sedimentary origin, commonly but not necessarily containing layers of chert." The definition thus includes noncherty rocks such as sulfide- and siderite-rich sediments.

Banded iron-formation (BIF) has a much more restricted meaning than iron-formation and is now accepted as "thinly layered or laminated rock in which chert or its metamorphic equivalent alternates with layers that are composed mainly of iron minerals" (James, 1983, p. 471). The iron minerals may include hematite and magnetite with a wide variety of silicates and carbonates. Goethite is found only in weathered rocks.

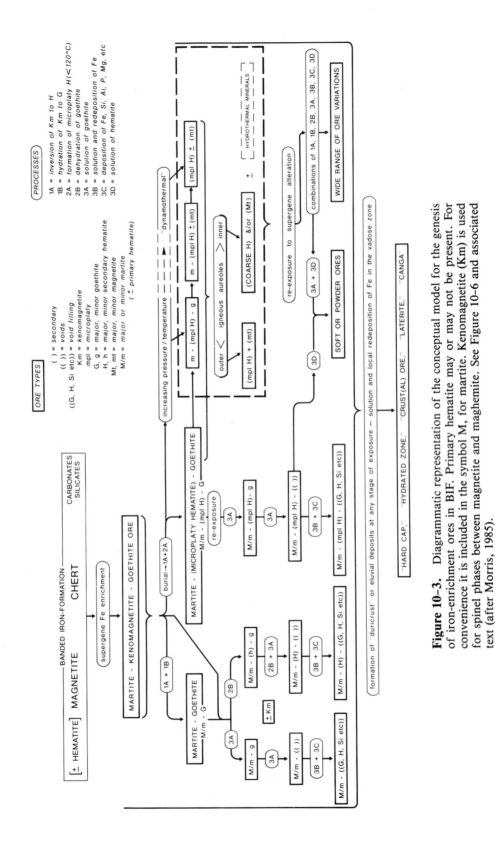

Figure 10-3. Diagrammatic representation of the conceptual model for the genesis of iron-enrichment ores in BIF. Primary hematite may or may not be present. For convenience it is included in the symbol M, for martite. Kenomagnetite (Km) is used for spinel phases between magnetite and maghemite. See Figure 10-6 and associated text (after Morris, 1985).

Iron Formation (capitalized, no hyphen) is used as a formal lithostratigraphic term, usually coupled with a specific name, as in Brockman Iron Formation, whereas *iron-formation* is used strictly as a lithologic term, equivalent, for example, to *shale*.

COMPOSITION

Unless otherwise stated, in this chapter BIF refers to the oxide-rich rocks and it is from these that the main bulk of enrichment iron ores have formed throughout the world. In common with BIF elsewhere, the Hamersley rocks contain four principal components in various proportions: chert (quartz), oxides (magnetite with or without hematite), silicates (stilpnomelane, ferron talc, minnesotaite, chlorite, micas, riebeckite, and crocidolite), and carbonates (siderite, ankerite, dolomite, and calcite). Apatite is a ubiquitous accessory mineral. Oxide BIF, the dominant type, consists mainly of chert with iron oxides, but a varying content of silicates and carbonates gives rise to many of the differences in texture, weathering properties, and ore types of the various Iron Formations. In North American and South African BIF, in particular, other silicates such as greenalite or grunerite are prominent components. A detailed summary of the mineralogy of BIF is given by Klein (1983).

TEXTURAL DATA AND ORE FORMATION

Supergene enrichment of BIF commonly results in remarkable preservation of both macroscopic and microscopic features of the parent rock by pseudomorphic replacement. Although metamorphism may destroy the microscopic details, delicate macroscopically visible features such as varved microbanding (Trendall and Blockley, 1970) are often perfectly displayed in ore (Fig. 10-4). Detailed textural data showing the transformation of BIF to supergene ore by oxidation and metasomatic iron enrichment have been provided by Morris (1980, 1983*b*, 1985) and are reviewed only briefly here (Fig. 10-5).

OXIDES

Primary hematite typically remains unaffected during supergene metasomatic enrichment and is usually readily recognizable in unmetamorphosed ores. However, supergene alteration of hematite to goethite during weathering of ore bodies, as described later in this chapter, produces significant changes to the textures of the ores.

Magnetite commonly provides excellent textural information despite the often complex oxidation, hydration, and recrystallization history of the mineral in ores. The mineral oxidizes by two similar mechanisms, both of which play some role in supergene ores (Fig. 10-6). First, magnetite may convert to hematite pseudomorphs (martite). According to the model of Davis et al. (1968), this conversion is accomplished by diffusion of iron to internal surfaces such as parting planes where, by reaction with oxygen, it forms hematite, giving rise to the well-known trellis pattern or to other growth-related textures

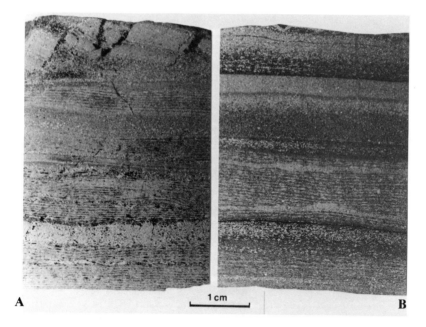

Figure 10-4. Preservation of banding in ore. (*A*) Metamorphosed hematite-rich ore [M-(mpl H)-(( ))] showing excellent preservation of microbands (varves). (*B*) Unaltered BIF with microbands, for comparison.

(Han, 1978; Morris, 1980, 1983*b*). The domains from which the iron migrated become metal deficient and may invert from γFe_2O_3 to αFe_2O_3 (hematite) to give solid martite.

The second mechanism involves migration of ferrous iron out of the structure into the groundwater to precipitate elsewhere, again leaving metal-deficient spinels in place of the original Fe_3O_4 (see Fig. 10-6). The end phase of the iron migration chain is γFe_2O_3 or maghemite, shown more explicitly as $Fe_{8/3}\square_{1/3}O_4$, in which the box represents cation vacancies.

Kenomagnetite is a convenient term for the various phases $(Fe_{3-x}\square_xO_4)$ between magnetite and maghemite, introduced by Kullerud et al. (1969) for synthetic material and applied to naturally occurring phases by Morris (1980). In polished section kenomagnetite is darker than magnetite and often distinctly pinkish-brown compared with the grey or fawn of fresh magnetite. Maghemite, typically with a pale bluish tint, is rare compared with kenomagnetite in oxidized BIF and immature ores. Kenomagnetite, once formed, may remain largely unaltered, oxidize further to maghemite, invert to hematite, or hydrate to goethite (see Fig. 10-6). The ratio of martite to kenomagnetite varies widely, and in consequence, the amount of goethite replacement is equally variable (Fig. 10-7).

Leaching of goethite pseudomorphs after kenomagnetite by groundwater, in preference to hematite, often leaves delicate martite lamellae almost unsupported in voids (see Fig. 10-7). Some magntite mesobands lose a significant part of their original iron by this process.

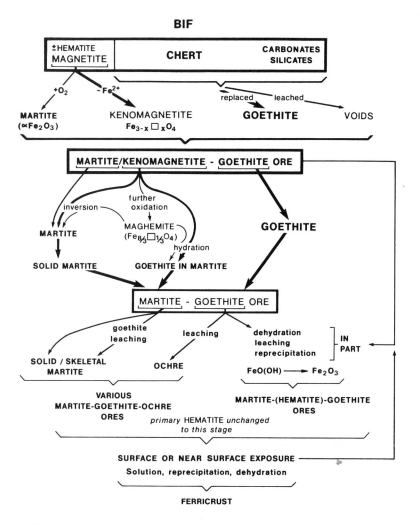

Figure 10–5.   Diagrammatic representation of the progress of iron enrichment and subsequent modifications during supergene alteration of BIF.

MATRIX MINERALS: METASOMATIC REPLACEMENT

Direct evidence for the supergene replacement of matrix minerals of BIF by iron hydroxyoxides is readily available in dissected outcrops below the selvedge of heavily weathered BIF. Such textures are also characteristic of the immature ores of the Hamersley Iron Province and are particularly common in ores derived from the Marra Mamba Iron Formation. They are also present in enriched BIF samples acquired from South Africa, Liberia, India, North and South America, and elsewhere in Australia. Mann (1953) described similar replacement in BIF of the Animikie Basin (United States) but ascribed the metasomatism to hydrothermal activity.

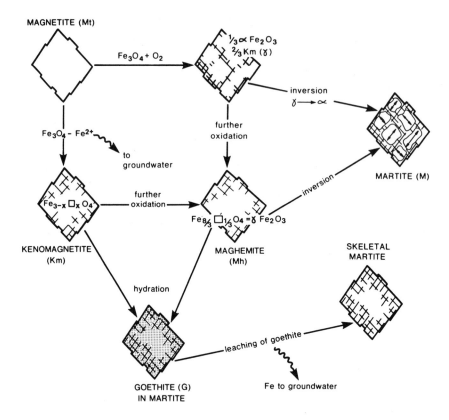

Figure 10-6. Simplified progression of alteration of magnetite during supergene processes (after Morris, 1985).

The fidelity of the replacement can be seen particularly in carbonate grains containing initial inclusions of silicates and chert (Fig. 10-8*a, b*). This clearly indicates a metasomatic mechanism, not merely one in which voids, formed by leaching, have been filled later by hydrous iron oxides. Silicate and carbonate replacement textures are the least equivocal features of metasomatic enrichment and often allow the recognition of the less clearly defined chert textures by association (Fig. 10-8*c*). Nevertheless, there is abundant direct evidence of chert replacement by iron hydroxyoxides (see Fig. 10-14) (Morris, 1980, 1985). The progression of replacement consistently follows a well-defined sequence: silicates first, overlapped by carbonates, and finally chert.

MODIFICATIONS TO THE INITIAL ORE BY CONTINUED SUPERGENE PROCESSES

LEACHING

The iron that gave rise to enrichment logically came from the now eroded BIF outcrop extension (see Fig. 10-13). Once this source of iron is exhausted or otherwise unavailable, groundwaters traversing the ore bodies will be un-

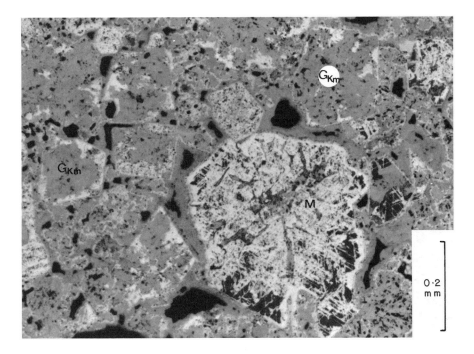

Figure 10-7. Ex-magnetite grains, now varying proportions of martite (white) and goethite-after-kenomagnetite (G_{Km}) in a goethite matrix. Skeletal martite textures result from leaching of goethite (voids, dark gray to black). Reflected light.

dersaturated in iron and will tend to dissolve the ore minerals. Since these are ferric compounds, solution will be slow unless aided by reducing or complexing agents such as organic matter. In general, goethite is preferentially leached, which results in the residual enrichment of hematite. Where the original textures are preserved, the leaching tends to dissolve the goethite pseudomorphs in the order ex-quartz, ex-silicates, then ex-carbonate (Fig. 10-8*a, b*). Thus, much of the leached, highly porous, yellow ochre-rich ores of the Marra Mamba Iron Formation consists of skeletal martite with the more resistant ex-silicate residuals and the carbonate pseudomorphs. Leaching of geothite, if taken to the extreme, can result in significant upgrading to hematite-rich ore, but at the expense of total Fe, and may give rise to slumping and brecciation within the deposits. These ore types are represented in Figure 10-3 as M-G, M-g, and M-(( )), indicating progressive leaching of goethite.

DEHYDRATION

In the Hamersley deposits, exposure of immature ores above the water table invariably produces some dehydration of the goethite. In such ores, clearly defined selective pseudomorphing of goethite-replaced minerals by hematite is common. The progression of dehydration follows the same sequence as the selective leaching: quartz, silicate, and finally carbonate pseudomorphs. The resulting hematite is commonly finely porous (goethite → hematite ~ 25%

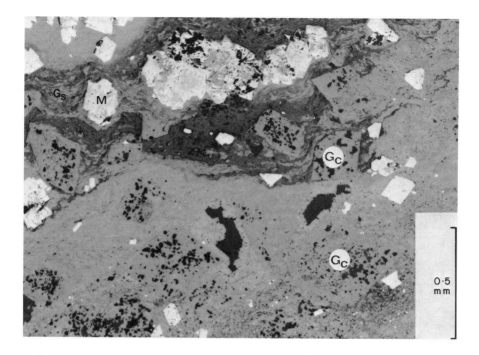

Figure 10–8a. Selective leaching of supergene ore has released goethite pseudomorphs after carbonate (G$_c$). Similar grains are visible in the more solid goethite (after silicates and quartz) by the presence of numerous voids (black) where goethite after quartz inclusions has been leached. White grains are martite (M). Reflected light.

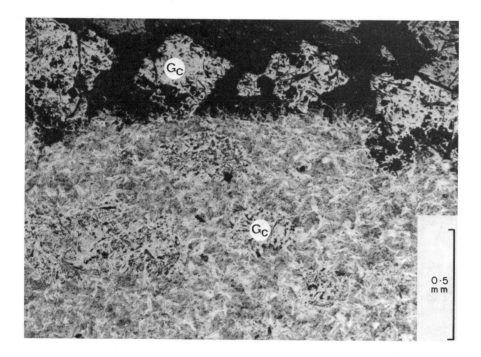

Figure 10–8b. Similar to Figure 10–8a but voids after fibrolamellar silicates are also present in the ex-carbonates. The porous matrix (lower) is goethite after felted chert-silicate. Reflected light.

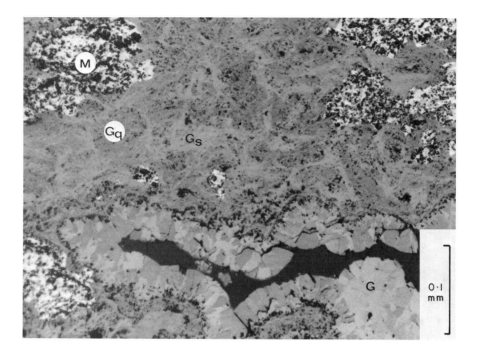

Figure 10–8c. Irregular skeletal martite in a matrix of goethite after chert (G_q) and silicates (G_s). Note the contrast between the replacement texture and the solution and reprecipitation texture of goethite (lower). Reflected light.

volume reduction) with a lower reflectivity than primary hematite (Morris, 1980, Fig. 11). In Figure 10–3 these ores are shown in the second column as M-(h)-g, and so on, where (H) or (h) represents secondary hematite.

SOLUTION AND REPRECIPITATION OF IRON AND OTHER COMPONENTS

Under vigorous groundwater attack, voids, caverns, and channels may develop in the ores. These may be subsequently completely or partly filled by goethite (see Fig. 10–8c), hematite, chalcedony, jasper, or clay minerals, typically with colloform habit. Secondary apatite or other phosphate minerals such as variscite or strengite, although scarce, may be locally prominent. In addition, clastic debris may be washed into voids and cracks in the upper parts of deposits. These various void-filling components are shown enclosed within double parentheses, (( )), in Figure 10–3.

WEATHERING OF ORE DEPOSITS

A profound difference exists between the products of prolonged weathering of ores and those of deep-seated metasomatic enrichment, even though both result from supergene activity. Recognizing the difference is simple. In the metasomatic ores, primary BIF texture is preserved, even though, in some, it may be modified by later metamorphism. With prolonged weathering, new

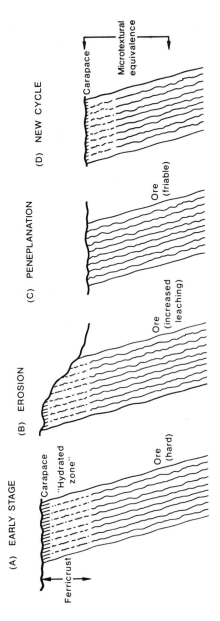

Figure 10-9. Idealized three-tiered weathering profile for typical Hamersley deposits. The section consists of a hard carapace with modified textures still comparable with unweathered ore, a zone of hydrated ore (ferricrete) up to 50 m in which primary textures have been degraded by repeated solution and reprecipitation of iron in the vadose zone, and the ore zone proper, with typically well-preserved BIF textures. Most Hamersley deposits are in the (B) phase of erosion (after Morris, 1985).

textures, characteristic of repeated solution and redeposition, form (ferricrete).

A three-tiered ore profile has long been recognized in the Hamersley deposits (Fig. 10–9). The surface zone, or carapace, is usually less than 2 m thick and contains clearly visible replaced BIF features such as banding. Underlying this carapace is a typically much thicker zone of degraded ore or ferricrete, which because of the prominence of goethite is often called the hydrated zone. The two zones, here called the ferricrust, are commonly referred to as *hard cap* and overlie the ore zone proper.

The carapace ores are zones of maximum surface dehydration, and the resulting high hematite content is accentuated by leaching of residual goethite by rain water. The dehydration commonly preserves and may even accentuate the original BIF texture.

The hydrated zone may result from seasonally controlled solution and redeposition of iron oxides in the vadose zone, presumably aided by the reducing effect of organic matter. In mature profiles, the replaced clearly defined BIF textures degrade to porous, often nonpermeable, ferricrete, rich in vitreous goethite and as thick as 50 m or more. Gross primary bedding may still be visible, but the finer laminae are usually destroyed.

The ore immediately below the hydrated zone is usually strongly leached and equally as friable as the typical Brazilian ores. Most of this disintegration probably occurred under the protecting hard cap when the water table was much higher and is no doubt occurring today where water movement and the reducing conditions required to dissolve ferric iron are adequate. Nevertheless, textural preservation is usually good.

Virtually all ore bodies in the Hamersley Iron Province show this basic subdivision into three horizons. The preservation of a carapace with its clearly visible ex-BIF textures would appear to be paradoxical because continued erosion of long exposed deposits should eventually remove this selvedge entirely, leaving only ferricrete at the surface. Possibly once the hard carapace is lost, rapid erosion cuts the less resistant material to base level, re-exposing BIF-textured ore and enabling the three-tiered profile to redevelop (see Fig. 10–9).

EFFECTS OF METAMORPHISM ON SUPERGENE ORE

GENERAL

Beginning in the 1980s, Australia and Brazil have competed for the position of the world's largest exporter of iron ore, with annual export levels around $70–80 \times 10^6$ tonnes. Most of this is high-grade hematite ore, characterized by the presence of abundant secondary microplaty hematite. Microplaty hematite ores (commonly designated as "specularite" ores in the Americas) are known from all the major BIF provinces of the world and, because of their quality, are the prime targets for exploration and exploitation.

The controversy surrounding the genesis of these ores has been discussed in detail by Park (1959), among others, and most recently by Morris (1985). The conflict can be simplified to a choice between two basic hypotheses to which a selection of subvariations may be attached: (1) The matrix minerals of BIF are replaced directly by hematite (or magnetite, in some cases) by addition of iron from igneous or metamorphic hydrothermal solutions, or (2) supergene concentrations of goethite-rich BIF-derived iron ore are recrystallized by regional metamorphism, mainly to hematite. The presence of major magnetite results from contact metamorphism.

Gruner (1937) and Dorr (1965) provided the most detailed arguments for the hypogene models, whereas the following summary from Morris (1985) argues for a modified version of the Van Hise and Leith (1911) hypothesis.

REGIONAL METAMORPHISM AND SUBSEQUENT LEACHING

The instability of goethite at mildly elevated temperatures is indicated by the fact that exposure of the mineral in the upper part of ore bodies to the hot, dry conditions of the tropical Hamersleys is sufficient to produce dehydration to hematite. Burial metamorphism (see Fig. 10-3, third column), however, produces a different and highly characteristic texture by the growth of microplaty hematite in the goethite (Morris, 1980, 1985). Nevertheless, the transformation can be sluggish at low burial temperatures. This situation probably results from the coarsening of the initially fine-grained goethite under increasing temperature and pressure, inhibiting the transformation to hematite, as suggested by studies on synthetic material by Langmuir (1971, 1972). Thus, some unleached zones of metamorphosed deposits in the Hamersleys, particularly at Paraburdoo, still contain significant matrix goethite associated with microplaty hematite (Fig. 10-10). The presence of this residual goethite is taken to indicate that burial temperatures did not significantly exceed about 100°C (Morris, 1980).

Similar conditions were experienced at the Tom Price and Whaleback deposits, but here, the exposure to weathering that has affected the Hamersleys since at least the Mesozoic resulted in preferential solution of most of the residual goethite by groundwater, leaving porous, virtually pure hematite [M-(mpl H)-(( ))] in the ore zones (Fig. 10-11). Unleached ores [M-(mpl H)-g], present only in places, indicate the original character of these deposits. Once the easily soluble goethite was removed, groundwaters attacked the contact points of the hematite to produce a variety of friable ore types from the so-called biscuit to the incoherent blue dusts. Postmetamorphic supergene leaching has been particularly prominent in the typically friable Brazilian ores, suggesting that the present high rainfall is probably a continuation of Tertiary conditions. The present arid climate of the Hamersley area may similarly reflect late Tertiary conditions and thus explain the higher lump-to-fines ratios of the high-grade ores compared with Brazilian ores. Nevertheless, blue dust ores are also present in Hamersley deposits, probably where channeling of groundwater increased solution of hematite.

Elsewhere throughout the world, similar metamorphic and later leaching processes have combined to produce variants of these microplaty hematite ores (see Fig. 10-3, center). Most, if not all, are probably Proterozoic. Higher grades of metamorphism than are found in the Hamersleys have affected many of these supergene ores (see Fig. 10-3, right-hand side), such as at Iron Knob in the Middleback Ranges of South Australia, increasing the goethite-to-hematite conversion. In Minas Gerais, higher metamorphism combined with shearing stress in some deposits probably increased the hematite content. Lo-

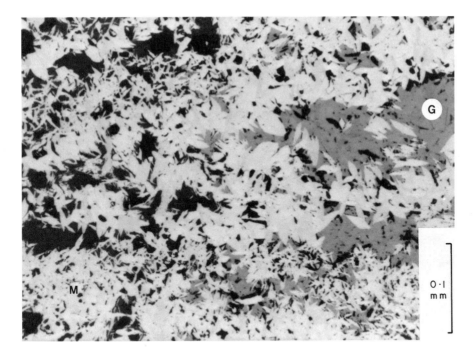

Figure 10-10.   Metamorphosed supergene ore [M-(mpl H)-g]. Secondary microplaty hematite has grown in the goethite-replaced matrix (G) during burial metamorphism. Later exposure has resulted in leaching of goethite, leaving voids (black). Reflected light.

cally in the Marquette Range (Michigan) significant deposits of schistose and "specularite" ores formed from supergene deposits, also apparently under tectonic stress. Petrographic data indicate that Precambrian microplaty ores occur in South Africa, Liberia, Gabon, Mauritania, Brazil, Venezuela, the United States, Canada, India, the USSR, and Australia.

CONTACT METAMORPHISM

Recrystallization of Proterozoic microplaty hematite ore has occurred along the margins of a 30 m wide dolerite intrusive in the Proterozoic microplaty hematite ore of the Channar deposit, about 19 km east of Paraburdoo. The contact ore consists of coarsely granular intergrowths of magnetite and hematite, the hematite carrying abundant blebs of magnetite and rare sulfide. Vugs containing coarse specular tablets of hematite are common. Contact effects diminish rapidly away from the dolerite, and samples 30 m from the dike edge show minimal effects. Similar magnetite-hematite recrystallization textures occur in the Aguas Claras deposit in Minas Gerais, Brazil (Morris, 1985).

Comparable material from much larger magnetite segregations in the Marquette Range were attributed by Cannon (1976) to hypogene enrichment of BIF during metamorphism. Gruss (1973) suggested that metasomatic enrichment of BIF by an intrusive gabbro was responsible for the El Pao magnetite deposit (Venezuela) and that metasomatism of BIF by granite produced the Bomi Hills magnetite-hematite deposit in Liberia.

Figure 10–11. Leached metamorphosed ore [M-(mpl H)-(( ))]. The ore has been upgraded by leaching of goethite (now represented by voids—black leaving martite (M) and microplaty hematite. Variations on this theme are present in most of the major BIF-derived metamorphosed ores of the world. Reflected light.

In arguing against the validity of BIF replacement by hypogene fluids, Morris (1985) suggested that contact metamorphism of a preexisting supergene-enrichment ore, involving the introduction of reducing agents (H_2, H_2S, CH_4, etc.) to form magnetite, is a more geologically consistent hypothesis. Such ores may also have been regionally metamorphosed before and after the contact episodes.

Secondary, now largely oxidized, magnetite of uncertain origin is a common minor component of the Minas Gerais hematite ores (Dorr, 1965; Morris, 1985). Magnetite is also a common but erratically distributed component in hematite ores from Carajas, Brazil. The Carajas deposits are attributed to Mesozoic to Recent leaching of silica from BIF (Tolbert et al., 1971). However, the presence of microplaty hematite textures with cross-cutting magnetite (now largely martite and kenomagnetite), suggests that supergene enrichment ores have been affected by at least two distinct periods of metamorphism—regional metamorphism producing microplaty hematite and a later igneous event that gave rise to the magnetite.

HEMATITE-CHERT RELATIONSHIPS

Gruner (1930, 1937), Guild (1953), Dorr (1965), Brandt (1973), Gruss (1973), and Sims (1973) are among the many authors who have supported direct replacement of BIF matrix (i.e., chert) by hematite, but no convincing petro-

Figure 10–12.   Recrystallization of the ferruginous matrix in a sandstone to hematite, Hainan Island, China. Note the minimal replacement of the quartz. Reflected light.

graphic evidence of this replacement has been published. Arguments are usually based on the fact that hematite now occupies space once occupied by silica and, hence, by assumption, that hematite replaced the chert.

Morris (1980) concluded that hematite was rarely, if ever, a direct replacement of BIF minerals (excluding magnetite) but instead formed from goethite that replaced the BIF matrix during supergene enrichment. Some of the most convincing "negative" evidence for nonreplacement of quartz by hematite can be seen in hematite-quartzites from Hainan Island, China (Fig. 10–12). In these rocks, as in comparable rocks from Australia and the United States, platy hematites, formed by recrystallization of the ferruginous matrix, cease their growth at the quartz margins. Magnetite in these samples, in contrast, grows readily into quartz. Other examples supporting the hematite-after-goethite-after-chert sequence are illustrated in Morris (1985, Figs. 74, 91, 94 through 98).

ENVIRONMENT FOR SUPERGENE ORE FORMATION

The formation of supergene metasomatic iron ores from BIF requires that vast quantities of dominantly siliceous components are removed in solution, while simultaneously, large amounts of iron are introduced to pseudomorph the gangue. Subsequent modifications, such as leaching or metamorphism, may improve the ore quality but, like so-called ferricrustation, usually act to obscure the basic process.

The movement of groundwater through the potential ore body is probably the most important controlling factor for enrichment. This movement, in turn, is affected by the mineralogy, stratigraphy, and structure of the BIF and is related to the topography, climate, and duration of exposure.

SOLUTION AND PRECIPITATION OF IRON

Iron is present in BIF mainly as Fe^{3+}, which is virtually insoluble in typical groundwater (pH 3–9). Thus, the high mobility of iron commonly observed in supergene conditions (e.g., Thornber, 1982, 1984) must be due to the reduction of Fe^{3+} to Fe^{2+} (or possibly to the formation of soluble iron-organic complexes). Ferrous iron, in turn, must have been reoxidized at depth to explain the ferric iron of the enrichment ores. The solution of ferric minerals near the surface can be attributed to organic agencies, but the precipitation of iron well below the water table has been a stumbling block for most supergene models. Probably for this reason many authors favored precipitation within the water table (e.g., MacLeod, 1966, 1973) or more complex mechanisms. For example, James et al. (1968) suggested repeated cycles of aridity with deep oxidation of iron minerals, alternating with pluvial conditions to remove silica. These postulated mechanisms of repeated solution and reprecipitation are not compatible with the petrographic evidence of metasomatic replacement in the ores.

An electrochemical mechanism for precipitation of iron at depth was proposed by Morris et al. (1980) and further amplified by Thornber and Morris (1983). Briefly, the mechanism requires that conductive layers (magnetite in BIF, carbon or graphite in IF) act as an electrical link between the driving force of oxygen reactions at the surface and the conversion of ferrous to ferric iron under anoxic conditions at depth (see Fig. 10–13A). The surface reactions can be summarized as the cathodic reduction of oxygen at the magnetite-groundwater interfaces in the outcrop,

$$4e^- + O_2 + 2H_2O \rightarrow 4OH^-,$$

providing the driving force for the corrosion cell by drawing electrons from the anodic oxidation of ferrous iron at depth:

$$Fe^{2+} \rightarrow Fe^{3+} + e^-.$$

The ferric iron reacts with water (hydrolysis) and precipitates as iron hydroxyoxides,

$$Fe^{3+} + 3H_2O \rightarrow Fe(OH)_3 + 3H^+,$$

releasing H^+, which attacks ferrous carbonates and silicates to increase permeability in the reacting zones. Charge balancing is achieved by electrolytic

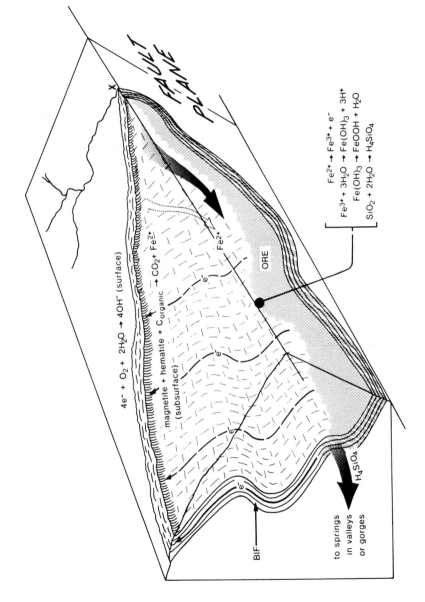

Figure 10-13a. An idealized diagram to illustrate the formation of supergene iron ore in a BIF. Initial reactions at X lead eventually to deep access of fluids along the fault and the beginnings of an artesian system. Reduction of oxygen on wet magnetite surfaces exposed in the outcrop (cathode) draws electrons from ferrous to ferric reactions occurring in the vicinity of exposed surfaces of magnetite at depth (anode), promoting growth of ore laterally and upward in the BIF.

255

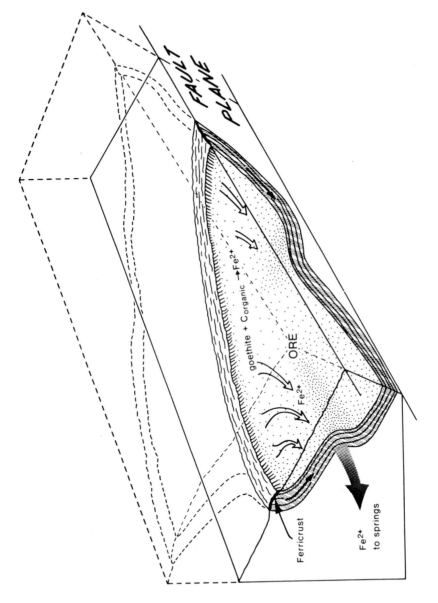

Figure 10–13b. Ideally, enrichment ceases only when the upward growth of ore meets the downward progression of erosion. Further groundwater movement then leaches iron from the ore (see Fig. 10–8a, b).

conduction in groundwaters to complete the electrochemical cell. The mechanism is quantitatively adequate to oxidize and precipitate all the iron needed for even the largest known ore bodies in reasonable geologic time (Morris et al., 1980).

SOLUTION AND REMOVAL OF SILICA

To produce large ore bodies with their well-preserved stratigraphy requires a fine balance over a long time between the precipitation of iron and the removal of silica. If iron is precipitated too rapidly, groundwater movement will be inhibited, thus slowing enrichment. If silica is leached much faster than iron is precipitated, extreme friability will develop, as in the near-surface BIF of Minas Gerais (see Fig. 10-1). These rocks, though residually enriched in iron, are certainly not equivalent to the metasomatic enrichment ores under consideration.

The solubility of silica in typical groundwaters (pH 3–9) is independent of Eh and pH and is about 10 ppm for quartz (Stöber, 1967); yet groundwaters traversing BIF in the Hamersleys consistently contain more than twice this level in solution. This excess is probably due to the breakdown of silicates to amorphous silica (solubility $\sim$ 120 ppm at 25°C). Theoretically, in the presence of quartz this excess silica should precipitate, but the equilibration is extremely sluggish. Once the silicates have been destroyed, the control of silica in solution should be the quartz solubility. For example, Ruckmick (1963) reported values of about 10.5 ppm SiO_2 in spring waters that had traversed leached BIF and ores at Cerro Bolivar in Venezuela.

Many workers have concluded that it is the rate at which quartz dissolves that controls ore formation. James et al. (1968) suggested that large ore bodies might take several million years to form; Ruckmick (1963), >20 m.y.; Trendall (1975), hundreds of m.y.; Morris (1985), 10–20 m.y. for each 100 m of downstructure extension of ore.

STRUCTURE

Data from the Hamersley deposits suggest that they represent the truncated remnants of confined hydrodynamic systems—that is, eroded local artesian basins—ranging up to about 10 km along strike. It seems equally probable that other iron ore deposits listed in the literature, consisting of various flat-lying, monoclinal, anticlinal, synclinal, or recumbent structural features, also represent residuals of larger aquifer systems.

The specific structural character of the system is thus unimportant. What does appear essential is that the BIF acts as an aquifer, with impervious horizons above and below to confine the groundwater movement, and that sufficient hydraulic head be maintained for adequate water flow while the system erodes downward for millions to hundreds of millions of years. One of many such possible systems is shown in Figure 10-13a, based partly on the Whaleback and Tom Price deposits.

MODEL FOR SUPERGENE ENRICHMENT
OF BIF

In this model the initial reactions are postulated as occurring at the outcrop of the BIF-fault contact, developing a permeable access zone in the BIF along the fault to the deeper strata. This permeability promotes higher reaction rates at depth associated with the exposed anodic magnetite than in the almost impermeable BIF closer to the surface. Cross-folding, fracturing in fold hinges, or intrusive contacts could give comparable initial water access. Once these early pathways are established, the ore body grows laterally and upward in the BIF. Ferric iron is dissolved from the near surface by bacterial or other organically mediated reducing processes and transferred in solution as ferrous iron through fractures and solution channels to the reacting zones. Here silica is slowly dissolved and simultaneously replaced by the precipitating hydrous iron oxides. The silica leaves the system in springs, forming proximal deposits at the surface, or exits to the drainage system.

As one pathway becomes blocked others open up, allowing slow but pervasive infiltration and eventual absorption of the refractory sections into the general progression. An arrested stage in the enrichment of a chert mesoband, shown in Figure 10-14, represents a microcosm of the suggested process. Provided the hydrodynamic system is maintained, the process should cease only when the upward growth of ore meets the downward progression of surface erosion as suggested in Figure 10-13*b*.

The concepts of this simplified diagrammatic model can be examined in the real world of the 4 East mine at Paraburdoo (Hamersley area) (Figure 10-15).

2 cm

Figure 10-14.   An arrested stage in the replacement of chert by iron hydroxyoxides (now goethite). The thin section is a two-dimensional microcosm of the hydrologic system hypothesized in Figure 10-13 and mapped in Figure 10-15.

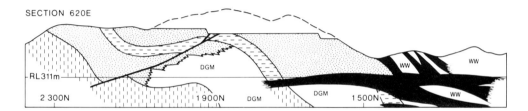

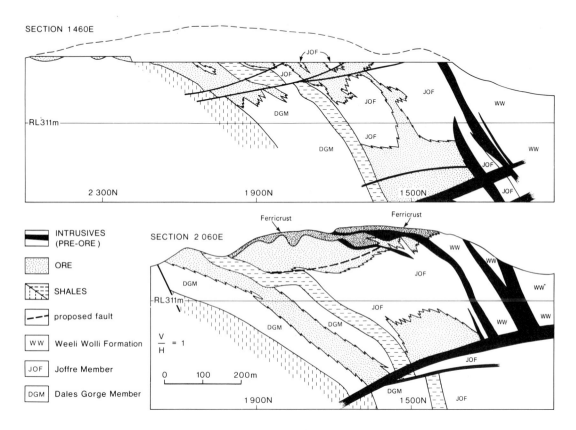

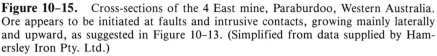

Figure 10-15. Cross-sections of the 4 East mine, Paraburdoo, Western Australia. Ore appears to be initiated at faults and intrusive contacts, growing mainly laterally and upward, as suggested in Figure 10-13. (Simplified from data supplied by Hamersley Iron Pty. Ltd.)

Here, the progression of enrichment began in the Proterozoic (Morris, 1980, 1985) and was interrupted at an advanced stage by sea level changes. Shallow burial by Wyloo Group rocks resulted in mild metamorphism of the deposit to microplaty hematite ore (see Figure 10-10).

Two levels of ore formation exist. In the upper level virtually all the BIF has been enriched to ore above the subhorizontal faults, with minor leakage downward. In the deeper zone the upward growth of ore from the margins of the pre-ore dikes did not reach completion at the eastern end of the ore body. This finding suggests that enrichment was initiated at the western end of the deposit.

AGES OF IRON ORE

Many authors have supported a Precambrian origin for the high-grade hematite ores, some on tenuous data and others on evidence more firmly based on stratigraphic relationships involving ore-derived clasts in conglomerates, but suggested ages range from Archean to Tertiary. Morris (1985) proposed that the earliest significant BIF-derived ores formed during the period 2,000 ± 200 Ma. The hypothesis was based on the abundance of BIF-derived ore pebbles among the BIF clasts of the Mt. McGrath Formation of the Wyloo Group and the absence of ore clasts from the conglomerates of the Beasley River Quartzite, an older unit of the same group that contains abundant BIF clasts. A correlation was drawn with major iron deposits in Minas Gerais (Brazil), Sishen (South Africa), and the Marquette Range (United States) (Fig. 10–16), but this correlation is tentative.

The 2,000 ± 200 Ma date coincides with the time when major BIF deposition appears to have ceased (e.g., Cloud, 1983), when the first evidence of *continental* oxidation is found (Hattori et al., 1983), and when the first major nondetrital sedimentary uranium deposits appeared (e.g., Robertson et al., 1978). All these situations are evidence in support of a significant change in concentration of atmospheric oxygen at that time (Fig. 10–17).

If the concept is valid, then conglomerates derived from supergene iron ore will also be younger than 2,000 ± 200 Ma. Thus, in any sequence of Proterozoic sediments and related unconformities in which BIF exposure has occurred, the lowest beds containing ore-derived pebbles are likely to correlate roughly with the age of the Mt. McGrath Formation (see Fig. 10–16). An important proviso is that the BIF must have been folded prior to exposure to provide suitable hydrologic systems for enrichment.

On the Hamersley Platform, the earliest ores are believed to be related to exposure of BIF along the gently folded margins of the McGrath Trough, which was active during Wyloo times (Horwitz, 1982, 1983) in the southern area of the platform. The presence of ore-pebble conglomerates in the Mt. McGrath Formation suggests that many deposits at that time were destroyed by erosion. Thus, the handful of major microplaty hematite deposits now known in the gently folded rocks of the Hamersley Iron Province were presumably preserved by burial until about the Mesozoic. They now represent the residues of a long period of erosion since that period. In Minas Gerais, Brazil, greater erosion has left small deposits of microplaty hematite ores as remnants in the exposed roots of the strongly folded, vestigial BIF structures that once covered a large area (Dorr, 1969, Plate 1). As discussed earlier, both ores and BIF in Brazil are extremely leached (see Fig. 10–1). The suggested age for these ores of the Iron Quadrangle, which on textural grounds are probably roughly contemporaneous with the much larger Carajas deposits in northern Brazil, is about 2,000 m.y. (see Fig. 10–16).

Ores of the M-G and M-(H)-G type that dominate the reserves of the Hamersleys, appear to have formed later than the microplaty hematite ores, as indicated by their goethite content and lack of metamorphic features. Where stratigraphic or other dating methods were unavailable, Morris (1980) suggested use of a maturity classification based on textural features. The least altered enriched BIF could be expected to show well-preserved pseudomorph textures and, hence, would be immature. Increasing maturity would be rec-

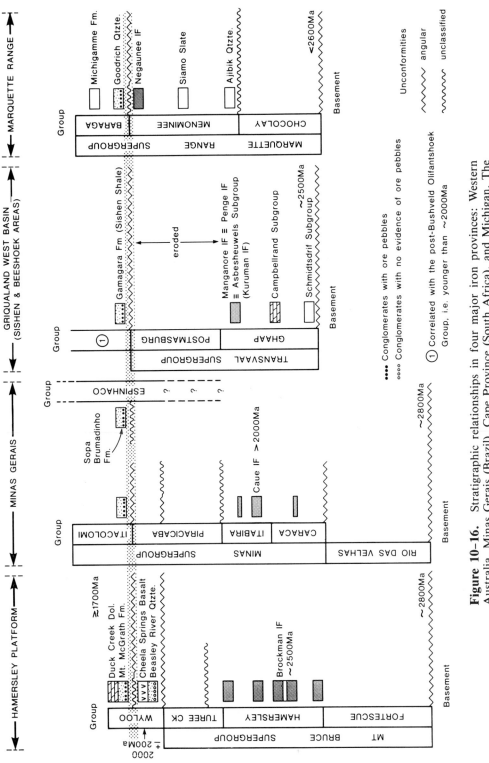

Figure 10-16. Stratigraphic relationships in four major iron provinces: Western Australia, Minas Gerais (Brazil), Cape Province (South Africa), and Michigan. The dot pattern is a tentative correlation of the first stratigraphic evidence of BIF-hosted supergene ores (after Morris, 1985).

261

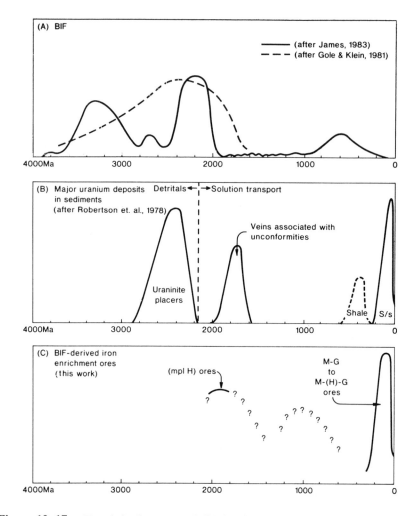

Figure 10-17. Trends in the temporal distribution of BIF, sediment-hosted uranium deposits, and BIF-derived iron-enrichment deposits, supporting a change in oxygen levels about 2,000 Ma.

ognized by various changes in the goethite including leaching, recrystallization, dehydration, and particularly metamorphism, leading to higher iron content and better ore quality. Conversely, weathering effects below the carapace (see Fig. 10-9) degrade the ore quality and could be equated with senility.

Though enrichment of BIF could have happened at any time after an oxidizing atmosphere formed, the fragmentary data available indicate that long exposure and other conditions required to form deposits large enough for preservation probably occurred on a worldwide scale only during certain periods. Morey (1983) suggested three major periods of ore formation in the Lake Superior area, the last two coincident with well-documented intense chemical weathering.

The first of the three periods may correspond to circa 2,000 Ma (Figs. 10-16 and 10-17); the third, during the Mesozoic, is consistent with the age of ores in Canada (Gross, 1968), the USSR, (Sokolov and Grigor'ev, 1974), and the Hamersley area (Morris, 1985). The second period, sometime in the middle late Proterozoic to late Cambrian, is less certain outside the United States, although the textural maturity of many ore bodies in the Hamersley Iron Province provides some support for a worldwide early Phanerozoic ore-forming period.

APPLICATION

This chapter is dominated by information from the Hamersley ores not only because of my familiarity with them but also because so little comparable information is available for deposits elsewhere. I can only hope that these descriptions will trigger the recognition of parallel features in BIF-derived ores outside Australia.

The model has been tested thoroughly as it applies to the Hamersley ores, and the mineragraphic classification of the left-hand side of Figure 10-3 has been developed into a bench and mine scale classification by industry geologists (Kneeshaw, 1984). This simple and practical pigeon hole system, the Pilbara Iron Ore Classification, can be extended to suit a wide variety of iron ores by adding further columns to suit local mineral suites and can be applied independently of the genetic implications of Figure 10-3.

ACKNOWLEDGMENTS

I am grateful to my colleagues in the iron ore industry, in particular to M. Kneeshaw, chief geologist of Mt. Newman Mining Co. Ltd., and R. A. Harmsworth, chief geologist of Hamersley Iron Pty. Ltd., and their staff, for their active participation in this project. Numerous colleagues in CSIRO have contributed help and advice, and I thank E. H. Nickel and M. J. Gole for constructive assessment of the manuscript, Irene Piercy for the typing, and C. Steel and A. Vartesi for drafting figures.

REFERENCES

Ayres, D. E., 1971. The hematite enrichment ores of Mount Tom Price and Mount Whaleback, Hamersley Iron Province, *Australasian Inst. Mining and Metallurgy Proc.* **238**:47–58.

Belevtsev, Y. N., 1973. Genesis of high-grade iron ores of the Krivoyrog type, in *Genesis of Precambrian Iron and Manganese Deposits,* Proceedings of the Kiev Symposium, 1970, UNESCO Earth Science Series, Vol. 9, pp. 167–180.

Berge, J. W., K. Johansson, and J. Jack, 1977. Geology and origin of the hematite ores of the Nimba Range Liberia, *Econ. Geology* **72**:582–607.

Brandt, R. T., 1973. The origins of the jaspilitic iron ores of Australia, in *Genesis of Precambrian Iron and Manganese Deposits,* Proceedings of the Kiev Symposium, 1970, UNESCO Earth Science Series, Vol. 9, pp. 59–66.

Campana, B., 1966. Stratigraphic-structural-paleoclimatic controls of the newly discovered iron ore deposits of Western Australia, *Mineralium Deposita* **1**:53–59.

Cannon, W. F., 1976. Hard iron ore of the Marquette range, Michigan, *Econ. Geology* **76**:1012–1028.

Cloud, P. E., 1983. Banded iron-formation—A gradualist's dilemma, in *Banded Iron-Formation: Facts and Problems,* A. F. Trendall and R. C. Morris, eds., Elsevier, Amsterdam, pp. 401–416.

Davis, B. L., G. Rapp, Jr., and M. J. Walawender, 1968. Fabric and structural characteristics of the martitization process, *Am. Jour. Sci.* **266**:482–496.

Dorr, J. van N., II, 1964. Supergene iron ores of Minas Gerais, Brazil, *Econ. Geology* **59**:1203–1240.

Dorr, J. van N., II, 1965. Nature and origin of high-grade hematite ores of Minas Gerais, Brazil, *Econ. Geology* **60**:1–46.

Dorr, J. van N., II, 1969. *Physiographic, Stratigraphic, and Structural Development of the Quadrilatero Ferrifero, Minas Gerais, Brazil,* U.S. Geological Survey Professional Paper 641-A, pp. 1–110.

Dorr, J. van N., II, and A. L. M. Barbosa, 1963. *Geology and Ore Deposits of the Itabira District, Minas Gerais, Brazil,* U.S. Geological Survey Professional Paper, 341-C, 110p.

Ewers, W. E., and R. C. Morris, 1981. Studies on the Dales Gorge Member of the Brockman Iron Formation, *Econ. Geology* **76**:1929–1953.

Gair, J. E., 1973. Iron deposits of Michigan, in *Genesis of Precambrian Iron and Manganese Deposits,* Proceedings of the Kiev Symposium, 1970, UNESCO, Earth Science Series, Vol. 9, pp. 374–375.

Gair, J. E., 1975. *Bedrock Geology and Ore Deposits of the Palmer Quandrangle, Marquette County, Michigan,* U.S. Geological Survey Professional Paper 769, 159p.

Gathman, Th., 1913. Beitrag zur Kenntnis der "Itabirite" Eisenerz in Minas Gerais (Brazilien), *Zeitschr. Prakt. Geologie,* **21**:234–240.

Gershoig, Yu. G., 1971. A genetic classification of the iron ores of the Krivbass (in Russian), *Geologiya rudn. Mestorozh.* **13**:3–17.

Gole, M. J., and C. Klein, 1981. Banded iron-formations through much of Precambrian time, *Jour. Geology* **89**:169–184.

Griffin, A. C., 1980. Structural geology and sites of iron ore deposition in Koolyanobbing Range, Western Australia. Abstract, Second International Archaean Symposium, Perth. Geological Society of Australia and IGCP, Archean Geochemistry Project, pp. 64–65.

Gross, G. A., 1965. *Geology of Iron Deposits in Canada, Volume 1, General Geology and Evaluation of Iron Deposits,* Geological Survey of Canada Economic Geological Report No. 22, 181p.

Gross, G. A., 1967. *Geology of Iron Deposits in Canada, Volume 2, Iron Deposits in the Appalachian and Grenville Regions of Canada,* Geological Survey of Canada Economic Geological Report No. 22, 111p.

Gross, G. A., 1968. *Geology of Iron Deposits in Canada, Volume 3, Iron Ranges of the Labrador Geosyncline,* Geological Survey of Canada Economic Geological Report No. 22, 179p.

Gruner, J. W., 1926. The Soudan Formation and a new suggestion as to the origin of the Vermilion ores, *Econ. Geology* **21**:629–644.

Gruner, J. W., 1930. Hydrothermal oxidation and leaching experiments: Their bearing on the origin of Lake Superior hematite-limonite ores, *Econ. Geology* **25**:697–719, 837–867.

Gruner, J. W., 1937. Hydrothermal leaching of iron ores of the Lake Superior type—A modified theory, *Econ. Geology* **32**:121–130.

Gruss, H., 1973. Itabirite iron ores of the Liberia and Guyana shields, in *Genesis of*

Precambrian Iron and Manganese Deposits, Proceedings of the Kiev Symposium, 1970, UNESCO Earth Science Series, Vol. 9, pp. 335–359.

Guild, P. W., 1953. Iron deposits of the Conghonas district, Minas Gerais, Brazil, *Econ. Geology* **48**:639–676.

Han, T.-M., 1978. Microstructures of magnetite as guides to its origin in some Precambrian iron-formations, *Fortschr. Minearlogie* **56**:105–142.

Harder, E. C., and R. T. Chamberlin, 1915. The geology of Central Minas Gerais, Brazil, *Jour. Geology* **23**:341–384, 385–424.

Hattori, K., H. R. Krouse, and F. A. Campbell, 1983. The start of sulfur oxidation in continental environments: About 2.2×10^9 years ago, *Science* **221**:549–551.

Horwitz, R. C., 1982. Geological history of the early Proterozoic Paraburdoo hinge zone, Western Australia, *Precambrian Research* **19**:191–200.

Horwitz, R. C., 1983. Palaeogeographic evolution of the Paraburdoo Hinge Zone: A summary of events, in *CSIRO Division of Mineralogy, Research Review 1983,* W. E. Ewers, ed., Floreat Park, Western Australia, pp. 77–79.

Irving, R. D., 1886. Origin of the ferruginous schists and iron ores of the Lake Superior region, *Am. Jour. Sci.* **32**:255–272.

James, H. L., 1954. Sedimentary facies of iron formation, *Econ. Geology* **49**:235–293.

James, H. L., 1983. Distribution of banded iron-formation in space and time, in *Iron-Formation: Facts and Problems,* A. F. Trendall and R. C. Morris, eds., Elsevier, Amsterdam, pp. 471–490.

James, H. L., C. E. Dutton, F. J. Pettijohn, and K. L. Wier, 1968. *Geology and Ore Deposits of the Iron River–Crystal Falls District, Iron County, Michigan,* U.S. Geological Survey Professional Paper 570, 134p.

Klein, C., 1983. Diagenesis and metamorphism of Precambian banded iron-formations, in *Iron-Formation: Facts and Problems,* A. F. Trendall and R. C. Morris, eds., Elsevier, Amsterdam, pp. 417–469.

Kneeshaw, M., 1984. The Pilbara Iron Ore Classification—A proposal for a common classification for BIF-derived supergene ore, *Australasian Inst. Mining and Metallurgy Proc.* **289**:157–162.

Kornilov, N. A., 1970. Age of rich hematite ores of Precambrian iron formations and the physiochemical conditions of Precambrian weathering, *Akad. Nauk SSSR Doklady* **195**:68–70.

Kullerud, G., G. Donnay, and J. D. H. Donnay, 1969. Omission solid solution in magnetite: Kenotetrahedral magnetite, *Zeitschr. Kristallographie* **128**:1–17.

Langmuir, D., 1971. Particle size effect on the reaction goethite = hematite + water, *Am. Jour. Sci.* **271**:147–156.

Langmuir, D., 1972. Correction: Paticle size effect on the reaction goethite = hematite + water, *Am. Jour. Sci.* **272**:982.

MacLeod, W. N., 1966. *The Geology and Iron Deposits of the Hamersley Range Area, Western Australia,* Western Australia Geological Survey Bulletin No. 117, 170p.

MacLeod, W. M., 1973. Iron ores of the Hamersley Iron Province, Western Australia, in *Genesis of Precambrian Iron and Manganese Deposits,* Proceedings of the Kiev Symposium, 1970, Paris, UNESCO Earth Science Series, Vol. 9, pp. 291–298.

Mann, V. I., 1953. The relation of oxidation to the origin of soft iron ores of Michigan, *Econ. Geology* **48**:251–281.

Miles, K. R., 1954. *The geology and iron resources of the Middleback Ranges area,* South Australia Geological Survey Bulletin, No. 33, 247p.

Morey, G. B., 1983. Animikie Basin, Lake Superior Region, U.S.A., in *Iron-Formation: Facts and Problems,* A. F. Trendall and R. C. Morris, eds., Elsevier, Amsterdam, pp. 13–68.

Morris, R. C., 1980. A textural and mineralogical study of the relationship of iron ore to banded iron-formation in the Hamersley Iron Province of Western Australia, *Econ. Geology* **75**:184–209.

Morris. R. C., 1983*a*. Genesis of supergene iron ores from banded iron-formation— A logical progression to different ore types, in *Abstracts, Regional Meeting,* R. Davy, C. R. M. Butt, and T. A. Ballinger, eds., Association of Exploration Geochemists of Australian Regional Meeting, **Abstracts vol.**:57–60.

Morris, R. C., 1983*b*. Supergene alteration of banded iron-formation, in *Iron-Formation: Facts and Problems,* A. F. Trendall and R. C. Morris, eds., Elsevier, Amsterdam, pp. 513–534.

Morris, R. C., 1985. Genesis of iron ore in banded iron-formation by supergene and supergene-metamorphic processes—A conceptual model, in *Handbook of Strata-Bound and Stratiform Ore Deposits,* K. Wolf, ed., Vol. 13, Elsevier, Amsterdam, pp. 73–235.

Morris, R. C., M. R. Thornber, and W. E. Ewers, 1980. Deep-seated iron ores from banded iron-formation, *Nature* **288**:250–252.

Park, C. F., 1959. The origin of hard hematite in itabirite, *Econ. Geology* **54**:573–587.

Robertson, D. S., J. E. Tilsley, and G. M. Hogg, 1978. The time-bound character of uranium deposits, *Econ. Geology* **73**:1409–1419.

Ruckmick, J. C., 1963. The iron ores of Cerro Bolivar, Venezuela, *Econ. Geology* **58**:218–236.

Sanders, B. H., 1933. Iron ores at Itabira, Brazil, *Inst. Mining and Metallurgy Bull.* **366**:1–23.

Schorscher, H. D., 1975. Entwicklung des polymetamorphen prakambrischen Raumes Itabira, Minas Gerais, Brasilien, Ph.D. dissertation, University of Heidelberg, 304p.

Schorscher, H. D., and P. F. Guimaraes, 1976. Estratigrafia e Tectonica do Supergrupo Minas e Geologia do Distrito Ferrifero de Habira, *29th Cong. Brasil Geol., Roteiro das Excursoes,* Belo Horizonte, pp. 75–76.

Sims, S. J., 1973. The Belinga iron ore deposit (Gabon), in *Genesis of Precambrian Iron and Manganese Deposits,* Proceedings of the Kiev Symposium, 1970, UNESCO Earth Science Series, Vol. 9, pp. 323–334.

Sokolov, G. A., and V. M. Grigor'ev, 1974. Deposits of iron, in *Ore Deposits of the USSR,* Vol. 1, V. I. Smirnov, ed., Pitman, London, pp. 7–113.

Stöber, W., 1967. Formation of silicic acid in aqueous suspensions of different silica modification, in *Equilibrium Concepts in Natural Water Systems,* R. F. Gould, ed., American Chemical Society Washington, D.C., pp. 161–182.

Thornber, M. R., 1982. Chemical aspects of gossan assessment, in *Geochemical Exploration in Deeply Weathered Terrain,* R. E., Smith, ed., CSIRO Institute of Energy and Earth Res. Div. Min. Floreat Park, Western Australia, pp. 67–72.

Thornber, M. R., 1984. Supergene alteration of sulphides VI. The binding of Cu, Ni, Zn, Co and Pb with gossan (iron-bearing) minerals, *Chem. Geology* **44**:399–434.

Thornber, M. R., and R. C. Morris, 1983. The formation of iron ore from banded iron-formation by an electrochemical weathering process, in *CSIRO Division of Mineralogy, Research Review 1983,* W. E. Ewers, ed., Floreat Park, Western Australia, pp. 84–85.

Tolbert, G. E., J. W. Tremaine, G. C. Melcher, and C. B. Gomes, 1971. The recently discovered Serra dos Carajas iron deposits, Northern Brazil, *Econ. Geology* **66**:985–994.

Trendall, A. F., 1975. Geology of Western Australian iron ore, in *Economic Geology of Australia and Papua New Guinea,* vol. 1, C. L. Knight, ed., Australasian Institute of Mining and Metallurgy, Monograph **5**:883–892.

Trendall, A. F., 1983. The Hamersley Basin, in *Iron-Formation: Facts and Problems,* A. F. Trendall and R. C. Morris, eds., Elsevier, Amsterdam, pp. 69–129.

Trendall, A. F., and J. G. Blockley, 1970. *The Iron Formations of the Precambrian*

Hamersley Group, Western Australia; with Special Reference to the Associated Cro-cidolite, Western Australia Geological Survey Bulletin No. 119, 336p.

UNESCO, 1973. *Genesis of Precambrian Iron and Manganese Deposits,* Proceedings of the Kiev Symposium, 1970, UNESCO Earth Science Series, Vol. 9, 382p.

Van Hise, C. R., and W. S. Bayley, 1897. *The Marquette Iron Bearing District of Michigan,* U.S. Geological Survey Monograph 28, Washington, D.C., 608p.

Van Hise, C. R., and C. K. Leith, 1911. *The Geology of the Lake Superior Region,* U.S. Geological Survey Monograph 52, 641p.

11

PALEOZOIC BEDDED BARITE ASSOCIATED WITH CHERT IN WESTERN NORTH AMERICA

Benita L. Murchey and **Raul J. Madrid**

U.S. Geological Survey
Menlo Park, California

Forrest G. Poole

U.S. Geological Survey
Denver, Colorado

ABSTRACT. In western North America, bedded barite associated with fine-grained siliceous sedimentary rocks is restricted to Paleozoic strata that were deposited in basins along the ancient continental margin. Siliceous belts with major bedded barite deposits include the northern Brooks Range belt in Alaska, the Selwyn Basin and Cassiar terrane in Canada, the Roberts Mountains allochthon in Nevada, and the Mazatán belt in Sonora. In these four regions, primary (?) and secondary barite occurs in multiple stratigraphic horizons. Stratigraphic and structural evidence supports the conclusion that barite formation at and/or below the sediment-water interface predated folding and thrusting of the basins. Barite formation was probably related to local uplift and possible vertical faulting during the basin histories. Evidence for these events include debris flows and turbidites with basin-derived chert and barite clasts. Sedimentary and/ or magma-driven exhalative hydrothermal systems appear to be the mechanism by which major barite deposits formed. The restriction of the barite deposits to continental margin environments and to the Paleozoic era suggests that biologic and/or oceanographic processes also controlled the distribution of bedded barite associated with siliceous sediments. Biologic productivity along continental margins is commonly high. In addition, intermediate-depth continental margin environments are sites where oxygen-poor marine waters impinge on the sediment-water interface. Conditions unique to the Paleozoic oceans include marine biotic composition and widespread early Paleozoic anoxic waters. Biological concentration of barium in marine shales as the result of high productivity and/or wide oxygen-minimum zones may have produced barium-enriched source rocks. Vertical faults provided a conduit by which barium-enriched hydrothermal fluids could migrate to or near the sediment-water interface, combine with sulfate from an oxygenated late Paleozoic ocean, and form bedded barite. In magma-driven hydrothermal systems, igneous rocks may also have been a barium source.

INTRODUCTION

In North America, bedded barite is associated wtih Paleozoic pelagic and hemipelagic siliceous rocks that discontinuously rim the Paleozoic margin of the continent. In western North America, these baritic siliceous belts occur in the northern Brooks Range in Alaska, the Selwyn Basin and Cassiar terrane in Canada, the Roberts Mountains allochthon (terrane) in central Nevada, and the Mazatán area in central Sonora, Mexico (Fig. 11–1). The bedded barite deposits are in eugeoclinal or miogeoclinal sequences that share many features including sedimentary facies, structural style, and similar tectonic histories. This chapter discusses the common features of barite-chert belts, as well as possible processes that lead to their formation.

Rock types characterizing the baritic siliceous belts include radiolarian and sponge spicule chert, siliceous shale, argillite, limestone, and siliciclastic sandstones and conglomerates. These lithologies are host rocks to bedded barite

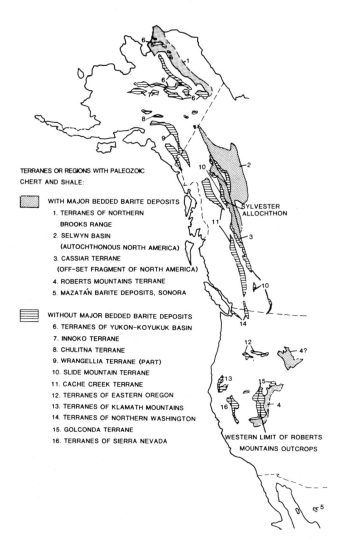

TERRANES OR REGIONS WITH PALEOZOIC
CHERT AND SHALE:

WITH MAJOR BEDDED BARITE DEPOSITS
1. TERRANES OF NORTHERN
   BROOKS RANGE
2. SELWYN BASIN
   (AUTOCHTHONOUS NORTH AMERICA)
3. CASSIAR TERRANE
   (OFF-SET FRAGMENT OF NORTH AMERICA)
4. ROBERTS MOUNTAINS TERRANE
5. MAZATÁN BARITE DEPOSITS, SONORA

WITHOUT MAJOR BEDDED BARITE DEPOSITS
6. TERRANES OF YUKON-KOYUKUK BASIN
7. INNOKO TERRANE
8. CHULITNA TERRANE
9. WRANGELLIA TERRANE (PART)
10. SLIDE MOUNTAIN TERRANE
11. CACHE CREEK TERRANE
12. TERRANES OF EASTERN OREGON
13. TERRANES OF KLAMATH MOUNTAINS
14. TERRANES OF NORTHERN WASHINGTON
15. GOLCONDA TERRANE
16. TERRANES OF SIERRA NEVADA

SYLVESTER
ALLOCHTHON

WESTERN LIMIT OF ROBERTS
MOUNTAINS OUTCROPS

Figure 11–1. Map of Western North America showing the distribution of autochthonous basins and allochthonous tectonostratigraphic terranes with Paleozoic chert and shale. Dotted pattern indicates areas with and striped pattern indicates areas without major bedded barite deposits.

occurrences. Barite is commonly associated with carbonaceous and phosphatic shale and chert. Lavas and (or) tuffs are also present in parts of the northern Brooks Range, Selwyn Basin, central Nevada, and central Sonora barite belts. Barite and lead-zinc deposits co-occur in the Brooks Range and Selwyn Basin, and locally, volcanic and volcaniclastic rocks also occur with these deposits.

PALEOGEOGRAPHY

In most paleogeographic reconstructions of the western margin of Paleozoic North America, the depositional sites of the barite-bearing siliceous belts are oceanward from the continental shelf. Barite deposition predates deformation and thrusting of associated siliceous sedimentary rocks. The barite belts are characterized by thrust faults that emplace the siliceous rocks over carbonate platform rocks. Time of thrusting varies from the Late Devonian and Early Mississippian in the Roberts Mountains allochthon in Nevada to the Mesozoic and Cenozoic in the Brooks Range and Selwyn Basin. The barite-bearing sequences are internally thrusted, folded, and structurally shortened. Therefore, the initial width of the depositional basins may have been hundreds of kilometers. For example, one palinspastic reconstruction of the northern Brooks Range foothills belt suggests that the late Paleozoic to early Mesozoic basin extended at least 500 km seaward from the northern margin of the shelf (Mayfield et al., 1983). Significant strike-slip displacement between the barite-bearing siliceous belts and the structurally lower rock sequences has not been postulated by most workers (Poole et al., 1977; Mayfield et al., 1983). In fact, Canadian geologists consider the Selwyn Basin sequences to be autochthonous (Cecile, 1982).

The structural position of barite-bearing facies in the northern Brooks Range suggests that they were deposited in a transitional zone between a shelf environment and a deeper off-shelf environment. For a distance of 1,100 km, a belt of barite-bearing pelagic and hemipelagic rocks trends eastward from the Chukchi Sea across the foothills of the northern Brooks Range (see Fig. 11-1). These upper Paleozoic and lower Mesozoic rocks consist of bedded chert, siliceous argillite, organic-rich shale, and fine-grained limestone (Mull et al., 1982). The pelagic and hemipelagic rocks of the northern Brooks Range occur in a series of imbricated thrust sheets (Mayfield et al., 1983) that formed during north-directed Mesozoic thrusting. The thrust sheets are structurally superposed above coeval platform rocks (Fig. 11-2), and the barite-bearing facies are confined to the structurally lowest thrust sheets in the tectonic stack (I. Tailleur, personal communication, 1984). The allochthonous barite-bearing rocks represent an environment inferred to be transitional between the Late Mississippian to Early Jurassic platform and coeval deeper-water off-shelf settings. Upper Mississippian to Jurassic carbonate and clastic platform rocks underlying the thrust sheets are, in part, organic rich and phosphatic. Coeval strata in the barite-bearing thrust sheets are also organic rich and phosphatic, although they are finer grained and more siliceous than the autochthonous sequence. Thrust sheets structurally overlying the barite-bearing units are more siliceous, less carbonaceous, less argillaceous, and less calcareous than the barite-bearing units. Overlying all these sedimentary units are thrust sheets with

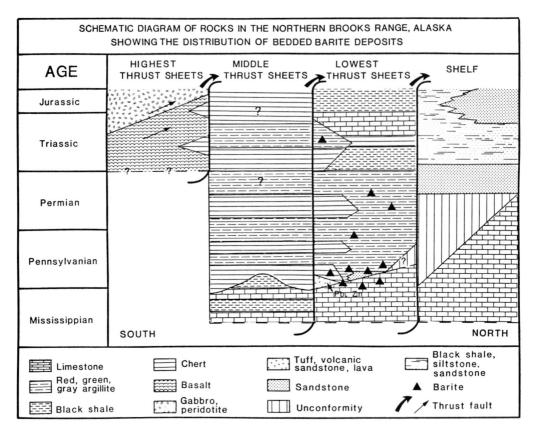

Figure 11-2. Schematic diagram showing the distribution of bedded barite deposits in Mississippian to Jurassic rocks of thrust sheets in the northern Brooks Range, Alaska. The highest thrust sheets correspond to region 2 (terranes of Yukon–Koyukuk Basin) in Figure 11-1. The middle and lowest thrust sheets correspond to region 1 (terranes of the northern Brooks Range) in Figure 11-1. The map scale does not permit differentiation between the barite-bearing lowest thrust sheets and the middle thrust sheets. The shelfal stratigraphic units crop out north of region 1 in Figure 11-1.

Paleozoic (?) and Mesozoic pillow basalt and thrust sheets with gabbro and peridotite (Mayfield et al., 1983).

In addition to being structurally confined to the organic-rich and carbonate-rich rocks in the lowest thrust sheets in the northern Brooks Range, the barite is also confined to specific facies within the lowest thrust sheets. The bedded barite occurs within a pelagic and hemipelagic chert and argillite sequence that is bracketed above and below by organic-rich, slightly phosphatic shale and limestone sequences. The lithologic boundaries between these units are time transgressive (Murchey et al., in press). In northern Alaska, barite occurs in Mississippian, Pennsylvanian, and Permian strata and locally in Triassic strata. However, barite appears to be most common in Mississippian and Lower Pennsylvanian rocks near the boundary between organic-rich fine-grained limestone and black spiculitic chert of the upper part of the Kuna Formation of Mull et al. (1982) and in green, gray, maroon, or variegated chert and argillite of the Siksikpuk Formation of Patton (1957) and its more siliceous equivalents. In the western part of the Brooks Range, the Kuna Formation is the host for stratabound lead-zinc mineralization and associated barite.

The upper Paleozoic sedimentary facies in the barite-bearing thrust sheets fluctuate between carbonate-rich and silica-rich sediments and between organic-rich and organic-poor sediments. These facies changes suggest vertical shifts in the calcite compensation depth (CCD) boundary and the oxygen-minimum zone boundaries relative to the depositional sites. Boundary fluctuations may have been related to sea level changes, regional changes in oceanic circulation patterns, or subsidence and uplift. The pre-Jurassic CCD may have been considerably shallower than it is now. A reasonable estimate of the possible range of basin-floor depths for this environment is about 100–1,500 m.

Paleozoic tectonostratigraphic terranes seaward of the barite belts lack significant bedded barite although many contain bedded chert (Murchey et al., 1983) (see Fig. 11–1). In addition to chert and shale, the barite-poor sequences commonly contain felsic volcanic and volcaniclastic rocks and (or) mafic volcanic rocks.

The Brooks Range, Alaska, is one of the few places where a structural contact between a barite-rich and a barite-poor belt is exposed. Fault-bounded lithostratigraphic terranes with Paleozoic and Mesozoic chert and mafic volcanic rocks rim the Yukon–Koyukuk Basin and, locally, structurally overlie upper Paleozoic rocks of the northern Brooks Range (see Figs. 11–1 and 11–2). At least some of the mafic volcanic rocks that are intimately associated with bedded chert in this area have geochemistry suggestive of a seamount setting (Pallister, 1985; Barker et al., in press). In the Yukon–Koyukuk Basin terranes, veinlets in chert commonly contain barite (Murchey, unpublished data), but no significant bedded barite deposits are known in these units. The Innoko terrane, south of the Yukon–Koyukuk Basin terranes but north of the right-lateral Denali fault, also lacks bedded barite. The original paleogeographic relationships between the chert-bearing terranes north of the Denali fault are not established.

In western Canada, the Devonian to Triassic Sylvester allochthon, part of the Slide Mountain terrane, structurally overlies cratonic rocks of the Cassiar terrane (Harms, 1986). The Cassiar terrane contains bedded barite, but the oceanic assemblages in the Sylvester allochthon do not. Harms suggested that the Sylvester allochthon (Slide Mountain terrane) contains structurally juxtaposed oceanfloor fragments that were not originally adjacent to one another.

South and west of the previously mentioned Alaskan and Canadian terranes lie tectonostratigraphic terranes with known lateral displacements of hundreds to thousands of kilometers, such as the Wrangellia, Chulitna, and Cache Creek terranes (see Fig. 11–1). These three terranes contain chert coeval with rocks in the barite belts but lack significant bedded barite deposits. Paleozoic chert in the Wrangellia terrane overlies a subsiding arc sequence (Murchey et al., 1983). In the Cache Creek terrane, Paleozoic chert locally overlies mafic volcanic rocks (Murchey et al., 1983). In the Chulitna terrane, Upper Devonian and Lower Mississippian radiolarian chert overlies pillow basalt, and higher in the section, Permian radiolarian chert overlies a volcaniclastic, chert-bearing conglomerate (Jones et al., 1980).

In the Sierra Nevada and eastern Klamath Mountains of California, Ordovician to Lower Mississippian bedded chert and arc-related volcanic rocks coeval with chert in the Roberts Mountains allochthon (terrane) of Nevada contain only minor bedded barite. The paleogeographic positions of these two areas in California relative to the Roberts Mountains allochthon have not been firmly established. Upper Paleozoic rocks in the Golconda allochthon (terrane) of central Nevada and in the terranes of the Sierra Nevada and eastern and western Klamath Mountains do not contain bedded barite.

The Sonora barite-chert belt is adjacent to cratonic rocks, but structural relationships between the chert belt and surrounding rocks are not well established. The presence of abundant siliciclastic rocks in the lower and upper Paleozoic sequence suggests formation near a continental margin.

In short, the sedimentary histories and structural positions of the baritic Paleozoic siliceous belts indicate that they formed along continental margins. The barite belts are either part of the North American craton or structurally overlie the craton. These basins may have formed by intracratonic rifting (Mayfield, 1980; Cecile, 1982) followed, in some or all localities, by intra-oceanic rifting. Island-arc environments or mid-ocean environments were not sites for the formation of significant bedded barite. The continental margin area (outer continental crust and inner oceanic crust settings), where most of the significant barite deposits occur, is characterized by a particular depositional environment as well as by vertical tectonics.

TIMING OF MINERALIZATION

Barite occurs in numerous stratigraphic horizons in all four regions under discussion. In the northern Brooks Range, barite occurs in Mississippian, Pennsylvanian, and Permian strata and locally in Triassic strata (Murchey et al., in press). In the Selwyn Basin, barite occurs in Cambrian to Mississippian rocks (Dawson and Orchard, 1982; Lydon et al., 1985). In Nevada, barite occurs in Cambrian, Ordovician, Silurian, Devonian, and Lower Mississippian strata (Coles, 1986; Madrid, Poole and Wrucke, unpublished data; Poole, 1986, and unpublished data). Barite in central Sonora, Mexico, occurs in Upper Devonian and Lower Pennsylvanian strata (Poole et al., 1983).

Several lines of evidence indicate that the bedded barite in these sequences formed during sedimentation in the basins:

1. Barite is typically conformable with adjacent strata and has been deformed along with the enclosing beds.
2. Undeformed rocks depositionally overlying deformed barite-bearing sequences do not contain barite.
3. Intrabasinal clastic rocks in Sonora (Madrid and Poole, unpublished data), Nevada (Shawe et al., 1969; Poole, 1986), and northern Alaska (Siok, 1985) contain clasts or grains of redeposited barite.
4. Finely laminated barite near the top of some units suggests barite deposition at the sediment-water interface (Dubé, 1986).

Bedded barite in these sequences probably formed both at and below the sediment-water interface. Barite commonly replaces or crosscuts fossils such as brachiopods, radiolarians, and sponge spicules. Less commonly, barite nodules crosscut sedimentary laminae. In contrast, sedimentary laminae also drape around some barite nodules. In the Pinecone assemblage of Coles (1986) in the

Toquima Range, Nevada (Roberts Mountains allochthon), sediments are compacted around radiolarian-bearing phosphatic nodules that formed at or near the sediment-water interface. Barite crystals crosscut the phosphatic nodules and some sedimentary structures and thus postdate the earliest sedimentary features in the Upper Devonian and Lower Mississippian part of the Pinecone assemblage. In the Tuscarora Mountains of northern Nevada (Roberts Mountains allochthon), barite rosettes in chert may have formed below but close to the sediment-water interface, while a thin layer of overlying laminated barite may have precipitated from seawater in an exhalative hydrothermal system (Dubé, 1986). Crosscutting relationships suggest multiple episodes of local baritization both close to the sediment-water interface and, possibly, deeper within the subsea sediments. Dean and Schreiber (1977) reported increasing amounts of barite with depth in some deep-sea cores and interpreted this trend as an indication of increased precipitation of barite during diagenesis.

Barite cement surrounding redeposited barite clasts in Mexico, Nevada, and Alaska also indicates multiple phases of mineralization in these sequences. Further evidence includes the presence of stratabound barite in rocks overlying barite-bearing sedimentary breccias and baritic conglomerates in Alaska and Nevada and the occurrence of multiple horizons of baritic conglomerates in Sonora.

The recognition that barite mineralization occurred either episodically or relatively continuously over millions of years in siliceous barite-bearing sequences suggests two alternative interpretations for the history of mineralization:

1. All stratabound barite had a hydrothermal barium source, and the hydrothermal systems were continuously or periodically active in the regions offshore Paleozoic North America for as long as 100 m.y. Hydrothermal barium may have been leached from buried strata, derived from magmatic sources, or both.
2. Some stratabound barite had a hydrothermal barium origin, whereas other barite in the same sedimentary sequence had a direct sedimentary barium source.

HYDROTHERMAL BARITE

Exhalative hydrothermal systems appear to be the mechanism by which major barite deposits formed. Both magma-driven exhalative systems and sedimentary exhalative systems have been proposed as models to explain the source of barium and the mode of deposition of bedded barite deposits.

In magma-driven convective systems, sediments and/or deeper fault-penetrated crustal rocks are heated and leached by contact with hot circulating fluids (Lange et al., 1980; Poole et al., 1983; Poole, 1986). Therefore, barium can be derived from a magmatic source and/or from leached submarine volcanic and sedimentary rocks.

The spatial association between barium enrichment in deep-sea pelagic sediments and the East Pacific Rise has been known for a long time (Arrhenius and Bonatti, 1965). The discovery of barite-precipitating hydrothermal vent systems associated with volcanism and oceanfloor rifting in the modern oceans

(Corliss et al., 1979) provides a model for the formation of barite in ancient marine sequences. Very thick (tens of meters) bedded barite intervals in the Paleozoic barite belts of western North America have been interpreted as being related to nagma-driven seafloor hydrothermal mineralization (e.g., Alaska: Lange et al., 1980; western Canada: Mortensen and Godwin, 1982; Nevada: Poole, 1986; Sonora: Poole et al., 1983). At a few localities in Alaska and western Canada, barite beds are spatially associated with massive sulfide deposits and with volcanic or volcaniclastic rocks.

In sedimentary exhalative systems, geopressured barium-enriched waters are exhaled at the seafloor when faults penetrate geopressured reservoir rocks, providing a pathway for fluid escape (Carne and Cathro, 1982; Mako and Shanks, 1984; Lydon et al., 1985). In this model, which is similar to some sedimentary exhalative models proposed for lead-zinc deposits, marine sediments are the barium source. For barite in the Selwyn Basin, Lydon et al. (1985) proposed that Proterozoic and lower Paleozoic clastic units were reservoirs for barium-enriched geopressured fluids and that chert and argillite were cap rocks. Based on the geochemistry of a lower Paleozoic formation considered to be a barium reservoir rock, Lydon et al. inferred that the formation's pore waters had anomalously high barium concentrations during its burial history. In the Selwyn Basin models, barium-enriched geopressured fluids escaped to the surface along rift-related extensional faults that penetrated the reservoir rocks during Devonian time. Similarly, Dubé (1986) interpreted bedded barite in the Tuscarora Mountains of northern Nevada as sedimentary exhalative deposits.

For large bedded barite deposits not directly associated with volcanic or volcaniclastic rocks, the source of barium in barite-precipitating fluids, whether from magma-driven or geopressured hydrothermal systems, is not certain. Faulting is a component of both models. All the barite-bearing basins show sedimentologic evidence for synsedimentary faulting associated with major barite horizons. In all four bedded barite regions, aligned and locally derived debris flows and turbidites (some with barite and chert clasts) indicate local uplift and probable syndepositional faulting (Gordey et al., 1982; Forrest, 1983; Mayfield et al., 1983; Poole et al., 1983; Siok, 1985; Poole, 1986) that may have resulted in a horst and graben topography.

Possible worm tubes and baritized and silicified brachiopods (Lange et al., 1980; Cloud and Boucot, 1971; Poole et al., 1983; Noll et al., 1984; Dubé, 1986; Poole, 1986) may represent vent faunas analogous to tube worm–mollusk faunas that have been found in hydrothermal systems on the modern ocean-floor.

Theoretically, both types of hydrothermal systems could generate barite deposits in a tectonically active continental margin basin. The only requirement for a magma-driven hydrothermal system is magmatic activity somewhere beneath the seafloor. A geopressured sedimentary exhalative system requires a barium-rich sedimentary sequence with permeable reservoir rocks and impermeable cap rocks. Such sequences are common in deep basins adjacent to continental margins. Not all stratabound barite can be directly or indirectly tied to a vent system by stratigraphic relationships. The barium source for thin barite beds, nodular barite horizons, or isolated barite lenses within pelagic and hemipelagic sequences is not clear. Barium could be derived from local strata that was biogenically enriched with barium or barite.

Depositional History

As stated, bedded barite occurs in rocks whose precursors were deposited in Paleozoic basins adjacent to continental margins. Because major bedded barite deposits are restricted to this particular depositional environment, a genetic relationship between bedded barite and its host rocks must be considered. Facies-related parameters that may be relevant to the formation of bedded barite include (1) biologically and (or) oceanographically controlled high concentrations of barium in the sediments and (2) the permeability of the sediments.

Biogenically Concentrated Barium

High barite concentrations beneath zones of high planktonic productivity in the modern oceans led Arrhenius and Bonatti (1965) and Church (1970) to postulate a relationship between the two. In the Pacific Ocean, the highest concentrations of barite occur in the eastern equatorial Pacific and in the southeastern Pacific Basin near the East Pacific Rise. Upwelling of nutrient-rich waters off the coast of Peru and along the equator results in high biological productivity and the deposition of calcareous and siliceous oozes where the sediments are not diluted by terrigenous material (Calvert, 1974; Kennett, 1982). Cronan (1974) and Dean and Schreiber (1977) found good correlation between the geographic distribution of barite in sediments on the seafloor and barite in sediments below the seafloor. Like seafloor barite, subseafloor barite is also associated with high organic content in the sediments.

A reasonable interpretation of the geographic relationship between high barite concentrations and high productivity in the modern oceans is that barium is concentrated from seawater by marine organisms. Many marine organisms have the ability to concentrate either barium or particulate barite by incorporating it into their test structure or by forming some type of loose bond with it. Shawe et al. (1969) discussed the possible biogenic origin for some Paleozoic bedded barite in central Nevada.

The Paleozoic barite-bearing siliceous rocks in basins along the continental margin of western North America were likely sites for high biologic productivity (see Chap. 2). The presence of organic-rich marine shales, phosphatic sedimentary rocks, and abundant radiolarians and sponge spicules all suggest upwelling and high productivity at times during the depositional histories of the basins. If barium is concentrated in significant volume by marine organisms, then the sediments of Paleozoic basins with histories of high productivity and/or wide oxygen-minimum zones were probably enriched with biogenically concentrated barium and barite.

Oxidizing and Reducing Chemical Environments on the Seafloor

Microscopic-scale (millimeters), outcrop-scale (meters), and map-scale (kilometers) variations in mineralogy indicate fluctuations between oxidizing (sulfate-precipitating) and reducing (sulfide-precipitating) environments temporally associated with barite ($BaSO_4$) mineralization. Interlaminated barite and sulfides at many localities indicate rapidly fluctuating oxidizing states in local microenvironments. In Alaska, Nevada, and Mexico, major barite horizons occur at or near boundaries between organic-rich black rocks and overlying green and/or red rocks.

If our premise is correct—that Paleozoic barite-chert belts formed in basins close to the continental margin—then depositional sites may have been mostly or entirely bathyal. The waters impinging on the sediment-water interface at bathyal depths commonly contain a dysoxic or an anoxic horizon. The vertical thickness and intensity of the oxygen-minimum horizon strongly influences the sites of deposition of organic carbon-rich and carbon-poor sediments.

The oxygen-minimum zone during Paleozoic time may have been substantially thicker than it is in modern oceans (Berry and Wilde, 1978). To account for widespread lower Paleozoic black shales, Berry and Wilde proposed that early Paleozoic oceans were poorly ventilated with only a thin surface layer of oxygenated water. As the result of successive glaciations that fed oxygenated cold water into deep ocean basins, the oceans became progressively more ventilated, and a residual anoxic water horizon became progressively more restricted. In the Berry and Wilde model, ocean bottom waters became oxidizing by Middle Devonian time. This model seems significant because the major horizons of barite mineralization in western Canada, Nevada, and Sonora are Upper Devonian. If the sulfate component of barite is derived from seawater, relatively little sulfate would have been available to form barite in pre–Middle Devonian sediments. The absence of oxidizing conditions in deep and intermediate-depth basins during most of the early Paleozoic may have produced barium-enriched sediments such as those inferred by Lydon et al. (1985) for lower Paleozoic strata in the Selwyn Basin. The barite belts of western Canada, Nevada, and Sonora all contain lower Paleozoic black shales and chert. The original relationship between fault-bounded upper Paleozoic barite-bearing rocks in the Brooks Range of Alaska and structurally underlying lower and middle Paleozoic rocks is not as well established.

Poole (1986) proposed that barium-bearing saline fluids from hydrothermal vents were pooled in local depressions beneath anoxic bottom waters. Barite was precipitated when seawater overlying these sites was ventilated. This model implies that the sill depths of local seafloor depressions or of the larger basin were initially within the oxygen-minimum zone. Another possibility is that many vent and mineralization sites lay near the upper (?) or lower boundary of the oxygen-minimum zone beneath oxygenated (oxic) or partly oxygenated (dysoxic) waters. Because the redox conditions within sediments are related to rates of supply of organic detritus, the organic-rich rocks associated with or below barite beds were not necessarily deposited beneath anoxic bottom waters (Dean and Gardner, 1982). In the Toquima Range, synsedimentary phosphate in a barite-bearing black chert and shale unit suggests upwelling coupled with oxidizing bottom waters (Coles and Snyder, 1985). Phosphatic rocks are common in all the barite belts. The presence of abundant siliceous sponge spicules in the organic-rich strata associated with Paleozoic barite also implies oxygenated bottom waters. Although oriented sponge spicules and spiculitic turbidites are evidence for transport of some sponge spicules within the chert-shale sequences, transport for all sponge spicules from shallower parts of the basin is not indicated. In situ casts of whole sponges occur in fine-grained limestone a few meters below barite horizons in the northern Brooks Range (Murchey, unpublished data). The boundary between oxidizing and reducing conditions, therefore, may have been slightly below the sediment-water interface in some bedded barite localities. Neither interpretation is mutually exclusive within a basin, and both conditions may account for local redox fluctuations.

PERMEABILITY

Although finely laminated barite may be precipitated at the sediment-water interface, replacement features in other barite occurrences suggest secondary mineralization below the surface of the seafloor. Therefore, permeability of sediments can be an important parameter controlling the mode of barite occurrence regardless of the barium source. In relatively impermeable chert and shale, stratabound barite tends to occur as concretions and rosettes or as lenses up to a meter in length. However, where the rock or original sediments were permeable, barite occurs as thick beds. Barite commonly cements, and may partly replace, conglomerate, sandstone, siltstone, and limestone beds. Carne and Cathro (1982) note that all barite mineralization at MacMillan Pass in Canada occurs near the transition from coarse clastics to overlying carbonaceous and siliceous shale. Similar relationships have been noted for occurrences in Alaska, Nevada, and Sonora.

Permeability, or lack of it, is an important component of the sedimentary exhalative model for barite mineralization. The model requires permeable reservoir rocks for barium-enriched formation waters and impermeable cap rocks (Carne and Cathro, 1982; Lydon et al., 1985). Whereas mid-ocean sedimentary sequences are commonly dominated by relatively impermeable fine-grained strata, both permeable and impermeable strata characterize the four barite-bearing basins discussed in this chapter.

DISCUSSION

Because almost all the world's bedded barite is Paleozoic (Brobst, 1970; Orris, 1985), the era must have been particularly conducive to barite mineralization. The parameters that made the Paleozoic an advantageous time for bedded barite formation may have been geologic, biologic, and (or) oceanographic.

In all the Paleozoic barite-bearing basins, extensional tectonics seem to have been the dominant tectonic process. Because extensional tectonic settings have characterized other continental margins during other geologic eras, additional parameters also seem to have controlled the formation of major bedded barite deposits. One geologic factor may have been an unproven difference between Paleozoic and post-Paleozoic rates of rifting and hydrothermal activity.

Biologic and (or) oceanographic conditions unique to Paleozoic time could have been critical factors that resulted in the formation of most of the world's bedded barite deposits by producing anomalously high concentrations of barium in pelagic and hemipelagic sediments. Microfossil assemblages in basinal rocks just seaward of Paleozoic continental shelves differ from those found off most Mesozoic and Cenozoic continental margins. Siliceous sponge spicules commonly form 10–100% of the Paleozoic fossils in siliceous rocks of the barite belts. In contrast, sponge spicules are relatively insignificant components of most Mesozoic and Cenozoic bedded silica deposits rimming the Pacific. Radiolarians, the most common test-forming pelagic organisms in the Paleozoic oceans, are abundant in the baritic sediments. The relative importance of radiolarians in contributing to pelagic and hemipelagic sediments decreased markedly following the middle Mesozoic explosion of calcareous planktonic organisms and the Cenozoic explosion of diatoms. Although barium does not appear to be incorporated in the siliceous tests of sponges or radiolarians, the organic matter in these organisms may have concentrated barium. Other Paleozoic marine organisms without tests or with chemically fragile tests also may have concentrated barium. Possible extensive oxygen-minimum zones in the early Paleozoic oceans may have been a critical factor in forming late Paleozoic age bedded barite deposits by concentrating barium in organic-rich sediments.

CONCLUSION

In North America, stratabound barite in siliceous sediments is largely confined to Paleozoic rocks, depositional basin environments along the continental margin, and extensional tectonic settings. While most stratabound barite appears to be related to hydrothermal activity, small barite occurrences may have formed when barium from locally enriched sediments combined with seawater sulfate. Paleozoic siliceous sequences seaward of the continental margin barite belts apparently lack significant stratabound barite even though these sequences have a history of volcanic hydrothermal activity. The barite belts contain thicker sequences of pelagic and hemipelagic rocks and associated clastic rocks than the more seaward Paleozoic settings. In addition, the sedimentary rocks in the barite belts contain more organic-rich strata than more seaward terranes. The western Canada, Nevada, and Sonora barite belts include organic-rich lower Paleozoic rocks that may have been anomalously enriched with barium. the Alaskan barite belt is thrust over organic-rich lower Paleozoic rocks. Dewatering of basinal organic-rich marine muds may have resulted in the migration of barium-enriched fluids that were eventually expelled at the seafloor. Permeable strata could have provided a conduit for the transport of barium-rich fluids both in deeply buried strata as well as in strata at the seafloor, and impermeable strata could have formed cap rock seals for geopressured reservoir rocks. Magma-driven hydrothermal systems may have derived barium from barium-enriched sedimentary rocks and from volcanic rocks and magma. A unique combination of tectonic, sedimentary, biologic, and oceanographic histories seems to have restricted the distribution of large barite deposits in space and time.

ACKNOWLEDGMENTS

We thank R. Earhart and J. Hein for helpful comments on this chapter. We thank I. Tailleur for providing the opportunity to visit the Brooks Range and for sharing his knowledge of regional geology in northern Alaska.

References

Arrhenius, G., and E. Bonatti, 1965. Neptunism and volcanism in the ocean, *Prog. Oceanography* **3**:7–22.

Barker, F., D. L. Jones, J. R. Boudahn, and P. Coney, in press. Ocean plateau-seamount origin for basaltic rocks of the Angayucham terrane, north-central Alaska, *Canadian Jour. Earth Sci.*

Berry, W. B. N., and P. Wilde, 1978. Progressive ventilation of the oceans—An explanation for the distribution of the Lower Paleozoic black shales, *Am. Jour. Sci.* **278**:257–275.

Brobst, D. A., 1970. Barite world production, reserves, and future prospects, *U.S. Geol. Survey Bull.* **1321**:1–46.

Calvert, S. E., 1974, Deposition and diagenesis of silica in marine sediments, in *Pelagic Sediments: On Land and Under the Sea*, K. J. Hsu and H. Jenkyns, eds., Special Publication 1. Blackwell, Oxford, pp. 273–299.

Carne, R. C., and R. J. Cathro, 1982. Sedimentary exhalative (sedex) zinc-lead-silver deposits, northern Canadian Cordillera, *Canadian Inst. Mining and Metallurgy Bull.* **75**:66–78.

Cecile, M. P., 1982. The lower Paleozoic Misty Creek Embayment, Selwyn Basin, Yukon and Northwest Territories, *Canada Geol. Survey Bull.* **335**:1–78.

Church, T. M., 1970. Marine barite, Ph.D. dissertation, University of California, San Diego, 133p.

Cloud, P. E., Jr., and A. J. Boucot, 1971. *Dzieduszyckia* in Nevada, in J. T. Dutro, Jr., ed., *Paleozoic Perspectives, A Tribute to G. Arthur Cooper,* Smithsonian Contributions to Paleobiology, 3, pp. 175–180.

Coles, K. S., 1986. Deposition and deformation of a mid-Paleozoic siliceous sequence, central Toquima Range, Nevada, *Geol. Soc. America Abs. with Programs* **18**:96.

Coles, K. S., and W. S. Snyder, 1985. Significance of lower and middle Paleozoic phosphatic chert in the Toquima Range, central Nevada, *Geology* **13**:573–576.

Corliss, J. B., J. Dymond, L. I. Gordon, J. M. Edmond, R. P. von Herzen, R. D. Ballard, K. Green, D. Williams, A. Bainbridge, K. Crane, and T. H. van Andel, 1979. Submarine thermal springs on the Galapagos Rift, *Science* **203**:1073–1083.

Cronan, D. S., 1974. Authigenic minerals in deep-sea sediments, in *The Sea*, Vol. 5, E. D. Goldberg, ed., Wiley-Interscience, New York, pp. 491–525.

Dawson, K. M., and M. J. Orchard, 1982. *Regional Metallogeny of the Northern Cordillera: Biostratigraphy, Correlation, and Metallogenic Significance of Bedded Barite Occurrences in Eastern Yukon and Western District of MacKenzie,* Canada Geological Survey Paper 82-1C, pp. 31–36.

Dean, W. E., and J. V. Gardner, 1982. Origin and geochemistry of redox cycles of Jurassic to Eocene age, Cape Verde Basin (DSDP Site 367), continental margin of northwest Africa, in *Nature and Origin of Cretaceous Carbon-Rich Facies*, S. O. Schlanger and M. B. Cita, eds., Academic Press, London, pp. 55–78.

Dean, W. E., and B. C. Schreiber, 1977. Authigenic Barite, Leg 41, in Y. Lancelot, E. Seibold, et al., *Initial Reports of the Deep Sea Drilling Project,* Vol. 41, U.S. Govt. Printing Office, Washington, D.C., pp. 915–931.

Dubé, T. E., 1986. Depositional setting of exhalative bedded barite and associated submarine fan deposits of the Roberts Mountains allochthon, north-central Nevada, *Geol. Soc. America Abs. with Programs* **18**:102.

Forrest, K., 1983. Geologic and isotopic studies of the LIK deposit and the surrounding mineral district, DeLong Mountains, western Brooks Range, Alaska, Ph.D. dissertation, University of Minnesota, 161p.

Gordey, S. P., J. G. Abbott, and J. J. Orchard, 1982. *Devono-Mississippian (Earn Group) and Younger Strata in East-Central Yukon,* Canada Geological Survey Paper 82-1B, pp. 93–100.

Harms, T. A., 1986. The Sylvester Allochton: A tectonized oceanic assemblage record of proto-Pacific telescoping and obduction, *Geol. Soc. America Abs. with Programs* **18:**114.

Jones, D. L., N. J. Silberling, B. Csejtey, Jr., W. H. Nelson, and C. D. Blome, 1980. *Age and Structural Significance of Ophiolite and Adjoining Rocks in the Upper Chulitna District, South-Central Alaska,* U.S. Geological Survey Professional Paper 1121-A, 21p.

Kennett, J. P., 1982. *Marine Geology,* Prentice-Hall, Englewood Cliffs, N.J., 813p.

Lange, I. M., W. J. Nokleberg, J. T. Plahuta, H. R. Krouse, B. Doe, Jr., and U. Jansons, 1980. *Isotopic Geochemistry of Stratiform Zinc-Lead-Barium Deposits, Red Dog Creek and Drenchwater Creek Areas, northwestern Brooks Range, Alaska.* U.S. Geological Survey Open-File Report 81-335, pp. 1–17.

Lydon, J. W., W. D. Goodfellow, and I. R. Jonasson, 1985. *A General Genetic Model for Stratiform Baritic Deposits of the Selwyn Basin, Yukon Territory and District of MacKenzie,* Canada Geological Survey Paper 85-1A, pp. 651–660.

Mako, D. A., and W. C. Shanks, III, 1984. Stratiform sulfide and barite-fluorite mineralization of the Vulcan prospect, Northwest Territories: Exhalation of basinal brines along a faulted continental margin, *Canadian Jour. Earth Sci.* **21:**78–91.

Mayfield, C. F., 1980, Comment on "Collision-deformed Paleozoic continental margin, western Brooks Range, Alaska," *Geology* **8:**357–359.

Mayfield, C. F., I. L. Tailleur, and I. Ellersieck, 1983. *Stratigraphy, Structure and Palinspastic Synthesis of the Western Brooks Range, Northwestern Alaska,* U.S. Geological Survey Open File Report 83-779, 58p.

Mortensen, J. K., and C. I. Godwin, 1982. Volcanogenic massive sulfide deposits associated with highly alkaline rift volcanics in the southeastern Yukon Territory, *Econ. Geology* **61:**1225–1230.

Mull, C. G., I. L. Tailleur, C. F. Mayfield, I. Ellersieck, and S. Curtis, 1982. New upper Paleozoic and lower Mesozoic stratigraphic units, central and western Brooks Range, Alaska, *Am. Assoc. Petroleum Geologists Bull.* **66:**348–362.

Murchey, B. L., D. L. Jones, and B. K. Holdsworth, 1983. Distribution, age, and depositional environments of radiolarian chert in western North America, in *Siliceous Deposits in the Pacific Region,* A. Iijima, J. R. Hein, and R. Siever, eds., Elsevier, Amsterdam, pp. 109–126.

Murchey, B. L., D. L. Jones, B. K. Holdsworth, C. D. Blome, and B. K. Wardlaw, in press. *Distribution Patterns of Facies, Radiolarians, and Conodonts in the Mississippian to Jurasic Siliceous Rocks of the Northern Brooks Range, Alaska,* U.S. Geological Survey Professional Paper.

Noll, J. H., J. T. Dutro, Jr., and S. S. Beus, 1984. A new species of the Late Devonian (Fammenian) brachiopod *Dzieduszyckia* from Sonora, Mexico, *Jour. Paleontology* **58:**1412–1421.

Orris, G. J., 1985. *Bedded/Stratiform Barite Deposits: Geologic and Grade-Tonnage Data Including a Partial Bibliography,* U.S. Geological Survey Open-File Report 85-447, 32p.

Pallister, J., 1985. Pillow basalts from the Angayucham Range, Alaska: Chemistry and tectonic implications. *EOS* **66:**1102.

Patton, W. W., Jr., 1957. *A New Upper Paleozoic Formation, Central Brooks Range, Alaska,* U.S. Geological Survey Professional Paper 303-B, pp. 41–45.

Poole, F. G., 1986. *Stratiform Barite in Paleozoic Rocks of the Western United States,* Abstract for the International Association on the Genesis of Ore Deposits, Seventh IAGOD Symposium and Nordkalott Project meeting, Lulea, Sweden: TERRA cognita, vol. 6, no. 3, p. 516.

Poole, F. G., B. L. Murchey, and J. H. Stewart, 1983. Bedded barite deposits of middle and late Paleozoic age in central Sonora, Mexico, *Geol. Soc. America Abs. with Programs* **15:**299.

Poole, F. G., C. A. Sandberg, and A. J. Boucot, 1977. Silurian and Devonian paleogeography of the western United States, in *Paleozoic Paleogeography of the Western*

United States, J. H. Stewart, C. H. Stevens, and A. E. Fritsche, eds., Pacific Section, Society of Economic Paleontologists and Mineralogists, Pacific Coast Paleogeography Symposium 1, pp. 38-65.

Shawe, D. R., F. G. Poole, and D. A. Brobst, 1969. Newly discovered bedded barite deposits in East Northumberland Canyon, Nye County, Nevada, *Econ. Geology* **64**:245-254.

Siok, J. P., 1985. Geologic history of the Siksikpuk Formation on the Endicott Mountains and Picnic Creek allochthons, north-central Brooks Range, Alaska, M.S. thesis, University of Alaska, Fairbanks, pp. 152-200.

Index